THE ISLANDS OF THE BAHAMAS

Jennifer McMorran

ULYSSES
TRAVEL PUBLICATIONS
Travel better... enjoy more

Editorial *Series Director:* Claude Morneau; *Project Supervisor:* Pascale Couture; *Editor:* Claude Morneau.

Research and Composition *Author:* Jennifer McMorran.

Production *Design:* Patrick Farei (Atoll Direction); *Proofreading:* Tara Salman; *Cartography:* André Duchesne, Patrick Thivièrge (Assistant), Marc Rigole, Isabelle Lalonde; *Layout:* Tara Salman, Stéphane G. Marceau.

Illustrations *Cover Photo:* Jeff Hunter (Image Bank); *Interior Photos:* Jennifer McMorran, André Vigneau (Reflexion), J. Greenberg (Reflexion); *Chapter Headings:* Jennifer McMorran; *Drawings:* Marie-Annick Viatour.

Special Thanks The author would like to thank the following without who's help this guide would not have been possible: Vacances Air Canada; Cherry Upton, Karine Sautier, Charity Armbrister, Donna McQueen, Ona Bullard and Jackie Gibson at the Bahamas Tourist Office; Felena S. Burrows at the Grand Bahama Island Tourism Board; Helen Fillmore at the Bahamas Out Island Promotion Board; Billy T. Greene; Sandra Eneas and Rachela Tirelli of Sun International Bahamas; Mark Major of the Radisson Cable Beach Resort; the staff of Small Hope Bay Lodge; the staff of Fernandez Bay Village; Ann and George Mullin of The Cove Eleuthera; Dwight Johnson of the Buccaneer Club; the staff of the Riding Rock Inn; Cliff Fernander of Fernander Tours; the staff of Stella Maris; the staff of Cape Santa Maria; and finally Alain Rondeau for his unfailing encouragement during the final hours.

Thanks to SODEC and the Department of Canadian Heritage for their financial Support.

Distributors

AUSTRALIA:
Little Hills Press
11/37-43 Alexander St.
Crows Nest NSW 2065
☎ (612) 437-6995
Fax: (612) 438-5762

BELGIUM AND LUXEMBOURG:
Vander
Vrijwilligerlaan 321
B-1150 Brussel
☎ (02) 762 98 04
Fax: (02) 762 06 62

CANADA:
Ulysses Books & Maps
4176 Saint-Denis
Montréal, Québec
H2W 2M5
☎ (514) 843-9882, ext.2232
or 1-800-748-9171
Fax: 514-843-9448
www.ulysses.ca

GERMANY AND AUSTRIA:
Brettschneider
Fernreisebedarf
Feldfirchner Strasse 2
D-85551 Heimstetten
München
☎ 89-99 02 03 30
Fax: 89-99 02 03 31

GREAT BRITAIN AND IRELAND:
World Leisure Marketing
9 Downing Road
West Meadows, Derby
UK DE21 6HA
☎ 1 332 34 33 32
Fax: 1 332 34 04 64

ITALY:
Centro Cartografico del Riccio
Via di Soffiano 164/A
50143 Firenze
☎ (055) 71 33 33
Fax: (055) 71 63 50

NETHERLANDS:
Nilsson & Lamm
Pampuslaan 212-214
1380 AD Weesp (NL)
☎ 0294-465044
Fax: 0294-415054
E-mail: nilam@euronet.nl

PORTUGAL:
Dinapress
Lg. Dr. Antonio de Sousa de Macedo, 2
Lisboa 1200
☎ (1) 395 52 70
Fax: (1) 395 03 90

SCANDINAVIA:
Scanvik
Esplanaden 8B
1263 Copenhagen K
DK
☎ (45) 33.12.77.66
Fax: (45) 33.91.28.82

SPAIN:
Altaïr
Balmes 69
E-08007 Barcelona
☎ 454 29 66
Fax: 451 25 59
E-mail: altair@globalcom.es

SWITZERLAND:
OLF
P.O. Box 1061
CH-1701 Fribourg
☎ (026) 467.51.11
Fax: (026) 467.54.66

U.S.A.:
The Globe Pequot Press
6 Business Park Road
P.O. Box 833
Old Saybrook, CT 06475
☎ 1-800-243-0495
Fax: 1-800-820-2329
E-mail: sales@globe-pequot.com

Other countries, contact Ulysses Books & Maps (Montréal), Fax: (514) 843-9448

Canadian Cataloguing in Publication Data
McMorran, Jennifer, 1971-
Bahamas
(Ulysses travel guides)
Includes index.
ISBN 2-89464-123-0
1. Bahamas - Guidebooks. I. Title II. Series.
F1652.M35 1998 917.29604 C98-940804-3

"There are here fish so unlike ours that it is a marvel; ... of the finest colours in the world, blue, yellow, red and of all colours, and others painted in a thousand ways, and the colours are so fine that no man would not wonder at them or be anything but delighted to see them."

– Christopher Columbus

TABLE OF CONTENTS

LIST OF MAPS

Help make Ulysses Travel Guides even better!

The information contained in this guide was correct at press time. However, mistakes can slip in, omissions are always possible, places can disappear, etc. The authors and publisher hereby disclaim any liability for loss or damage resulting from omissions or errors.

We value your comments, corrections and suggestions, as they allow us to keep each guide up to date. The best contributions will be rewarded with a free book from Ulysses Travel Publications. All you have to do is write us at the following address and indicate which title you would be interested in receiving (see the list at the end of guide).

Ulysses Travel Publications
4176 Rue Saint-Denis
Montréal, Québec
Canada H2W 2M5
www.ulysses.ca
E-mail: guiduly@ulysse.ca

TABLE OF SYMBOLS

(ship symbol)	Ulysses' favourite
☎	Telephone number
⇄	Fax number
≡	Air conditioning
⊗	Ceiling fan
≈	Pool
ℜ	Restaurant
⊛	Whirlpool
ℝ	Refrigerator
K	Kitchenette
ℑ	Fireplace
⌂	Sauna
#	Screen
⏲	Exercise room
tv	Colour television
sat tv	Satellite television
pb	Private bathroom
sb	Shared bathroom
ps	Private shower
hw	Hot water
MAP	Modern American Plan (lodging + 2 meals)
AP	American Plan (lodging + 3 meals)
bkfst	Breakfast

ATTRACTION CLASSIFICATION

★	Interesting
★★	Worth a visit
★★★	Not to be missed

HOTEL CLASSIFICATION

The prices in the guide are for one room, double occupancy in high season, not including taxes and service charges.

RESTAURANT CLASSIFICATION

$	$10 or less
$$	$10 to $20 US
$$$	$20 to $30 US
$$$$	$30 and more

The prices in the guide are for a meal for one person, not including taxes, drinks and tip.

All prices in this guide are in American dollars.

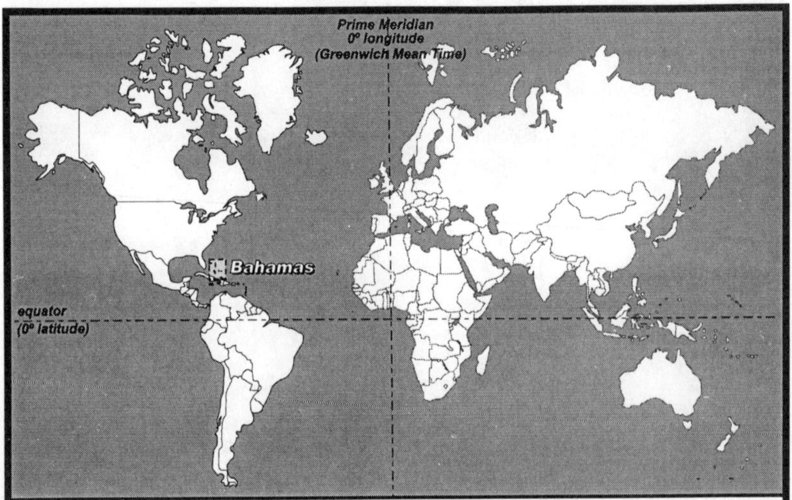

Where are The Bahamas?

THE ISLANDS OF THE BAHAMAS
Capital: Nassau
Population: 284,000 inhab.
Language: English
Currency: Bahamian dollar
Area: 13,930 sq. km. 5400 sq. mi.

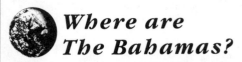

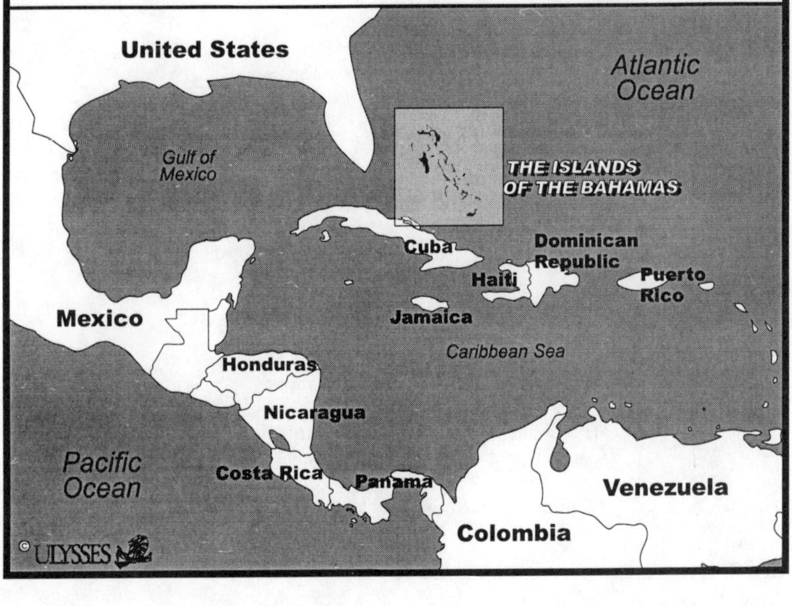

PORTRAIT

Pink sand, blue holes and Blackbeard... Seven-hundred islands and 2050 cays... An engaging, proud, sophisticated and unpretentious people... Whether you are exploring the beaches and prized diving sites of the charming Out Islands, the colonial architecture of the capital city of Nassau or the casinos and shops of Freeport, this stunning archipelago has something for island-hoppers of all types.

Perhaps like Columbus, who remarked, "so many that I did not know how to decide which one to go to first...", you are having trouble choosing from this string of sunny islands? First you should know that The Bahamas are like two different countries. One includes Nassau (New Providence) and Freeport (Grand Bahama) and offers up the fast-paced glitz of casinos, bars, cruise ships, expensive boutiques, luxurious yachts and mega-resorts. The other is a much quieter collection of sparsely populated islands called the Out Islands. The Ministry of Tourism prefers the name Family Islands, which does seem fitting when you hear Nassauvians or Freeporters speak of where they were born as being their family island. Family is certainly one of the most important features of life on these far-flung paradises. The most visited of the Out Islands are the Biminis, Abacos, Eleuthera and Exumas, and the majority of the visitors are sailors, fishers and divers. Some hamlets only recently got electricity, so the day goes by at a considerably slower pace than on New Providence and Grand Bahama. There is little nightlife to speak of and few attractions beyond what the sea brings in, both above and below water. In fact, many of the country's natural treasures are here, including Great Inagua's flamingo reserves.

To help you decide between following the tourists, the tradewinds, the marlin, the angelfish, the flamingoes or the tanning rays, here is a brief sum-up of the best of each of The Islands Of The Bahamas.

New Providence (pop. 170,000) is home to the country's capital, historic Nassau, and the majority of its inhabitants. Most tourists to New Providence, and The Bahamas for that matter, stay either at Cable Beach, east of downtown, or on the more upscale Paradise Island. Both boast beautiful beaches, golf courses, casinos (Paradise Island has the country's best), nightlife, dining, services, easy access to downtown and *lots* of tourists. Paradise Island also has its own airport, though Cable Beach is not far from Nassau International Airport. A number of tourists stay right in Nassau close to what is arguably the island's biggest draw: its colonial architecture and old-world feel. The hotels in Nassau proper are less expensive but the beaches are less accessible, save the British Colonial's small stretch of sand. The other highlights that (dare we repeat ourselves) you will be sharing with hordes of other tourists include spectacular diving and great shopping.

Grand Bahama (pop. 50,000) has much to recommend it, especially for families: there are idyllic Gold Rock Beach, Lucayan National Park with its walking and kayaking excursions, unbeatable duty-free shopping, two casinos, the typically Bahamian settlement of West End and the renowned UNEXSO diving centre. It is unfortunately lacking that essential sense of place that can make a destination. The proximity of the United States might make you wonder if you aren't in Florida. The International Bazaar is just too put on, the town centre is boring and much of the development borders on the tacky. Few hotels, most of which are in need of a facelift, actually border the island's beautiful beaches. The redevelopment of the Lucayan Beach Resort & Casino and Grand Bahama Beach Hotel announced in 1997, should spruce up the islands' image.

The Abacos (pop. 10,000), often referred to as simply Abaco is actually a grouping of islands and cays, the second-largest in the country. With a strong Loyalist history, you'll find some of the best such architecture in the islands. Green Turtle Cay, Elbow Cay, Great Guana Cay and Man O' War Cay each has its own village, complete with local galleries, museums and shops; lodging possibilities are most numerous on the first two. Marsh Harbour is mainly a service centre with hotels and marinas, but not much in the way of beaches. Treasure Cay is a major residential and resort complex with some beautiful beaches. Boatbuilding was the mainstay of the Abacos for many years and it is now a noted sailing and fishing destination, with many well-equipped marinas. Abaco National Park has fine walking and birding. There is even whale-watching off Elbow Cay.

Eleuthera (pop.10,000) is so long it is served by three airports. Modern Bahamian history began here with the Eleutherian Adventurers in 1648. Most tourists stick to the north end flock to Harbour Island's pink sand beach or Dunmore Town to admire its Loyalist architecture. The luxurious resorts along Eleuthera's stunning coastline that once attracted royalty and millionaires are mostly closed down, but there is talk that they will once again welcome the rich and famous. Nevertheless, the "mainland's" grand seascapes and exquisite beaches can be enjoyed from a handful of hotels down the coast. Highlights include the pink sand, the Pink Sands Resort, the Glass Window, Surfer's Beach and the picturesque villages of Gregory Town and Tarpum Bay.

The Biminis (pop. 1,600) are two islands: North and South Bimini. The famed favourite haunt of Ernest Hemingway, these islands in the stream host countless sport-fishing tournaments each year. The proximity to the United States makes them popular with spring-break sun-seekers, the majority of which head to the smaller, more developed North Bimini and pass most of their time at either the Compleat Angler or the End of the World Bar. There are no sights, besides these two watering holes, and the beaches are nothing to write home about.

The Berry Islands (pop. 700) are a cluster of 30 tiny islands and cays with very few hotels and a certain upscale seclusion about them. Most of the visitors to these secluded beaches arrive on sailing or sport-fishing yachts and stay in private homes.

Andros (pop. 8,000) is the largest island in The Bahamas, the least developed and perhaps the most fascinating. Unexplored forests and mangrove swamps cover most of this island outpost, which is actually two islands, separated by a shallow tidal river called a bight. Visitors are mostly fishers and divers attracted by bonefishing flats, blue holes and the third-largest barrier reef in the world, other highlights include hand-made Androsia batik fabrics and basketry from Red Bays. The facilities are limited compared to the other islands, but there are choices for every budget.

The Exumas (pop. 3,500) are a chain of sandy cays, lined with secluded beaches many of which are protected in Exuma Cays Land & Sea Park. The park protects an underwater treasure trove. There are also good bonefishing flats west of the chain, and this sport is more popular than diving. Sailing, however, is the religion here and most visitors are boaters who congregate near the marina facilities of George Town, especially during the month of April when they join Bahamians from throughout the archipelago for the annual inter-island Family Island Regatta.

Cat Island (pop. 1,600) is a quiet island in the southeastern Bahamas. Colourful traditional clapboard and limestone cottages dot the island. There are only a handful of accommodations options (nothing grand-scale) but plenty to do: Cat has the highest point in The Bahamas, Mount Alvernia, topped by Fra. Jerome's Hermitage; besides diving and bonefishing, you can also go hiking, birding and kayaking. The Cat Island Regatta on August 1st is another highlight.

San Salvador (pop.1,200) is round and strewn with lakes, both fresh and saline. Believed to be the first landfall of Christopher Columbus in 1492, there are no less than four monuments commemorating the event. The working lighthouse, plantation ruins and wall-diving prove more fascinating than the monuments, however. Fine beaches and Club Med have produced a tourist boom in recent years.

Long Island (pop. 4,500) has minimal facilities, but does nevertheless boast two very good resorts, both in the northern end of the island, which organize diving, snorkelling, sport-fishing and bonefishing and a few good finds further south. Many of the island's beautiful churches are the work of Father Jerome.

Crooked Island & Acklins & Ragged Island Range (pop. 1,000) are remote islands that receive very few visitors, save perhaps the flamingoes and nesting turtles that stop by regularly. Only Crooked has facilities for tourists, who come generally for the diving and snorkelling.

Mayaguana (pop. 600) has virtually no facilities, **Great Inagua** (pop. 1,200), on the other hand, has facilities in Matthew Town, as well as flamingoes. The Inaguas are actually two islands, Great and Little Inagua, the latter being entirely protected by the Bahamas National Trust and the former being mostly covered by parkland as well. The flamingoes can be seen November to June on Great Inagua, along with many other winged species as well as hawksbill turtles.

GEOGRAPHY

A string of islands extending over an area 885 kilometres long and 320 kilometres wide, running in a southeasterly direction from about 80 kilometres off the coast of Florida to about 113 kilometres from the coast of Haiti, make up The Islands Of The Bahamas. They lie between longitudes 72°35'W and 80°30"W and latitudes 20°50"N and 27°30"N, an area of about 256,000 square kilometres (100,000 square miles). The islands themselves cover an area of about 14,000 square kilometres (5,382 square miles), about the same size as Jamaica or the State of Connecticut. Traditionally, the country is said to be made up of 700 islands and 2000 cays or islets. An 1864 survey counted 29 islands, 661 cays and 2387 rocks. The rocks are nothing more than outcroppings of limestone. "Cays" are a little trickier. The word is adapted from the Arawak word *cairi*, meaning island; however, the word as it has been adopted by the English language - as "cay" (pronounced "key"), more precisely refers to a small island. Some islands are actually groups of islands, while others are so small that they should more correctly be called cays. Nevertheless, commonly accepted wisdom puts the number of islands at a more accurate 700.

The Land

The Islands Of The Bahamas are generally flat and rocky. The rock is oolitic limestone, formed from the remains of countless marine organisms, which accumulated prior to the last ice age when this entire area was a giant sea and the islands lay completely submerged. The ocean's surface lay 90-120 metres (300-400 ft.) higher during the last ice age, some 50,000 years ago. As the ice melted, the mountains, whose peaks today form the islands, were slowly engulfed. This phenomenon continues even today at the rate of about one inch per century. The rocky composition and mere five centimetres of topsoil is not conducive to agriculture. In certain areas where sand has accumulated, vegetation has taken hold and the cycle of growth and decay enriches the land.

Caribbean or Not

The Islands Of The Bahamas are not in the Caribbean Sea, though they are often considered a Caribbean destination. The archipelago actually lies in the Atlantic Ocean, with the swift-moving Gulf Stream separating it from Florida. It is more accurate to say that The Bahamas are part of the West Indies.

The Sea

The spectacular seas surrounding The Islands Of The Bahamas are easily their main attraction, varying from gin-clear to brilliant turquoise blue and green, before trailing off into the inky blue of the ocean. Named *baja mar*, or shallow sea, by the first Europeans, the archipelago is indeed surrounded by mostly shallow water, except for a few exceptions, like Exuma Sound and the Tongue of the Ocean, the latter east of Andros and more than one mile deep. The Tongue also happens to be flanked by the second (or third depending on who you talk to) longest barrier reef in the world.

Close to shore, those gin-clear waters remain so because of a constant shifting of the sands by the tides, making it impossible for any vegetation to take hold. Further out, sea-grasses, sponges and molluscs thrive in sheltered locations. Another inhabitant of these waters is the coral polyp, preferring waters over 21°C (70°F) and shallower than 24 metres (80 ft.). Colonies of coral polyps come in all colours, shapes and sizes, and bear evocative names like finger coral, brain coral and staghorn coral. On the leeward side of an island, coral forms what are called shoals or coral heads, while on the windward side they are known as fringe reefs. They provide shelter and feeding grounds for the abundance of underwater life, and protect the islands from erosion.

FLORA

Despite poor soil conditions, The Bahamas are home to over 1,370 species of plants, including 121 that are not found anywhere else in the world. The northern islands are dominated by Caribbean, Bahamian and Australian (casuarina) pines, while in the south, hardwood forests, called "coppices", predominate. These contain species such as the lignum vitae (the national tree and heaviest of all woods), mahogany, horseflesh, logwood and cascarilla (used to flavour campari). Smaller islands are covered mostly with dense shrubs and low trees. Palm trees also abound throughout the islands; the royal, silver thatch (used in weaving) and coconut are some varieties found both inland and along the beaches.

Many of the trees, bushes and magnificent flowers that grow here are prized houseplants in cooler climates. These include hibiscus, orchids, oleander, poinsettia, gardenia, jasmine, frangipani and poinciana, to name but a few. The national flower is the yellow elder. The leeward coasts and inland waterways, such as on Andros, are for the most part lined with mangrove trees of which all four New World varieties are represented.

Hibiscus

Tasty fruits of all kinds, some familiar some not, grow here. There are the familiar pineapples, bananas, limes and papaya, and the not so common tamarind, guinep, sapodilla, sugar apple, breadfruit, pigeon plums and seagrape. The tamarind fruit is a long, brown, pod-like fruit with a greenish pulp that can be used as a sauce; the guinep is the most popular fruit amongst islanders, it grows in clusters, has a crisp green skin and is about the size of a plum and similar in taste; known locally simply as "dilly", the sapodilla has a brown skin and a sweet pink flesh, much like a melon, inside are several shiny black seeds; also called sweetsop, the sugar apple resembles a grenade, and often splits open when it falls from the tree, the creamy white flesh is dotted with black seeds and is often used in ice cream; breadfruit was brought to the Caribbean from the South Pacific by Captain Bligh in 1793, its meat is rather bland and is often cooked as a vegetable; pigeon plums grow on bushes with dark purple or green skin, the white flesh is chalky if not ripe, be sure the fruit is good and soft before eating; finally, sea grapes grow by the sea on large bushes in green, grape-like clusters and are used in jellies and preserves.

Casuarinas

One of the species of pine trees found throughout The Bahamas is the Australian pine or casuarina. This species of pine with its willow-like appearance is not indigenous to the islands but was imported during colonization. Casuarinas grow very quickly and line beaches thoughout the islands. Their long needles blanket the earth, preventing indigenous plant species from growing. Many casuarinas have been uprooted in an effort to encourage native species.

FAUNA

The Bahamas are rich in fauna. When it comes to wildlife observation, it might seem logical to assume that scuba divers and snorkellers are the luckiest, but birders will also find a variety of spectacular winged species, including several endangered treasures, to marvel at.

Starting underwater is the obvious plethora of colourful tropical fish. These include abundant grunts, tiny silvery fish with yellow stripes and yellow fins that are easily approached. These fish are the first to colonize artificial reefs. Bright-blue damselfish are another plentiful small reef fish. The unmistakable angelfish, with its compressed body, comes in a variety of colours and sizes. The rock beauty is the most common type and is easily identifiable by its distinctly black and yellow markings and blue rim around its eyes. The most striking angelfish is probably the queen angelfish, which you can identify by its blue ringed freckled spot or "crown" and all-yellow tail. Parrotfish are another colourful fish. Growing to up to 50 centimetres in length, their distinctive beak gives them their name. While underwater you can hear them munching away at the coral. The males are usually bluish-green, while the females are a dark reddish-brown. Another common fish is the trumpetfish. It comes in lots of different colours, but is easy to spot thanks to its trumpet-like snout. It can grow to up to 75 centimetres and is carnivorous.

Other species that are common to Bahamian reefs are: Groupers, which seem ferocious but are quite harmless, and moray eels, which like to poke their noses out of reef walls. Keep your eyes open for barracudas, porcupine fish, stingrays, marine turtles, sharks and dolphins. Special diving excursions where you can swim with these last two species can be arranged on most islands. And all of these creatures thrive thanks to a healthy reef. Corals of all colours and shapes support curious worms, including the aptly named Christmas-tree worm and flamingo worm, among others. While diving and snorkelling, watch for the telltale tracks of the queen conch on the sandy bottom. This large marine sea snail, served

Frigatebird

up in just about every Bahamian restaurant, inhabits a spectacular pink shell.

Humpback whales and blue whales can be spotted on occasion in Bahamian waters on their way to warmer mating waters. Deeper waters are also home to a wealth of prized game fish. These include tarpon, wahoo, kingfish, billfish, tuna, amberjack, sailfish and marlin.

The Bahamas are inhabited by a mere 13 indigenous land mammals. There are 12 bat species and one terrestrial specie, the hutia. This large rodent is endangered and strictly protected by the Bahamas National Trust. It was thought to be extinct until it was rediscovered in the 1960s. Feral pigs, cattle and cats are the only other mammals in The Bahamas.

The islands are home to 44 species of reptiles, the most common being lizards. The ubiquitous curly-tailed lizards flit about everywhere. You'll also spot tiny geckos and much bigger anoles. Red, blue and black land crabs, along with hermit crabs lumbering about in mismatched shells, are also common sights throughout the islands, especially after rain. Much bigger and more impressive are Iguanas, in particular the endangered Bahamian dragon, which can grow to up to five feet and inhabits a handful of protected islands in the Exuma cays.

Last, but certainly not least, are the winged species of The Bahamas. Intrepid birders will want to make the trip south to Great Inagua to view the largest flock of West Indian (Caribbean) flamingoes in the western hemisphere. Fifty thousand of these pink beauties, The Bahamas' national bird, thrive among the salt ponds of this isolated island. Those who don't make the trip can still see flamingoes on both New Providence and Grand Bahama. The Bahama parrot, also called the Abaco parrot, is another endangered species. These ground-nesting bright green and red parrots, once plentiful throughout the islands, are now only found in Abaco National Park on Great Abaco. The Bahamas is also home to a handful of hummingbird species, including the Bahamian woodstar, with a white breast, dark red throat and brilliant-green head and back. Also keep your eyes peeled for great herons, cattle egrets, red-legged thrushes, cormorants, ospreys, frigatebirds, pelicans, terns, white-crowned pigeons, vireos, red-tailed hawks, turkey vultures, barn owls and mockingbirds, just some of the 230 different species of birds that inhabit The Bahamas.

HISTORY

Early Bahamian history is often glossed over in favour of the "discovery" of the New World and of The Bahamas by Christopher Columbus. The Genoese navigator is truly revered in the islands despite the fact that his discovery was the catalyst for the destruction of the native peoples of The Bahamas and the Caribbean in general. The hundreds of years it took for these islands to be truly settled have given them a unique history, and it is only in the last 40, with the advent of black rule, that the country and Bahamian society have come into their own.

The Lucayans

The nomadic peoples that crossed the Bering Strait 12,000 years ago slowly worked their way across a vast land and evolved into powerful civilizations throughout what we now call the Americas. The region that concerns us, the islands of the Caribbean and western Atlantic, was inhabited later on by groups that are believed to have migrated here from southern Mexico and Central and South America. They were actually three tribes in this area. The Lesser Antilles (those islands located between Trinidad and the Virgin Islands) were inhabited by cannibalistic warrior Caribs; the Greater Antilles (Cuba, Hispaniola, Jamaica and Puerto Rico) and The Bahamas were inhabited by a peaceful people called Arawaks; Cuba was also home to a more primitive tribe called the Ciboneys.

The Islands Of The Bahamas were called Guanahaní by the Lucayans, the "island people" who arrived here around AD 700. The Lucayans spoke of having come from Hispaniola, which they called Haiti. Although they spoke the same language, used the same tools and weapons and had similar customs and beliefs as the Arawaks of Hispaniola, called Tainos, they did not physically resemble them, which led some to speculate that they were descendants of the Ciboneys. Nevertheless, they were a peaceful people. The Europeans were struck by their beauty, noting their strong lean bodies, naked save decorative markings, and in particular their foreheads, which were bound and flattened in infancy and thus seemed large to European eyes. They lived in small settlements of no more than 15 houses that were called *canayes*, which consisted of a round timber structure with a conical thatched roof. The *canayes* were all built around that of the chief or cacique. One example of this hierarchical society has survived to modern times: thirteen ceremonial wooden stools, called *duhos* and probably used by the caciques, have been found in Bahamian caves. *Zemis*, or good spirits, were worshipped with hand-carved idols, remnants of which have also been found. All was not sweetness and light for the Lucayans, however, for they were terrorized by the cannibalistic Caribs to the south who frequently raided Guanahaní. The systematic flattening of children's foreheads may have been to make them appear ugly so that the Caribs would not rape or eat them.

Tierra! Tierra!

Meanwhile in Europe, Christopher Columbus dreamed of sailing to the Orient. He had trouble selling the idea but finally convinced King Ferdinand and Queen Isabella of Spain to finance the expedition. On August 3, 1492, three

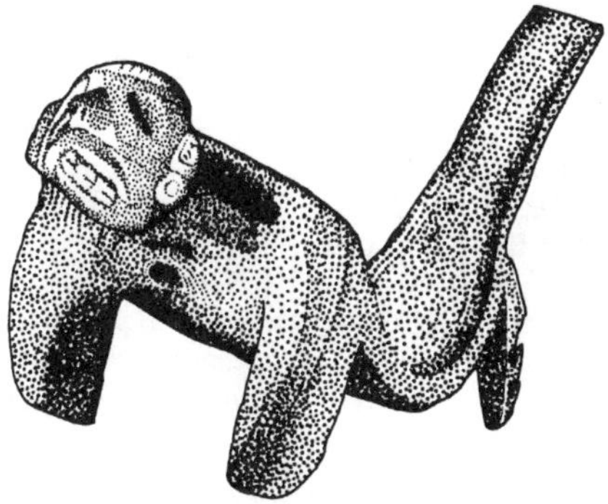

Duho

ships, the *Santa Maria*, the *Niña* and the *Pinta* set sail for the New World. Thirty-three days later, in the early morning hours of October 12, 1492, the cry went out.

The Spanish, though friendly at first, proved just as deadly as the Caribs. Columbus made landfall and named five islands: from San Salvador he sailed south to Santa María de la Concepcíon, west to Fernandina, southeast to Isabela and then southwest to Islas de Arena. He and his crew spent only 15 days in The Bahamas, long enough to note that this was not the coveted Orient, that no wealth lay in the soil of Guanahaní and that the timid Lucayans "should be good servants", in Columbus' words. Columbus was, however, more impressed by the natives of Fernandina, his third stop, describing them as "a somewhat more tractable and domesticated people... they know better how to bargain". The generally accepted wisdom is that Columbus' first landfall in the New World was on the present-day island of San Salvador. Although that island has its share of monuments commemorating the landing, there is irrefutable evidence to suggest that San Salvador as we know it today is not the island that Columbus named as such. The most convincing case against San Salvador finds favour with uninhabited Samana Cay and is made in the November, 1986, edition of National Geographic magazine. The article claims that evidence pointing to present-day San Salvador ignores the inevitable leeway, or sideways slide of a sailboat, and when considered brings Columbus ashore at Samana Cay. Evidence on the islands of Lucayan settlements as well as geographical features also point to Samana. The article is worth a look.

Whichever island was the first to receive European visitors, what ensued is undeniable. Columbus kidnapped a handful of Lucayans and continued on to Cuba and Hispaniola (present-day Haiti and the Dominican Republic). There he met other natives, but more importantly he confirmed that there was gold on Hispaniola. The Spanish contingent left on Hispaniola was brutally killed and Spanish retaliation was just as brutal. After making quick use of Cuba and Hispaniola's native populations in the gold mines, the Spanish returned to the Bahamas and enslaved the Lucayans. Within about 25 years, they made their way through the estimated 40,000 Lucayans. Bishop Bartolomé Las Casas' *History of the Indies*, written in 1530, advocated better treatment of the slaves. He recommended that any Lucayans left in the Bahamas be resettled with their brethren in Hispaniola and allowed to live free. After three years of searching the islands, only 11 Lucayans were found. The Bahamas would remain devoid of human settlement for more than 100 years.

Spain claimed the islands because their ships, laden with gold, passed them to catch the favourable winds back across the Atlantic. Legends of the miraculous fountain of youth held the only possibility of anything worthwhile as far as the Spanish were concerned. They dispatched Ponce de Leon to the island of Bimini in 1513, but neither he nor his successors ever found anything. Leon did discover the powerful Gulf Stream, however, and followed it to Florida. In doing so, he noted the Grand Bahama Bank and named the area *baja mar*, meaning "shallow sea". No real Spanish foothold was ever established in The Bahamas, instead the islands sheltered privateers employed by envious European powers intent on sharing in the riches that Spain was taking from the Americas. As Spain's might waned, so did her supremacy in the Americas. England and France eventually made their own claims on the Bahamas. In 1629, England claimed the uninhabited isles, then in 1634 Cardinal Richelieu did the same for France. Still no one came.

Religious Freedom: Eleuthera

Meanwhile, the winds of change were blowing in England and the establishment of a state church was at the eye of the storm. Religious freedom was precious to those who abandoned the traditional church and created their own independent congregations. Persecution and ridicule ultimately drove many of them into exile, including the famous pilgrims who settled in Massachusetts in 1620. Throughout the British Empire, groups of independents, including Oliver Cromwell's New Model Army, were calling for change. The group that concerns us is a small one in Bermuda. Located almost 1,300 kilometres to the northeast of The Bahamas, Bermuda was settled in 1612. The Bermuda Independents wanted to "enjoy Christie in the puritye of his ordinance, without this Bermudian embitterment" and decided to resettle in The Bahamas.

In 1644, a ship sent to the Bahamas in search of suitable land never returned, a year later another ship headed southwest and returned with news of favourable land for settlement. An ex-governor of Bermuda, Captain William Sayle, and 25 others founded the "Company of Adventurers for the Plantation of the Islands of Eleutheria", *eleutheria* being the Greek word for freedom. They had grand plans and their Articles and Orders, which called for religious freedom, a governor, council and senate, amounted to what could be considered the first republic of the New World and the first constitution of The Bahamas. Sayle is probably the only one of the original adventurers to ever set foot on Eleutheria, now Eleuthera. In 1648, he and some 70 settlers set sail in the *William*. It was not smooth sailing, on board was one Captain Butler whose concept of religious freedom did not gel with those of most of the colonists. Sayle is thought to have anchored at one of the small islands near Eleuthera and left Butler and his gang there. The *William* continued to Eleuthera but was wrecked on the reefs fringing the northern end of the island. All but one of the colonists made it to shore, taking refuge in Preacher's Cave, a cave since named as such because the pulpit-like boulder was used in religious services. All the provisions had been lost in the wreck of the *William* and the meagre existence afforded by the natural surroundings threatened the survival of the colonists. Sayle thus set off for Virginia for supplies. Still, the settlement struggled and finally in 1650 the Puritans of New England sent supplies, and as a show of gratitude the colonists sent 10 tons of timber to Boston, the proceeds of which were given to Harvard College.

Colonists from Bermuda came and went. Those who found Eleutheria too much of a struggle left, while others arrived. The colonies of New England, Virginia and Bermuda are all believed to have exiled troublesome slaves and free blacks to the island. Sayle himself returned to Bermuda in 1657. Those that stayed survived just barely from the land and the sea, and settlements were established along the shore of Eleuthera, and at Spanish Wells and Harbour Island.

Settlement on New Providence

Meanwhile, sailors from Bermuda were populating the island of New Providence, then called Sayle's Island, which had much to recommend it in the early 1600s. Though it was small, they were not so much interested in the island itself. Its protected harbour and strategic location were what most attracted them. Spanish galleons laden with treasures sailed through the Providence Channel on their way back to Spain, and the treacherous reefs and lack of lighthouses claimed their fare share of ships. Farmers from Bermuda also came to Sayle's Island and renamed it Providence because they were sure the land would be fruitful. Providence being a popular name, the New was added later to distinguish this one from the others. Feeling a certain responsibility for the courageous Eleutherian settlers and Bermudans on New Providence, the crown granted the islands to the six Lords Proprietors of Carolina in 1670. By that time there were 300 people in the main settlement, Charles Towne, named for King Charles II of England. The Lords Proprietors were absentee landlords who took little interest in their latest charges, except for profit. The Proprietors envisioned plantations, but the seamen continued as they had salvaging wreck goods and collecting ambergris, and generally ignored the Proprietor-appointed governors.

Wreckers made up the majority of the islands' population. Salvaging the goods from a wreck and even privateering in time of war were acceptable occupations. They weren't acceptable to the Spanish, however, who still claimed the title over The Bahamas and whose fortunes too often made their way into the hands of Bahamian wreckers. Not only did the wreckers take their fortunes, but they often attacked the Spanish ships sent out later to salvage the goods. This was viewed as out and out piracy by the Spanish who wasted little time in retaliating. In 1684, they attacked and destroyed the settlement on New Providence, as well as the original settlement of Eleuthera. Charles Towne was deserted.

The rebuilding of Charles Towne was slow and it was not until Governor Nicholas Trott arrived in 1694 that Nassau came into being. A new town and a new fort were both built and named for William, Prince of Orange-Nassau who became King William III of England in 1689. The fort guarded the harbour from where the British Colonial

Hotel now stands. The town consisted of 160 houses and a church.

Privateers' and Pirates' Republics

As luck would have it for Nassauvians, England was at war with France and the pickings for privateers were plentiful. It is important here to make the distinction between privateers and pirates. Privateers were commissioned or encouraged by a government to wage war on the enemy. This saved on expenses for the public treasury and the privateers could keep all or most of the spoils. Privateers held a letter-of-marque that authorized their actions and gave them immunity. When the Treaty of Ryswick was signed in 1697 and the war came to an end, those privateers that weren't already committing piracy, for many did so to stay alive, became pirates. It seems everyone was involved in piracy in some way, including the governors. During peacetime pirates were a liability, taking any ship they could, leading to repeated retaliatory attacks. It became clear that the colony was undefendable and ungovernable.

The War of Spanish Succession began in 1701 and England and the rest of Europe were allied against France, whose prince was the strongest contender for the Spanish Crown. Spain was no longer the New World power she had once been. Privateers out of Nassau profited greatly at the expense of France and Spain and in 1703, these two nations got together for a swift and brutal strike on Nassau. It was burnt to the ground. The last governor sent to the islands by the Proprietors returned to Carolina in 1703, leaving a lawless land behind.

For the next 14 years, privateers and then pirates held sway over The Bahamas. The legal niceties of privateering sanctioned the actions of most, but when the war ended in 1714, once again the moral privateers became immoral pirates who invariably chose the lawless Bahamas as a safe haven. The "Pirates' Republic" lasted for the next three years. All the buying and selling occurred in Nassau, and the Out Islands provided secret hideaways. Few records remain from that time, but it is believed some 1,400 pirates operated out of Nassau, which was regularly sacked by the French and Spanish. The original settlers that remained fled to the Out Islands, in particular Exuma and Long Island.

Expulsis Piratis - Restituta Commercia

Finally in 1717, the situation had so degenerated that the House of Lords advised the King to take over the governing of the Bahamas. The Lords Proprietors surrendered all but ownership of the land, and the British government offered to pardon all pirates who turned themselves in before September 5th, 1718. Now a royal colony, The Bahamas needed a royal governor. Woodes Rogers, himself a privateer, was chosen to clean up house and rid Nassau of piracy. Rogers' goal, *Expulsis Piratis - Restituta Commercia* (Pirates Expelled - Commerce Restored), became the country's motto. His reputation as a privateer preceded him, and when he arrived at the mouth of Nassau's harbour, his ultimatum of "death or pardon" was taken seriously. There was a brief skirmish in the harbour but eventually all took an oath or were chased away or executed.

Woodes Rogers set about cleaning up Nassau, which was in shambles. He formed a Council and outfitted Fort Nassau with 50 cannons. The threat from former pirates and war with Spain

Famous Pirates

The first of Nassau's great pirates was Captain Henry Jennings who was busy looting Spanish treasure as a privateer, completely unaware that the Treaty of Utrecht had been signed ending War of Spanish Succession. He fled the gallows in Jamaica and took up refuge in The Bahamas, where he lorded over the mayhem that was Nassau.

Edward Teach, a.k.a. Blackbeard, is the most famous pirate to have sailed from The Bahamas. He patrolled the waters in search of prey from his tower at the eastern edge of town. By all accounts, Blackbeard was a scary formidable man, draped as he was with cutlasses and pistols, his long black beard tangled with colourful ribbons and twisted around his ears and his wild eyes barely perceptible through the smoke circling his head from the slow-burning fuses strung from his hat. He was the self-appointed magistrate of Nassau and plied Bahamian waters in his ship *Queen Anne's Revenge*. He died off the coast of the Carolinas in 1719.

A final trio of pirates have an important place in Bahamian heritage: Calico Jack Rackham and two of his crew, female pirates Anne Bonney and Mary Read, who apparently dressed like men to the point where they fooled each other, but were also known to parade around topless. Bonney and Rackham are reported to have been lovers. They were all captured in Jamaica and executed.

required it. Rogers had indeed accomplished much in Nassau, for the Spanish were held off in 1720. Rogers stayed in Nassau for just under three years, having incurred much debt rebuilding Nassau and encouraging agriculture, he ended up in debtor's prison and bankrupt. He returned in 1729 though, and called for a 24-member Assembly, the beginnings of the parliament that still sits in The Bahamas today. Rogers served as Governor until his death in 1732.

Governor Fitzwilliam followed but is not remembered fondly, having achieved little besides scaring off the few farmers working Bahamian land. War between England and Spain brought prosperous times during the governorship of John Tinker. Fort Nassau was again rebuilt and Fort Montagu and a sea battery to guard the eastern entrance to the harbour were built. The War of Austrian Succession in 1748 and then the Seven Years' War in 1756 ensured continued economic stability. In 1760, the ex-governor of Massachusetts, William Shirley, took up the position in The Bahamas. His successful term was marked by many improvements, funded mostly by privateering. When his brother Thomas took over in 1768, England was at peace and economic depression followed like clockwork. The treasury was empty and government was simply not functioning.

Americans and Loyalists

Of course, there was more to this economic depression than the lack of privateering possibilites. The Bahamas, which depended on trade with the mainland colonies, found itself in the middle of a disagreement between England and 13 of her North American colonies. The Bahamas began as an

Slavery in The Bahamas

The success of the plantations is attributed mainly to the slaves brought in to work them. Sold by African chiefs, literally stacked into the holds of slave ships and sent across the ocean, the majority of these unfortunate souls never made it to the Americas. The bounty of the sea, both natural and salvaged, accounted for most of the economic activity in The Bahamas before the arrival of the Loyalists, who were the first ones to engage in any large-scale and profitable agricultural enterprise. This does not mean there weren't any slaves in The Bahamas. Free blacks and troublesome slaves were sent to Eleuthera where they joined other free blacks who arrived with the original settlers. The few Bermudian farmers who made a go of it on New Providence in the 1670s also had slaves. And then the booty salvaged or taken by privateers and pirates was often slaves. Around 4000 arrived with the Loyalists. The demand for slaves rose as their cotton plantations prospered, but by that time cries for reform were already being heard. The failure of the plantations put an end to that demand. Nevertheless, about 3,000 slaves arrived before 1804 when the last arrivals were recorded.

Though it is impossible to trace the tribal origins of black Bahamians today, when their ancestors arrived in The Bahamas they maintained the languages and traditions of their tribes, which included Yoruba, Congo, Ibo, Mandingo, Fulani and Hausa, among others. More often, however, they were separated and found themselves with other slaves whose languages were just as foreign to them as English. Accounts of the time do not dismiss the fundamental problem of slavery, but do maintain that Bahamian slaves were treated well, much better than in the other islands of the West Indies.

In Britain, abolitionist William Wilberforce was instrumental in the passing of a law ending the slave trade on British ships in 1807. Part of the law required that slaves be registered, and the 1822 registration found there to be 10,808 slaves in The Bahamas. The Abolition of Slavery Act became law in 1833, stating that slavery would end on July 31, 1834. August 1st is celebrated throughout the islands, except curiously in Fox Hill, where it is celebrated two weeks later, since that is how long it took for the news to reach residents. After trading was outlawed and well into the second half of the century, British ships stopped traders, released their African captives and resettled them. About 6,000 Africans came to The Bahamas this way and settled in free black villages, including Adelaide, Carmichael, Gambier, Grant's Town, Bain Town, Creek Village and Fox Hill on New Providence. These freed Africans joined the approximately 11,000 blacks already in The Bahamas, which means that about 35% of the black population in the mid-1800s had never known slavery.

After emancipation, freed slaves still had four years of apprenticehship to endure. They still had to work for their former masters but came to be seen and to see themselves as employees, receiving wages in some cases. Complete freedom was finally theirs on August 1, 1838.

extension of the Carolinas when it was granted to the Lords Proprietors, and when the American Revolution broke out in 1775, choosing sides was not a clear-cut question. Besides economic considerations many Bahamians had family on the mainland. Nevertheless, Bahamians remained loyal and suffered through rebel raids and occupation. The American Navy wanted gunpowder and though the Bahamians succeeded in sending it away, they could not hold back the rebels who occupied Nassau for two weeks and imprisoned the governor. Vulnerable Nassau was left with no arms and no gunpowder, and in 1778 they attacked again.

Nassau was not a priority for the English during the American Revolution, and Spain and France, who had been trounced by England in 1763, took advantage of this by attacking the city in 1782. The Spanish fleet, led by the governor of Havana, included some 600 soldiers as well as American warships. Bahamians had always hated the Spanish, and racial, linguistic, religious and cultural differences made the year-long Spanish occupation that much more difficult to bear. In 1783 the Loyalist colonel from South Carolina, Andrew Deveaux, mounted an army to free Nassau. Every able man from Eleuthera and Harbour Island volunteered and set out for Nassau. The small army of 200 should have been no match for the Spanish, but Deveaux tricked the Spanish: the Harbour Island fishing boats going back and forth appeared to the Spanish to be unloading a much larger army than they actually were. Deveaux's troops took Fort Montagu, and after some negotiation, the Spanish surrendered Fort Nassau. This was a great victory for Bahamians, who would never be lorded over by another occupying force. A victory for the rebels on the mainland proved to have equally important consequences. Residents of the 13 rebel colonies who wished to remain loyal to the British crown were branded as traitors at home and had little choice but to relocate to the other British colonies in North America. In 1782, before the end of the revolution, there were 3,950 people in The Bahamas, and by 1788 the population had risen to 9,300. The Loyalists brought their slaves with them and for the first time there was a black majority. The mostly destitute Loyalists could not afford to purchase land, and though the Crown wanted to grant it to them it wasn't theirs to grant. During the scurrilous pirate years, the Lords Proprietors had surrendered control of the islands but they still owned the land. Thus in 1787, ownership was transferred to the Crown for the sum of £12,000. Lands were grabbed up and plantation homes were built. Cotton promised and delivered: at its height nearly a million pounds were grown each year. And then the pesky little chenille worm and red bug made their way to The Bahamas. The chenille chomped its way through plants and the red bug stained fibres, destroying the 1789 and 1794 crops. By the 1830s, with the failure of the cotton plantations and the abolition of the slave trade and then of slavery, most of the plantations had been abandoned.

Peaks and Valleys... Blockade Running

While cotton fortunes were being lost and won and slaves were being freed, the treacherous reefs of The Bahamas were still claiming ships, thus wrecking was alive and well. Then the War of 1812 between England and the United States broke out and privateers were busy once again. This war ended in 1814, but all was not calm in the United States. The American Civil War broke out in 1861 and in an effort to defeat the Confederacy, Abraham Lincoln declared a complete sea blockade of the Southern States, and this is where The Bahamas come in. Ocean-crossing vessels could not enter blockaded harbours, but light, fast and shallow-draft runners out of The Bahamas could. Nassau became a trans-shipment point supplying the war machine of the South and the hungry mouths of Southerners.

Tourism was a growing concern in Nassau at the time. In 1851, the government approved a subsidy for steamship service between New York City and Nassau. The first ship arrived in 1859, the year construction began on the Royal Victoria Hotel. The hotel was completed just in time to become the favourite haunt of deal-making buyers, sellers and runners. So much money was being made that shops and businesses flourished along Bay Street, homes were built and the public debt was eliminated. But alas, easy come, easy go. In 1865, the war, the blockade and the boom were over.

Once again, Bahamians turned to the land and the sea. But these two gave as much as they took. The depression that followed the blockade was compounded by the devastating hurricane of 1866. The old standby wrecking could not even be relied upon. Charts and lighthouses made Bahamian waters safer than they had ever been before. Despite very poor soil, sisal, pineapples and citrus fruits also enjoyed success. Sisal was a promising enterprise. Promoted by Sir Ambrose Shea, governor in 1887, it seemed such a sure thing that Neville Chamberlain, future Prime Minister of Great Britain, had a plantation on Andros. There was no getting around the Bahamian soil, however, and all the sisal plantations failed. In 1900, 7,000,000 dozen pineapples were exported. Again, there were complications: the fruit was fragile, the yield low and the soil quickly exhausted, but the decisive blow came from the mainland in the form of large import tariffs. A winter freeze in Florida in 1894-95 resulted in a peak year for citrus fruits, but American tariffs soon claimed that industry as well. In 1896, sponging took off, spawning a healthy boatbuilding industry, and lasted a good 40 years before disease and overfishing led to the closing of the sponge beds. At the turn of the century, the situation boiled down to three choices: subsistence farming, sponging or emigrating to Florida; twenty percent of the population chose the latter.

A New Century and Rum-Running

The excitement that drew thousands of Bahamians to Florida was the construction of the railroad by Henry Flagler. As it turned out, this affected The Bahamas in more ways than one. Flagler became the first major foreign investor in Bahamian tourism with the opening of his Colonial Hotel in 1900 on the site of Fort Nassau. That same year a winter steamship service between Miami and Nassau started.

Of the 700-odd Bahamians who fought in the First World War, there were 37 casualties. Effects of this conflict nevertheless went beyond the front lines. The market disturbances contributed to the failure of sisal and sponges and disrupted the fledgling tourist industry. Throughout the islands hundreds of residents donated their time and money to the war effort.

As per usual, events in the United States were increasingly more influential than those in Europe as far as The Bahamas were concerned. In 1920 it became illegal to manufacture, sell, import and export liquor in the United States. Prohibition was just the shot in the arm The Bahamas needed. Instead of being shipped to the United States, intoxicating liquors were shipped to Nassau and from there runners brought the illicit liquor to the mainland, or rather to "Rum Row", a floating liquor store in international waters about six or seven kilometres off the Jersey shore. The deals were made in Nassau, which experienced another boom, while the liquor was stored on Bimini, Grand Bahama, Gun Cay and Cat Cay, those islands closest to the United States. Naturally, liquor imports into The Bahamas rose (from 1917 to 1922 they increased thirty-five times over) and so did the government's revenue from duties. Even though they lowered the duty to encourage imports, duties payed off the public debt and left a healthy surplus behind. So much so that the harbour was dredged, year-round steamer service between Nassau and New York was assured and the Fort Montagu Hotel and a casino were opened. Though the Colonial Hotel burned down in 1922, there was enough money to rebuild: the New Colonial Hotel opened in 1923 and has been in operation ever since. Before too long, however, the US Coast Guard stepped up patrols of "Rum Row" and the United States claimed 12 miles instead of three as terrestrial waters. Finally in 1933, Prohibition ended.

The end of Prohibition coincided with the failure of the sisal crops and shortly thereafter the sponge beds were closed. The Bahamas had yet to know everlasting economic success, most of the population was therefore used to getting along with what the land and the sea could provide. The 1930s were difficult years, but the growing importance of tourism (Pan-Am started its first flights between Nassau and Miami in 1929) was paving the way for the modern Bahamas that we know today. But first there was a war to fight.

HRH the Governor

Bahamians contributed greatly to the Second World War at home and abroad. This time around there were enemy submarines to watch out for and 500 men volunteered for The Bahamas Defence Force. The strategic location of the islands led to the construction of two US naval bases in The Bahamas to monitor the movements of German submarines. One of the most significant effects of the war in The Bahamas, however, was the arrival of the Duke and Duchess of Windsor. King Edward VII abdicated the throne of England for the love of divorcee Wallis Simpson. As Duke and Duchess, the couple posed something of a problem for the British government. His new bride was not accepted in England, but unsupervised the Duke was seen as a security risk to the government. Rumours of his involvement with the Germans persisted; apparently the Germans were plotting to kidnap him and restore him to the throne as a puppet king; Edward was also believed to have been sympathetic to the Nazis. So to keep him out of harm's way, and perhaps to ensure he behaved, the former King became Governor of The Bahamas in 1940. Bahamians were certainly honoured to have him, for it lent their islands a certain stature and respectability. The Duke's legacy as Governor of The Bahamas is controversial. He is as revered for promoting equality, self-sufficiency and full employment for the black population as he is reviled for backing the mostly white Bay Street Boys, a group of merchants and lawyers whose businesses and offices were located on Nassau's Bay Street.

It was not until the Americans officially joined the war, however, that the negative repercussions of the conflict were

The Murder of Sir Harry Oakes

Sir Harry Oakes was a wealthy Canadian mining magnate with huge real-estate holdings on New Providence and a major hand in countless tourist development projects before the war. He built a small airstrip, the Cable Beach Golf Course (the country's first golf course) and the Bahamas Country Club. On July 8th, 1943, he was found brutally murdered in his bed. Theories and rumours were many: for one, Sir Harry Oakes had been a member of the Legislative Assembly and was opposed to the opening of casinos in The Bahamas, perhaps Miami mobsters had ordered a hit on him. The Miami detectives flown in to solve the case, however, felt that Oakes' son-in-law, Alfred de Marigny, was the killer, and so arrested him. After a sensational trial, de Marigny was acquitted and the mystery remains unsolved.

felt in The Bahamas. Up until then the tourist industry had continued to grow, and there were plenty of jobs keeping the Allied war machine going. The bombing of Pearl Harbour in 1941 forced the United States into the war, and once again events in that country were keenly felt in The Bahamas. In 1942 work began on "The Project", a flight-training facility, base and a pair of air fields on New Providence, one of which is now Nassau International Airport. More than 2,000 jobs were created but Bahamian construction workers were not paid as much as their American counterparts. The problem was that the Bahamian minimum wage was ridiculously low compared to the American rate. Blaming the government, angry workers rioted on and sacked Bay Street in June of 1942. Racial strife lasted through the week-long curfew that was imposed and afterward. At the end of the month the daily minimum wage was raised from four shillings to five shillings plus a free meal.

Towards Self-Determination

The post-war era in The Bahamas was marked by the rise of party politics and the establishment of the tourist industry. We will address the former first. The Progressive Liberal Party (PLP), formed in 1953 and led by Lynden Pindling, was the first political party in The Bahamas. It represented the black majority and challenged the authority of the Bay Street Boys, the white members of the House of Assembly who purported to represent the Out Islands but all lived in Nassau and worked on Bay Street. In 1956 the Anti-Discrimination Resolution was passed allowing blacks access to all public places. Then in early 1958 a general strike by mostly black workers brought the tourist industry to a grinding halt. The Bay Street Boys thus got together and formed the United Bahamian Party (UBP). The PLP slowly gained seats in the House of Assembly, but still the UBP won more seats. In 1964 a new constitution was drawn up that saw the creation of a cabinet by the majority party of the Assembly. The UBP named the country's first premier, Sir Roland Symonette.

The cries of the civil rights movement in the United States were heard in The Bahamas where, though the legislature was now more representative, the electoral process remained unfair: electoral boundaries favoured whites and only male property-owners were allowed to vote. The opposition, the PLP,

The Grand Bahama Port Authority

Before American financier Wallace Groves set his sights on Grand Bahama, there was not much to recommend the island. But in 1946, Groves decided there was money to be made there and he purchased the Abaco Lumber Company's mill. He rebuilt the mill and expanded his operations and the settlements on Grand Bahama. By 1955 his vision for the island was expanding: he set in motion the eventual passing of the Hawksbill Creek Agreement that year. Groves became president of the Grand Bahama Port Authority, which was granted 50,000 acres of land to be developed as an international deep-water port and free zone. Another 99,000 acres were later acquired for the development of a hotel and eventually a casino.

protested in the House of Assembly by violating the rules of debate, throwing the Speaker's mace and the hourglass used for timing speeches out the window and finally boycotting the House. They succeeded in eliminating the property qualification, and in 1961 suffragettes led by Doris Johnson fought for and won the right to vote. The 1967election was very close but represented a victory for the PLP, which named Lynden Pindling premier.

Let us now take a look at the establishment of the tourist industry. After the Second World War, it became clear that tourism was one of the only industries on which the Bahamian economy could rely. In 1950 the calling of a development board headed by Stafford Sands marked the government's serious commitment to tourism. By the mid-1950s, air-conditioning was standard in all new hotels, enabling tourists to enjoy year-round comfort. In 1957, the new Nassau International Airport was opened. The general strike of 1958, which closed down all tourist facilities, served to underline the industry's importance. The 1961 US Embargo on Fidel Castro's communist Cuba sent a lot of business The Bahamas' way. Banking was promoted and the country's status as a tax haven drew a lot of heavy hitters. The fledgling new town of Freeport was exempted from gambling laws and a casino opened there in 1963. Nassau's harbour was dredged and the new Prince George Wharf was built, ushering in a new era of cruise ship travel to The Bahamas. In 1968, one million tourists came to The Bahamas.

Independence

Contrary to what one might expect, the desire for independence was neither unanimous nor very enthusiastic. It seemed to be an inevitability. Britain encouraged it and the PLP was for it, but the UBP along with the descendants of Loyalists in Eleuthera and the Abacos were strongly against it. Nevertheless, Pindling's government sought the people's support, and during the 1972 election a vote for the PLP was understood to be a vote for independence. The PLP won a resounding victory over the Free National Movement, a new party formed by the UBP and two spinoffs of the PLP, the National Democratic Party and the Free PLP.

On July 10, 1973, The Commonwealth of The Bahamas gained its independence after 325 years of colonial rule. The Queen remained the official

Important Dates in the History of The Bahamas

12,000 years ago: Nomadic tribes cross the Bering Strait and populate the Americas in successive waves of migration, finally occupying the islands of the Caribbean and the present-day islands of the Bahamas around the year AD 700.

October 12, 1492: Columbus makes landfall on the Lucayan island of Guanahaní, which he renames San Salvador. He spends the next 15 days exploring the islands of Santa Maria de la Concepcion, Fernandina, Isabela, and the Islas de Arena.

1513: Spain's Ponce de Leon explores Bimini in search of the fountain of youth, he discovers the Gulf Stream instead.

1517: Just 25 years after Columbus' arrival, nothing remains of the Lucayans, the islands' native population, who were wiped out by disease and enslavement.

1629: England claims possession of the Bahamas, but has no settlement plans as yet for the still uninhabited islands.

1648: The Eleutheran Adventurers, a group of Bermudians seeking religious freedom, led by Captain William Sayle, settle on Eleuthera and create the first Republic of the New World.

1656: New Providence is settled by Bermudian seamen.

November 1, 1670: The Bahama Islands are granted to the six Lords Proprietors, marking the beginning of Proprietary Rule.

1703-1717: Privateers and pirates hold sway over the islands attacking French and Spanish ships that regularly sack Nassau.

1718: The First Royal Governor, Woodes Rogers, arrives to rid Nassau of piracy.

1776, 1778, 1781: Americans attack and capture New Providence as part of the American Revolution.

1782-1783: The Spanish occupy Nassau until Colonel Andrew Deveaux chases them out and Spain cedes the islands with the signing of the Treaty of Versailles.

1783: With the end of the Revolutionary War in the United States, Loyalists flee the new republic, many end up in the Bahamas.

1807: The slave trade is abolished on British ships.

1834: The Abolition of Slavery Act ends slavery throughout the British Empire.

1851: The government approves a subsidy for a steamship line to Nassau, laying the foundation for what would become the islands' most important industry.

1861-1865: Abraham Lincoln proclaims a sea blockade of the Confederate States as part of the American Civil War, and blockade running brings tremendous but short-lived prosperity to the islands.

1862: The Royal Victoria Hotel opens and is the centre of society and business during the blockade.

1866: A major hurricane sweeps across the entire chain.

1900: This is the most prosperous year of pineapple growing, with the export of seven million dozen pineapples. The Colonial Hotel opens and a winter steamship service starts.

1920-1933: Prohibition in the United States makes The Bahamas a centre for bootlegging and rum-running. The economy picks up, but collapses just as quickly when Prohibition is repealed.

1940: The Duke of Windsor is sent away from warring Europe to become governor of the Bahamas.

1955: The Hawksbill Creek Agreement is signed creating Freeport, Grand Bahama.

1956: Anti-discrimination Resolution is passed, allowing blacks free access to all public places.

1958: General strike over opening of Nassau's international airport closes down all tourist facilities for 19 days.

1964: Sir Roland Symonette is chosen as the Bahamas' first Premier.

1967: The People's Liberation Party (PLP), lead by Lynden Pindling, is elected by a slim margin putting an end to the rule of the mostly white United Bahamian Party (UBP).

1968: A landslide election victory for the PLP establishes black rule in The Bahamas.

July 10, 1973: The Bahamas gains independence from Britain.

1992: The Free National Movement lead by Hubert Ingraham defeats longstanding Prime Minister Pindling amidst rumours of corruption in the Pindling government.

1994: Paradise Island, formerly known as Hog Island, is sold by American entertainment mogul Merv Griffin to Sun International which opens the ever-expanding Atlantis mega-resort and casino.

1997: The Free National Movement is re-elected in a landslide victory.

though symbolic head of state, but her flag was replaced with the black, turquoise and gold of the Bahamian flag.

Coming of Age

Though Lynden Pindling led his country into nationhood, he could not escape controversy. His efforts to encourage the tourism and banking industries were successful, but to the average Bahamian, foreigners were getting a free ride, so to speak. Without this preferential treatment, however, the economic picture was not so rosy and there were allegations of corruption within the government by the former chairman of the PLP, Hubert Ingraham. Then along came the drug trade. Like in Prohibition, The Bahamas became a trans-shipment location, this time for illicit narcotics on their way from South America to the United States, and as with Prohibition, drugs brought money into the islands. But they also brought American news reporters and shame to Pindling. In 1984, it was revealed that government officials were in cahoots with Colombian drug lords. With the government crackdown and the involvement of American drug enforcers that followed, no one wanted to touch The Bahamas.

The 1992 election brought the FNM to power and made Hubert Ingraham prime minister. The previous government had taken over many hotels in an effort to keep them open, and now these were sold off at bargain prices. This prompted a huge injection of foreign capital and the opening of a whole slew of refurbished mega-resorts throughout the islands. The most recent election, in April 1997, was a landslide victory for the FNM.

POLITICS

The Islands Of The Bahamas has a commonwealth government. It gained its independence from the United Kingdom on July 10, 1973. Its national holiday is celebrated each year on this day. The head of government is Prime Minister Hubert Alexander Ingraham of the Free National Movement (FNM), the other major party is the Progressive Liberal Party (PLP). The most recent election, held in April 1997, was a landslide victory for the FNM, which was initially brought to power in 1992. The PLP, formerly led by Sir Lynden Pindling, had been in power since independence. Queen Elizabeth II is the chief of state, she is represented by the governor-general whom she appoints. The bicameral Parliament is made up of a 16-member senate appointed by the governor general and a 49-seat House of Assembly appointed by democratic vote.

The domination of the white Bay Street Boys was particularly irksome to Lynden Pindling ever since he was elected to Parliament in 1956. He became premier in 1967 as Bahamian independence was becoming more and more likely. The Crown offered The Bahamas independence in the late 1960s, and in 1972 Bahamians voted for total independence, but chose to remain part of the Commonwealth and to retain the Queen as the official head

Bahamian-US Relations

When it comes to US-Bahamian relations, it is something of a love-hate relationship. Too often it seems that the fate of The Bahamas has been sealed by events in the United States. It started with the Revolutionary War. Trade with the mainland was the lifeblood of The Bahamas, yet war precluded that. The attacks and occupation by the fledgling American army that followed only added insult to injury. The Americans even helped the Spanish invade Nassau in 1782. Then when war broke out between the United and Confederate states, Nassau's fortunes again came to depend on the Americans as blockade running boomed and then died. Agriculture finally bore fruit in the late 19th century, with citrus fruits, pineapples and sisal, but American protectionism ruined any chance those crops might have had. Prohibition in the US brought another boom to Nassau, but its repeal ended the boom as quickly as it had started it. During the Second World War, US participation in the conflict had serious repercussions in The Bahamas. Bahamian construction workers were not paid as much as their American counterparts for work on major military installations in Nassau, and this lead to a serious riot in 1942. Finally, there is the issue of tourism. The proximity of the United States has meant that the industry depends tremendously on American tourists and certainly the country has benefited greatly from the influx of capital from hotel developers and tourists themselves. It is central to the fact that The Bahamas enjoys the third highest standard of living in North America. Bahamians love to take weekend trips to Miami, and there is no denying the Americanization of Bahamian culture. Proud Bahamians are not so enthusiastic about this, however, and the bad hand that the Americans have dealt them in history is not forgotten.

of state. Despite bringing the country to independence, Pindling's years as Prime Minister were marked by accusations of corruption.

ECONOMY

According to the US Department of Commerce, The Bahamas is a stable, upper-middle-income developing nation. It boasts the third highest standard of living in North America. The Bahamas National Investment Policy reads as follows: "The Bahamas levies no taxes on capital gains, corporate earnings, personal income, sales, inheritance or dividends. This tax freedom is available to all resident corporations, partnerships, individuals and trusts." This tax haven is thus a major centre for offshore banking. All this financial activity still takes second place to tourism, however, the industry that is responsible for more than 50% of the GDP and that directly or indirectly employs 40% of the workforce. More than 15% of Caribbean tourist dollars are spent in The Bahamas.

The GDP is $4.8 billion (1995 estimate, purchasing power parity) with a real growth rate of 2%. Consumer price inflation has risen slightly in recent years and at the start of 1996 stood at 2.2%. Services, including tourism and banking, account for 62% of the GDP, industry for 35% and agriculture for 3% (only 1% of the land is arable). The main industries besides these three are cement, oil refining and transshipment, salt production, rum, aragonite, pharmaceuticals and spiral-welded steel piping.

One of the main goals of the government's economic policy is to foster growth in other sectors such as agriculture and manufacturing so as to lessen the dependence on tourism and imports, which stand at about $1.1 billion versus about $224 million in exports. The United States is the country's major trading partner (imports: US 55%, Japan 17%, Nigeria 12%, Denmark 7%, Norway 6%; exports US 51%, UK 7%, Norway 7%, France 6%, Italy 5%).

Various investment incentives exist to encourage both foreign and domestic investment. Foreign investors are attracted by the tax-free status of income, the free repatriation of profits, the accessibility of international financing and finally the stability of the economy and the currency, which is matched to the US dollar on a 1:1 ratio. Hotel developers are exempt from customs duties on raw materials and equipment. The same exemptions are also available to manufacturers of certain approved products (the garment industry, food processing, handicraft, souvenir and cottage industries, spirits and beer production) and to those industries that intend to export at least 95% of their products. Agricultural businesses are also encouraged with similar customs exemptions.

The Bahamas' tourism industry began with the opening of the Royal Victoria Hotel in 1861 during blockade-running days, and became an official industry in 1898 with the Hotel and Steam Ship Service Act. Fortunes have been lost and won in this industry, which has nevertheless always remained the country's most important. In the late 1960s, this was the place to hobnob with royals and millionaires. During the slump that followed, the government actually purchased and ran many hotels to save them from closing. The new government in 1992 instigated a new policy to sell most of these hotels off at bargain prices. This prompted a huge injection of foreign capital and the appearance of a string of refurbished mega-resorts throughout the islands. The favourable investment environment and proximity to the United States have bolstered confidence in the destination and once again made it a leader in the region.

The Ministry of Tourism has been promoting the Family Islands as a destination. Though an Act of Parliament officially changed the name from Out Islands to Family Islands, the Ministry of Tourism prefers Family Islands as it emphasizes the relaxed and remote atmosphere of these unique islands. Ecotourism has also become a hot item, contributing to the image of The Bahamas as a an activity destination and not just a beach destination.

In 1995, 3,238,255 foreigners came to The Bahamas, a decline over previous years. Despite the decreasing numbers, the estimated total visitor spending has increased. More than 50% of visitors arrive in Nassau, the other 4% arrive either in Grand Bahama or the Family Islands.

With no income tax and all these incentives, one can't help but wonder where the government gets all its money. Unfortunately, all of these exemptions do not apply to the average Bahamian, as fairly high duties and taxes are imposed on many standard goods and services like vehicles and food. Tourism revenue is what drives the Bahamian economy.

If tourism is the bread of the Bahamian economy, banking is butter, accounting for roughly 8% of the GDP. Most banks and trust companies are non-resident or

A Few Statistics

Population:	254,685 (1990 census); 259,367 (1996 estimate)
Age Structure:	0-14 years 28%
	15-64 years 67%
	65 years and over 5%
Birth rate:	18.73 births/1,000 population
Death rate:	5.74/1,000 population
Infant mortality rate:	23.3 deaths/1,000 live births
Fertility rate	1.97 children
Life expectancy rate:	total population 72.53 years
	Male 67.98 years
	Female 77.16 years
Literacy:	total population 98.2%
	Male 98.5%
	Female 98%

(Source: The World Factbook; all 1996 estimates unless otherwise indicated)

offshore companies that manage the assets of wealthy individuals and do not generate any Bahamian dollar earnings.

Agricultural production, concentrated in the Abacos, Andros and Grand Bahama, involves citrus fruits, winter vegetables and poultry. Pork, mutton and dairy farming are being encouraged.

Freeport, a 230-square-mile free-trade zone established in 1955, is operated by the Grand Bahama Port Authority. Its port is currently the closest offshore port to the United States and well-positioned between Europe and the Americas. The tax-free status of the zone and facilities encourage international investment. The port is also currently undergoing major renovations through a partnership project with Hong Kong; the completion, set for 1998, of the deepwater port will make it the finest facility and the transshipment hub of the western hemisphere.

Unemployment is 10% (1996). There is no minimum wage in The Bahamas, though wages are among the highest in The Caribbean. The Fair Labour Standards Act has established standard daily and weekly work hours, vacation and overtime pay.

PEOPLE AND CULTURE

The original inhabitants of the islands now known as The Bahamas were Lucayans. A mere half-century after Columbus' landfall, the entire population had been destroyed by disease and enslavement in the gold mines of Cuba and Hispaniola, and the pearl fisheries of Cubagua and Margarita. The islands remained unpopulated for the next 100 years, and without any permanent settlement until 1684. Of the original Eleutheran Adventurers, only a handful actually remained, these included the Adderley, Albury, Bethell, Davis, Sands and Saunders families, who were later joined by poor whites, rebel slaves and free blacks from Bermuda. The greatest population influx occurred following US independence, due to the arrival of Loyalists and their slaves. From then on

Culture in The Bahamas

Bahamian playwright and lawyer Winston Saunders made this rather telling statement in an essay in the book *Modern Bahamian Society* published in 1989:

"Culture in The Bahamas today is an amalgam of our British heritage, and the effects of our closeness to North America. Our language is English, our Parliament follows the judicial procedure set down in England... Our courts follow the English system... Marry the above with the practice of *obeah*, the girating movements of the ring-play, the pulsating rhythm of Junkanoo and the goat-skin drum, the hand-clapping jumpers, the use of bush medicine, the songs and the drinking of a wake and the consequent outpouring of public grief at the death of a loved one, our African-inspired neighbourhood banking system called *asue*, and you almost have a Bahamian. The final touches come in the form of the American Jerri curl, the American Afro, American television, American and Japanese technology, the American system of higher education and its graduate degrees, hamburgers and hot dogs, Coca-Cola, the Chevrolet... the satellite dish. Frivolous though some of these things may seem, they fuse to form a representative catalogue of our cultural heritage and the patterns that dictate our reaction to any given situation."

blacks formed the majority and a Creole society evolved during this period. Running the cotton plantations of the late 18th century required labourers, and more slaves were brought to the islands. The failure of these plantations prompted many white Loyalists to leave The Bahamas, thus tipping the population scales further in favour of blacks. Following the abolition of the British slave trade in 1807, African slaves liberated from foreign ships settled in The Bahamas. Between 1808 and 1860, about 6,000 Africans, mostly Yoruba and Congolese, were freed and settled in The Bahamas. At least eight free black villages existed by Emancipation in 1834. Despite hard times, African Bahamians survived by thrifty habits and the custom of *asue*, a neighbourhood banking system from Africa still popular in contemporary Bahamas, and by "Friendly Societies" that offered mutual assistance in hard times.

An increased demand for labour in the sponging and farming industries in the late 19th and 20th centuries brought Greeks, Chinese, Lebanese and other West Indians. During Prohibition, the latter group sensitized black Bahamians to the political movements elsewhere in the Caribbean. The largest minority in The Bahamas, the Haitians, began arriving in the 1950s, and they are still coming in significant numbers. Despite intermarriage, these various ethnic groups still form distinct communities.

"Conchs" is often used today for white Bahamians in general, but a true "conchy-Joe" is a descendant of the original settlers of Eleuthera. They were given this nickname by Loyalists who arrived following the American Revolution who blamed their predecessor's lack of economic success on the fact that they were as lazy and slow-moving as those giant molluscs.

The last census was taken in 1990 and found the population of the Bahamas to be 254,685; 1996 estimates put the figure at 259,367. Eighty-five percent of the population is black, primarily of West African descent. These are the descendants of people brought to the islands as slaves. The other 15% of the population is white, the majority being descendants of original settlers

ARTS

Visual Arts

Pre-Columbian art in The Bahamas is limited to a scattering of artifacts and descriptions by Europeans of the Lucayans prior to their extinction. A ceremonial wooden stool called a *duho* was discovered in a cave on Long Island and is an example of the Lucayans' ability to carve with simple and primitive tools. They are also known to have carved intricate designs with live hardwood coals. Finally, petroglyphs have been found, most notably on Rum Cay. They painted their skin many colours for cosmetic reasons, to ward off evil spirits and to protect their skin from the sun and insects. They wore woven headbands and waist bands and jewellery made of gold, sea-shell and coral. The Lucayans were clearly an artistic people; however, there does not seem to be a distinction between art and necessity, art was simply a part of their daily lives.

Before and after Columbus' famous landfall in 1492, European artistry of this part of the world did not amount to more that cartography wherein myths of mermaids, the fountain of youth, buried treasures and ocean monsters were created. Once the islands were settled, the inhabitants displayed artistic talent with boat-building and distinctive architecture. The first settlers were Puritans and Protestant Loyalists, who rejected the Roman Catholic worship of idols, and thus the carving skills of Africans were not valued or encouraged as they were in Catholic Hispaniola. Any artistic piece in the islands was brought from America. It is really only in the early 1800s with emancipation that an African influence was felt, and ultimately, with independence that a true Bahamian style found its way.

The American War of Independence and the blockade running that followed drew many artists to The Bahamas. Most notable among these is the American artist Winslow Homer, who was sent here in 1884 to illustrate a story of the bustling new tourist destination of Nassau; he returned on his own in 1888. His watercolours provide a candid look at the black population of the time.

Horace Wright is considered the father of modern Bahamian art. His watercolours raised the awareness of art appreciation in the islands. Don Russell's famous painting of the Queen's Staircase hangs in the lobby of Princess Margaret Hospital in Nassau. His Academy of Fine Art produced many fine artists including Max Taylor, Brent Malone and Jackson Burnside.

The African influence is difficult to identify and is more easily perceptible in the colours, rhythms, shapes and themes. Intuitive and naive artists include Amos Ferguson (referred to as the "Grandma Moses of Bahamian art"), Tony Mackey and Eric Ellis are most representative of an African influence. Amos Ferguson, born in 1920, is perhaps the most intriguing. This former house- and basket-painter was discovered by an American woman who purchased one of his painted baskets in Nassau's straw market in the 1980s. He paints by "divine instruction" from God, and his pieces of colourful naive art now sell for thousands of dollars.

Other Bahamian artists that are very popular with the public and considered highly collectible include Alton Lowe and Eddie Minnis. Lowe paints realist and scenic landscapes of his native Green Turtle Cay. Minnis's very colourful oils preserve images of present-day and historical Bahamas. His two daughters Roshanne and Nicole also use striking realism in their work.

The struggle for self-determination that followed independence is discernable in the visual arts. A searching for, and identification with their African roots has greatly affected contemporary Bahamian artists whose works exhibit stylized realism and experimental and eclectic tendencies.

Music and Dance

Music is central to the culture of The Bahamas where stories are more often sung than spoken. In these "islands of song", as they are known, even the language is melodic. The musical and dancing heritage of The Bahamas is truly a result of the marrying of European and African customs. A rich tradition of three- and four-part harmonies is alive and well throughout the islands, such as in the telling of legends and stories with re-occurring themes of faith, optimism, patience, weariness and fighting Satan. The same themes persist in the religious hymns and antebellum slaves songs brought by Loyalists and their slaves from the United States. In the tradition of American gospel, hymn-singing in churches is usually accompanied by hand-clapping, dancing and spirit possession, the latter two being remnants of West African worshiping styles.

Secular music in The Bahamas is called **goombay**, a corruption of the West African word *gumbay*, which means drum, a goatskin drum in The Bahamas. "Goombay" was called out as the signal to begin the drumming and singing during ring dances and African fertility dances, which were seen by priests and missionaries as sinful because of the hip movements and coupling of members of the opposite sex. Lyrics were equally frowned upon. Today, goombay has a rolling rhythm accompanied by a "click" rhythm and a piano, guitar or saxophone melody. As far back as the early 1800s, the Bahamian quadrille and heel-and-toe polka, unique combinations of European and African styles, were accompanied by **rake and scrape** bands. These bands were formed by slaves using make-shift instruments like saws and goat-skin drums, made from pork barrels over which was stretched a goat-skin, occasionally there was also an accordion, probably a donation from the master. Rake and scrape bands persist today using modern technology but still creating essentially the same sound. **Junkanoo** music is a livelier version of Goombay that includes cowbells and whistles along with the traditional goat-skin drums; it originated during the long-awaited yuletide holiday granted to slaves, which explains its louder, more enthusiastic and almost hypnotic rhythms. Junkanoo has become to The Bahamas what reggae is to Jamaica and son to Cuba.

For an excellent introduction to traditional Bahamian folk music, Smithsonian Folkways Recordings has recently released a compilation disc called *The Bahamas Islands of Song*, which is available throughout North America. While in The Bahamas, a few names to look out for are Eddie Minnis, the renowned painter whose music follows the story-telling and rake-and-scrape traditions, and Bahamen, a group that has had a lot of success in Europe with their African-American hip-hop and rap sound.

Literature

The first Bahamian literature could be considered to go back as far as Christopher Columbus' log book in which he described the Lucayans and their islands. True Bahamian literature, however, is a much more recent invention arising from a self-determination on the part of Bahamians and an assertion of an authentic Bahamian culture. This new awareness created a need to express and articulate the collective experiences of being Bahamian. This does not mean that all things written deal with these experiences, rather the common forms and themes reflect the customs, lifestyles, environment and folklore that bind the writers and their works. Giving voice to these elements of Bahamian culture valorizes the culture and contributes to the growth of the community.

Folk forms employ a colloquial style and dramatic conventions that are familiar to the audience. The fact that the audience relates quickly to these tales makes them more than simple stories – they often end with a moral and thus take the form of popular children's tales. Brer Bookie and Brer Rabbit are favourite folk characters that are examples of the Bahamians' African heritage. Later stories deal with social and political concerns but nevertheless employ the folk form, offering the people moral guidance, they thus offer readers insight into their ways. Eugene Dupuch's *Smokey Joe*, the stories of Mizpah Tertullien, and the poetry of Susan J. Wallace, *Ole Zeke* in particular, all offer a humourous though inspired look at Bahamian voices, attitudes and society in general.

Themes such as social attitudes, action and national pride are popular with contemporary writers. Robert Johnson celebrates everything about being a Bahamian, no matter how trivial. This assertion of a Bahamian culture in a broader context with familiar imagery is also found in Patrick Rahming's work.

No look at Bahamian literature would be complete without considering works not necessarily written by Bahamians but very much about the islands nonetheless. While in Bimini, Ernest Hemingway spent a lot of time fishing, working on his reputation and writing *Islands in the Stream*, thus introducing the island to the world. His novel *To Have And Have Not* was also written in Bimini. Evans W. Cottman's *Out-Island Doctor*, published in 1963, is the story of an American doctor who travelled between the Out Islands providing medical care in the 1940s, 50s and 60s. It may not be timely, but its peek at Out-Island living is still fascinating.

ARCHITECTURE

Climatic elements and available materials have always been the main variables in Bahamian architecture. The islands' first inhabitants, the Lucayans, lived in small villages of *canayes,* round houses with timber walls and conical thatch roofs supported by a central pole. The circular shape and flexible construction was more resistant to weather. The single entrance and roof opening encouraged the ventilation of cool air from the ground up.

Early settlers had their own preconceived notions of construction and architecture, though architecture was probably the last thing on their minds as they struggled to provide shelter for themselves in this singular geography with limited materials. Before the need for public buildings arose, there was the classic Bahamian cottage. This vernacular style is common throughout the Caribbean; in The Bahamas, the simple clapboard-sided building shows particularly fine craftsmanship with the clapboard ends joined with pegs, not nails. Later cottages, like those on Harbour Island, feature fine woodworking details. Storm shutters were necessary for hurricane winds and rains that occasionally hit the islands; as a sub-tropical country, the northern islands also occasionally get quite cool. Awning-style push-out shutters, when opened, provided shade as well as directed airflow into a building that generally had many large windows to increase cross-ventilation, and were situated so as to take advantage of tradewinds. Before screens, and still today as a matter of fact, trellising and jalousied windows provided shade and ventilation but also privacy. Galleries also help provide shade. Structures were raised onto wood pilings or stone piers to allow cooling breezes under the house and also to protect from floods. Another common feature is the lack of roof overhangs, which holds the roof during strong winds. Verandas and galleries are generally dispensable additions.

Though the islands were a British colony, their architecture was more strongly influenced by the American east coast, and more remotely by Bermuda, than by Britain. Each island developed its own style, due at least in part to the provenance of its settlers. The clapboard cottage was more common in the northern islands where most inhabitants were from Bermuda; in the southern islands, houses were built of stone as in the American South. The majority of the building was done by African hands and their influence is seen in the outdoor stone ovens and the thatch and timber construction. Both plantation houses and tiny square slave quarters were made of coral limestone cut into precise blocks in the former and quarried stones in the latter. Both used lime burnt down in a lengthy process from limestone or from conch shells, as mortar, plaster and whitewash. Eleuthera and the Abacos are noted for their wooden homes. Cat Island has an equally important place in the history of Bahamian architecture. Father Jerome, aka the Hermit of Cat Island (see p 256), was also an accomplished architect who built six spectacular churches and a handful of other buildings throughout the islands.

The arrival of the Loyalists increased the population considerably, thus creating a need for public edifices and churches and lending some sophistication to the islands. The classical style reminiscent of England resulted and gave Nassau some of the finest colonial architecture in the English-speaking Caribbean. The Gothic, Byzantine and Romanesque styles were also employed in some of Nassau's finest architectural gems. Interestingly, the same elements of necessity found in the Bahamian clapboard cottage (jalousies, galleries, awning-style shutters and limestone and lime) turn up again and again throughout the Bahamas, no matter what the function or style of the building.

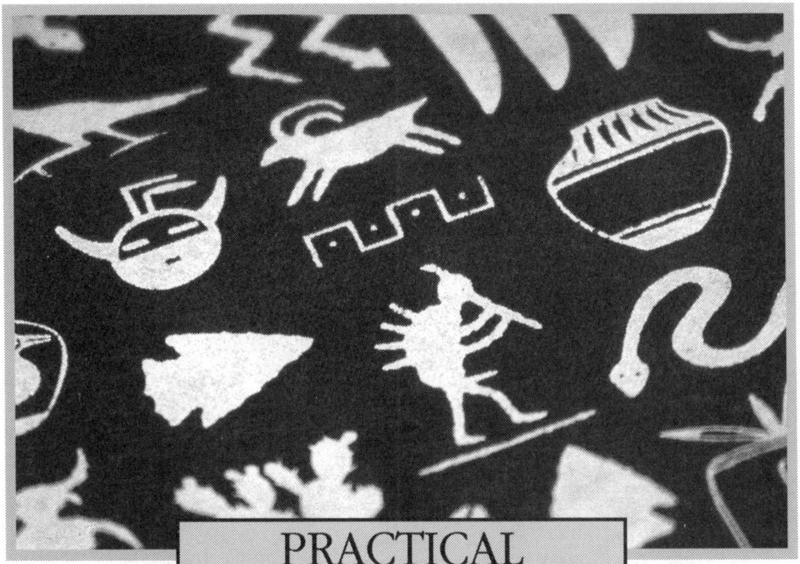

PRACTICAL INFORMATION

As if to stress the geography of the country, "The Islands Of The Bahamas" is its official name. For brevity's sake, however, we will simply use The Bahamas in this guide. This does not simplify the fact that this island nation has its own set of logistics when it comes planning a trip. Whether you're planning to island-hop in your own little plane, to sail or cruise between cays or to relax at one of the all-inclusive resorts, this chapter will tell you how, by providing general information and practical advice.

ENTRANCE FORMALITIES

Before leaving home, be sure you have the official documents that will allow you to enter and leave The Bahamas. Though the requirements may seem lax, without the proper documents you will not be able to travel within the country. Safeguard these documents and always have them on your person. Since entrance formalities can change without warning, be sure to verify that the requirements mentioned below still apply before your trip.

Bring a photocopy of your important documents (passport, driver's license, health insurance, etc.), and leave other copies with someone at home. Also take note of your passport number and its expiry date. This will make it easier to replace any official documents that might be lost or stolen. In the event that you lose an important piece of identification, contact your country's consulate or embassy (see below).

Passport

Canadian travellers and citizens of the UK and Commonwealth countries staying less than three weeks and US travellers staying less than eight months do not need a passport to enter The Bahamas. A certified birth certificate, photo identification, proof of citizenship and a return ticket are required. All other travellers are required to have a passport valid for at least six months as well as a return ticket; they may require visas for longer stays (see below). Canadians and Americans should note, however, that a passport is the best and most accepted form of identification, and citizens of the UK will require their passport to re-enter the UK.

Visa

Visitors from EU member countries and South Africa need a visa for stays of more than three months. Citizens of Belgium, the United Kingdom, Switzerland, Luxembourg, Greece, the Netherlands, Norway, San Marino and Spain may stay for up to eight months. Other visitors should contact their nearest Bahamas High Commission or Tourist Office.

This visa is valid for three months.

Departure Tax and Port Tax

Everyone leaving The Bahamas must pay a departure tax of $15 ($18 from Grand Bahama). Children under six are exempt. It is collected at the airport when you check-in for your return flight. Be sure to have this amount in cash (US$ or Bahamian $), credit cards are not accepted. The tax for visitors travelling by cruise ship, called the port tax, is payed by the cruise ship and is usually included in the price of the cruise.

Customs

Those entering the country must fill out and sign an immigration card, keeping a portion of the card until departure. Each adult visitor may have in their possession personal effects, clothing, and toiletries; 1 quart (approx. 1 l) of alcoholic beverage and 1 quart of wine; 50 cigars, 200 cigarettes or 1 pound (2.2 kg of tobacco); articles up to a value of $100 and food in airtight containers. Narcotics and firearms are, of course, forbidden.

An import permit is required to bring any animal into The Bahamas. Dogs and cats must have a veterinary certificate issued no less than 48 hours before arriving in the country, a valid rabies certificate as well as proof of vaccination.

BAHAMAS OVERSEAS MISSIONS

In Canada
Bahamas High Commission, 360 Albert St., Suite 1020, Ottawa, Ont., K1R 7X7, ☎(613) 232-1724, ⇄(613) 232-0097.

In the United Kingdom
Bahamas High Commission, 10 Chesterfield St., London W1X 8AH, UK, ☎0171 408-4488, ⇄0171 499-9937.

In the United States
Embassy of the Commonwealth of The Bahamas, 2220 Massachusetts Ave. N.W., Washington D.C., 20008, ☎(202) 319-2660/7, ⇄(202) 319-2668.

Bahamas Consulate General, Bahamas House, 231 East 46th St., New York, NY, 10017, ☎(212) 421-6420, ⇄(212) 759-2135.

Coat of Arms

Bahamas Consulate General, Ingraham Building, 25 SE 2nd Ave., Suite 818, Miami, FL, 33131, ☎(305) 373-6295, ⇄(305) 373-6312.

Visitors from other countries should contact the Bahamas Tourist Offices for official documents and tourist information.

FOREIGN EMBASSIES AND CONSULATES IN THE BAHAMAS

Embassies, consulates and high commissions representing your home country can provide valuable assistance in the event of health emergencies, legal problems or the death of a travel companion. Only urgent cases are dealt with, however. Visitors are responsible for any costs incurred as a result of services provided by these official bodies. You can also receive mail here.

Austria
Honorary Consul: PO Box SS-6519, Nassau, ☎363-2929.

Belgium
Honorary Consul: PO Box N-52, Nassau, ☎/⇄323-7421.

Canada
Honorary Consul: PO Box SS-6371, Nassau, ☎393-2123/4, ⇄393-1305.

Denmark
Honorary Consul: PO Box N-4005, Nassau, ☎323-8779.

Germany
Honorary Consul: PO Box N-3035, Nassau, ☎322-8032/3.

Great Britain
British High Commission: BITCO Building (3rd Floor), East St., PO Box N-7516, Nassau, ☎325-7471/4.

Italy
Honorary Consul: PO Box CB-11608, Nassau, ☎322-1928, ⇄323-8600.

The Netherlands
Honorary Consul: PO Box N-44, Nassau, ☎323-5414.

Spain
Honorary Consul: PO Box N-838, Nassau, ☎362-1271 or 362-1412.

Switzerland
Honorary Consul: PO Box SS-6312, Nassau, ☎325-1531.

United States
Embassy: Mosmar Building, Queen St., PO Box N-8197, ☎322-1181.

TOURIST INFORMATION

Abroad

In Canada
Bahamas Tourist Office, 121 Bloor St. E., Suite 1101, Toronto, Ont., M4W 3M5, ☎(416) 968-2999 or 1-800-667-3777.

In Germany
Bahamas Tourist Office, Leipziger Strasse 67d, D-60487 Frankfurt/Main, ☎(069) 97 08 340, ⇄(069) 97 08 34 34.

Out Island Promotion Board, c/o Basic Service Group Am Scleifweg 16, D-55128 Mainz, ☎(061) 319 9330, ⇄(061) 319 9331.

In Great Britain
Bahamas Tourist Office, 3, The Billings, Walnut Tree Close, Guilford, Surrey GUI 4UL, ☎(01483) 448900, ⇄(01483) 448990.

Nassau / Cable Beach / Paradise Island Promotion Board, Suite 301, Parkway House, Sheen Lane, East Sheen, London SW14 8LS, UK, ☎(0181) 878-5569, ⇄878-7854.

In Italy
Bahamas Tourist Office: Via Cusani, 7, 1-20121 Milan, ☎(02) 7202 2526, ⇄(02) 7202 3123.

In the United States
Bahamas Tourist Office, 8600 W. Bryn Mawr Ave., Suite 820, Chicago, IL 60631, ☎(312) 693-1500, ⇄(312) 693-1114.
or
3450 Wilshire Blvd., Suite 208, Los Angeles CA 90010, ☎(213) 385-0033, ⇄(213) 383-3966.
or
150 East 52nd St., 28th Floor North, New York, NY 10022, ☎(212) 758-2777, ⇄(212) 753-6531.
or
One Turnberry Place, 19495 Biscayne Blvd., Suite 242, Aventura, FL 33180, ☎(305) 932-0051 or 937-0585, ⇄(305) 682-8758.

On the Internet

Official site of the Bahamas Ministry of Tourism:
www.interknowledge.com/bahamas.

Bahamasnet site run by Etienne Dupuch Jr. Publications, publisher of free maps and mini-guides for travellers: www.bahamasnet.com

The Bahamas Accommodations and Travel Resource site provides hotel listings and practical information: www.bahamas-mon.com

The Bahamas Online at www.thebahamas.com provides general information on the country, plus links to other sites.

For links to every site imaginable as well as practical general information, try www.bahamasvg.com/links.html

In The Bahamas

For tourist information once in the islands, there are Bahamas Tourist Offices in Nassau, Freeport, Governor's Harbour (Eleuthera), Harbour Island, Marsh Harbour (Abaco) and George Town (Exuma). See the specific chapters for phone numbers and locations.

Resorts on the other islands are usually good sources of on-site information.

Bahamahost

The majority of people working in tourism in The Bahamas, whether it is the guides at the tourist information office, the taxi drivers and sometimes even the hair-braiders, have participated in the Bahamahost training program. In order to improve the welcome and service given to visitors, participants learn about the country's history, culture and places of interest.

TOUR COMPANIES

When planning a trip to The Bahamas (or to almost anywhere else, for that matter), travellers have to decide what they have in mind, and this in turn will determine whether a tour package or independent travel is more suitable.

Those who are mostly interested in relaxing by the beach will often end up staying at the same hotel and in the same area for most of their visit, and this is where it makes the most sense to consider buying an air-and-hotel package, which in some cases costs only slightly more than airfare alone. Some of these packages are based on the all-inclusive formula, with meals, drinks and certain activities included in the price. While this is useful in controlling costs, it may lock you into taking nearly all your meals at hotel buffets whose offerings can get boring. Air-and-hotel packages usually can be bought only through travel agencies or, in some cases, from the tour divisions of airline companies.

For visitors who plan to island hop, the options are package tours, independent travel or a combination of the two. Bahamasair offers an island tour package, which includes a stop in New Providence and Grand Bahama. If you choose to visit several islands and don't have your own private yacht or plane, it will cost quite a bit. Some charter companies offer packages with stops in two, three or four islands.

Independent travel will appeal to many visitors because it allows almost infinite flexibility in the choice of itineraries and a sense of freedom that no package tour can offer. Travellers also have considerable leeway in choosing accommodations and meal arrangements that suit their budgets and tastes. Paying as you go generally costs more, especially if you choose to stay in the resorts. Package deals are always less expensive than the rack rates in hotels.

Even some independent-minded travellers may want to consider combining package tours with do-it-yourself travel.

One possibility is to get to The Bahamas with an air-hotel package, but only take one week in the hotel and move around on your own for the rest of your trip.

GETTING TO THE BAHAMAS

By Plane

The majority of visitors to The Bahamas arrive by plane. Many major North American carriers offer direct flights to Nassau, Freeport and some of the Out Islands. Other flights, including those from Europe, go through Miami or Fort Lauderdale. Some of the more remote Out Islands are only accessible on flights through Nassau.

Nassau International Airport (see p 81) and **Freeport International Airport** (see p 119) receive most of the flights, though there are international flights to many of the Out Islands.

Air Canada offers direct flights from Toronto and Montreal to Nassau every day and every Saturday, respectively. Delta, USAir, American Airlines, Carnival, Gulfstream, American Eagle and Comair offer flights from major American cities. Finally, Bahamasair, the country's national airline flies out of Fort Lauderdale and Miami.

The following airlines provide flights from Europe: Martin Air from Amsterdam; Aeroflot from Shannon, Ireland; British Airways from London; AOM from Paris; Condor Air from Frankfurt and Air Europe from Milan.

For the local phone numbers of these airlines, please see the appropriate chapter later in the guide.

Contact your travel agent or any of these airlines directly for more precise information.

Private pilots arriving internationally can land at any of the airports that are designated as ports of entry. Visitors with their own plane are advised to purchase the *Pilot's Guide to the Bahamas*.

By Cruise Ship

The rest of the visitors to the islands arrive by sea, either as passengers on a cruise ship or on a private boat.

Cruises can be an interesting way for travellers with a limited amount of time to visit as many as four or five islands in the Caribbean. Cruises to The Bahamas usually include a stop in Puerto Rico and Miami, some head further south to Cuba and the Lesser Antilles. If you have never taken a cruise before, there are a few things to consider. First and foremost, the most important and unpredictable variable is your shipmates - for some this unknown is part of the fun, for others it can be a show-stopper. Next, on some cruises you disembark at each stop for just a few hours, while in others, called the fly-and-cruise vacation, you spend a week on board and then another week on an island. While on board, you'll have the choice between filling your days with more activities than you can bargain for, or simply sitting back and soaking up the sun and the sea. Of course, each cruise puts the emphasis on one or the other, so it is worth doing a bit of research. Whichever way you go, cruise ships are like all-inclusive resorts. Cost-wise, the fly-and-cruise packages will cost less than if you purchased the portions separately, though you might get stuck in a mediocre hotel. A cruise itself can be made more economical by opting for the

Ports of Entry

Whether entering the Bahamas by air or by sea it must be at a port of entry. There are ports of entry for boats, land planes and/or sea planes at the following places:

Abaco: Grand Cay, Treasure Cay, Marsh Harbour, Sand Point, Green Turtle Cay.
Andros: Congo Town, Fresh Creek, San Andros.
Berry Islands: Chub Cay, Great Harbour Cay.
Bimini: Alice Town.
Cat Cay
Cat Island: The Bight.
Eleuthera: Governor's Harbour, Hatchet Bay, North Eleuthera, Rock Sound, Cape Eleuthera.
Exuma: Moss Town.
Grand Bahama: Freeport, West End.
Harbour Island: Dunmore Town.
Inagua: Matthew Town.
Long Island: Stella Maris.
Mayaguana: Abraham's Bay.
New Providence: Nassau, Paradise Island.
San Salvador: Cockburn Town.

smaller inside cabins. If you plan on participating in a lot of activities, you won't be spending much time in your room anyhow. And remember that rolling and pitching is less marked in midship cabins. Most cruises start in Miami, though there are departures from New York and Los Angeles as well.

The following major cruise lines make stops in The Bahamas:

Carnival Cruise Lines with their ships *Fantasy* and *Ecstasy*; Celebrity Cruises with their ships *Horizon*, *Meridian* and *Zenith*; Commodore Cruise Lines/Crown Cruise Lines with their ship *Crown Dynasty*; Costa Cruise Lines with their ships *Costa Romantica*, *Costa Allegra* and *Costa Classica*; Dolphin Cruise Lines/Majesty Cruise Line with their ships *Royal Majesty*, *Dolphin* and *Seabreeze*; Holland American Line with their ships *Westerdam*, *Wyndam*, *Statendam*, *Naasdam*, *Veendam*; Norwegian Cruise Line with their ships *The Norway* and *The Leeward*; Premier Cruise Lines with their ships *Oceanic* and *Atlantic*; Princess Cruises with the ships *Star Princess - Princess Cays*, *Crown Princess - Princess Cays*, *Sky Princess - Princess Cays* and *Sun Princess - Princess Cays*; and Royal Caribbean Cruise Line with their ships *Nordic Empress* and *Sovereign of the Seas*.

By Private Boat

Boaters must use designated ports of entry and go through immigration and customs upon entering the country. A six-month cruising permit is issued to the captain after all the passengers show proof of citizenship. Only the captain may go ashore until everyone has cleared customs. Keep the cruising permit in a safe place as it must be presented upon request.

GETTING AROUND THE ISLANDS

By Car

Cars drive on the left in The Bahamas, however, most cars have their steering wheels on the left as well. This makes driving a challenge no matter where you come from. Traffic is generally not a problem, however. Just remember to **KEEP LEFT**!

Distances that can be travelled by car are short in The Bahamas. Most people who rent cars do so for a day or two to explore whichever island they are visiting. Roads on New Providence, Paradise Island and Grand Bahama are generally in good condition. Some secondary roads on these islands and many of the roads on the Out Islands have a lot of potholes or are simply not paved. Only streets and roads in built-up areas are lit. It is best to avoid driving at night.

Car Rental

Renting a car in The Bahamas is easy. Expect to pay between $50 and $100 per day, not including insurance. This may seem like a lot, but when you consider the high cost of taxis and the lack of public transportation outside of Nassau and Freeport, it is less costly than you think. The major North American car-rental agencies have offices on New Providence and Grand Bahama at the airports, downtown and near the resorts. A whole slew of local companies also rent cars on these two islands and are your only option in the Out Islands.

Many travellers prefer renting from the major companies because of easy toll-free reservations lines and the better general condition of their vehicles. If you do reserve in advance, you can save up to 25%, just remember to confirm your reservation a few days in advance. Only local companies rent cars in the Out Islands, and these outfits often have agreements with Out Island hotels. Inquire when reserving your hotel about renting a car from a local company. It is generally more expensive to rent in the Out Islands, where the choice of vehicles is more limited.

Less-expensive compact cars are readily available in Nassau and Freeport. Rentals can range from dune buggies, Jeeps and Volkswagen Beetles to huge American sedans. Mopeds and motorcycles are a very popular option (see below).

To rent a car you must be at least 21 or 25 (depending on the company), have a valid driver's license (North Americans do not need an international driver's license), a major credit card and a cash or credit-card security deposit of $300 to $500. The major rental companies all take credit cards, but many of the smaller outfits in the Out Islands only accept cash. These companies are, however, sometimes associated with local hotels, in which case the rental cost can be added to your hotel bill.

Be sure to take sufficient insurance to cover the costs of an accident. Some credit cards automatically insure the card-holder, though not for all types of vehicles; your own car insurance at home might also insure you on a rental car – check on these things before you leave home. The collision damage waiver (CDW) is sometimes included in the rental price but not always; the major car-rental companies will make a

Traveller's Joy

PRACTICAL INFORMATION

point of trying to sell you extra insurance, while the smaller guys might not even mention it, so make sure you ask.

Insurance against injury or death liability is mandatory.

Before signing the rental contract, ensure that the method of payment is clearly indicated. Remember that when you sign, your credit card must cover not only the rental cost but also the insurance deductible.

Driving and the Highway Code

Having your own set of wheels (two or four) in The Bahamas is certainly not a necessity, though it can be a great way to discover secluded beaches and off-the-beaten-track villages. You'll probably have more trouble adjusting to driving on the left and avoiding potholes than dealing with aggressive Bahamian drivers. Traffic is only a problem in Nassau at rush hour when tempers may flare up. Bahamians do like to use their horns, though not always to register their discontent. A short toot is usually just to say hello; if someone really leans into it, then you know you've done something wrong!

Highways in The Bahamas are two-lane roads that vary in size and condition. There are generally no shoulder or passing lanes. On New Providence and Grand Bahama, these roads are well paved. In the Out Islands, the thin layer of asphalt has crumbled away in many places causing potholes and leaving sand-covered tracks in its place. Children, chickens, dogs, speed bumps in villages and small land crabs, depending on the season, are just some of the obstacles you'll encounter on Bahamian roads.

Road signs are few and far between outside of urban areas. Car-rental agencies in Nassau and Freeport can give you quite good maps for touring these two islands, and many of the resorts in the Out Islands offer their guests maps for seeing all the major points of interest. You can also buy the *Atlas of The Bahamas* at bookstores in Nassau or Freeport. Make sure you have precise directions before heading out.

Seat belts and child seats are both mandatory.

There are no tolls on Bahamian roads except the $2 toll for cars on the Paradise Island Bridge.

Parking can be difficult in downtown Nassau. Pay special attention to parking signs as tickets can be costly. There are parking metres in some places and a few parking garages, the latter cost about $2 an hour. Most hotels have valet parking service or parking lots. Though many Bahamians in the Out Islands will leave their cars unlocked and sometimes even leave the keys in the ignition, better to err on the side of caution and keep things locked up and valuables out of sight.

Gas

Gas (petrol) stations are plentiful in Nassau and Freeport. They are not as easy to come by on the Out Islands. The location of gas stations on these islands is indicated in each chapter, make sure you note where and when you can get gas before heading out, and note that many of these places do not take credit cards. As distances are not that great, getting stranded is unlikely, nevertheless think ahead. Gas is much more expensive than in the United States and Canada and only slightly more than in Europe.

Accidents

If you get into an accident, phone the police and ask them to come to the scene, or go to a police station. You will need a police report for insurance purposes.

By Taxi

There are many taxis in Nassau, Paradise Island, Cable Beach, Freeport and Port Lucaya, so many you can usually hail one from the sidewalk. Most taxis charge by zone while others are metered. There are fixed rates for some trips, for example to and from downtown and the airports. Taxis in the Out Islands are not metered and rates should be determined before you get in. Here, the cars are often a little more run down and some taxis are shared. Taxis usually meet flights at port of entry airports, but don't count on it, also some Out Island resorts arrange pick-ups of their guests at the airport. Taxis can be very expensive throughout The Bahamas, so check with your hotel about land transportation upon arrival.

Here are some sample fares: Nassau International Airport to Cable Beach is $10 to $15, to downtown Nassau about $15, to Paradise Island $20 to $25; from Freeport International Airport to International Bazaar is about $6, to Port Lucaya is about $10. Fares from Out Island airports can be anywhere from $10 to $50.

Taxis can also be hired for tours. Prices vary considerably, but it is generally less expensive if you get a few people together. As all taxi drivers must follow the Bahamahost (see p 43) training program, they are generally able to give you some information about their island. If you do plan on hiring a driver for a tour, ask your hotel or the tourist office to recommend someone.

By Bus (Jitney)

There are public buses, called jitneys, in Nassau. Jitneys are minibuses that run between about 6:30am and 7pm. The fare is 75¢ for adults and 50¢ for children. Bus drivers do not give change. Buses on Grand Bahama operate around the International Bazaar and Port Lucaya areas. The fare is $1. Some hotels also offer their own free bus service to downtown Nassau or to Grand Bahama's beaches.

There is no coach service in The Bahamas.

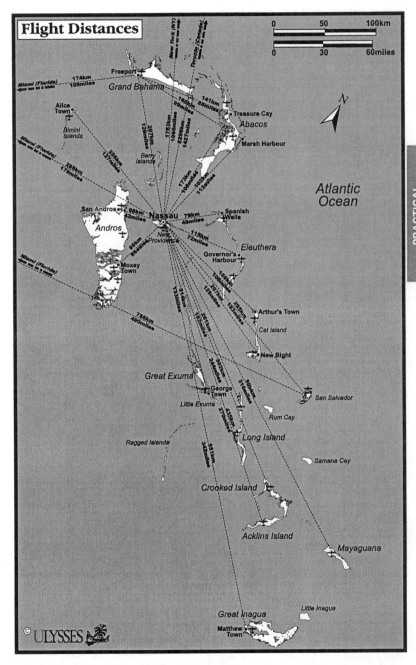

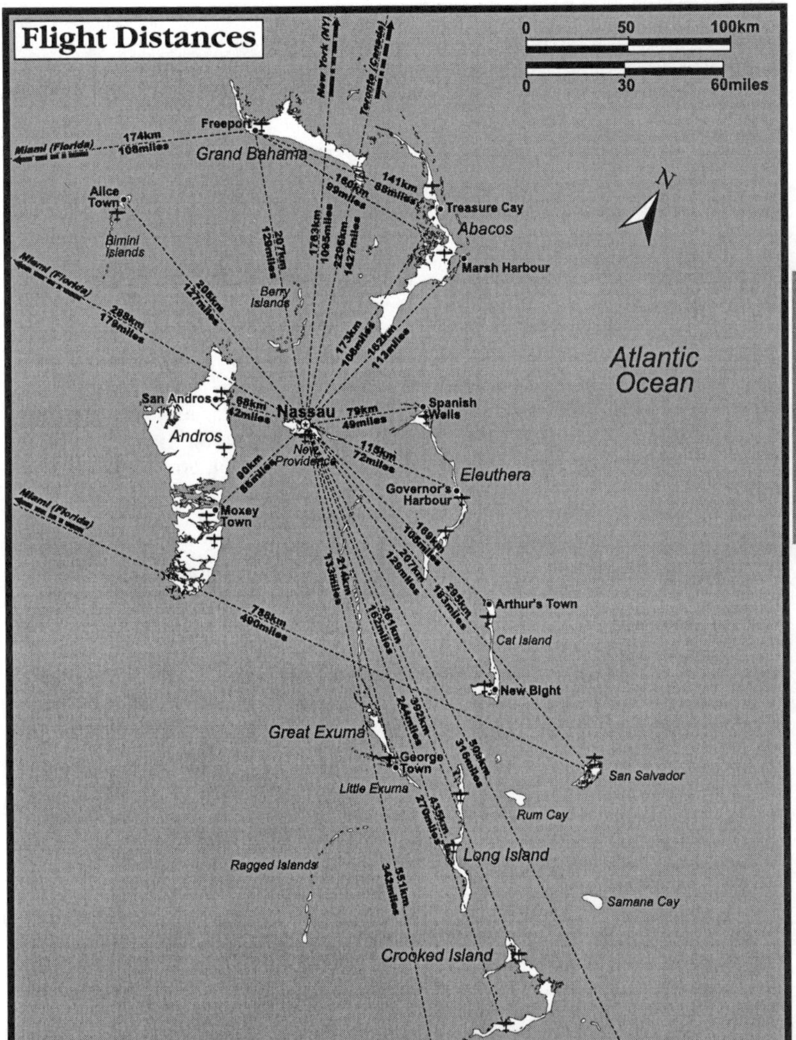

PRACTICAL INFORMATION

Hitchhiking

Hitchhiking is fairly common in The Bahamas, especially in the Out Islands where cars are scarce. You will often see people waiting by the road for the next car to pass. Once again, it is best to err on the side of caution. You just never know these days.

By Plane

Flying is really the only way to truly see a lot of the country. A handful of airlines, including Bahamasair, the national airline, offer flights to the Out Islands. Most islands are only an hour's flying time from each other. All flights, however, originate in Nassau, Miami, Palm Beach, Orlando and Fort Lauderdale, and flying between the Out Islands necessitates a stop in Nassau, unless you charter a plane. Providing you can arrange a good connection, the flying time between the Out Islands takes a minimum of three hours and often much more. Flights cost about $100 to $150 return.

Bahamasair *(reservations ☎1-800-222-4262, in Nassau ☎327-5505, ⇨377-7408/9, in Freeport ☎352-8341/6, ⇨352-2180)* has international flights from Orlando, West Palm Beach, Fort Lauderdale and Miami to Freeport, Nassau, Abaco, Exuma, San Salvador and Long Island. All of Bahamasair's domestic flights originate in Nassau; there are flights to Freeport, Andros, Abaco, Acklins and Crooked Island, Eleuthera, Exuma, Long Island, San Salvador, Cat Island, Mayaguana and Great Inagua. Bahamasair offers the most complete air service between the Out Islands, and though delays are frequent, their service is more economical and safety standards stricter than the other option between the Out Islands: charter companies. Bahamasair requires passengers to check in at least one hour in advance for international flights and 45 minutes for domestic flights, and they mean it: if the plane happens to be ready early and everyone is on board except you then it will simply leave without you. Bahamasair reserves the right to cancel your reservation if you are late, so make sure you aren't.

Charter flights within The Bahamas are more expensive than Bahamasair; however, groups of four or more people might find a charter more economical. Either way, charters are more convenient and offer more flexibility. Many hotels in the Out Islands have their own planes and can arrange transfers from other islands or from points in Florida (Small Hope Bay Lodge, Andros, see p 237; Stella Maris Resort, Long Island, see p 280, Fernandez Bay Village, Cat Island, see p 263).

General charter services operating in the islands include the following:

Pan Am Air Bridge, ☎(305) 371-8628 or 1-800-424-2557.
Abaco Air, ☎367-2266.

Cherokee Air, ☎367-2089.

Congo Air, ☎377-5382.

Island Air Charters, ☎1-800-444-9904.

Island Express, ☎(954) 359-0380.

Major Air, ☎352-3778.

If you have your own plane or are chartering one, remember that you may only enter the Bahamas at ports of entry. Not all islands have ports of entry. Of course, if you are flying from another island, you can use any airstrip. The *Bahamas Pilot's Guide* is strongly recommended to pilots.

By Mailboat

If it isn't the casinos, cruise ships and duty-free shops that have brought you to The Bahamas, then getting around the islands by mailboat might just be for you. A fleet of more than 20 government-subsidized private boats makes weekly runs to all the islands. They carry the mail bags along with cargo and passengers. A return passage is between $40 and $80 (one-way passage is available). The mailboat is the most inexpensive transportation to the Out Islands and is used mostly by Bahamians. Instead of deck chairs, you'll find yourself lounging on crates of building supplies, between refrigerators, eggs and tires, as the flat calm of the deep blue passes by, dotted occasionally by small, idyllic deserted islands. On longer hauls there are usually small cabins (4 to 6 people) and mediocre food is included. Snacks and coffee can be purchased on shorter trips. There is not much to do, so bring a good book or a deck of cards, motion-sickness medication is a good idea as well. All boats leave from Potter's Cay, under the Paradise Island Bridge in Nassau; remember this is The Bahamas, so schedules are subject to change. The schedules are given in later chapters in this guide or check with the dockmaster at Potter's Cay *(☎393-1064)*.

ACCOMMODATIONS

Lodging possibilities in The Bahamas vary widely depending on where you are. Generally speaking, you must add 10% to 20% to room prices for government taxes and service charges (water and energy charges, housekeeping, etc.). It is also the norm to leave a dollar or two per day for the housekeeping services.

The rate listed in this guide is the rack rate for one room, double occupancy in the high season, not including taxes and service charges. Note that package deals are always less expensive than rack rates, so check with your travel agent. There is also a considerable difference between low- and high-season rates, between 20% and 60% in some cases. If you are travelling between mid-April and mid-December, enquire about low-season rates.

Beware of words like deluxe, first-class, villa and guesthouse, for they are often used with a lot of imagination. Not all establishments are waterfront, though they usually offer transportation to the beach if they aren't. The more modest establishments often have arrangements with fancier hotels allowing their guests to use the other's facilities; sometimes there is a fee. Crashing at a hotel can be risky, but usually if you go for a drink or lunch you can get away with hanging around all afternoon.

Most hotels accept credit cards, those that do not are indicated as such in the description.

Resorts

From world-wide chains to family-run resorts, The Bahamas has many establishments offering the whole deal. Golf courses, tennis courts, beaches, watersports, snorkelling, scuba diving, swimming pools, water slides, parasailing, fitness clubs, nightclubs and casinos are some of the extras offered by resorts. Those in New Providence, Paradise Island and Grand Bahama usually have most of the above, while the perks offered by those in the Out Islands vary greatly from one place to the next. If they don't offer a particular activity on site, they can make arrangements for you or refer you to somewhere that does. Air conditioning is standard in the majority of resorts, but there are still a fair number in the Out Islands that rely on ceiling fans and sea breezes.

All-inclusive deals are becoming more and more popular with hotels and guests. Meal plans include breakfast (European Plan), breakfast and dinner (Modified American Plan) or three meals (American Plan); drinks are also often part of the deal. These plans are more common in the Out Islands where other dining facilities are limited.

Prices range from $150 to $1000 per night.

Hotels-Motels

Some establishments that fall into this category might call themselves hotels or resorts, but in reality resemble the typical North American motel more than anything else. Rooms are pretty standard and feature stock hotel furniture and acceptable but not exceptional decor. Sometimes these are older places that could use some freshening up, or brand-new places that, perhaps in an attempt to make North Americans feel at home, have charmless rooms. They usually have a small pool and sometimes a small restaurant and bar. These places are not all bad, in fact their greatest assets are often the people running them. Some are air-conditioned, some have fans and others have both. Prices range from $45 to $150 per night.

Guesthouses

Guesthouses are the closest things to bed and breakfasts that you'll find in The Bahamas. Some establishments that would seem to fit into the previous category call themselves guesthouses. Actually, there are really only three true guesthouses in the Bahamas, Dillet House (see p 101) in Nassau, Lochabar Beach Lodge (see p 286) on Long Island and Dolphin Beach Resort (see p 163) in the Abacos. Prices range from $45 to $150.

Youth Hostels

There is only one genuine youth hostel in The Bahamas, the International Travellers' Lodging in Nassau (see p 99).

Vacation Homes (Rentals)

If you are planning to stay in the same place for one week or more, you might consider renting a fully-equipped apartment, condominium, cottage, villa or even a whole island. Prices range from $300 to $30,000 per week!

Camping

Camping is permitted in certain national parks.

RESTAURANTS

Restaurants serving all sorts of fare, from local to international, abound near the major tourist sites. Service is always very courteous and friendly, whether you're in a fine restaurant or a small eatery. Many establishments automatically add a 15% service charge to restaurant bills. If the service was particularly exceptional, you can leave extra. Ask, if you aren't sure, whether the tip has already been included in the bill. Prices mentioned are for a meal for one person, not including drinks and tip.

$	$10 and less
$$	$10 to $20
$$$	$20 to $30
$$$$	$30 and more

BAHAMIAN CUISINE

Beside the international dishes listed on many menus in The Bahamas, you'll spot native dishes as well as old favourites that have been given an island twist. The marrying of British, Spanish, African and American cultures has given The Bahamas a cuisine all its own, and this cuisine goes beyond the fried conch and peas 'n' rice you may have heard about.

With all that water around it is no wonder that seafood and fish are staples of the Bahamian diet and central to the country's cuisine. Local fruits and vegetables, which are surprisingly abundant and diversified, figure prominently in native dishes. Chicken, pork and mutton are also prime ingredients. Imports include North American favourites like pizzas and burgers. All the beef that is served in restaurants is imported.

Fish and Seafood

The most famous Bahamian food to come from the sea is the conch (pronounced *konk*). This national delicacy is the firm, white meat of a large ocean mollusk (the shell is the one we traditionally put up to our ears to listen to the ocean). Conch meat is actually quite chewy and has to be tenderized, either by being pounded or cured, before being eaten. Fresh, uncooked conch is delicious in conch salad, where the meat is marinated in lime juice and Old Sour Sauce (hot sauce) and served with diced red peppers and onions. "Cracked conch" is prepared by pounding the meat to tenderize it, dipping it in a batter and deep frying it. It is usually served with French fries. "Conch fritters" are a favourite appetizer. These deep-fried little balls are made with small pieces of conch combined with chopped sweet peppers, onions and tomatoes in a corn batter. "Conch chowder" is the other favourite conch variation. Ingredients of this thick and sometimes spicy soup include tomatoes, bacon, sweet peppers, carrots, potatoes, onions, and thyme.

If you are visiting between early April and late August, you can try fresh Bahamian lobster, a spiny variety often called a rock lobster, and a true delicacy. It has no claws; only the tail is eaten. When it is fresh it is broiled, grilled or sometimes curried with local ingredients like coconut and lime juice. It is also served in salads. Land crabs are another tasty shellfish prepared in The Bahamas. Summer rains bring these critters out, and you can often see them scurrying about after dark. The meat is combined with bread crumbs, eggs and spices and baked in its shell.

The preferred fish in The Bahamas is grouper. This mild, white fish lends itself well to various different seasonings. Steamed with mango salsa, Creole hot sauce or white wine sauce are a few possibilities. It is also served as a breaded filet or as the popular "grouper fingers". So-named because the fish is cut in thin strips, fingers are breaded, deep-fried and served as an appetizer with a tangy dipping sauce.

Bonefishing is a popular sport in The Bahamas and the bonefish is usually served baked and seasoned with hot sauce. Other fresh catches that make their way to Bahamian restaurants include shark, swordfish, tuna, and red snapper.

Turtle soup and turtle stew are still served in some Out Islands despite the animal's endangered species status. Try to avoid this dish if possible.

Other Specialities

"Peas 'n' Rice" is the standard accompaniment in The Bahamas. Very inexpensive to make, it is a staple in the local diet. It is prepared with pigeon peas (like lima beans) and rice and seasoned with spices, tomatoes, onions and bacon.

"Johnny cake" is a pan-cooked bread that was once prepared by ship captains, who probably used to call it journey cake. It is sometimes referred to as moon bread, because of its round shape. Many bakeries also prepare Bahamian bread, a beautiful, airy white bread that makes great French toast.

A variety of tasty soups are also served: hearty conch chowder described above; creamy split pea and ham soup; and unique to the Caribbean and The Bahamas, souse, which is a more watery soup whose only ingredients are meat (can be ox-tail or pigs' feet), water, onions, peppers, celery and lime juice.

Finally, wild boar, game birds like ducks and pigeons, local vegetables like sweet potatoes, cassava, okra, corn and peppers and the typical local seasonings of lime juice, fresh pineapple and coconut all usually make their way onto a Bahamian menu somewhere.

Desserts

Besides the typical desserts found on most buffet tables in The Bahamas, you'll also find "guava duff". A duff is a boiled pudding in Britain, and each former colony has its own duff. The Bahamas' one is particularly tasty. It resembles a jelly roll, the jelly being made of guava puree and the cake part a sweet cake made with cinnamon and nutmeg. It is time-consuming to prepare and therefore a real treat.

Drinks

The water throughout The Bahamas is potable. It can be brackish in some areas. Many visitors prefer to buy bottled water, which is available everywhere. Water is filtered by reverse osmosis and barged to New Providence from the Out Islands. Some hotels filter and chlorinate their water a second time, giving it a peculiar taste that won't appeal to everyone.

The standard North American soft drinks are widely available. But so are some local choices, including Goombay Punch, a very sweet, carbonated fruit punch. The beer of The Bahamas is a light and wheaty beer called Kalik. The Kalik brewery is located in Nassau (see p 94), Heineken is also brewed there. Besides these two brews, all bars also serve American beers. Another refresher popular with true Bahamians is coconut water blended with condensed milk and gin. Of course, The Bahamas has its own cocktails too: there is the Caribbean favourite, planter's punch, prepared in The Bahamas with lime juice, rum, Triple Sec and bitters; the Bahama Mama is made with rum, coconut rum, pineapple juice, orange juice and grenadine; the Yellowbird is made with rum, banana liqueur, apricot brandy, pineapple and lime juice, and finally the Goombay Smash is made with coconut rum, pineapple juice, lemon juice, Triple Sec and rum. Rum is the liqueur of choice in the islands, and Nassau Royale is the local brand. It comes in dark, coconut and banana varieties.

The legal drinking age in The Bahamas is 21.

ENTERTAINMENT

Casinos

There are four casinos in The Bahamas: the Atlantis Resort and Mariott Crystal Palace Resort & Casino in Nassau/Paradise Island, and the Bahamas Princess Resort Casino and Lucayan Beach Resort & Casino in Freeport. Thousands of slot machines along with blackjack, baccarat, craps, roulette, stud poker and big six tables keep gamblers busy 24 hours a day. The high-rollers only come out after 10pm, when gambling tables take their first bids. You must be 18 to gamble in The Bahamas, and appropriate dress is required. Gambling is illegal for residents of The Bahamas. Keep an eye on your valuables while in the casinos as pickpockets are common.

Bars, Nightclubs and Theatres

All of the big resorts have their own nightclubs and many organize Las-Vegas-style cabaret shows. There are also a few hot spots in Nassau and Freeport. The Out Islands are decidedly quieter. Many resorts hire local bands for a little evening entertainment, while the friendly atmosphere at others makes for fun and casual evenings among new friends. Local theatre groups and church choirs in Nassau, Freeport and the Out Islands round out the cultural offerings.

Festivals and Cultural Events

January 1 New Year's Day Junkanoo Parade (Nassau, Freeport and other islands). Celebrations and a parade (a repeat of the one held on Dec. 26). Times vary on other islands. Call ☎322-3140 for information.

Late April Annual Family Island Regatta (Exuma). Locally built sloops representing different Bahamian islands gather in Elizabeth Harbour for four days of races. Activities, native foods and crafts. Call ☎336-2430 for more information.

May National Arts Festival (Nassau). Local artists in music, drama and dance display their talents. Call ☎356-2691/2 for more information.

Late May Annual Long Island Regatta (Long Island). Once again, locally made sloops vie for cash and prizes while onshore, music, food and activities create a festive mood.

Early June Annual Eleuthera Pineapple Festival (Gregory Town, Eleuthera). Four-day celebration of this tasty local fruit, with crafts, dancing and a pineapple recipe contest. Call ☎332-2142 for more information.

July 10 Independence Day (all islands). Barbecues, parties and festivities in all villages.

July or August Jazz Festival (Grand Bahama Island). Talented international artists perform. Call ☎352-6721 for more information.

First Monday in August Emancipation Day (all islands) celebrates the end of slavery in 1834. The Junkanoo rushout starts at 4am in Fox Hill, where celebrations occur one week later on **Fox Hill Day**, which commemorates the fact that residents only learned of Emancipation one week after it was announced. Highlights include "climbing the greasy pole" and plaiting the maypole.

October Discovery Day (all islands). All islands celebrate the arrival of Columbus in the New World. In McLean's Town, Grand Bahama, there is a Conch Cracking Contest to see who can crack the most conchs in the shortest amount of time.

November 5 Guy Fawkes Day (all islands). Celebrations include the hanging and burning of an effigy of Guy Fawkes, the malfeasant involved in a plot to blow up the British Parliament.

December 26 Junkanoo Boxing Day Parade (all islands). This is the real Junkanoo: the parade starts at 2am, and revellers in colourful crepe paper costumes celebrate in the streets to the sounds of goatskin drums, whistles and cowbells. Prizes are awarded at 8am. Call ☎322-3140 for information.

Besides these events, there is usually a regatta or fishing tournament just about every weekend somewhere in The Bahamas.

Every two weeks (Wednesdays at 10am) is the **changing of the guard ceremony** on the grounds of Government House in Nassau, the residence of the governor general. A tradition of pomp and circumstance, the ceremony sees the renowned Royal Bahamas Police Force Band decked out in their leopard-skin tunics and pitch helmets.

Another traditional ceremony, this one four times a year (in January, April, July and October), is the **opening of the Supreme Court**, when a white-wig-clad Chief Justice inspects the Royal Bahamas Police Force Guard-of-Honour in Rawson Square, Nassau. The ceremony begins at 10am.

Finally, there is the monthly **People-to-People tea party** at Government House (see below).

SHOPPING

Straw Markets

Straw markets and straw goods are so plentiful in The Bahamas, that it really isn't a problem if you forget your hat! Nassau's market, started in the 1930s, was the first. Now there are markets in every place where there are tourists. Straw hats, baskets, handbags, place mats and coasters, along with shell and beaded jewellery and of course t-shirts and sweatshirts are sold. Because of the ever-increasing demand, not everything in the straw markets is handmade, the way it once was. Be aware that many of the items were actually made in China or Taiwan, and these have only been decorated by hand in The Bahamas.

What to Bring Home

Certain islands specialize in different types of crafts and different types of straw-work. The straw work for sale in Nassau and Freeport comes from all over the islands; you'll find pieces made from straw, sisal, Peel Top Plait and Silver Top Plait. Abaco is known for its ceramics and Eleuthera has its pineapples. The locally produced

Nassau Royale rhum is available throughout The Bahamas.

Duty-Free

Nassau and Freeport are both full of duty-free shops. Fairly good prices can be had on alcohol and perfume. The Bahamas is also a goldmine for jewellery, china, crystal and cigar stores. Prices are as much as 40% lower than in the United States. Americans particularly appreciate the Cuban cigars for sale here.

Bargaining

Bargaining is part of the fun of visiting the markets. If you are nice enough and try hard enough, a cheaper price can be negotiated. If you have no intention of buying something, don't bargain just to see how far you can go.

CLIMATE

The Bahamas has a tropical maritime climate. The Tropic of Cancer passes through Great Exuma and Long Island accounting for slight temperature variations from north to south in the Islands. The Gulf Stream blows along the western islands bringing clear warm waters. Polar air does make its way down to the islands in the winter but only succeeds in lowering temperatures by a few degrees. Winter temperatures in the central Bahamas, including New Providence, rarely fall below 15°C (60°F) and average about 24°C (75°F) in the afternoons. In the summer, night-time temperatures rarely fall below 25°C (78°F) and often top 32°C (90°F) in the afternoons. Winter temperatures vary by 10° from north to south. Summer temperatures are pretty similar throughout the islands.

Summers are very humid in The Bahamas. It can rain at any time throughout the year, though the months from May to October are generally wetter. The quick afternoon showers and thunderstorms usually clear up fast. The northern islands receive 20% more rain than the southern ones.

Hurricane season runs from June to November, with August, September and October being the greatest risk months.

Tar Stations

Tar washes up on some beaches in the Out Islands. This sticky situation is somewhat alleviated by tar stations at the beach's edge for cleaning your shoes and feet and by cleaning products in some guest rooms.

Packing

What you pack depends on what you plan on doing while in The Bahamas. Generally speaking, loose-fitting, cotton c clothing is best. You will probably spend most of the time in your swim suit or shorts, though short shorts and beachwear are frowned upon in casinos and hotel lobbies. More formal attire is a good idea if you plan on visiting any casinos, churches or fancier restaurants. For cooler evenings, a long-sleeved shirt or jacket will come in handy. Dress is much more casual in the Out Islands. Long pants are also a good idea for buggy evenings or walks in the woods. A small umbrella or raincoat will protect you from showers. Some hotels have health clubs, so running shoes and exercise gear are a good idea. Scuba diving gear can be rented in all the islands; however,

Average temperatures (maximum, °C/°F) and rainfall (cm/in)

January	25.2/77.4	4.7/1.85
February	25.3/77.5	4/1.57
March	26.5/79.7	4/1.57
April	27.7/81.9	5.4/2.13
May	29.2/84.6	11.6/4.57
June	30.7/87.3	23.3/9.17
July	31.7/89	15.8/6.22
August	31.8/89	21.6/8.5
September	31.3/88.3	17.1/6.73
October	29.7/85.4	17.6/6.93
November	27.7/81.9	5.7/2.24
December	25.9/78.6	5.2/2.36

snorkellers and divers may want to bring their own mask and snorkel to ensure a good fit. Most hotels provide guests with beach towels.

Besides a name tag, put a tag on your luggage indicating what hotel you are staying at and the dates you will be there. Lost luggage is common when you fly with smaller airlines, especially to the Out Islands, and this way airport staff can forward your luggage on to your hotel when it finally shows up. It is also a good idea to bring a few essentials (medication, toothbrush, contact lense solution, etc.) in your carry-all bag. Finally, note that many of the planes that serve The Bahamas are small and have limited space for carry-on luggage. Enquire about this when making reservations.

As far as laundry is concerned, most of the bigger hotels have laundry and dry-cleaning service. This can be quite expensive, however. A small amount of laundry detergent and a clothesline will therefore come in handy.

When to Go

There is a very big difference between the high season (winter) and the low season (summer) in The Bahamas. The number of visitors and the costs of accommodations are the two main variables. High season in The Bahamas runs from mid-December to mid-April. Cooler temperatures, spring break and holiday festivities like Junkanoo attract a lot of vacationers. Hotel reservations during this period are essential. Reserving your car is not a bad idea either. Hotel rates in the low-season can be an astonishing 20% to 60% lower, representing major savings for cost-conscious travellers. Another advantage for some are the smaller crowds. And if you are worried about the weather, don't be. Breezy trade winds mean it's always June in The Bahamas. See Festivals and Cultural Events p 55.

MONEY AND BANKING

Currency

The legal currency of The Bahamas is the Bahamian dollar. It is fixed to the

Exchange Rates

$1 CAN	= $0.64 US	$1 US	= $1.55 CAN
1 £	= $1.64 US	$1 US	= 0.61 £
$1 Aust	= $0.58 US	$1 US	= $1.73 Aust
$1 NZ	= $0.49 US	$1 US	= $2.03 NZ
1 guilder	= $0.49 US	$1 US	= 2.03 guilders
1 SF	= $0.66 US	$1 US	= 1.50 SF
10 BF	= $0.27 US	$1 US	= 37 BF
1 DM	= $0.56 US	$1 US	= 1.80 DM
100 pesetas	= $0.66 US	$1 US	= 152 pesetas
1000 lire	= $0.56 US	$1 US	= 1,774 lire
1 Euro	= $1.10 US	$1 US	=0.91 Euro

American dollar and both are accepted everywhere. It is common to pay and receive your change in a combination of the two. Though the two currencies are on par, the Bahamian dollar may not necessarily be worth as much as the U.S. dollar once you get back home. For this reason it is best to stick to U.S. dollars unless you are sure you are going to spend all of your Bahamian currency in The Bahamas.

All prices in this guide are in Bahamian (U.S.) dollars.

Banks and Automatic Tellers

Banks are usually open Monday to Thursday from 9:30am to 3pm and Friday from 9:30am to 5pm. Banks in the Out Islands keep more restricted hours and in some cases are only open once a week (see the chapter on the particular island for more specific information)

There are banks on all of the inhabited islands and most will exchange major currencies, cash traveller's cheques and give cash advances on your credit card.

Automatic teller machines can be found in the airport (Nassau), in downtown areas, near the casinos and in some major hotels on New Providence, Paradise Island and Grand Bahama. There are no bank machines on the Out Islands. These machines only give Bahamian dollars.

Exchange Offices

There are very few exchange offices in The Bahamas. You can exchange money or travellers' cheques at hotel front desks and at banks. There is usually, though not always, a service charge of either 1% or $1 per travellers' cheque.

Travellers' Cheques

Travellers' cheques are the safest way to carry money. They are accepted in large hotels and restaurants and in most stores on New Providence, Paradise Island and Grand Bahama. It is always best to carry cash in the Out Islands, especially if you plan on renting a car from a local company. Cheques in a currency other than American dollars generally enjoy a better exchange rate than cash in that currency. There is usually a small fee (either 1% or $1) when exchanging traveller's cheques at banks. Get your travellers' cheques in U.S. dollars to avoid the hassle of searching out the best rate.

Keep a list of your serial numbers separate from your cheques (leave this information with someone at home as well) so that they can be cancelled and replaced if they are lost or stolen.

Credit Cards

Visa and MasterCard are the most widely accepted credit cards. American Express and Diners Club are also accepted, but to a lesser extent. Do not rely solely on credit cards as many small merchants, particularly in the Out Islands, do not accept them. Once again, even if you have a credit card and travellers' cheques, always carry some cash.

TIPPING

Tipping can be tricky in The Bahamas. The tip or service charge (usually 15%) is often included in restaurant bills, however, if the service has been especially good it is customary to leave a little extra. Keep in mind that tipping is a way of showing your appreciation for good service. If you aren't sure if the tip has been included, simply ask.

Porters and other staff in fancier or all-inclusive hotels sometimes do not accept tips. It is best to offer about $1 per bag, nonetheless. Between $1 and $2 per day for housekeeping services is the norm, plus a bit more for any special services rendered. Taxi drivers, ferry captains, tour guides, hairdressers, etc. usually receive about 10%-15% extra.

TELECOMMUNICATIONS

The area code in The Bahamas is 242. It changed only recently from 809 and many establishments have yet to redo their brochures and advertisements. Phone numbers in The Bahamas have seven digits.

Telephone services in The Bahamas are, for the most part, first rate. International and local calls can be placed from pay phones found in many public places, from **BaTelCo** offices, which are located on almost every island, or from your hotel for a considerable fee. Public phones, either coin-operated or debit-card, are plentiful. The former are gradually being phased-out. The latter use debit cards available in $5, $10, $20 and $50 denominations from BaTelCo offices and from some hotels. These cards can be used for local and long-distance calls and are a worthwhile investment. The cards keep track of your balance, which is shown, along with the price of your call, on the electronic display of the telephone. Local calls cost 25¢ and long-distance calls up to $1.25 per minute to North America and up to $4 per minute to Europe. Calls placed from BaTelCo offices are calculated and paid for after the call. You must pay cash. Calling from your hotel should be avoided unless it is urgent! Hotels charge anywhere from 50¢ to $1.50 for local calls, and $2 to $5 for collect, third party or calling-card long-distance calls, on top of long-distance charges.

For information: BaTelCo Centralized Telephone Office, East St., Nassau, ☎323-6414.

Only BaTelCo in Nassau, Freeport and certain larger offices can send faxes and telexes. Otherwise, most hotels have fax machines. BaTelCo charges a minimum of $5, while hotels can charge up $10 plus long-distance charges.

Telegrams are sent from the Bahamas Post Office *(main post office: Shirley St., Nassau, ☎322-3344).*

Long-Distance Calls

When calling long-distance, either to another country or to another Bahamian island, you can pay Bahamian phone rates or the phone rates of your phone company with a calling card. Direct-dial calls will always go through a Bahamian operator. Collect and credit-card or calling-card calls can go through a Bahamian operator or by using an international access number, through an operator in another country.

To direct-dial the United States or Canada dial 1, the area code and the phone number; to direct-dial The Bahamas or from one Bahamian island to another, dial 1-242 and the seven-digit phone number.

To direct-dial another country dial 011 for the international operator, the country code (see below) and the area code and phone number.

Country Codes:

Australia 61
Great Britain 44
New Zealand 64
Belgium 32
Switzerland 41
Italy 39
Spain 34
Germany 49
Holland 31

International access numbers allow you to use an operator in your country. Some of these operators allow you to use any calling card, while others are only for card-holders of that phone company.

Canada Direct: 1-800-463-0501 (be aware that this number only seems to work from private phones and coin-operated pay phones).
AT&T Canada: 1-800-389-0004.
AT&T US: 1-800-872-2881.
MCI Call USA: 1-800-964-8218.
Sprint USA: 1-800-389-2111.
British Telecom Direct:
1-800-389-4444.

Useful Telephone Numbers

Bahamas Directory Assistance: 916
Police and Fire Emergencies: 919
Crisis Centre: 328-0922
Bahamas Air/Sea Rescue: 322-3877
Weather: 915
Time: 917

MAIL

There are post offices in Nassau, Freeport and at both airports; offices are fewer and farther between in the Out Islands. They are open Monday to Friday 8:30am to 5:30pm in Nassau and Freeport and may only be open a few days a week in the Out Islands. Most hotels can also mail your letters and sell you stamps. The mail can be a bit slow, especially if you have sent something from the Out Islands. Many hotels have U.S. addresses and it is a good idea to use them if you are trying to make reservations. It costs 40¢ to send a postcard and 45¢ for a letter to Canada and the United States and 50¢ for a letter to Europe.

See p 51 for information on the mailboats.

PRACTICAL INFORMATION

HOLIDAYS

The following is a list of public holidays in The Bahamas. Most administrative offices, banks and stores are closed on these days. Holidays that fall on a Saturday or Sunday are usually observed on the preceding Friday or the following Monday.

New Year's Day
Good Friday
Easter Monday
Whit Monday (seven weeks after Easter)
Labour Day (first Friday in June)
Independence Day (July 10)
Emancipation Day (first Monday in August)
Discovery Day (Oct. 12)
Christmas Day (Dec. 25)
Boxing Day (Dec. 26)

BUSINESS HOURS

Stores are closed on holidays. As mentioned above, holidays that fall on a Saturday or Sunday are usually observed on the preceding Friday or the following Monday. Stores are generally open Monday to Saturday, from 9am to 5pm. Some stores close early on Thursday afternoons, and only a handful of shops on Nassau's Bay Street are open on Sundays. Banks are open Monday to Thursday from 9:30am to 3pm and on Fridays from 9:30am to 5pm.

INSURANCE

Health Insurance

Health insurance is the most important type of insurance travellers can get. A comprehensive health insurance policy that provides a level of coverage sufficient to pay for hospitalization, nursing care and doctor's fees is recommended. Keep in mind that health care costs are rising quickly everywhere. The policy should also have a repatriation clause in case the required care is not available in The Bahamas. As patients are sometimes asked to pay for medical services up front, find out what provisions your policy makes in this event. Always carry your health insurance policy with you when travelling to avoid problems if you are in an accident, and get receipts for any expenses incurred.

Theft Insurance

Most residential insurance policies cover a percentage of personal belongings against theft if the items are stolen outside the country. If you plan on travelling with valuable objects, check your policy or with an insurance agency to see whether additional baggage insurance is necessary. To file an insurance claim for a theft incurred while on holiday, you will need a police report from the country you are visiting.

Cancellation Insurance

This type of insurance is usually offered by your travel agent when you purchase your air tickets or tour package. It covers any non-refundable payments to travel suppliers such as airlines, and it must be purchased at the same time as initial payment is made for air tickets or tour packages. Trip cancellation insurance comes into effect if a traveller has to call off a trip for valid medical reasons or because of a death in the family. This type of insurance can be useful, but weigh the likelihood of your using it against the price.

Life Insurance

By purchasing your tickets with certain credit cards you also get life insurance. However, many travellers already have another form of life insurance and do not need extra insurance.

HEALTH

The Bahamas is a wonderful country to explore and boasts top-rate medical facilities. You do not need any vaccinations to enter the Bahamas, unless you have recently visited an area where Yellow Fever is common.

Cases of illnesses like Hepatitis B, AIDS and certain venereal diseases have been reported; it is therefore a good idea to be careful. Condoms are the best protection against these illnesses.

Remember that consuming too much alcohol, particularly during prolonged exposure to the sun, can cause severe dehydration and lead to health problems.

If you do get diarrhea, soothe your stomach by avoiding solids; instead, drink carbonated beverages, bottled water, or weak tea (avoid milk) until you recover. As dehydration can be dangerous, drinking sufficient quantities of liquid is crucial. Pharmacies sell various preparations to treat diarrhea, with different effects. Pepto Bismol and Imodium will stop the diarrhea, which slows the loss of fluids, but they should be avoided if you have a fever as they will prevent the necessary elimination of bacteria. Oral rehydration products such as Gastrolyte will replace the minerals and electrolytes that your body has lost as a result of the diarrhea. In a pinch, you can make your own rehydration solution by mixing one litre of pure water with one teaspoon of sugar and two or three teaspoons of salt. After, eat easily digested foods like rice to give your stomach time to adjust. If symptoms become more serious (high fever, persistent diarrhea), see a doctor as antibiotics may be necessary.

Nutrition and climate can also cause problems. Pay attention to food's freshness, and the cleanliness of the preparation area. Good hygiene (wash your hands often) will help avoid undesirable situations.

Insects

A nuisance common to many countries, bugs can be a big problem in The Bahamas, particularly mosquitoes and sand flies. Mosquitoes are generally more numerous in the summer when there is more rain, and at nightfall. Sand flies, also called "no-see-'ems" by locals because they are so small (they can even get through screens), are perhaps the most annoying. They also come out at nightfall and are particularly prevalent near windless beaches on the lee side of an island. Their bite does not so much itch as burn. The best way to deal with these two critters is with a good insect repellent. Repellents with DEET are the most effective. The concentration of DEET varies from one product to the next; the higher the concentration, the longer the protection. A concentration of 35% DEET will protect for four to six hours, while 95% will last from 10 to 12 hours. New formulas with DEET in lesser concentrations, but which last just as long, are available.

To further reduce the possibility of getting bitten, do not wear perfume or bright colours. Sundown is an especially active time for insects. When walking in wooded areas, cover your legs and ankles well. Insect coils can help provide a better night's sleep. Before bed, apply insect repellent to your skin and to the headboard and baseboard of your bed. If possible, get an air-conditioned room, or bring a mosquito net.

Lastly, since it is impossible to completely avoid contact with mosquitoes, bring along a cream to soothe the bites you will invariably get. And try not to scratch - scratching a bite will only activate the allergen and make things worse. A bite that is left alone will go away much faster.

There is also a small risk from black-widow spiders, which are found in The Bahamas. The bite of these spiders, identifiable by the red hourglass shape on the female's underside, is lethal. Their webs are characteristically asymmetrical and more gauzy than a typical spider web. They are to be avoided at all costs.

The Sun

Its benefits are many, but so are its harms. Always wear sunscreen. Many creams on the market do not offer adequate protection; ask a pharmacist. Too much sun can cause sunstroke (dizziness, vomiting, fever, etc.). Be careful, especially the first few days, as it takes time to get used to the sun. Take sun in small doses and protect yourself with a hat and sunglasses. Many people don't realize the risk of sunburn while snorkelling - a good waterproof sunscreen is imperative.

First Aid Kit

A small first aid kit can prove very useful. Bring along sufficient amounts of any medications you take regularly; it can be difficult to find certain drugs in the Out Islands. Also, bring a valid prescription in case you lose your supply. Finally, don't forget self-adhesive bandages, disinfectant cream or ointment, analgesics (pain-killers), antihistamines (for allergies), anti-itch cream, an extra pair of sunglasses or contact lenses and medicine for upset stomach.

SAFETY AND SECURITY

When it comes to safety, The Bahamas is like two countries. Grand Bahama and New Providence in one and the Out Islands in the other. Bahamians are very friendly people, the kind who say hello to strangers in the street. However, this can lead to a false sense of security in Nassau and Freeport, where you should take the same precautions you would in any big city. Itinerants and drugs are becoming more common in these two cities; drug dealers hang around Bay Street, west of the British Colonial Hotel and should be avoided. Travellers, especially women, should avoid deserted side streets and walking around alone at any time of the day (an attempted mugging at 11am in downtown Nassau is something this author would like to forget). Bay Street and most of downtown Nassau are deserted after dark so stay away. The jitneys stop running around 7pm, so if you plan on heading out take a taxi. Pickpockets are common in the casinos.

As for the Out Islands, the likelihood of encountering malfeasants is pretty small, except perhaps in Bimini, where drugs are more prevalent thanks to the proximity of Florida. Many Out Islanders leave their car keys in the ignition, a practice we don't recommend. A fair number of Out Island hotel rooms don't lock and you are strongly encouraged to leave your valuables in the front desk's safe.

Wherever you end up, a degree of caution can help avoid problems. For example, do not wear too much jewellery, keep your electronic equipment in a nondescript shoulder bag slung across your chest, avoid revealing the entire contents of your wallet when making a purchase, don't bring anything of value with you to the beach, but if you must, keep a close eye on it. Most hotels have either private safes in the rooms or one at the front desk - use it for all your valuables and at all times. If you rent a car, make sure it is locked at all times and never leave anything of value visible inside.

A money belt that goes under your clothes can be useful for hiding money, traveller's cheques and passports. Follow the "never put all your eggs in one basket" principle: put your money in many different places, so that if any one bag is lost or stolen, you have not lost everything. Be discreet, and remember - the less attention you draw to yourself, the less chance you have of being robbed.

WOMEN TRAVELLERS

The question of women travelling on their own is never black and white, as what one woman considers offensive, another may not even notice. Friendly Bahamians say hello to most people, and will pay special attention to women, particularly women travelling alone. However, this attention is not generally aggressive, and ignoring it is probably your safest bet. Observe the basic safety rules for all foreign travel, and you should not have any problems. Be careful what you wear and avoid questionable or poorly-lit areas, especially in Nassau and Freeport.

LANGUAGE

English is the official language of The Bahamas. The Bahamian accent, however, is altogether different: a mix of British and African, with a distinctly island ring. The vocabulary is similar to standard English in England and her former colonies.

TIME DIFFERENCE

The Bahamas is on Eastern Standard Time, like the east coast of North America. The islands are five hours behind Greenwich Mean Time and six hours behind continental Europe. When it is noon in Nassau it is also noon in Montreal and New York City, 9am in Los Angeles, 5pm in London and 6pm in Paris. The Bahamas observe daylight savings time (+1 hour) from the first Sunday in April to the last Sunday in October.

GAY LIFE

Being openly gay or lesbian in The Bahamas is not the best idea. Homosexuality is formally forbidden by the State and can lead to imprisonment. There are a few clandestine gay bars in Nassau and Freeport, but they are difficult to find.

GENERAL INFORMATION

Religion

The majority of Bahamians are first Baptist, then Anglican and Catholic, and most of them go to church. Religion is very important in the Islands, and attending a church service is a wonderful cultural experience. Most churches are open to visitors. Ask at your hotel for some suggestions. The following religions are also represented: Assembly of God, Ba'hai Faith, Brethren, Christian & Missionary Alliance, Christian Science, Church of God of Prophecy, Greek Orthodox, Jehovah's Witness, Jewish, Latter Day Saints (Mormon), Lutheran, Methodist, Muslim/Islamic, Pentecostal, Presbyterian, and Seventh-Day Adventist.

Broadcasting

The Broadcasting Corporation of The Bahamas operates four public radio stations. ZNS-1 (107.1 FM or 107.9 FM in the southeastern Bahamas) with adult contemporary music and talk shows; ZNS-2 (1240 AM, 6am to 12am) with religious and educational programming; ZNS-FM (104.5 FM) with contemporary music and sports; and ZNS-3 (810 AM) serves the northern Bahamas with similar programming to ZNS-1. A handful of private radio stations also operate out of Nassau, including 100 JAMZ (100.3 FM), with island and North American popular music, MORE FM (94.9 FM) offers an "eclectic" format, and LOVE 97 (97.5 FM) has an adult contemporary format.

There is also a ZNS television station, Channel 13, which shows local news, soap operas and public interest programmes, including sessions of parliament. Most hotels also have satellite television capabilities, offering guests channels from Canada, the United States, and many European countries.

Newspapers

There are two national daily newspapers, *The Nassau Guardian* in the morning and *The Tribune* in the afternoon. They are published Monday to Saturday. Both are widely available in Nassau and Freeport, and have limited and delayed circulation in the Out Islands. The *Freeport News* is published daily (Mon to Fri) in Freeport. The weekly paper *The Bahama Journal* is available throughout the islands. Finally there is the tabloid-style *The Punch* published every Thursday.

Besides the local papers, U.S. papers (primarily *USA Today*, *The New York Times*, *The Wall Street Journal* and Miami newspapers) are flown into The Bahamas everyday. Newspapers from Canada and Britain are available, though they are harder to come by and quite expensive.

Electricity

Electrical appliances run on an alternating current of 110 volts (60 cycles), just as in North America. Travellers from Europe and Asia will need both a converter and an adapter with two parallel flat pins for any appliances they plan to bring along.

Drugs

The Bahamas' proximity to the United States makes it a favourite place of drug runners, and drugs in general are becoming a major problem. Possession, importation and trafficking of drugs are serious offenses and carry heavy penalties. Drug dealers often approach tourists on the streets and should be avoided at all costs.

People-to-People

The People-to-People program, run by the Bahamas Ministry of Tourism, matches visitors and volunteers with similar interests, age groups and professions. Your hosts might invite you to see the sights, to attend their church, or maybe even for an authentic Bahamian meal in their home. There is also a monthly tea party at Government House hosted by the wife of the governor-general of The Bahamas. To participate in the program, contact the closest Bahamas Tourist Office at least three weeks before your trip. You'll be asked to fill out a form so that you can be matched up with someone in The Bahamas. If you are already in Nassau and want to participate, visit the tourist office in the Nassau Airport or at Rawson Square, or call the Ministry of Tourism at ☎326-5371, 328-7810 or 326-9772. In Freeport visit the tourist office on the International Bazaar or call ☎352-8044. The program is also available in Eleuthera, Exuma, Abaco, Bimini and San Salvador.

Getting Married in the Bahamas

How romantic and idyllic to tie the knot in paradise. Well, it is much easier than one would think to get married in The Bahamas. The People-to-People program can help with arrangements, whatever you have in mind. You could say "I do" underwater in scuba gear, on the beach in your bikini, in your shorts on the deck of a fabulous yacht, or if you prefer a more traditional wedding, in one of the islands' pretty churches. They'll also help with the reception, cake, flowers and champagne. Contact the People-to-People program coordinators directly (see above) for their assistance.

Couples can be married after just one day. You will need a marriage license, which can be obtained on the day of the wedding from the registrar general *(in Nassau, P.O. Box N532, ☎322-3316, ⇌322-5553; in Freeport, PO Box F4602, ☎352-4932, ⇌352-4060)* or from the Commissioner's Office of any of the Out Islands. To obtain a license the following requirements must be met: you must have proof of your date of arrival in The Bahamas; if either party is less than 18 years of age parental consent is required; if either party has been divorced, the original decree or a certified copy must be produced; if either party is widowed, a death certificate must be produced; if either party is unmarried, a declaration certifying this (by a notary public) must be produced; both parties must have photo identification issued by a government office in their country of residence. The license costs $40 and a marriage officer $175. Photographers, flowers and music cost extra.

Weights and Measures

The Bahamas, like the United States uses the Imperial system. Gas is sold by the U.S. gallon. The following conversion table may be useful.

Weights
1 pound (lb) = 454 grams (g)
1 kilogram (kg) = 2.2 pounds (lbs)

Linear Measure
1 inch = 2.2 centimetres (cm)
1 foot (ft) = 30 centimetres (cm)
1 mile = 1.6 kilometres (km)
1 kilometre (km) = 0.63 miles
1 metre (m) = 39.37 inches

Land Measure
1 acre = 0.4047 hectare
1 hectare = 2.471 acres

Volume Measure
1 U.S. gallon (gal) = 3.79 litres
1 U.S. gallon (gal) = 0.83 imperial gallon

Temperature

To convert °F into °C: subtract 32, divide by 9, multiply by 5

To convert °C into °F: multiply by 9, divide by 5, add 32.

OUTDOORS

The Islands of The Bahamas is a country of land and sea. Some 700 islands or cays make up the country and have an estimated land mass of about 14,000 square kilometres (5,400 square miles) that extend over a marine territory of 256,000 square kilometres (100,000 miles), an area almost twice the size of Spain. The possibilities for outdoor pursuits are thus endless and varied. Crystal-clear waters, abundant animal and plant marine life and rich terrestrial flora and fauna can be enjoyed on each island. Twelve national parks, proof of The Bahamas commitment to environmental conservation, protect a variety of ecosystems and habitats like pine forests, wild dunes, wetlands, barrier reefs, impenetrable mangrove swamps and semi-arid salt pans. The world's largest breeding colony of pink flamingoes on Inagua, the second (or third, depending on how you define it) largest coral reef in the world off Andros, and the longest known underwater cave and cavern system in the world on Grand Bahama are just some of the wonders Mother Nature has placed in The Bahamas. Spectacular underwater gardens make The Bahamas a premier diving destination. Strong and constant winds are behind the sailing tradition, and each island has its own annual open regattas. Finally, those spectacular waters are home to some of the biggest and most elusive game fish in the world. There are tournaments year-round where you can test your hook against over 50 world records. Championship golf courses and unbeatable scenery also draw their share of outdoors enthusiasts.

This chapter provides information on what to expect in The Bahamas in terms of outdoor activities. In the following pages, you'll find tips and safety information for various activities. **The addresses of outfits offering these activities can be found in the chapters on each of the islands**.

PARKS

Established in 1959, the Bahamas National Trust administers more than 129,500 hectares (320,000 acres) in 12 national parks and protected areas in The Bahamas. The work of this small non-profit organization has contributed to the preservation of the West Indian flamingo, turtle conservation work, white-crowned pigeon management and rediscovery and propagation of the hutia, the islands' only indigenous land mammal. The country's natural resources are not their only concerns; they are also responsible for the preservation and restoration of historic public buildings and the valorization of the cultural and folkloric heritage.

The 12 national parks and protected areas in The Bahamas are as follows: on Abaco, Pelicans Cays Land and Sea Park (see p 155), Black Sound Cay, Abaco National Park (see p 156) and Tiloo Cay; on New Providence, The Retreat (see p 90); on Grand Bahama, The Rand Nature Centre (see p 124), Lucayan National Park (see p 125), Peterson Cay National Park (see p 125); on Conception Island, Conception Island National Park (see p 273); on Exuma, Exuma Cays Land and Sea Park (see p 206); and on Inagua, Inagua National Park (see p 299) and Union Creek Reserve (see p 300).

Some of these parks offer walking trails and information panels, while others are simply protected areas. For information on these areas contact the Bahamas National Trust at PO Box N-4105, ☎393-1317, ⇌393-2848.

BEACHES

With so many islands, The Bahamas is truly a beach-lover's paradise. Though you might hear otherwise from the fancy resorts, all beaches in The Bahamas are public and therefore open to everyone. It is the access to the beach that can be private: if the property fronting the beach is private then, for all intents and purposes, you can't get to the beach. Some resorts, however, do allow non-guests to use their facilities for a daily fee. The only other way onto such beaches is by boat. It is actually to allow stranded boaters to reach land that all beaches in The Bahamas are public.

Around 80% of beaches in The Bahamas are deserted stretches of virgin sand lined with pristine vegetation and washed by crystalline waters free of any motorboats and crowds. The other 20% are generally crawling with sunbathers most of the year, places where you can partake in some windsurfing, parasailing, banana-boating, water-skiing, cocktail sipping, hair-braiding, t-shirt buying or any of a number of festive, tropical pastimes. Some of these beaches are guarded by staff employed by the hotels that line them. A handful have changing rooms and other facilities. Currents can be strong, so keep an eye out for warning flags. Small jellyfish can also be a problem in summer. Never swim alone or at night.

OUTDOOR ACTIVITIES

Scuba Diving

Scuba diving is an exciting way to explore new horizons. Experienced divers as well as those who've never

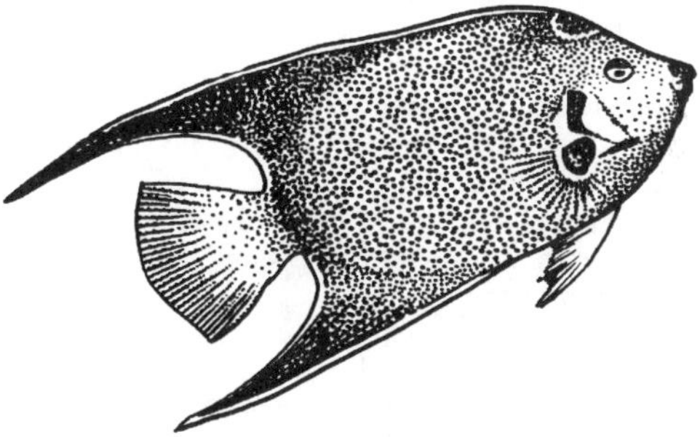

Angelfish

strapped on a mask can easily enjoy this adventure in The Bahamas, one of the premier diving destinations in the world. With 5% of the world's coral reefs (more than Australia's Great Barrier Reef) within its boundaries and incredible 30-metre (100-ft.) visibility, the possibilities are endless. Beyond these barrier reefs, the waters drops off to the dizzying depths of the Atlantic Ocean, making for exceptional wall and shelf dives. The diving opportunities don't stop at the shore: inland are the celebrated blue holes, deep sea pools up to 60 metres (200 ft.) across that are fed by the ocean via natural underground passages, tunnels and caverns. And then there are the shark dives, where those who dare can swim with these amazing creatures; softies can choose to frolic with the dolphins instead. Shipwrecks and night dives are two more exciting options.

Diving is not a dangerous activity; however, these adventures, whether new or old hat, should be taken seriously, since a successful dive requires planning and caution. Remember: plan the dive and dive the plan! Those who have never dived can take what's called a resort course (often included free of charge at many hotels), which involves a short introduction to the basics and then a shallow dive accompanied by an instructor. You will learn how to equalize the pressure in your ears, how to clear your mask, how to breathe underwater and, most importantly, not to hold your breath. Always choose a reputable dive shop, and don't let a macho dive master goad you into diving beyond your capabilities or level of comfort. Insist upon your instructor's undivided attention during the dive. Besides the one-shot resort courses, complete certification courses (NAUI and PADI) as well as guided dives and live-aboard excursions are also available to more experienced divers, as are equipment rentals for your own unguided adventures.

Remember that the underwater environment you are entering is fragile and should be respected by following a few simple guidelines: do not touch anything or stick your hand into any obscure areas (sea urchins' spikes can cause injury and biting eels like to hide in the darndest places); do not take pieces of coral with you (it takes years to grow and is much prettier in the water than out, where it dies and discolours); do not disturb any creatures; do not hunt; do not feed the fish; be careful not to disturb anything with your fins and, of course, do not litter. Finally, just enjoy the feeling of weightlessness and the tremendous bounty of underwater creatures before you, from schools of bright blue chromis fish to the spectacular coral formations of all shapes and colours. If you want a souvenir of your underwater experience, consider purchasing an underwater disposable camera, or even better, see if you can rent an underwater still or video camera from the dive shop or hotel.

Two favourites of divers in the know are the variety of shark and dolphin experiences offered by UNEXSO in Grand Bahama (see p 128) and the extraordinary barrier reef and blue holes of Andros.

Snorkelling

Those for whom scuba diving is too adventurous can still enjoy the wonders of the ocean by snorkelling. It doesn't take much: a mask, a snorkel and some fins. Just offshore from many beaches lie spectacular underwater gardens inhabited by coral and tropical fish. Many dive operations organize snorkelling trips to prime spots and at some hotels equipment is complimentary. If you plan on snorkelling while in The Bahamas, however, you may consider investing in your own mask and snorkel; there's nothing like ill-fitting equipment to ruin a day in the water. Remember that the same environmental guidelines apply to snorkellers as divers (see above). Finally, make sure you use plenty of sunscreen. Spending the day with your face in the water and your back to the sun can lead to a painful sunburn if you aren't well protected.

Just about every island figures on the Ministry of Tourism's list of top 10 snorkelling spots in The Bahamas: the northern and southern Abacos, Andros, Bimini, Cat Island, Eleuthera, the Exumas, Harbour Island, Long Island and San Salvador.

Several resorts in the Out Islands offer the Jean-Michel Cousteau Bahamas Out Islands Snorkelling Adventures. This program, created in conjunction with Jean-Michel Cousteau (son of Jacques), involves a day of discovery on the reefs offshore from whichever island you are staying on. Guided groups are introduced to the marine world, its ecology as well as local history. The cost is $97 per person, which includes two guided snorkelling trips and a souvenir t-shirt. For information on which hotels offer the program, contact the Out Island Promotion Board, or the nearest tourist office (see p 42).

Surfing and Windsurfing

The Bahamas are not necessarily known for windsurfing. Despite this, many outfits and resorts on the islands rent out the equipment, or offer it to their guests. Grand Bahama is one of the best places for windsurfing in the islands; Cable Beach and Harbour Island are two other spots where you'll find boards for hire. Surfing is another story, and die-hard surfers know that some of the finest waves break in the vicinity of Gregory Town, Eleuthera. Called the "second-best wave in the world", Surfer's Beach (see p 187) brings them in from as far away as Australia. If you have never tried either of these two sports before, here are a few pointers: choose a relatively calm day with little surf; do not head too far from shore but steer clear of swimmers; if you get into trouble make the distress signal by waving both your arms above your head, and finally, wear shoes to protect your feet.

Sailing and Cruising

The Bahamas is one of the most sought-after sailing destinations in the Atlantic. Skippers from The Bahamas and elsewhere rig up their dinghies and yachts to ply Bahamian waters, drop anchor in an idyllic cover, make for port in superb marinas or match their tactical wits against other racers in any of 30 local regattas. The Abacos and Exumas are particularly popular with yachties and salties alike during their many annual regattas. The major regattas are discussed in the specific chapters of this guide.

Many resorts have small sailboats available for the use of their guests, otherwise they can be rented on most of the bustling resort beaches (Lasers, Sunfish or Hobie-Cats for about $25 per day). Other cruising options are available in all of the islands. You can watch the ocean floor go by from a glass-bottom boat, take a dinner cruise under the stars, charter a crewed, captained or barefoot yacht for a carefree vacation at sea (anywhere from $300 to $3000 per day!) or hire a small motorboat (Boston Whalers for about $50-75 a day) to explore deserted islands just offshore. Note that it is forbidden to drive a motor boat in the 200-foot zone of water directly offshore from any Bahamian island unless you are approaching or leaving a dock.

Fishing

Bahamian waters are teeming with game fish and food fish. World-record game fish caught in The Bahamas include amberjack, bonefish, dolphin and wahoo, though these records change quickly. The latter is the fastest gamefish in the world, and then there are the giant tuna and the favourite of Ernest Hemingway, the enormous blue marlin. Hemingway is surely the most famous fisherman to try his luck in the Bahamas, and his favourite haunt, Bimini, is considered home to lures and lore and the deep-sea fishing capital of the world, as its Hall of Fame attests. Tournament fishing attracts anglers from all over the world, and this all year-round. Bahamas Tourist Offices can provide you with a calendar of local fishing events. In some cases, like the succulent grouper and jack, you might find an agreeable chef to prepare your prize catch just the way you like it.

The following game fish can be caught at the following times of the year and in the following areas:

- Allison tuna: year-round but best in June, July and August; in deepwater;
- Amberjack: November through May; reef areas;
- Barracuda: year-round; near reefs and in shallow water;
- Blackfin tuna: May to September; around Nassau;
- Bluefin (giant) tuna: May 7 to June 15; Bimini, Cat Cay and West End, Grand Bahama;
- Blue marlin: throughout the year but best in June and July; off Bimini, Cat Cay, Walker's Cay, off Andros in the Berry Islands near Chub Cay, Exuma Sound and in the Atlantic from north Eleuthera to Green Turtle Cay;

- Bonefish: year-round; in shallow flats throughout the islands, best in Andros;
- Dolphin: winter and spring; in deep water;
- Grouper: year-round; all reefs;
- Kingfish: May, June and July; throughout the islands but best in the Berry Islands and western Abaco;
- Sailfish: summer and fall; Berry Islands, Chub Cay, Bimini, Cat Cay, West End, Walker's Cay and Exuma Sound;
- Tarpon: year-round; Andros and Bimini;
- Wahoo: November to April, especially January and February; Exuma Sound, lower end of Eleuthera, also in Northeast Providence Channel from Nassau to Spanish Wells and Northwest Providence Channel around Berry Islands and off Abaco;
- White marlin: winter and spring; Bimini to Eleuthera and Walker's Cay to Exuma Sound, deep water.

Fishing for spiny lobsters (crayfish) and stone crabs is also popular. The season is closed for the former from April 1 to July 31, and for the latter from June 1 to October 15. Removing sponges and hawksbill turtles from Bahamian waters is strictly forbidden. Note that foreign vessels intending to sportfish must have a permit and can only have six lines in the water at one time. You do not need a permit if you are planning to participate in a sportfishing excursion with a company in The Bahamas, the company itself is responsible for the permit. For license information contact the Department of Fisheries, East Bay St., P.O. Box N-3028, Nassau, ☎393-1014/5. For addresses of outfitters see the respective chapters in the guide.

Jetskiing

These high-speed contraptions, known to some as personal water-crafts, are common off the beaches of New Providence, Paradise Island and Grand Bahama; they are less common in the Out Islands. Learning to drive one is fairly easy, and it certainly is a lot of fun to wheel about the waves. They have their opponents, however: those who claim they make too much noise and are dangerous. Caution and respect are therefore important considerations when hopping on a personal watercraft. Watch out for swimmers and scuba divers (dive boats fly a red flag with a white diagonal stripe) and always give the right of way to smaller, less manoeuvrable boats. Jet-skis can be rented on the bustling resort beaches for about $30 per half-hour; for insurance reasons, however, they are not rented by the hotels.

Horseback Riding

Horseback riding is not a huge thing in The Bahamas. Trail rides through wooded areas and along spectacular beaches are offered on New Providence and Grand Bahama at a few stables. These stables also offer lessons plus a choice of English or Western saddle. An hour ride runs between $30 and $40 with pick-up at your hotel.

Hiking

Hot temperatures and relatively flat terrain mean that hiking is not one of the islands' big drawing cards. The short hike up Mount Alvernia on Cat Island, the highest point in The Bahamas, is about as strenuous as it gets. Besides this, the best walking is on Grand Bahama, where both Lucayan

National Park and Rand Memorial Nature Centre have a series of well-maintained and well-marked nature trails. The particular flora, fauna and geology are highlighted in each of these parks.

Bicycling

The highest point in The Bahamas lies a mere 61.8 metres (206 ft.) above sea level, which makes the islands ideal for nice bike rides. Bikes can be rented from most resorts or small towns for about $10 a day and are the perfect way to explore the country. Shade can be hard to come by in certain places, so bring water and be sure to wear a hat.

Golf

Location, location, location. Imagine sinking that perfect put with the multi-hued blue ocean as a backdrop, a winning score is that much sweeter in a place like The Bahamas. Among the dozen courses are championship ones designed by names like Joe Lee and Robert Trent Jones. There are courses on New Providence, Paradise Island, Grand Bahama and Abaco. Fees are about $60, plus $35 for cart rentals. Reservations are a must. Hotel guests often play for free.

Tennis

Most of the major resorts, particularly those on New Providence, Paradise Island and Grand Bahama, have tennis courts. If your hotel does not have one, inquire at the front desk about courts at neighbouring hotels, which are generally open to non-guests for a fee of about $15 to $25 per hour, more at night when the lights have to be turned on. Rarely is equipment available for rent, so bring your own if you plan on hitting a few volleys.

Fitness Clubs

With such extraordinary natural surroundings and endless possibilities of things to do outside, fitness clubs are not a necessity, even for die-hard exercise freaks. Nevertheless, a fair number of the resorts on New Providence, Paradise Island and Grand Bahama do have them. These offer weight-training equipment and aerobics classes to guests; non-guests can usually participate for a small charge. There is also Gold's Gym in Nassau (see p 98), which offers classes and weights. The accommodations sections throughout this guide include information on fitness facilities where applicable.

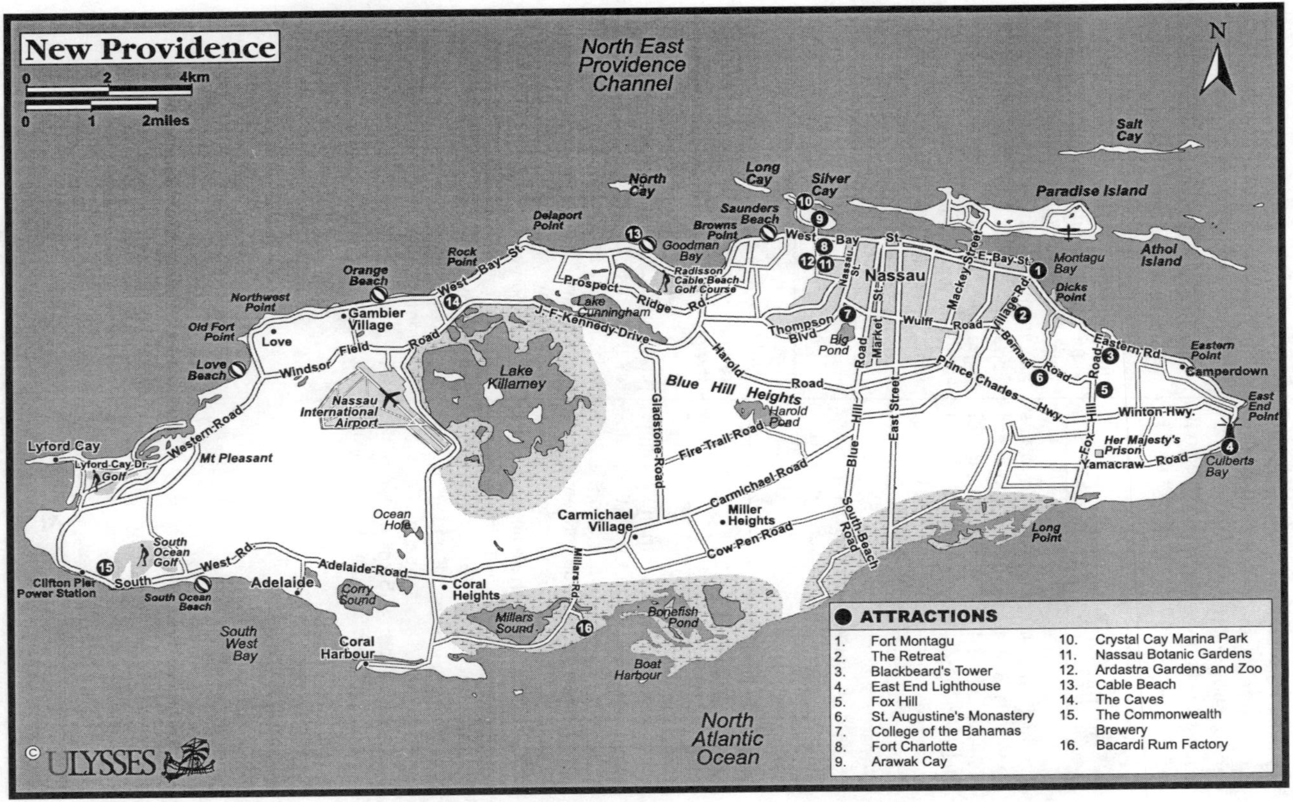
New Providence
0 2 4km
0 1 2miles
N
North East Providence Channel
North Atlantic Ocean
Salt Cay
Paradise Island
Athol Island
Long Cay
Silver Cay
North Cay
Delaport Point
Rock Point
Orange Beach
Northwest Point
Old Fort Point
Love Beach
Love
Gambier Village
Saunders Beach
Browns Point
Goodman Bay
Radisson Cable Beach Golf Course
Prospect Ridge Rd.
Lake Cunningham
J. F. Kennedy Drive
West Bay St.
Nassau
Nassau St.
Market St.
Mackey Street
E. Bay St.
Montagu Bay
Dicks Point
Village Rd.
Bernard Road
Wulff Road
Thompson Blvd
Big Pond
Eastern Rd.
Eastern Point
Camperdown
East End Point
Culberts Bay
Her Majesty's Prison
Yamacraw Road
Winton Hwy.
Fox Hill Road
Prince Charles Hwy.
East Street
Blue Hill Road
South Beach Road
Harold Road
Blue Hill Heights
Harold Pond
Fire Trail Road
Gladstone Road
Carmichael Road
Miller Heights
Cow Pen Road
Carmichael Village
Windsor Field Road
Nassau International Airport
Lake Killarney
Western Road
Mt Pleasant
Lyford Cay
Lyford Cay Dr.
Golf
South Ocean Golf
Clifton Pier Power Station
South West Rd.
South Ocean Beach
Adelaide
Adelaide Road
Ocean Hole
Corry Sound
Coral Heights
Coral Harbour
South West Bay
Millars Rd.
Millars Sound
Bonefish Pond
Boat Harbour
Long Point
ULYSSES
ATTRACTIONS
1. Fort Montagu
2. The Retreat
3. Blackbeard's Tower
4. East End Lighthouse
5. Fox Hill
6. St. Augustine's Monastery
7. College of the Bahamas
8. Fort Charlotte
9. Arawak Cay
10. Crystal Cay Marina Park
11. Nassau Botanic Gardens
12. Ardastra Gardens and Zoo
13. Cable Beach
14. The Caves
15. The Commonwealth Brewery
16. Bacardi Rum Factory

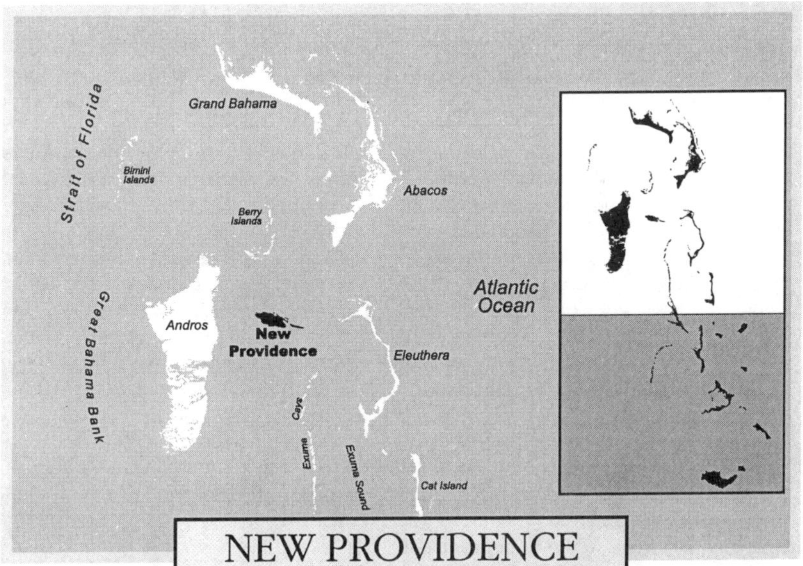

NEW PROVIDENCE AND PARADISE ISLAND

New Providence ★★★ is The Bahamas' most important island, and in more ways than one. Its main city, Nassau, is the country's capital; more than two-thirds of the population resides here, and finally more than 70% of tourists to The Bahamas come here, drawn by the best colonial architecture in the British West Indies, the action of Bay Street's duty-free shops, superb white sand beaches, excellent diving and marina facilities and the mega-resorts and casinos of Cable Beach and Paradise Island ★★★. And curious visitors can complete their visit by seeking out the true-true Bahamian side of New Providence with a visit Over-the-Hill.

While some say the real Bahamas can only be found in the laid back Out Islands, some travellers prefer a little more action. If you are one of these types and casinos and duty-free shopping are all you're after then you might settle for grand Bahama. However, if you are looking for more from your vacation, New Providence and Paradise Island win hands down. Nowhere else in the country will you find the colonial charm of Nassau, surely its greatest asset and what sets it apart from Grand Bahama and the rest of the West Indies for that matter.

New Providence and Paradise Island, though separate islands, are just a stone's throw apart and a visit to one necessitates a visit to the other. It is only natural, therefore to discuss them in the same chapter. Paradise Island may be a mammoth mega-resort, but one of the huge attractions is still the Old World charm of Nassau.

Small, oval-shaped New Providence is a mere 34 kilometres long and 11 kilometres wide at is widest point. The city of Nassau lies on its northern shoreline and its downtown core extends inland about four blocks and runs about two dozen blocks from east to west. Most of Nassau's budget hotels (with the exception of the exceptional Graycliff) are downtown where they enjoy a great location by day, come nightfall, however, the downtown area is not the ideal place to be. About five kilometres west of the city centre is Cable Beach, New Providence's best beach and location of the island's biggest concentration of hotels. Continuing west are some of the island's poshest residential areas, including the very private Lyford Cay. To the south lie Nassau's middle- and lower-income suburbs. This handful of communities is collectively referred to as Over-the-Hill. East of Nassau, East Bay Street is shaded by the grand trees of some of the island's most sumptuous residences. But before you go that far, there is the Paradise Island Bridge.

Over the bridge is Paradise Island, six-and-a-half kilometres long and just under one kilometre wide at its widest point. At a point about level with downtown Nassau, its western end narrows into a slender, sandy peninsula. Its resorts are clustered in the middle portion of the island along its northern shore and face. The airport and golf course take up the eastern part of the island.

Paradise Island and Cable Beach both have casinos, beautiful beaches and mega-resorts. They are two very different places, however, as Paradise Island retains the aura of exclusivity that made it famous, thereby attracting a slightly more sophisticated and certainly more moneyed clientele than comfortable Cable Beach. Not to knock Cable Beach, mind you, which boasts excellent facilities.

Of course, neither New Providence nor Paradise Island are the natural wonders that the neighbouring Out Islands are, but untouched pockets of wilderness do exist. Much of Paradise Island remains wooded, providing shelter for a variety of birds. New Providence, for all its population, still has vast areas of undeveloped land. Its inland lakes are also prime birding spots. And of course, nature-seekers will marvel at the wealth of marine life that thrives just offshore.

Nassau is a curious combination of American consumerism and British propriety tempered by tropical indolence. The mood here is perhaps best epitomized by the suited banker hurrying past the uniformed police officer directing traffic, the Bible-reading taxi driver waiting for his next fare and the domino-playing Bahamians, all in the shadow of massive, gleaming-white cruise ships.

A Short History

Nassau's history is very much the history of The Bahamas. It begins in 1648 with the intrepid group of Eleutheran Adventurers who stopped here en route to establish their settlement on Eleuthera and the first republic of the New World. Their leader, Captain William Sayle, later purchased the island and gave it his name. But Sayle's Island remained unsettled until 1656, when Bermudian seamen began using it as a base and a few farmers drifted over. By 1666, the main settlement, Charles Town, was populated by unsavoury types from pirates to prostitutes. Pirates put in at the protected harbour for repairs to their ships and to survey the spoils of their marauding. A small portion of the settlers farmed – they were the ones who renamed the island Providence, adding the New later to avoid confusion with other Providences. When the British crown granted The Bahamas to the six Lords Proprietors in 1670, Charles Town had a population of 300.

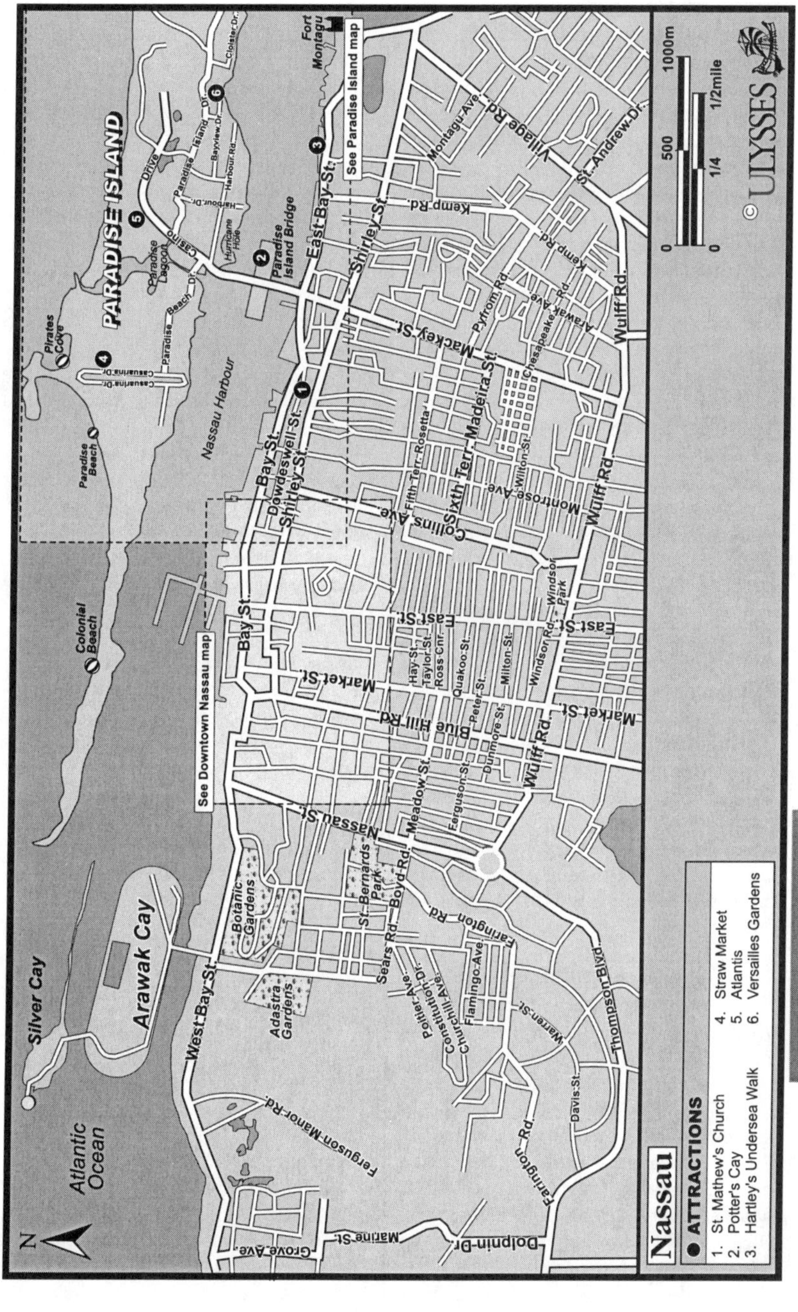
Nassau
ATTRACTIONS
1. St. Mathew's Church
2. Potter's Cay
3. Hartley's Undersea Walk
4. Straw Market
5. Atlantis
6. Versailles Gardens
0 500 1000m
0 1/4 1/2mile
© ULYSSES
N
Atlantic Ocean
Silver Cay
Arawak Cay
Colonial Beach
Paradise Beach
Pirates Cove
PARADISE ISLAND
Paradise Lagoon
Hurricane Hole
Nassau Harbour
Paradise Island Bridge
Fort Montagu
See Paradise Island map
See Downtown Nassau map
Casuarina Dr.
Paradise Beach Dr.
Casino Drive
Paradise Island Dr.
Harbour Dr.
Harbour Rd.
Bayview Dr.
Cloister Dr.
West Bay St.
Bay St.
East Bay St.
Dowdeswell St.
Shirley St.
Nassau St.
Market St.
East St.
Blue Hill Rd.
Collins Ave.
Mackey St.
Kemp Rd.
Village Rd.
St. Andrew Dr.
Montagu Ave.
Wulff Rd.
Madeira St.
Sixth Terr.
Fifth Terr.
Rosetta
Montrose Ave.
Wilton St.
Chesapeake Rd.
Arawak Ave.
Pyfrom Rd.
Windsor Park
Windsor Rd.
Hay St.
Taylor St.
Ross Cnr.
Quakoo St.
Peter St.
Milton St.
Dunmore St.
Ferguson St.
Meadow St.
Boyd Rd.
Sears Rd.
St. Bernards Park
Botanic Gardens
Adastra Gardens
Farington Rd.
Flamingo Ave.
Poitier Ave.
Constitution Dr.
Churchill Ave.
Warren St.
Thompson Blvd.
Davis St.
Ferguson Manor Rd.
Grove Ave.
Marine St.
Dolphin Dr.

The swash-buckling ways of the pirates and the retaliatory attacks by the French and Spanish got the most of the farmers, however, who were chased away, most of them to the Out Islands. The first attack was in 1684, when Charles Town was levelled by the Spanish. It wasn't until ten years later with the arrival of Governor Nicholas Trott that Charles Town was rebuilt. Trott set about building a fort to protect the settlement from future attacks. Fort Nassau kept watch from where the British Colonial Hotel now stands. He also renamed the city, calling it Nassau for William, Prince of Orange-Nassau who became King William III of England in 1689.

A new name and a new fort didn't change the fact that Nassau's population was still made up essentially of wreckers and pirates, and with England at war, the Spanish attacks continued. The city was again leveled in 1703 and the during the ensuing 14 years, pirates and privateers held sway over the island. Finally in 1718, Woodes Rogers, the first Royal Governor, arrived to chase the pirates away and restore order. This was no easy task, and Nassau remained in disarray until 1760 when Governor Shirley set about cleaning the place up, draining the mosquito-breeding swamps and laying out streets.

The next big story for Nassau was the American Revolution. The blockade imposed on the mainland affected The Bahamas, which relied heavily on it for trade. It also placed the islands in the firing line. The Americans attacked in search of gun powder and then the Spanish invaded Nassau and occupied it for a year. The Revolution proved to have an even more lasting influence on Nassau and The Bahamas, however, when the 13 American colonies won their independence and Americans wishing to remain loyal to the Crown began pouring in. The Loyalist legacy, both in traditions and architecture, is surely one of Nassau's greatest assets. The Loyalists also brought with them their slaves, and forever changed the face of The Bahamas. There was little farming on Nassau, therefore fewer slaves. Nassau's elite, nevertheless, had their share of domestic slaves.

Fortunes rose and fell in Nassau over the next 150 years, and invariably at the mercy of the Americans. Blockade runners prospered during the US Civil War (1861-1865) by supplying the Southern states, and rum-runners got their turn during Prohibition (1920-1933). During both these periods, Nassau boomed. Warehouses were stocked with goods and the Treasury filled up with export duties. This was the start of tourism to Nassau as grand hotels including the Royal Victoria were erected.

Nassau was on the map now. In 1940, its new governor, the Duke of Windsor arrived, sending all of Nassau into a state. After the Second World War, it soon became clear that tourism would be the big industry in The Bahamas.

Enter Paradise Island. Originally called Hog Island because it was used for raising pigs, it had already become a haven for the rich and famous in the early 1900s. This group of millionaires formed the exclusive Porcupine Club. In 1939, Axel Wenner-Gren bought up much of the island and built his "Shangri-La" and his terraced Versailles-style gardens. He sold everything for $11 million to newspaper magnate Huntington Harford II, who built the posh 52-room Ocean Hotel and decided that the name Hog Island just wouldn't do. He convinced the Bahamian government that Paradise Island was much more a propos. He had a clear vision of the exclusivity he wanted on Paradise Island, stating firmly, "There will be no automobiles, no roulette wheels, no honky-tonks on Hog Island."

There were only so many rich people who met the criteria, and in 1967 the island was sold off to the Mary Carter Paint Company, which started to transform the island into what it is today. The Paradise Island Bridge was built and the Paradise Island Casino opened its doors. The brashness that Huntington Hartford had feared reached its peak when Donald Trump and Merv Griffin took over and built more resorts and the airport.

These days, however, Paradise Island's reputation is once again that of an exclusive resort, a turnaround that can be attributed to Sun International. Atlantis Paradise Island Resort & Casino, the posh Ocean Club, Paradise Paradise and the Pirate's Cove Resort are all part of Sun International's ongoing transformation of Paradise Island.

Back in Nassau, the upswing in tourism has prompted just about every hotel on Cable Beach to undertake renovation, refurbishment or expansion projects. Not to mention the addition of several real showpiece hotels, namely the luxurious Sandals Royal Bahamian and the marvellous Compass Point.

FINDING YOUR WAY AROUND

By Plane

Nassau International Airport

Nassau International Airport *(☎377-7035)* is served by direct flights from many cities in the United States, Canada, England, France, Holland, Ireland, Germany and Italy. The national airline, Bahamasair, is based here and offers flights to the Out Islands (charter flights to Bimini depart Paradise Island). The airport is located about 13 kilometres southwest of downtown Nassau.

There are two separate terminals here, the newer and flashier international terminal and the aged and modest domestic terminal. Both have snack bars and small gift shops. Services including a tourist information desk, car-rental counters, a bank with an automatic teller machine and a BaTelCo office separate the two. Private charters arrive at and fly out of the General Aviation Terminal, a short cab ride to the east of the airport.

Paradise Island Airport

Paradise Island Airport is a tiny affair at the eastern end of the island. It is served by Pan Am Air Bridge from Miami and Bimini and Paradise Island Airlines from Fort Lauderdale, Miami and West Palm Beach.

By Boat

By Mailboat: Mailboats to each of the Out Islands depart at least once a week from Potter's Cay (under the Paradise Island Bridge). Cabins are available on some of the longer hauls. For information call the Dockmaster's Office at ☎393-1064.

Marinas

Browns Boat Basin, East Bay Street, ☎393-3331.

Claridge Marina, South Nassau, ☎364-2218.

East Bay Yacht Basin, East Bay St., ☎322-2218.

Lyford Cay Club (private), Lyford Cay, ☎362-4131.

Nassau Harbour Club, East Bay St., ☎393-0771.

Nassau Yacht Haven, East Bay St., ☎393-8173.

Hurricane Hole Marina, Paradise Island, ☎363-3600.

Ferries

The Paradise Island Ferry runs between Woodes Rogers Walk and the Canal Wharf on Paradise Island (just west of the bridge) every 30 minutes between 9:30am and 6pm. The fare is $2 one way. Water taxis can be hired to run you closer to your hotel.

By Bus

Jitneys, white or beige minibuses, cover most of downtown Nassau. They run between about 6:30am and 7pm. The fare is 75¢ for adults and 50¢ for children. Pay as you get off. Bus drivers do not give change. There are bus stops along the route, but you can also flag the bus down from the sidewalk.

From Cable Beach, buses number 10 and 38 go to Prince George Wharf via Over-the-Hill – it is an interesting ride.

There are no jitneys on Paradise Island. There is the "Casino Express" which makes the rounds of the hotels. The fare is $1. To get downtown, you'll have to walk across the bridge and catch bus number 24 or 30 heading west to Prince George Wharf.

By Car

Downtown Nassau's narrow and congested streets can be a challenge, especially if you've never driven on the left. Traffic remains fairly heavy the whole length of Bay Street. In the rest of the island, however, the roads are virtually empty, leaving you the chance to explore at your leisure. Parking is difficult right downtown. There are parking lots on Charlotte Street and Elizabeth Avenue.

There is a $2 toll on the Paradise Island Bridge.

Car Rentals

Dollar Car Rental, airport, ☎-377-7231.
Avis Rent-A-Car, airport, ☎326-6380, Cable Beach ☎322-2889, Marlborough St., ☎326-6380.
Budget Rent-A-Car, airport, ☎377-7405.
Hertz Rent-A-Car, ☎377-8684.
Orange Creek Rentals, ☎323-4967.
Wallace's, ☎393-0650.

By Taxi

Taxis hang around the major hotels, and in general have to be called by telephone. Fares are set by the government.

Lil Murph & Sons Limousine Service ☎325-3725.
Bahamas Taxi Cab Union, ☎323-4555.

Here are some sample fares: Nassau International Airport to Cable Beach is $10 to $15, to downtown Nassau about $15, to Paradise Island $20 to $25. Cable Beach to downtown is $9 to $12, Paradise Island to downtown is $9.

By Surrey

Historic horse-drawn surreys tour *(Nov to Apr, every day 9am to 1pm and 2pm to 4:30pm; May to Oct, every day 1pm to 3pm)* downtown Nassau in about 30 minutes. You can hire one at Prince George Wharf for $5 per person, a great deal!

PRACTICAL INFORMATION

Tourist Information: Bahamas Ministry of Tourism Information Office on the north side of Rawson Square, is open Mon to Fri 8:30am to 5pm, Sat 8:30am to 4pm, Sun 8:30am to 2pm, ☎327-9781.
The magazine *What-to-do* lists the latest entertainment and dining offerings. It is available around town in hotel lobbies and shops.

Banks: There are plenty of banks in Nassau and they are generally open Monday to Thursday from 9:30am to 3pm, and Friday from 9:30am to 5pm:
Scotiabank, Rawson Square, Cable Beach.
CIBC, Cable Beach.
Barclay's Bank, Bay Street.
Royal Bank of Canada, Bay Street, East Bay Street, Airport, Cable Beach.

Police: East St., ☎919 or 332-4444.

BaTelCo: East St., beside the police station, open every day 7am to 10pm, ☎323-6414.

Post Office: East Hill St. at Parliament St., ☎322-3025.

Hospital: Princess Margaret Hospital, Shirley St., ☎322-2861.

Travel agency: Playtours, Shirley St., ☎322-2931, ⇒325-1780.

Guided Tours: Walking tours of historic Nassau depart from the Bahamas Tourist Office on Rawson Square twice an hour, every day from 10am to 4pm for $3 per person. They are given by Bahamahost guides and by the Ministry of Tourism. The tours don't necessarily run like clockwork, however, so it is a good idea to call ahead to make sure they are running according to schedule. Call ☎328-7811 or 322-8634.

Majestic Tours *(Hillside Manor, Cumberland St., ☎322-3606)* offers a variety of tours in and around Nassau. They have a two-hour city tour for $20 and a four-hour city and country tour for $25. The most unique tour they offer is a nightclub tour, complete with limbo dancing and fire-breathing, the cost is $25, or $55 with dinner. These tours can usually be booked through your hotel's tour desk.

EXPLORING

Downtown Nassau Walking Tour ★★★

Start your tour at **Prince George Wharf**, Nassau's cruise-ship dock where 1.6 million visitors are unloaded each year. Nassau harbour's first wharf was built in the 1920s to accommodated blockade runners during US Prohibition, it was named for Prince George, the Duke of Kent who visited in 1928. But this was a far cry from the ships that began calling at Nassau as of 1969, when a new wharf was put in and a deep-water harbour was dredged.

Few cruise-ship passengers will make it past the **Hair Braiding Centre** untransformed! The hair-braiders used to operate in the Straw Market until the government created this open-air pavilion where there are women with their toolkits full of different-coloured beads. A single braid is $2 and, depending on how much hair you have, you can get your whole head done for $20. Don't forget to put sunscreen on your scalp in between the braids.

The new **Junkanoo Expo** ★★ *(every day 9am to 5pm, closed holidays, Prince George Wharf, ☎356-2731)* is full of winning Junkanoo costumes and noisemakers from years gone by. Junkanoo is the annual festival and parade held on Boxing Day and New Year's Day each year. Its history is recounted here.

Rawson Square ★★, just up from the wharf, is the centre of town. Flanked to the north by the main **Tourist Information Office** *(Mon to Fri 8:30 am to 5pm, Sat 8:30am to 4pm, Sun 8:30am to 2pm, ☎326-9781)*, the square contains a few sculptures. There is a **bronze bust of Sir Milo Butler**, the first black Bahamian to be named governor general, and the first governor-general of the newly independent Bahamas. There is also an interesting bronze statue called ***Bahamian Woman***. Benches and shady trees surround the leaping dolphins of **Sands Fountain**.

The main Bahamian branch of the **Royal Bank of Canada** ★★ is on the south side of Bay Street to the west of the square. The Greek Revival stone building dates from 1919 and was built after the Royal Bank took over Bank of Nassau in 1917. An equally imperious-looking Greek-Revival building is the **Masonic Lodge** across the street.

Bay Street divides Rawson Square to the north from **Parliament Square** ★★★ to the south. It is hemmed in on three sides by the hallowed halls of the Bahamian government, lovely pink and white Georgian neoclassical buildings that were based on Governor Tyron's Palace in New Bern, the ancient capital of North Carolina. They were all erected between 1805 and 1813 and were once described as the most beautiful in colonial America. The white **Queen Victoria Statue**, in the centre, shows a youthful queen, it was unveiled May 24th, 1905 by then Governor General Sir William Wilson. The **House of Assembly**, on the western side, is where sessions of Parliament are held. Visitors can sit in on the proceedings *(you must call ahead, ☎322-7500)*, with all their pomp and ceremony. The square originally overlooked the waterfront, along which Bay Street ran.

Cut through the southeastern corner of Parliament Square to Bank Lane.

The facade of the **Supreme Court** boasts four Tuscan columns supporting a Classical portico. Judges and lawyers still don those strange white wigs, as they have since these courts were built in 1921. The grand palm trees and flowering bushes surround a cenotaph to Bahamian soldiers who have died while serving their country.

At the other end of the Garden of Remembrance is the wonderful, octagonal **Nassau Public Library and Historic Museum** ★★★. Erected around 1798, this was Nassau's first jail, complete with its own dungeon. Prisoners were housed in cells on the first and second floors. Assembly meetings were held on the third floor, whose gallery roof was added later. In 1873, the prisoners moved out and bookshelves took their place. This small historical museum has lots of old documents and drawings from colonial times, a model of a rumrunning ship, plus a scattered collection of artefacts; the second floor is dedicated to the Lucayans.

The **Parliament Inn** across the way on Parliament Street dates from 1937. Just below it is the attractive **Magna Carta Court** ★★★, which dates from

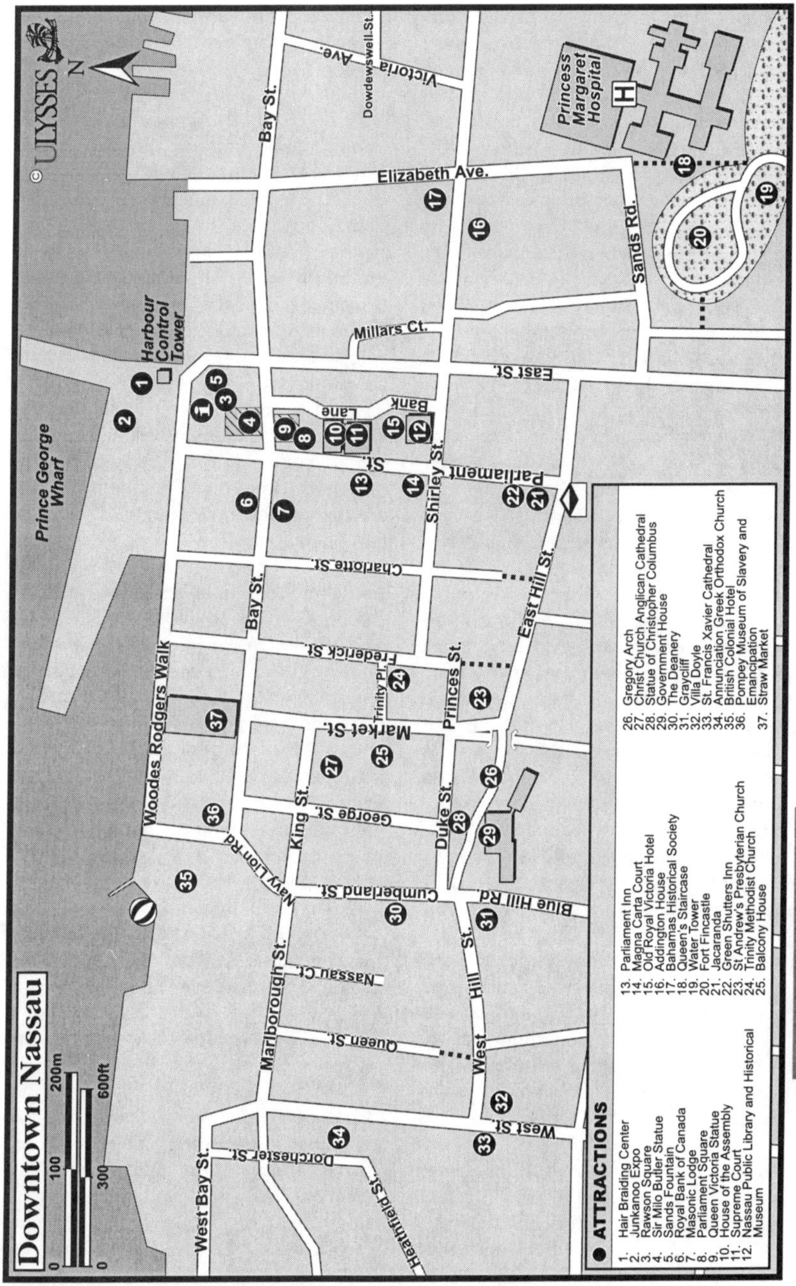
Downtown Nassau
0 100 200m
0 300 600ft
© ULYSSES
N
Prince George Wharf
Harbour Control Tower
Woodes Rodgers Walk
West Bay St.
Bay St.
Marlborough St.
Navy Lion Rd.
King St.
Duke St.
Princes St.
Shirley St.
East Hill St.
West Hill St.
Blue Hill Rd.
West St.
Dorchester St.
Heathfield St.
Queen St.
Nassau Ct.
Cumberland St.
George St.
Market St.
Trinity Pl.
Frederick St.
Charlotte St.
Parliament St.
Bank Lane
East St.
Millars Ct.
Elizabeth Ave.
Sands Rd.
Victoria Ave.
Dowdeswell St.
Princess Margaret Hospital
H
ATTRACTIONS
1. Hair Braiding Center
2. Junkanoo Expo
3. Rawson Square
4. Sir Milo Butler Statue
5. Sands Fountain
6. Royal Bank of Canada
7. Masonic Lodge
8. Parliament Square
9. Queen Victoria Statue
10. House of the Assembly
11. Supreme Court
12. Nassau Public Library and Historical Museum
13. Parliament Inn
14. Magna Carta Court
15. Old Royal Victoria Hotel
16. Addington House
17. Bahamas Historical Society
18. Queen's Staircase
19. Water Tower
20. Fort Fincastle
21. Jacaranda
22. Green Shutters Inn
23. St Andrew's Presbyterian Church
24. Trinity Methodist Church
25. Balcony House
26. Gregory Arch
27. Christ Church Anglican Cathedral
28. Statue of Christopher Columbus
29. Government House
30. The Deanery
31. Graycliff
32. Villa Doyle
33. St. Francis Xavier Cathedral
34. Annunciation Greek Orthodox Church
35. British Colonial Hotel
36. Pompey Museum of Slavery and Emancipation
37. Straw Market

the early 1800s, a time when its cut-stone exterior would have been very costly. Note how the stonework does not line up and the difference in the stone arrangement of the lintels between the southern and northern parts of the building, suggesting that it was constructed in two sections. Then take a stroll along Shirley Street to see its contrasting rear wooden facade.

The venerable **Royal Victoria Hotel** occupied the site immediately to the north of the library. The hotel opened in 1861, just in time to cash in the flood of people pouring into Nassau as the US Civil War raged on and blockade running became a very profitable business. The hotel's construction had put the government into serious debt, but the Treasury swelled so much with import and export duties that this and all its other debts were quickly wiped out. The hotel was a haven for Confederate officers, merchants who made deals, spent money and lolled away the afternoons on its verandah, gazing out at its tropical **garden** ★ with over 200 varieties of exotic plants and shrubs. Unfortunately, this is about all that remains of the hotel, which closed in 1971 and was later claimed by fire. A few of its outbuildings now house government ministries. The centrepiece of the garden is a huge silk tree.

Head east along Shirley Street. On your right, before you reach Elizabeth Avenue, a sweeping lawn leads up to a lovely old home, now abandoned. This is **Addington House**, the former official residence of the Anglican Bishop of Nassau. It was built in the mid-1800s.

Across the street at the northwest corner of Shirley and Elizabeth streets is the **Bahamas Historical Society** ★ *($1; Mon, Tue, Wed, Fri 10am to 4pm, Sat 10am to noon, ☎322-4231)*. A few old photos and relics relate the natural and social history of The Bahamas. Of particular note are the old dug-out canoe and the model of the Spanish Galleon, the *Santa Lucerno*.

Walk up Elizabeth Avenue towards the **Queen's Staircase** ★★. You'll pass the Princess Margaret Hospital on the way. Each of the 66 steps, which were cut from solid limestone by slaves starting in the 1790s, represents a year of Victoria's Reign. The stairs were made to provide an escape route from Fort Fincastle into town. Mosses and plants sprout from the moist walls of the narrow canyon, and palm trees stretch up to the sun. Souvenir stalls line the walk up to the steps where tour guides vie for your ear. If you don't want to pay them, then don't let them tell you anything about the steps. The steps can be slippery in wet weather.

Sixty-six steps later and you are up at the Water Tower and Fort Fincastle. The **Water Tower** ★ *(50¢; every day 8am to 5pm)* was erected in 1928 to maintain water pressure in the city. It rises some 70 metres above sea level, and is 42 metres tall. A long winding staircase or an elevator lead to the top from whence you will have a sweeping view of Nassau and a great perspective of **Fort Fincastle** ★★ below. Shaped like a paddle-wheel steamer, it was built in 1793 by Lord Dunmore. You can climb up to the top where old cannons, which date from 1855, point out to sea. The fort never saw any fire and later served as lighthouse and signal station. Tour guides hang around here as well.

A path and stairs lead west of the fort to Sands Road, turn right on East Street, then left on East Hill Street. You'll walk through a small corner of the modest residential part of Nassau known as "Over the Hill" if you head this way.

Nassau's **Main Post Office** will be on your left as you make your way to **Jacaranda** ★ *(at the northwest corner of Parliament and East Hill)*. Built in the 1840s, the house was later purchased by the widow of Sir Harry Oakes, Lady Eunice. Two balconies with fine latticework adorn its facade.

Just a few doors down, the **Green Shutters Inn** on Parliament is the only true English pub in The Bahamas. It was built by shipwrights who put it together with glue and wooden pegs. It became a restaurant and bar in the early 1970s.

Take the white steps down towards Frederick Street. Turn on Princes Street to **St. Andrew's Presbyterian Church** also known as **The Kirk** ★★★. Nassau's Scottish Presbyterians, lead by Michael Malcolm, petitioned the St. Andrew's Society of Scotland for funds to build their own church. They were successful, and in 1810 work commenced on this church. It was the first non-Anglican church in The Bahamas. Its Romanesque and Gothic features are complemented by a beautifully ornate cast-iron railing.

Head back to Frederick Street and up it to **Trinity Methodist Church** ★. Construction on this church was begun in 1861, but with the start of the US Civil War, builders could not procure the lumber necessary to continue, then an yellow fever epidemic claimed the lives of four of the six builders. It finally opened in 1865, only to be destroyed one year later by a hurricane. It was rebuilt, but damaged again by the 1928 hurricane.

Turn left on Trinity Place and walk to Market Street.

One of the loveliest and most unique houses in Nassau lies a few doors to your left. **Balcony House** ★★★ *(donations; Mon, Wed, Fri 10am to 1pm and 3pm to 4pm, Market St., ☎326-2566 for information)* is a restored early Loyalist (1790s) merchant's house. Its furniture and design recapture the elegance and glory of a bygone era. Built of American soft cedar, wooden-knee braces support the namesake second-floor balcony. There is a slave kitchen on the premises and the house's interior staircase is believed to be from a ship. The house is now a historical museum.

Look south along Market Street and you'll see the **Gregory Arch**, which was opened 1852. Head north on Market and turn left on King Street to come up alongside **Christ Church Anglican Cathedral** ★★ *(at the corner of George St. and King St.)*. The first Anglican church in Nassau was destroyed by the Spanish in 1684, subsequent churches were also sacked or lost to termites and bad weather. The present church is the fifth on this site. The Gothic square tower predates the rest of the church, which was built in 1837. Inside, large stone columns support a solid timber-trussed roof.

Walk south on George Street, to Duke Street. An 1830 **statue of Christopher Columbus** towers over the steps up Mount Fitzwilliam to **Government House** ★★, the official residence of the Queen's representative in The Bahamas, the Governor General. Governor Fitzwilliam was the first governor to set up house on this hill, in 1737. This house was leased to the government and continued to house governors until Lord Dunmore built his own manse to the west. After his term ended, he leased his house to the government until it finally acquired the Mount Fitzwilliam site and built a new Government House there in 1806. This house was badly damaged in the hurricane of 1929 and had to be torn down. The present Government House dates from

1932. The lavish decor dates from the time of the arrival of the Duke of Windsor as governor-general in 1940. You can ask the guards for a closer look or get an invitation to the monthly tea party at Government House hosted by the wife of the governor-general as part of the People-to-People program (see p 66).

Make a short detour up Cumberland Street to **The Deanery**. This stone building, with its wrap-around wooden galleries, is one of Nassau's oldest residences. The separate kitchen and slave quarters still stand on the property.

Back up on West Hill Street, **Graycliff ★★★** was built in the 1720s by Captain John Howard Graysmith on the ruins of the a church destroyed in 1694 by the Spanish. The house began operating as a guesthouse in 1844 as Victoria House, later it was known as French's Hotel serving "Best Porter, Ale, Wine, etc, etc, etc." In the 1920s, one of Al Capone's friends, Polly Leach, ran the place as Graycliff and attracted such famous guests as the Duke and Duchess of Windsor and Sir Winston Churchill. It is now owned and run by Enrico Garzaroli and is one of Nassau's most elegant establishments (see p 100).

Continue along West Hill Street, which boasts several stunning houses. At the southwestern corner of West Hill and West Street is the lovely **Villa Doyle ★**. In major need of restoration, this former home of Sir William Doyle, Chief Justice of the Supreme Court and the first Bahamian to be knighted, is the future home of the National Art Gallery of The Bahamas, whose opening date is still a ways away. The house was built in the 1860s, its design is more reminiscent of the antebellum South than colonial Nassau. The house was also owned by Nancy Oakes, whose husband was accused of murdering her father Sir Harry in the country's most famous murder trial.

St. Francis Xavier Cathedral ★★★ stands along the west side of West Street. Opened in 1886, this was the first Catholic church in The Bahamas. Protestants who objected to its construction saw the "Hand of God" in the mishaps surrounding its opening. Lightning struck and killed a workman during the construction and then the minister of St. Andrew's Presbyterian, Kirk Rev. Robert Dunlop, who had sold the land to the Catholics for the church, had a heart attack and died at the pulpit of his church. The slightly tapered square tower and main structure overlook a lovely garden. Inside the long pulpit lies the middle of the church.

From here you have two options to reach Marlborough Street: either by West Street or Queen Street.

On West Street you'll find the lovely **Annunciation Greek Orthodox Church ★** or Kuriko. The Byzantine-style domed church has a beautiful interior and still serves a small Greek community. Down Queen Street, you'll see enclosed gardens of lush tropical plants and shrubs, wooden cottages and white picket and latticed fences. Present-day Shirley Street was once called Queen Street, but was renamed in honour of Governor William Shirley, at which point the name was transferred to this quiet little street. The stairs at its southern end keep the car traffic down to a minimum.

The **British Colonial Hotel ★** lies south of Marlborough Street. Fort Nassau, the town's first defence, once occupied this site. Governor Nicholas Trott, who arrived in 1694, renamed the town Nassau and began construction of the fort to protect the Western entrance to the harbour. It was completed in 1697,

Pompey Museum

but destroyed by a combined French and Spanish attack in 1703. It was rebuilt by Governor Tinker and finally torn down in 1837. Military barracks occupied the site until the Colonial Hotel was built in 1899. This original was destroyed by fire in 1922, and the fireproof New Colonial Hotel was built in 1923. Sir Harry Oakes purchased this and renamed it the British Colonial Hotel. A small beach fronts the hotel, which Sheraton is currently restoring.

From here head east along Bay Street.

The **Pompey Museum of Slavery and Emancipation ★★★** *($1; Mon to Fri 10am to 4:30pm, Sat 10am to 1pm, Bay St., ☎326-2566 or 326-2568)* is located in Vendue House, also known as the Bourse. The marketplace was established sometime before 1769, and at the time was simply a roofed open area; the present building was erected in 1807. Slaves were among the commodities auctioned off here. Before the museum, the building accommodated the Telegraph, Telephone and Electrical departments. The museum is named for an Exuman slave named Pompey who defied relocation plans for slaves after the abolition of slavery. The museum is dedicated to the African experience in The Bahamas with artefacts and documents, and its second floor houses a permanent exhibit of the naive paintings of noted Bahamian artist, Amos Ferguson.

Make your way along shop-filled Bay Street, to the **Straw Market ★★★**. Nassau's straw market, started in the 1930s, is the biggest in the islands. Handmade straw baskets, place mats, coasters, bags and hats can be purchased here, as well as conch and other shell jewellery, wood carvings, tons of t-shirts and other souvenirs. You'll even spot some of the 160 vendors making some of the items on site.

Exit the market on the water side and finish your walking tour on **Woodes Rogers Walk** ★. More stalls line the waterfront and sell more souvenirs and crafts. Horse-drawn surreys offering tours of the city also depart from here.

Island Tour ★★

If you have rented your own car, take a day to tour the island. Some of the sights below are still relatively close to downtown Nassau and a few are accessible by jitney. Head east on Bay Street

Heading east out of downtown, just before the intersection of Bay and Dowdeswell Streets is **St. Matthew's Church** ★. Opened in 1802, this church is the oldest church building in The Bahamas. Its attractive octagonal tower and spire rise above the low roof, built that way to avoid hurricane damage. The chancel, organ room, vestry room and stained-glass windows were added in 1887. The lovely setting boasts mature trees shading the churchyard and old cemetery.

Bay Street becomes East Bay Street at the **Paradise Island Bridge**, built in 1967. **Potter's Cay** ★★ is a manmade island under the bridge but a world away. Boats from the Out Islands pull in here to unload their fresh catches of conch, grouper, lobster, turtle, and to sell it alongside fresh limes, pineapples, tomatoes, avocados and other fruits and vegetables. This is where to come for the freshest food in The Bahamas and a lively atmosphere unlike anything you'll see while in Nassau. Simple snack foods like cracked conch and conch salad can also be bought here.

Head east on East Bay Street.

The Nassau Yacht Haven and Nassau Yacht Club are here, along with a handful of scuba diving outfits. **Hartley's Undersea Walk** *(departures at 9:30am and 1:30pm, in Nassau Yacht Haven, ☎393-8234)* is a strange experience indeed. Called helmet-diving, it involves putting an ancient-looking brass helmet over your head and heading underwater. Your hair doesn't even get wet! You'll be whisked out to a shallow reef where you can swim and explore the marine world.

Fort Montagu keeps watch over the eastern entrance to the harbour. The first fort on this site was erected in 1728, the present fort dates from 1741. This is the oldest fort of those that are still standing on New Providence. You can't get into or onto the fort, so there isn't much to see.

East Bay Street becomes Eastern Road at Village Road. Turn right on Village to the **Retreat** ★★ *($2; Village Rd., ☎393-1317)*. This is the headquarters of the Bahamas National Trust. A superb collection of 176 different types of exotic palm trees, some very rare, is the highlight here. And growing amongst these are delicate orchids, ferns and hardwoods. In 1986, the collection lost one of its prize specimens when the Ceylonese talipot palm ironically exploded into a profusion of blooms before dying. You can wander about this 11-acre property on your own or join the half-hour tours given on Tuesdays to Thursdays at 11:45am.

Head back up to Eastern Road and turn right.

Eastern Road faces Montagu Bay. Just inland and parallelling the shoreline is a ridge lined with sumptuous homes known as the Montagu Foreshore. About half a kilometre south of Fox Hill Road there is a narrow road next to a green and white house called "Tower

Leigh". Follow it up and you'll come to **Blackbeard's Tower** ★. This crumbling stone tower was supposedly used as a lookout by the notoriously ferocious pirate Edward "Blackbeard" Teach. It was actually built in the late 1700s, however, after the scoundrel had met his maker. There's no denying the terrific **view** ★★ he might have enjoyed from here.

Continue around the eastern shore to and around East End Point atop which sits **East End Lighthouse**. Turn right on Yamacraw Hill Road. You will notice as you head inland that most of the houses are of wood. At **Her Majesty's Prison**, turn right on Fox Hill Road.

Today **Fox Hill** is a suburb of Nassau, but in the mid-1700s it was established as a settlement for freed slaves called Creek Village and New Guinea. **St. Anne's Church** *(Fox Hill Rd.)* was built in 1848, but the first church on this site was a small wooden church erected in 1740. The present, simple stone exterior hides lofty interior space, with slender cast-iron columns supporting the heavy timber frame. Emancipation Day celebrations in Fox Hill take place in Freedom Square at Freedom Par at the intersection of Fox Hill and Reeves; interestingly, they occur one week after Emancipation on Fox Hill Day to commemorate the fact that it took one week for the news about Emancipation to reach the settlement.

Turn left on Bernard Road.

St. Augustine's Monastery *(donations appreciated; Bernard Rd.)* was designed by Father Jerome, the Hermit of Cat Island, and built in 1946. This Mission-style monastery and college is still lived in by Benedictine monks who tend small gardens around the property. Latin is still taught at the adjoining boys' college. The monks give interesting guided tours.

Continue east on Wulff Road which becomes Poinciana Drive before meeting Blue Hill Road.

Several government buildings line the way including the **College of The Bahamas**, the highest school in the country.

To the north is the area known as **Over-the-Hill**, bounded by Blue Hill Ridge (East Hill Street) to the north, Blue Hill Road to the west, East Street to the east and Prospect Ridge to the south. Settlement on the island started on the northern shore. After the abolition of slavery, freed slaves were resettled in a handful of villages, including Bain's Town, Fox Hill and Grant's Town, all located to the south over the ridge known as Blue Hill. This is still a poor area, whose black population is for the most part descended from those slaves. These days they live in small wooden cottages and shacks, running from tumbledown, tin-roofed hovels with littered front yards to small colourful and well-cared-for homes festooned with flowers.

Continue west on Poinciana Drive to Nassau Street and turn right. Follow it all the way to West Bay Street. Turn left. Turn left at the first road and follow it up to Fort Charlotte.

Construction on **Fort Charlotte** ★★★ *(tours every half-hour 9am to 4:30pm)* was begun in 1787 and completed 1789. It is named for wife of George III. This huge fort and moat was literally cut from the surrounding limestone. Its virtually indestructible walls were then buttressed with cedar. The animated tour guides dressed in period costumes offer up amusing anecdotes as they point out the soldiers names carved into the rock while they waited for Napoleon to strike and the torturous stretching rack.

Arawak Cay is a small artificial island, just offshore in the vicinity of Chippingham Road and Fort Charlotte. The island was created as storage for the fresh water that is freighted in daily from Andros. It has become the place to hangout with the locals, especially at lunch and on weekends, when the colourful stalls are set up, the music is turned up and the cracking begins, of the conchs that is. You can get conch salad, conch with hot sauce and other conchy snacks, and wash it all down with a favourite island concoction: coconut water, condensed milk and gin.

Crystal Cay Marina Park and Underwater Observatory *($16, $8 for guests of Nassau Mariott and Nassau Beach hotels; every day 9am to 6pm; shuttle from Cable Beach and ferry from Paradise Island and Woodes Rogers Walk, ☎328-1036)* lies off Silver Cay, which is just off Arawak Cay. Here, instead of recreating a natural habitat in an aquarium and bringing the marine world to you, you are literally immersed in a natural marine habitat. Lying 20 feet below the surface, this underwater marine observatory bills itself as the greatest show of natural marine life. Visitors can peer out at fish, coral and sponges; note that the visibility is best on calm and clear days. Children get hands-on experience with starfish in the Encounter Pool, and can feed turtles and stingrays too. In the Shark Encounter pool you can see sharks being fed. Paths lead around the private island.

Head back to West Bay Street and turn left, then left again to the Botanic Gardens.

Nassau Botanic Gardens *($1; Mon to Fri 9am to 4:30pm, Sat and Sun 9am to 4pm; Chippingham Rd., ☎323-5975)* are 26 acres of chirping birds, flowering paths, lush forest and cool breezes. There are more than 600 species of plants, shrubs and trees here plus a recreated Lucayan village, a fantastic conch-shell ceilinged tunnel, ponds and a Chinese fountain.

Ardastra Gardens and Zoo *($10; every day 9am to 5pm, last admission at 4:30pm; marching-flamingo show three times a day at 11am, 2pm and 4pm; ☎323-5806)*. The gardens cover 5.5 acres with low limestone walls draped in moss, gnarled vines, climbing tall fruit trees, a 60-year-old Banyan tree, paths, footbridges and the cages of 300 animals. There are reptiles, rare rock iguanas, sloths, lemurs, agoutis, ocelots, a boa constrictor named Benji, endangered Bahama parrots, Caribbean flamingoes, macaws, red-tailed hawks and peacocks strutting about. The cages are a bit small, but then the real reason to come here is for the marching flamingoes. Commander Joe runs his charges through their drill three times a day. After the show you can hold Benji the boa.

Continue west along West Bay.

Cable Beach ★★★, comes second after Paradise Island as far as self-sufficient resorts on New Providence go. This endless stretch of fine gold and white sand is lined with high-rise hotels. Crystal Palace Casino, a small straw market and the beach just about sum up Cable Beach, named for the underwater cable from Florida that was laid in 1892.

Continuing west, you'll pass through residential areas and right along the shore with beautiful turquoise waters to your right and some caves to your left just before the Orange Hill Beach Inn (see p 101). Called simply **The Caves**, these dark and dank passages were once used as a burial site by Lucayans.

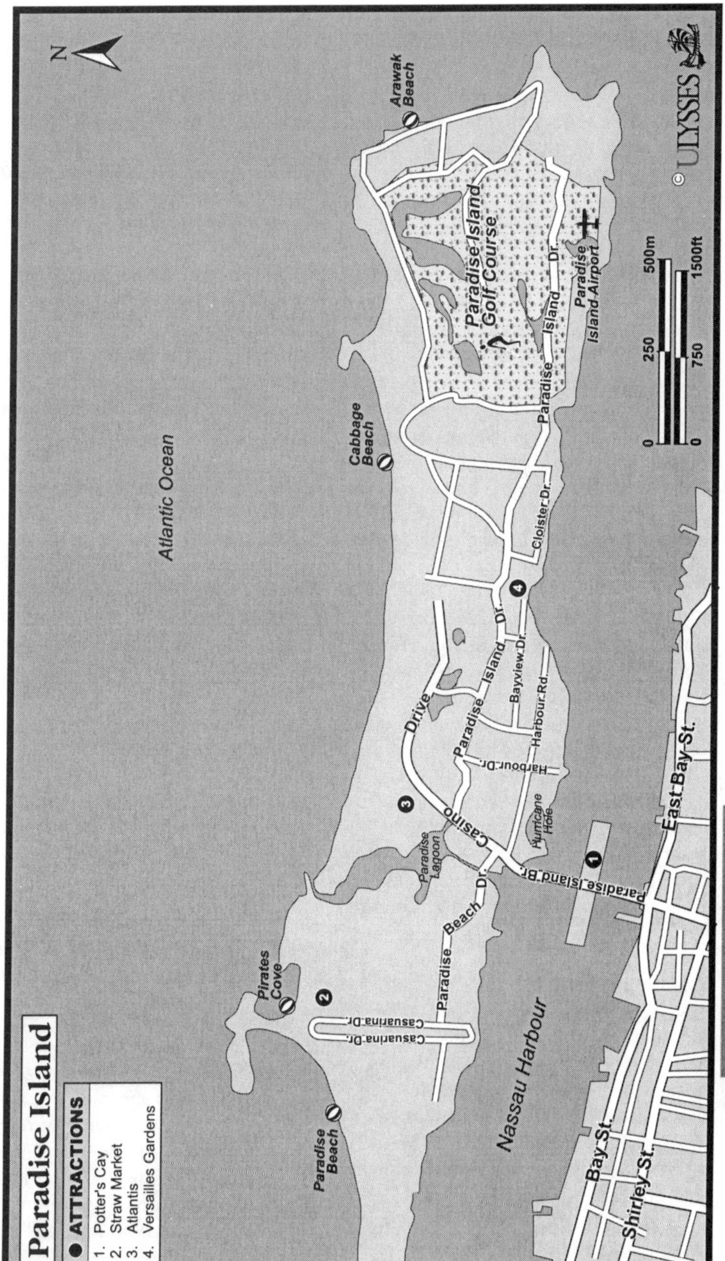
Paradise Island
ATTRACTIONS
1. Potter's Cay
2. Straw Market
3. Atlantis
4. Versailles Gardens
N
Atlantic Ocean
Nassau Harbour
Paradise Beach
Pirates Cove
Cabbage Beach
Arawak Beach
Paradise Island Golf Course
Paradise Island Airport
Casuarina Dr.
Paradise Beach Dr.
Paradise Lagoon
Casino Drive
Paradise Island Dr.
Hurricane Hole
Harbour Dr.
Harbour Rd.
Bayview Dr.
Cloister Dr.
Paradise Island Br.
East Bay St.
Bay St.
Shirley St.
0 250 500m
0 750 1500ft
© ULYSSES

Gambier Village is another settlement established for freed-slaves after the abolition of slavery. Stands sell home-made bread here, otherwise the village slumbers peacefully immediately to the south of West Bay Street, right before colourful Compass Point (see p 101). Worth a peek even if you aren't hungry.

At Northwest Point the road heads south alongside Love Beach. Soon you're back amongst the wealthy developments, notably **Lyford Cay**, a very private and very rich area. You can only go there if you have an invitation and unless you are a close and personal friend of Sean Connery's or Eddie Murphy's, you can forget that. The Cay was developed by Canadian E.P. Taylor. Scenes from *Jaws Revenge* were filmed around here.

The road heads inland and is lined on both sides with thick bush. There are some plantation ruins to the west, but these are best not explored without a guide. Eventually the deep-blue of what's called the South Ocean appears on the horizon and you'll pass the Clifton Pier Power Station and the **Commonwealth Brewery**, where Kalik, the beer of The Bahamas, and Heineken are brewed. The South Ocean Golf & Beach Resort offers the only accommodations down here.

Continuing east, the main road once again leaves the shoreline, which is riddled with creeks and mangrove swamps in this area. **Adelaide** is another settlement founded for slaves freed from foreign slave ships, in this case a Portuguese ship in 1807. This little village thrived thanks to a navigable creek and plenty of lobster, conch and fish. Several factors, both natural and man-made, threatened and eventually destroyed the creek and surrounding wetlands. Thankfully, the damage was not permanent. The Bahamas National Trust, with tremendous help from this and other communities all over the island, cleaned up the piles of garbage that had been dumped here, and on Earth Day in 1990, the mouth of the creek was cleared and it once again filled with water. Nature has taken its course and today the creek is once again teeming with young marine life.

Return to the main road, now called Adelaide Road, and continue east. **Coral Harbour** is another residential community, this one full of vacationing or retired expats. Continue east and turn right on Millars Road.

The **Bacardi Rum Factory** *(free tours on Mon and Thu at 11am and 2pm, Fri at 11am, ☎362-1412)* offers half-hour guided tours of the facility which explain the rum-making process from sugar cane all the way to rum and coke. The tours are only given for eight people or more, but even if you can't get enough people together, check it out anyway. There are free samples in the visitors pavilion.

The quickest way back downtown from here is back to Carmichael Road and then left and straight up Gladstone Road.

Paradise Island ★★★

Many guides cover Paradise Island completely separately from New Providence, despite the fact that they are practically a stone's throw apart. Just because you are staying at one doesn't mean a visit to the other is a grand excursion. It only takes about 45 minutes to walk from downtown Nassau to Paradise Island, much less by jitney, ferry or taxi.

Once over the bridge, head west from the roundabout on Paradise Beach Drive and then right on Casuarina Drive if you want to visit the island's **Straw Market**. If you have been to or are planning on going to Nassau's Straw Market, you can give this much smaller version a miss.

The most exciting attraction on the island is **Atlantis ★★★** *(free admission; open 24 hours, guided tours 10pm, 1pm and 4pm, Atlantis Resort, ☎363-3000)* and its famous Waterscape. Anyone can come for a tour of this open-air aquarium, the world's largest. The highlight has to be the 30-metre-long plexiglass underwater viewing tunnel, which runs through the Predator Lagoon & Reef, home to more than 100 sharks, plus graceful spotted and eagle rays, barracudas and thousands of other fish. You can also see all these creatures from up above on the swinging Suspension Bridge. Shark feedings are on Tuesdays, Thursdays, Saturdays and Sundays at 10am, predator feedings occur daily at 3pm, and fish feedings are daily at 4pm; these times are subject to change, though, so you might want to call ahead. Aquarium staff occasionally give guests a look behind the scenes.

For a change of pace head over to the **Versailles Gardens ★★★** at the foot of Ocean Club Drive. The tiered gardens were laid out by Swedish financier Axel Wenner-Gren who installed classical statues amidst the tropical flowers. The masterpiece of the gardens are the 14th century Augustinian **Cloisters ★★★** overlooking the harbour. This delicate stone gazebo was purchased by American newspaper magnate Randolph Hearst, who ordered it dismantled and shipped piece by piece to his estate in San Simeon, California. It was never put back together, and when Huntington Hartford purchased it and brought it to Paradise Island, it took sculptor Jean Castre-Manne two years to figure out how all the un-numbered pieces fit together. It is a favourite and idyllic wedding locale (see p 67).

The island's northern and eastern shores are one long, virtually unbroken stretch of fine white sand divided into **Colonial Beach ★★★**, **Paradise Cove ★★**, **Pirate's Cove ★★**, **Cabbage Beach ★★★**, **Snorkeler's Cove ★★★** and **Smuggler's Beach** (see below).

BEACHES

The closest beach to downtown Nassau is the **Western Esplanade** which starts at the British Colonial Hotel and carries on westward. There is no surf to speak of and the closer you are to town, the dirtier the sand is. It gets a bit better past Nassau Street. There are restrooms, changing rooms and a snack bar.

On Paradise Island, the northern shore is almost one long beach. It starts in the west with **Colonial Beach ★★★**, which borders the thin western tip of Paradise Island and boasts white powdery sand. **Paradise Cove ★★** curves up to Hog Point at its eastern end. Club Med and a few smaller guesthouses face this beach. **Pirate's Cove ★★** is a picturesque and very protected little cove, great for families. **Cabbage Beach ★★★** is the best beach on the island. Over three kilometres long, it is wider than the others. The waters are not too rough and jet skiing, parasailing, sailing and banana boat rides are all possible. With Atlantis, the Radisson, the Sunrise Beach Club, the Ocean Club and the Mariott, there are lots of people on this beach, its eastern end is quietest. Even more secluded and quiet is superb **Snorkeler's Cove ★★★**. Head there early in the morning or in the afternoon to avoid the excursion groups that come here for the great snorkelling. Finally, **Smuggler's Beach** lines the eastern shore and is almost always deserted.

Cable Beach ★★★ is lined with high-rise hotels and so packed with all of their guests. Things are quieter and cleaner to the east, where local families come on weekends. Further east, **Saunders Beach ★** is another popular beach with Bahamians. It is not as wide and near the road, but much quieter.

West of Cable Beach, the road follows runs alongside a string of small beaches. The first is **Orange Hill Beach ★★★**, in front of the inn of the same name. It was in the news lately when the owners of the inn cut down the casuarinas. These trees are not indigenous and the blanket of needles they shed crowds out native plants like sea grapes and palms. Locals love this beach, however, and obviously liked the casuarinas too. **Love Beach ★★**, beyond Old Fort Point, has sand and limestone and great snorkelling.

South Ocean Beach ★ is a secluded and narrow stretch of sand on the south side of the island.

OUTDOOR ACTIVITIES

Scuba Diving and Snorkelling

The waters off New Providence offer a great variety of diving possibilities. The **Lost Blue Hole** to the east begins at only 15 metres. Groupers and moray eels are among the creatures that inhabit the coral heads around its edge. The aptly-named **Fish Hotel** is just teeming with colourful tropical fish, plus lovely soft corals and sea fans. At the **Barracuda Shoals**, north of Paradise Island, you can view a healthy and vibrant reef plus a few shipwrecks. The steamship ***Mahoney*** lies at two different depths, providing both deep and shallow divers with a great wreck dive. The fairly shallow **Southwest Reef** boasts tall coral heads with elkhorn and staghorn formations, and swirls of tropical fish. **Goulding Cay** is another shallow dive with beautiful elkhorn coral. Deep-water diving is best in the South Ocean where reefs line the drop-off into the dizzying Tongue of the Ocean. Notable dives here include the **Shark Wall**, where bull, lemon and Caribbean-reef sharks are fed right before your eyes. Shipwrecks abound here including the **James Bond Trawler** sunk for the filming of a 007 movie.

Bahama Divers *(☎398-DIVE in Nassau or 1-800-398-DIVE in North America, mailing address: PO Box SS-5004, Nassau)* offers everything from certification courses to resort courses. They'll pick you up at your hotel and rent or sell you equipment. A one-tank dive is $40, two-tank dive is $60, a half-day snorkel is $20, a resort course is $60.

Sun Divers *(☎325-8927 or 1-800-258-4768, mailing address: PO Box N-10728, Nassau)* is a smaller operation. A half-day snorkel with them will cost you $20, a two-tank dive $55, and scuba equipment rental $30.

Divers Haven *(East Bay St., ☎393-0869 or 393-3285, ≠393-3695, mailing address: PO Box N-1658, Nassau)* has one-tank dives for $35, two-tank dives for $65, and half-day snorkelling trips for $25. An introductory scuba course is $65, they also offer certification levels and accept referrals for open-water check-outs.

Stuart Coves Dive South Ocean *(☎362-4171 or 1-800-879-9832, at South Ocean Golf & Beach Resort, mailing address: PO Box CB11697,*

Nassau's octagonal former prison, which dates from the 1790s, now houses Nassau's Public Library and Historic Museum. *(Jennifer McMorran)*

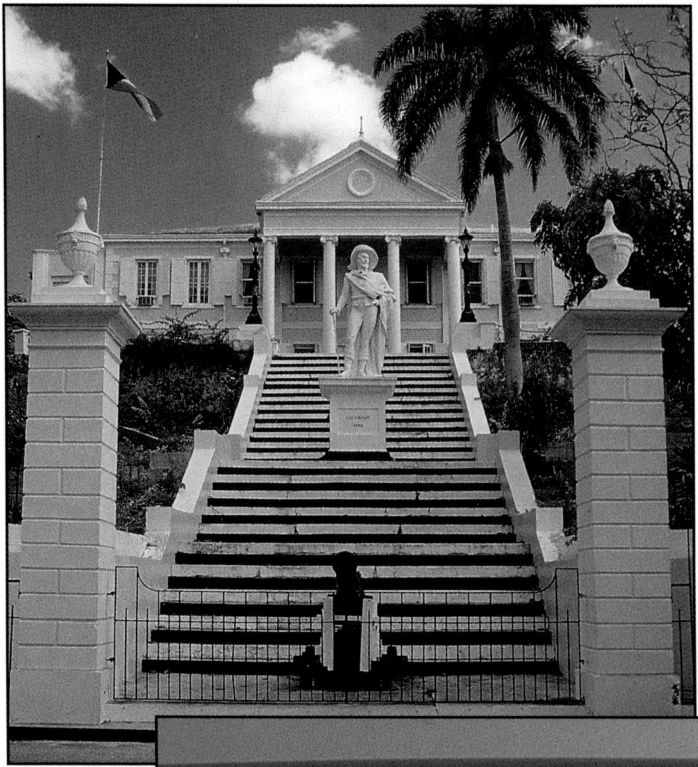

Nassau's Georgian Government House is the official residence of the Bahamas' governor-general. The statue of Christopher Columbus dates from 1830. (*J.M.)*

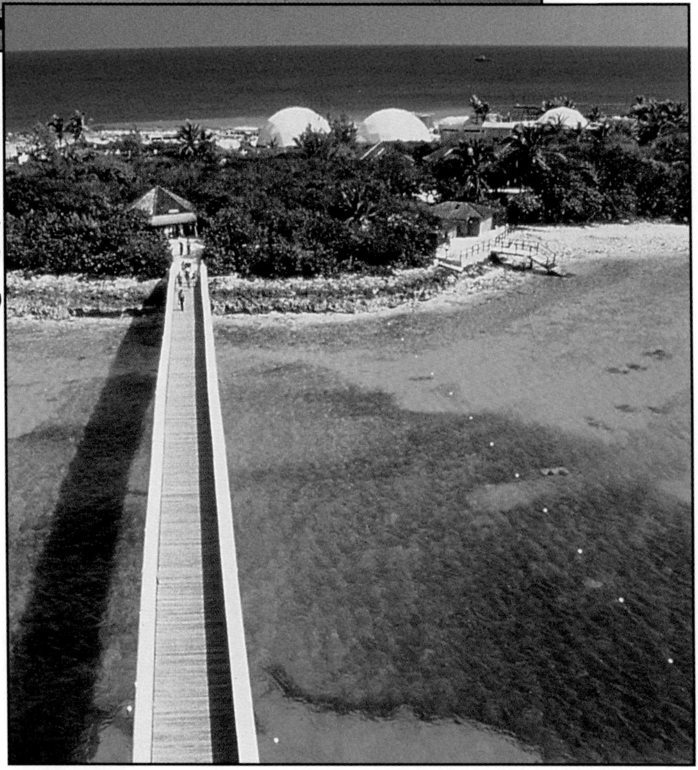

Bridge leading to the futuristic Crystal Cay Marine Park in Nassau, an underwater marine observatory. *(J. Greenberg)*

Nassau) offers a two-tank dive for $70, an introductory scuba course for $85, a snorkel trip for $30, a two-tank shark dive is $115. You can rent scuba gear as well as still and video cameras.

Fishing

Your hotel staff should be able to make any arrangements for sportfishing trips. Boats can also be hired at the local marinas (see p 81). One of the most recommended companies on the island is Charter Boat Association *(☎363-2335)*. You can expect to pay between $500 and $600 for a full day on the high seas.

Horseback Riding

Happy Trails Stables *(☎362-1820, Coral Harbour)* has rides along secluded beaches and through wooded areas. Reservations are required and they will pick you up at your hotel. A 90-minute ride costs $50, the whole excursion will take three hours. No children under eight years of age.

The **Cantalupa Riding School** *(Carmichael Village, ☎361-7101)* has pony rides for the little ones. Trail rides are also available.

Cruises

Here is just a sampling of the countless cruises and boat excursions that you can join from new Providence and Paradise Island. Your hotel's tour desk can suggest others if nothing tickles your fancy.

Discover Blue Lagoon *(☎363-3577)* is one of the most popular trips. A 30-minute ride from Nassau along the pristine beaches of Blue Lagoon Island. All sorts of activities and water sports, including spectacular snorkelling are available here. There is even a gift shop, a straw market and hair braiding. The best thing about these trips is the chance to swim with dolphins and stingrays.

Nassau Cruises *(☎363-3577)* offers half-day "Dolphin Encounters" on Blue Lagoon Island where you'll get a half-hour swim with these amazing creatures. The cost is $85. The "Stingray Snorkel" is $45.

Seaworld Explorer *($29; ☎358-2548)* is a semi-submarine that visits the Sea Gardens Marine Park, an underwater nature preserve. You'll see coral, colourful exotic fish (yellowtail snapper, sergeant majors, parrot fish, queen angelfish), and a 70-year old ship wreck. The vessel does not actually submerge, you can sit up on deck or down in the air-conditioned underwater observatory which lies at five feet below the surface.

Historical Harbour Cruise *($20; ☎363-3577)* is a 90-minute historical tour around Paradise Island.

There is also **Hartley's Undersea Walk** (see p 90), which includes a cruise on a 57-foot catamaran.

The **Atlantis Submarine Adventure** *($75; hotel pick-ups included; ☎327-7157)* has you board a 28-passenger submarine that then heads into the deep for an up-close look at magnificent corals as well as a wreck used in the James Bond movie *Thunderball*.

Golf

There are three championship 18-hole golf courses on New Providence and Paradise Island.

The **Radisson Cable Beach Golf Course** *(☎327-6000 or 1-800-451-3103)* is a 7,040-yard par-72 course designed by Joe McCormick. It is known for its many lakes and sand traps. The one and only Arnold Palmer is actually the manager of this course. Green fees are $60 ($45 for 9 holes), cart rental is $50 and club rental is $25.

The **South Ocean Golf Course** *(☎362-4391 or 1-800-223-6510)* is PGA-rated and considered one of the best and most challenging in The Bahamas. Its ocean views certainly are exquisite. It was designed by Joe Lee and is 6,707 yards long. Green fees are $80 including the cart rental, guests of the South Ocean resort pay $65. Reservations are recommended.

The **Paradise Island Golf Course** *(☎363-3925 or 1-800-321-3000)* has water (the ocean) just about everywhere and five bunkers per hole over its 6,776-yard length. The course was designed by Dick Wilson. Green fees are $80, $50 in the low season, including cart rental.

Spas and Fitness Clubs

In case your hotel doesn't have the facilities to pamper you properly, **Windermere Day Spa and Salon** *(Mon to Sat 9am to 6pm, Sun 10am to 3pm; Harbour Bay Shopping Centre, ☎393-0033 or 393-8788)* can help you relax after a hard game of tennis or day of windsurfing. A one-hour Swedish massage is $55, an aromatherapy massage is $60, honeysuckle algae scrubs are $40, an after-sun wrap is $30. There is also a small gym. A full-day pass ($20) includes access to cardiovascular equipment. Full salon services, including waxing, are also available.

There is a superb full-service spa and gym at the **Sandals Royal Bahamian** *(☎327-6400)* with massages, algae scrubs, mud baths and aromatherapy. The gym at the **Radisson Cable Beach** is open to everyone.

Gold's Gym *(Bay St. at Mackey St., ☎394-6975)* has a large weight room, a variety of cardiovascular machines and aerobics classes. Non-members can use the facilities for $5.

Birdwatching

Parts of Paradise Island still attract flocks of birds. Kingfishers, herons, snowy egrets, Bahama woodstar hummingbirds, moorhens and Caribbean coots have been spotted. On New Providence, the Retreat (see p 90) is a good spot for birding as are the shores of Lake Killarney for waders. The Bahamas National Trust *(☎393-1317)* can give you information on guided walks and local species.

Adventure Excursions

Pedal & Paddle Ecoadventures *(☎362-2772, ℻362-2044)* offers full-day cycling and kayaking trips to the more remote corners of New Providence. This is a great way to escape the throngs at the beach and along Bay Street.

Lakes Nancy and Killarney are popular with canoeists. Call ☎356-4283 for information on trips.

ACCOMMODATIONS

Downtown Nassau

International Travellers Lodging *($26 per person, bkfst incl.; 14 rooms, sb, ⊗, K; 23 Delancey St., ☎323-2904, PO Box CB-13558, Nassau)* is the only youth hostel in The Bahamas. Associated with VIP Backpackers, this hostel has modest dormitory beds, as well as private double ($50) and single ($40) rooms. It has a good location in a residential part of town, just a few blocks from Bay Street. Continental breakfast is served in the pretty colonial house along with the cats and bird.

The **Park Manor Guest House** *($45; 18 rooms, ≡, ⊗, ≈, K; Market St., ☎356-5471, ⇒325-3554, PO Box N-4164, Nassau)* is more like an apartment-hotel than a guesthouse. This is a decent budget self-catering option in the downtown area. The pool is small and lacks greenery.

The Towne Hotel *($50; 46 rooms, pb, sat tv, ℜ, ≡, ≈; 40 George St.; mailing address: PO Box N-4808, Nassau, ☎322-8450, ⇒322-1512)* is still the budget place it was when my parents spent their honeymoon here, though its gotten a bit dingy over the years. Rooms are small and modest and the interior courtyard has a tiny pool.

The Parthenon Hotel *($56, low $46, continental bkfst $3; ≡, tv, 18 rooms; West St., ☎322-2643, ⇒322-2644, PO Box N-4930, Nassau)* is a quiet and pleasant budget option near the heart of downtown Nassau. The small, two-story, blue-and-white, L-shaped building overlooks a pretty garden. Rooms are carpeted and a bit dated but quite large.

The **Parliament Inn** *($60; pb, ≡, ℜ; Parliament St., ☎322-2836, ⇒326-7196, mailing address: PO Box N-4138, Nassau)* boasts decent-sized rooms with the standard tropical prints and rattan furniture. They are pretty basic but you can't beat the location for its proximity to downtown.

Rooms at the **Astoria Hotel** *($75; 70 rooms, ℜ, ≡, ⊗, pb, sat tv, ≈, ℝ; West Bay and Nassau St., mailing address: PO Box N-3236, Nassau, ☎322-8666 or 227-593-997 in Holland, ⇒322-8660)* are a bit on the dingy side, despite the kitschy bright-red carpet and brilliantly flowered bedspreads. Each room has one king-sized or two double beds, a balcony and views of either the pool or the ocean. Only some rooms have refrigerators. The five-story U-shaped hotel surrounds a large pool, and the beach is right across the street. In-room safes are $2.50 per day.

Buena Vista Hotel *($90, low $60; 5 rooms; pb, sb, ≡, sat tv, ℑ, ℜ; PO Box N-564, Nassau, ☎322-2811, ⇒322-5881)* lies at the end of a long driveway in one of Nassau's fine old historic mansions. The rooms are large and individually decorated, but their elegance is fading. One of them has a fireplace. The hotel's restaurant is recommended (see p 108).

El Greco Hotel *($87, low $77; 26 rooms, pb, ≈, ≡, ℜ; PO Box N-4187, Nassau, ☎325-1121, ⇒325-1124)* is much more appealing than the Astoria down the street. Rooms are set around a cosy and leafy courtyard with a small pool. They are spacious and very clean, and those on the second-floor have balconies. A friendly Greek family runs the place.

Best Western British Colonial Beach Resort *($139, low $89; 355 rooms, pb, ≈, ℜ, ≡, sat tv; 1 Bay St., PO Box*

Ulysses' Favourites

Accommodations

Best Value for Your Money:

Dillet's Guest House (see p 101), El Greco Hotel (see p 99), Paradise Paradise (see p 104) and Howelton Rose House (see p 104).

Warmest Welcome:

Dillet's Guest House (see p 101) and Compass Point (see p 101).

Best Resort for Tennis Buffs:

Club Med Paradise Island (see p 104) and Atlantis Paradise Island Resort & Casino (see p 105).

Best Resort for Golfers:

South Ocean Golf and Beach Resort (see p 103).

Best Swimming Pool:

Atlantis Paradise Island Resort & Casino (see p 105) and Radisson Cable Beach Casino & Golf Resort (see p 102).

Best Resort for Families:

Pirate's Cove Beach Resort (see p 104) and Atlantis Paradise Island Resort & Casino (see p 105).

Best Resort for Honeymooners:

Club Med Paradise Island (see p 104), Ocean Club (see p 106), Sandals Royal Bahamian (see p 103), Graycliff (see p 100) and Compass Point Beach Club (see p 101).

Best Overall Decor:

Compass Point Beach Club (see p 101), Sandals Royal Bahamian (see p 103) and Ocean Club (see p 106).

N-7148, Nassau, ☎322-3301 ≠322-2286), the only downtown hotel with its own beach, is in the midst of a major million-dollar refurbishment. Some major sprucing up is in store for every guest room, the lobby, the exterior, the pool and the grounds. Rooms come in a variety of shapes and sizes.

Graycliff Hotel *(rooms $150 to $290, cottages $170 to $365; 13* *rooms, ≡, pb, ≈, ℜ, sat tv; PO Box N-10246, Nassau, ☎322-2796/7, ⇌326-6110)* is the only Relais & Chateaux establishment in the West Indies and at the height of luxury right in Nassau. Set in a historic mansion (see p 88), each of the nine rooms in the main house and five cottages has its own unique and elegant decor and superb bathrooms. The creme de la creme, the Mandarino Suite, has an Oriental decor, large bathroom, private balcony, jacuzzi and sauna. The lush tropical gardens are the ideal spot to while away an afternoon with a good book. The lounge and dining room are stuffed with antique furniture and paintings. Guests are picked up at the airport in a Mercedes limousine. The food here comes highly recommended (see p 108). The cheapest room is the Dunmore.

Island Tour

West of Downtown Nassau

The motto of the **Arawak Inn** *($50, $35 for two or more nights; 6 rooms, sat tv, ⊛, ≡, K; West Bay St., PO Box N-3222, Nassau, ☎322-2638, ⇌328-4014)* is "go native". The rooms here are on the small and rudimentary side, with a dated motel-like decor. They have small kitchenettes. There is a large whirlpool tub outside. Children are not allowed here.

Dillet's Guest House *($50; 7 rooms, pb, ≡, K, ≡, ⊗, sat tv, ℝ; Dunmore St., at Strachan St., PO Box N-204, Nassau, ☎325-1133, ⇌325-7183)* is the only true guest house on New Providence. Set in a historic house, one of five built on the estate of an English businessman in the 1920s, the house is run by Iris Dillet-Knowles. Mature palm trees, each one identified, line the front walk, and there are hammocks slung here and there. Once inside, the centrepiece of the comfy living room is a huge fireplace, for those cool winter evenings. Works by local artists adorn the walls, some of it is for sale. Rooms are quite simple but very homey and either have kitchenettes or refrigerators.

Orange Hill Beach Inn *($90, low $80; 32 rooms, ≡, ℜ, K, ≈; PO Box N-8583, Nassau, ☎327-7157, ⇌327-5186)* has been described as the "Fawlty Towers" of Nassau. This family-run resort is across the road from small Orange Hill Beach. Rooms overlook the ocean or the large pool at the centre of the property. They are nothing special: large, with cool white-tile floors, but a bit drab and dark. The lounge where movies are played, the rustic restaurant and pool area are usually pretty lively, however. Studios with kitchenettes are $120. There is a daily shuttle to the jitney that heads into town. Free laundry facilities.

One look at **Compass Point Beach Club** *($175, low $135; 18 rooms, pb, ≈, sat tv, ⊗, ℝ; West Bay St., PO Box N-4599, Nassau, ☎327-4500, 1-800-OUTPOST, ⇌327-3299)* and either you'll wish you were staying here or you'll be glad you are. The brightly coloured cottages and cabanas are just divine, inside and out. The interiors boast simple wooden furniture, one-of-a-kind batik bedspreads, bathrobes, stereos and a selection of CDs. Showers are all al-fresco, and some of the cottages have outdoor kitchenettes (all have mini-bars). The "West Point" cottage has the best view of the water. There is a small sand and coral beach at the western end of the property. The restaurant is just as funky (see p 108). Compass Point is part of the Chris Blackwell empire, which includes Island Records (there is a studio across the street) and the glorious Pink Sands

Resort on Harbour Island (see p 190). Some people have complained that the pool here is too small and the roadside location is a bit noisy.

Cable Beach and Surroundings

Casuarinas Of Cable Beach *($95; 86 rooms, sat tv, pb, ≈, ≡, ℜ; PO Box CB-13225, Nassau, ☎327-7921/2, 327-8153, ⇒327-8152)* is squeezed between West Bay Street and a narrow little beach, with other units across the street. Rooms, each one named for one of the Family Islands, surround the pool and face either it or the beach, they are simply furnished, some with refrigerators. This family-run hotel gets a lot of repeat customers, including many Bahamians.

Radisson Cable Beach Casino & Golf Resort *($115; 669 rooms, pb, ≡, ≈, ℜ, sat tv, ⊛; Cable Beach, PO Box N-4914, Nassau, ☎327-6000, ⇒327-5969)* was completely renovated in 1996 with new room furnishings, and a redesigned pool area, which now includes hammocks slung between palm trees, three large pools, waterfalls and a swim-up bar. The lobby is bright, modern and tropical. Rooms are also bright and attractive, they all have balconies and 80% of them have ocean views. Fine dining is possible at a handful of restaurants. There are tennis courts and a championship golf course. All-inclusive packages are available, and with a minimum of four nights, one of your meals can be taken somewhere else. This hotel is connected to the Crystal Palace Casino.

Forte Nassau Beach Hotel *($160; 408 rooms, ≡, ℜ, sat tv; PO Box N-7756, Nassau, ☎327-7711 or 1-888-627-7282, ⇒327-7615)* has a quieter, more refined atmosphere than its glitzy all-inclusive neighbours, even though its facilities are in need of some sprucing up, something they are getting as this book goes to press. The rooms are already quite lovely, especially those in the east wing. The Georgian touches and colonial feel make for a pleasant stay. The refurbishment project will spruce up the hotel's exterior and public spaces. A large pool is among the improvements. Many Canadians are among its return guests. Cafe Johnny Canoe is on site (see p 108).

Nassau Marriott Resort & The Crystal Palace Casino *($165, low $95; 867 rooms, pb, ≡, ≈, ⊘, sat tv, ℜ; PO Box N-8306, Nassau, ☎327-6200 or 1-800-333-3333, ⇒327-6801)* is visible for miles around no matter what time of day it is. The profusion of hot pink and grey of this hotel is getting tired as is the neon rainbow that lights up its facades each night! The rooms, which were redone in 1997, are comparatively sedate and attractive in forest green and beige. They are spacious and each one has a private balcony. Bathrooms are large. The hotel has a large pool and gym. And of course there is the Crystal Palace Casino.

Breezes Superclubs *($220; 391 rooms, sat tv, ℜ, pb, ≡, ≈, ℜ; PO Box CB-13049, Nassau, ☎327-6153 or 1-800-330-8272, ⇒327-5356)* is the all-inclusive resort extraordinaire. From the moment you enter the open-air lobby with its brilliant hand-painted tiles, everything is just full-on! Just beyond the lobby, pool tables and ping-pong tables are given place of honour, while outside there is always something going on in the five swimming pools. There is also a trapeze. This is a singles and couples resort, with lots of young people out for a good time, and crazy activities like pyjama parties and beauty contests try to do just that. Despite the flash of the lobby, the rooms are pretty drab. Not all have balconies, and the bathrooms are very small. Everything is included here, from airport transfers to rum cocktails.

Sandals Royal Bahamian *($580 per person, all-incl.; 196 rooms, ≡, pb, ℜ, ≈, ⊙, sat tv, ⊛; PO Box N-10422, Nassau, ☎327-6400 or 1-800-726-3257, ⇌327-1894)* has maintained the level of luxury that visitors have come to expect from this location, once occupied by the prestigious Balmoral Club and then by Le Meridien Royal Bahamian. For a sense of what awaits you here, you need only consider that the Sandals chain has been lauded as the "World's Best All-Inclusive Resort" and the "Top Caribbean Group", and this particular Sandals is their flagship property. Spacious rooms, which come in six categories, are spread about the property in villas and the Manor House. They boast formal mahogany furniture, ceiling and wall mouldings and king-sized beds. The free-form pool is surrounded by classical columns. The resort has fine dining facilities, an authentic English pub, a full-service spa, and all sorts of watersports. This is a couples-only resort.

East of Downtown Nassau

The Little Orchard Hotel *($65 for apartment, $100 for cottage; 28 rooms, ≡, pb, ≈, K, sat tv; Village Rd., PO Box N-1514, Nassau, ☎393-1297, ⇌394-3562)* is an attractive little property with cottages and apartments and lots of trees. Rooms are comfortable and each has a balcony. Shops and local restaurants are all close at hand in this residential area. Montagu Beach is a five-minute walk away, and bus number 17 goes downtown. There is no restaurant, but the onsite Tree Frog Bar is a neat place.

Red Carpet Inn *($74; 32 rooms, ≡, sat tv, ≈ pb, ℜ, K; Bay St., PO Box SS-6233, Nassau, ☎393-7981, ⇌393-9055)* is a motel-style U-shaped place set around a pool with clean, comfortable and otherwise non-descript rooms. It is popular with divers because of its proximity to the Nassau Yacht Haven and all the dive shops. A standard room has one double bed, for $85 you can have two beds or a kitchenette and for $95 you can have both. All rooms have safes and come with coolers so that you can bring your lunch with you.

Southern New Providence

South Ocean Golf & Beach Resort *($145; 250 rooms, sat tv, ≡, ⊛; PO Box N-8191, Nassau, ☎362-4391/2, ⇌362-4728)* offers the only luxury accommodations on this secluded coastline. It was recently upgraded, which adds a bit more finesse to the rooms. The older rooms border the pool, while the newer, more modern rooms line the beach. These are brighter, airier and more appealing. Ornate balconies evoke the plantations of old. With the best golf course, the resort has a certain exclusivity about it. A shuttle runs guests to Cable Beach, Nassau and Paradise Island for $5. There are golf and children's packages.

Coral Harbour Beach House & Villas *($65; 8 rooms, pb, ⊛, ≡; PO Box N-9750, Nassau, ☎362-2210, ⇌361-6514)* is for those who really want to get away from the action. On a small beach, looking out over the South Ocean, are eight compact rooms with fairly standard island decor. Second-floor rooms have showers and balconies.

Paradise Island

Sivananda Yoga Retreat *(cabin $60, campsite $40; 40 rooms, pb, sb, ℜ; PO Box N-7550, Nassau, ☎363-2902 or*

1-800-783-9642, ⇄363-3783) is not your typical Paradise Island lodging option. Daily meditation and yoga set the mood here. You can pitch your tent here or stay in one of the simple cabins on the beach or in the garden. Two lacto-vegetarian meals are served a day.

The Howelton Rose House *($90, bkfst incl.; 4 rooms, pb, ≡; PO Box N-1968, Nassau, ☎363-3363, ⇄393-1786)*, also known as Pink House, is a real find. Located adjacent to the Club Med property, this Georgian-style B&B is surrounded by greenery. Minnie Winn is the most gracious of hosts, and her touch is evident in each of the four guest rooms and the lounge.

Chaplin House *($95; 7 rooms, K ≡, ⊗, pb; PO Box SS-6034, Nassau, ☎/⇄363-2918)* is a quiet and quirky self-catering option on the western side of Paradise Island. Three rustic cottages are set amidst trees and birds. They are fully equipped and comfortable. What an escape!

Paradise Paradise *($120; 100 rooms, sat tv, pb, ≡, ℜ; PO Box N-4777, Nassau, ☎363-3000 or 1-800-321-3000, ⇄363-2543)* is a less ostentatious, less expensive and less noisy version of its sister hotel, Atlantis. Guests here can use the facilities at the Atlantis and enjoy free transportation back and forth between the two hotels. The hotel is set amidst trees, a short distance from the beach.

Club Med Paradise Island *($130 per person to $210, all-incl.; 300 rooms, pb, ℜ, ≈, sat tv, ⊘, ≡; PO Box N-7137, Nassau, ☎323-2640 or 1-800-258-2633, ⇄363-3496)* is a sprawling 23-acre all-inclusive resort that runs from Nassau Harbour clear across the island to Paradise Beach. Rooms are located in small 3-story bungalows unless you opt for the gingerbread-trimmed "House in the Woods", a favourite with honeymooners. Children are welcome here, but there are no planned activities so they'll probably get bored. The decor is in soft earth tones with white wicker furniture. All activities are included, with special mention going to the tennis. The facilities are top-rate and top tennis players occasionally give seminars.

Paradise Harbour Club & Marina *($130; 16 rooms, sat tv, ℜ, pb, ≡, K; PO Box SS-5804m, Nassau, ☎363-2992, ⇄363-2840)* on the southeastern shore of the island with a view of the Paradise Island Bridge, is secluded and quiet. The rooms are modern and they all have kitchenettes. You'll have to walk to the beach.

Pirate's Cove Beach Resort *($150; ≈, sat tv, ℜ, ≡, 564 rooms; PO Box SS-6214, Nassau, ☎363-2100, ⇄363-3386)* is a fantastical place for children, from the pirate ship in the pool to the Captain Kids program. Also, the beach in front faces protected Pirate Cove, a great place for swimming with little ones. The run-of-the-mill hotel rooms are comfortable and clean but nothing more. This place was recently acquired by Sun International and is due to become fully incorporated into the Atlantis experience.

Comfort Suites *($159; 150 rooms, pb, sat tv, ≈, ℜ; PO Box SS-6202, Nassau, ☎363-3680 or 1-800-228-5150, ⇄363-2588)* lies in the middle of Paradise Island, and is almost surrounded on all sides by roads. Rooms are quite attractive in this almost motel-style establishment. They are all suites, with coffee machines, refrigerators and minibars. They offer views of the bougainvillea, the pool or the rest of the island. Guests have site privileges at

Atlantis, making this place a good value for the money.

Bay View Village *($160; 43 rooms, ≡, pb, K, ≈, sat tv; PO Box SS-6308, Nassau, ☎363-2555, ⇒363-2370)* boasts a flowery property and nicely furnished efficiency units. You are right in the middle of the island here, but the harbour, bridge and Cabbage Beach are easy walks away. There are rooms with kitchenettes and balconies, or villas and townhouses that can sleep four or six. There is a simple snack bar beside the pool.

Paradise Island Fun Club *($160; 250 rooms, pb, ≡, sat tv, ℜ, ≈; PO Box SS-6249, Nassau, ☎363-2561 or 1-800-952-2426, ⇒363-3803)* is an all inclusive resort that offers surprisingly good value for the money. It isn't as glitzy, sophisticated or expensive as Club Med, but all the activities are on offer including plenty of stuff to keep the young ones occupied. It faces the harbour and has a small and unpicturesque beach; Cabbage Beach is much better, and worth the walk.

Sunrise Beach Club & Villas *(studio $213, one-bedroom $299; 92 rooms, sat tv, pb, ≈, ⊗, ≡ ℝ; PO Box SS-6519, Nassau, ☎363-2234 or 1-800-451-6078, ⇒363-2308)* is popular with Europeans. These two-story townhouse-style units resemble Mediterranean villas, combined with the two free-form pools traversed by footbridges, the lush property and the occasional hummingbird create an attractive setting. The interior decor is a bit dated in some cases and quite exquisite in others. A short walk under the weepy casuarinas and you're at Cabbage Beach, which at this point is usually virtually deserted.

Club Land'or *($215; 72 rooms, ≈, ≡, K, sat tv, ⊗, ℜ; PO Box SS-6429, Nassau, ☎363-2400 or 1-800-346-8200, ⇒363-3403)* is a time-share club with efficiency units available for rent. The nicely landscaped property has a small pool and overlooks Paradise Lake. There is a free shuttle to Paradise Beach. Units are a bit cramped, but attractively furnished with fine attention to detail. They have full kitchens, but no bathtubs – only showers.

Radisson Grand Resort Paradise Island *($235, low $185, 342 rooms, pb, ≈, ≡, ℜ, sat tv; PO Box SS-6307, Nassau, ☎363-2011 or 1-800-333-3333, ⇒363-3193)* is a huge high-rise on a quiet section of Cable Beach. Its pool deck blends almost seamlessly with the beach. It offers a whole slew of services including a beauty salon and a travel agency. Rooms were recently updated, the decor is still fairly standard, but attractive. Each room has its own private balcony, in-room safe and minibar. Several restaurants and eateries and a disco round out the offerings.

Atlantis Paradise Island Resort & Casino *($300, low $130, MAP $43; 1,150 rooms, pb, ≡, sat tv, ≈, ℜ; PO Box N-4777, Nassau, ☎363-3000 or 1-800-321-3000, ⇒363-2543)* is *the* megaresort on Paradise Island, thanks mostly to its showpiece 14-acre waterscape featuring an open-air aquarium. This place is run by Sun International which is gradually grabbing up property around Atlantis. Atlantis Phase II should be completed by the end of 1998. Let's consider Phase I for now. Standard rooms are in either the Beach Tower or the Coral Tower, the latter having received the most recent refurbishment. More luxurious rooms are in the Reef Club. All the rooms feature attractive decors in coral pink and pale yellow tones, large bathrooms, balconies and special touches like turn-down service. But with so much to keep you busy here, forget the rooms.

Head down to the Predator Lagoon, inner-tube down the Lazy River Ride, swim and slide into the three swimming pools. There are also a casino, 12 restaurants, cabaret and comedy shows to fill any spare moments, or a fine endless beach to while away the hours.

The Ocean Club *($595, low $335; 58 rooms, pb, ≡, ⊗, ≈, sat tv, ◎, ℜ; PO Box N-4777, Paradise Island, Nassau, ☎363-3000 or 1-800-321-3000, ⇒363-2543)*, also part of the Sun International holdings on Paradise Island, combines luxurious rooms, exquisite gourmet cooking (see p 110) and Old World charm. Augustinian gardens filled with Classical statues surround a large pool, while hammocks sway under the shade of beach-side casuarinas. Colonial-style mahogany pieces, like a four-poster "pineapple" bed and a wardrobe, and his-and-hers marble bathrooms, contribute to the elegance of this exclusive getaway. The property straddles the island with the rooms and pool facing the ocean and the Versailles Gardens (see p 95) sweeping all the way to the harbour. There are 12 tennis courts and guests here have access to Atlantis' facilities.

RESTAURANTS

Downtown Nassau

For a real espresso or cafe latte and some authentic Cuban cigars, head upstairs from the Flamingo Trading Company on Bay Street, to **La Casa del Habano Coffee & Tea Bar** *($)*; they also sell a few pastries. **Jitters Coffee House** *($; ☎356-9381)* across the street and upstairs from the Girls from Brazil swimsuit shop, also makes a good cup of Jo, along with soups, salads and sandwiches.

Rosalie's *($; Nassau St.)* is reputed to have the best take-out. This small shack is in Over-the-Hill on the northeastern corner of Nassau Street and Boyd, just look for the crowds at lunchtime. The cracked conch and chicken in a bag and are good and greasy.

Bahamian Kitchen *($-$$; Trinity Pl. off Bay St., ☎325-0702)* is the downtown favourite for Bahamian home-cooking. They are famous for their okra soup, but also serve pan-fried turtle steaks, boiled fish, curried chicken and conch salad. You can get yours to go or eat in. Good value for the money in a nice unpretentious place.

Conch Fritters Bar & Grill *($-$$; Marlborough St., ☎323-8778)* is Nassau's answer to McDonald's. Except here the fast food of choice is cracked conch, of course. Conch chowder, conch fritters and other quick and greasy snacks are available.

The **House of Wong** *($-$$; Marlborough St., opposite British Colonial, ☎326-0045)* is the best Chinese restaurant in town. The hot and sour soup and shrimp toasts are good to start. After that, take your pick from a wide selection Szechuan and Cantonese dishes with vegetables, beef, chicken and seafood. There are even a few Polynesian and Hawaiian offerings. The ambiance is modern and bright.

The Shoal Restaurant *($-$$; Nassau St., ☎323-4400)*, is very popular with locals and visitors alike who appreciate its Bahamian breakfasts, lunches and dinners served like at home, "not prettied up". Their local claim to fame is the best boiled fish in the islands.

Sugar Reef Harbourside Bar & Grille *($-$$; Bay St. at Deveaux St., ☎356-3065)* has an original decor of

Ulysses' Favourites

Restaurants

Best True-true Bahamian Cooking:

Rosalie's (see p 106), Bahamian Kitchen (see p 106), Traveller's Rest (see p 109), Tamarind Hill Bar & Restaurant (see p 109) and The Island Restaurant (see p 110).

Finest Dining:

Cafe Matisse (see p 108), Graycliff (see p 108), Sun And... (see p 110), Compass Point (see p 108), Villa d'Este (see p 111) and Cafe Martinique (see p 111).

Funkiest Ambiance:

Compass Point (see p 108), Cafe Johnny Canoe (see p 108), Rock 'n' Roll Cafe (see p 109) and Sugar Reef Harbourside (see p 106).

colourful mosaics, lots of plants and a patio facing the harbour. Great for lunch. A tempting array of appetizers starts the meal, for mains there are lot of seafood choices, including authentic Bahamian, Caribbean and a few contemporary offerings. Reservations recommended for dinner.

Green Shutters Inn *($-$$$; closed 8pm on Sun, 48 Parliament St., ☎325-5702)* is an authentic English pub complete with English beers on tap and all the fish 'n' chips, steak-and-kidney pie and shepherd's pie you could ever want. The 190-year-old house and leather wing chairs certainly add to the charm. Bahamian fare and simple sandwiches are also cooked up.

The Cellar *($$; Charlotte St., ☎322-8877)* has a pub-like atmosphere with a beamed ceiling and is in the historic 18th-century stone kitchen of a former residence on Charlotte Street. It is only open for lunch when you can sample English pot and meat pies, or try the more innovative artichoke bake with cheddar cheese or the crepe of the day. Conch, grouper, sandwiches and pasta dishes are also served, as well as a good old soup and salad combo. Wines are available by the glass and there is patio seating in an interior courtyard.

Europa *($$-$$$; West Bay St., ☎322-8032)* is the only place in town to get your fill of wiener schnitzel, bratwurst and sauerbraten. They also cook up a few Italian dishes, fondue and Bahamian fare. The ambiance is relaxed and the service particularly helpful.

Gaylords *($$-$$$; Dowdeswell St., ☎356-3004)* is part of a renowned Indian restaurant chain that has recently opened a location in a lovely 125-year-old Bahamian home just east of downtown. They cook up wonderful Tandoori, Punjabi, Nepalese and Mughalo dishes. Reservations are recommended.

Pick-A-Dilly at the Parliament *($$-$$$; closed Sun; 18 Parliament St., ☎322-2836)* has outdoor seating and a menu of Bahamian favourites, most of which are blackened, grilled or steamed. A few more original choices are on offer as well. The dessert specialties are key lime pie and the famous Banana-à-la-Dilly, a banana rolled in puffed pastry, sprinkled with cinnamon, deep-fried and served with ice cream.

Silk Cotton Club *($$-$$$; Market St. off Bay St., ☎356-0955)* offers casual dining on continental, mostly Italian and Bahamian fare. You can do both by starting with the zesty bruschetta and finishing with the sinful guava duff. Live bands play mellow jazz and smooth blues during dinner and lively dance music after.

Cafe Matisse *($$$; Bank Lane, behind Parliament Sq., ☎356-7012)* is a study in Mediterranean decor from the concrete walls with their pale-yellow wash, the ceiling fans and the Matisse prints. The menu lists dish after dish of inventive Italian-flavoured dishes including mouthwatering suggestions like grilled lobster with asparagus tips and lemon butter sauce, roasted breast of duck with white port sauce and peaches and the subtle, but delicious, scallops with saffron cream sauce on rice. Pastas and pizzas, both traditional and with seafood, are also recommended. Home-made Italian biscotti are served with coffee. The service is a tad unsure but sincere. The lunch menu is just as good and very reasonably priced. Reservations recommended for dinner.

Buena Vista *($$$$; Delancey St., ☎322-2811)* boasts the terrific ambiance of an historic Nassau mansion. The fixed-price menu offers a wide variety of appetizers and soup, entrees and dessert and drinks. You can start with avocado pear stuffed with lobster or foie gras; the entree choices include grouper à la Bimini, roast duckling au pamplemousse or rack of lamb, and for dessert cherries jubilee perhaps.

Graycliff *($$$$; West Hill St., ☎322-2796)* is the only five-star restaurant in The Bahamas, and it more than meets up to the distinction. The table is set with the finest silverware, china and crystal, worthy receptacles for wines from the best cellar, with some 175,000 bottles in the Caribbean and Chef Philippe Bethel's acclaimed creations. He uses the finest and freshest of Bahamian ingredients in his savoury and hearty dishes. Seafood, lobster in particular, is the specialty here. Host Enrico Garzaroli's collection of Cuban cigars is offered for your after-dinner enjoyment. Cuban cigar-roller Avelino Lara might even be on hand to roll a Cohiba right before your eyes.

Island Tour

Cable Beach and West of Downtown Nassau

Cafe Johnny Canoe *($-$$; next to Nassau Beach Hotel, ☎327-3373)* has a funky, colourful decor and lively ambiance in keeping with its namesake Junkanoo festival. The menu is Bahamian plus American favourites like burgers and fries. This is a good place for hearty breakfasts.

Compass Point *($-$$$; West Bay Rd., ☎327-4500)* has the funkiest restaurant and menu offerings on New Providence. Even more interesting is the fact that it offers one of the best values for your money. A popular hangout of supermodels and recording stars, the colourful dining room of this even more colourful hotel is open for breakfast, lunch and dinner. At lunch you can chose between phat Thai, jerk chicken salad or maybe Caribbean chicken roll-ups with cashews. The dinner menu is yet more interesting with Bahamian sushi rolls as a starter, and then lobster angolotti or Washington rack of lamb with guava roasted garlic glaze.

Caripelago Gallery and Restaurant *($$; Cable Beach, ☎327-4749)* sells hand-made crafts and the work of local painters from its location in Cable Beach. Most of the space, however, is given over to the restaurant, which serves island cooking. They have traditional Bahamian-style fried chicken or more innovative and wonderfully seasoned steamed grouper with mango salsa. They also roast their own coffee here.

Rock 'n' Roll Cafe *($$; between Breezes SuperClubs and Nassau Beach Hotel, ☎327-7639)* is a fun spot with rock 'n' roll collectables on the walls, a WWII fighter plane and a tropical sports bar ambiance. The food is not stellar, but the potato skins, chicken wings, nachos and the like are in order in a place like this. You can eat indoors or out on the terrace with its ocean views. Things liven up here as the night progresses, especially on Friday's Junkanoo Night.

Dicky Mo's *($$-$$$; next to the Radisson, Cable Beach, ☎327-7854)* is a casual, family-style place with Bahamian dishes and seafood. Prime rib of beef and sirloin steaks are also served. The decor is very seaworthy featuring all sort of collectables, and the staff donned in captain's outfits also seem to have gotten their sea legs. Fun ambiance.

Traveller's Rest *($$-$$$; near Gambier, West Bay St., ☎327-7633)* enjoys an awesome seaside setting surrounded by sea grapes and palm trees. The locals arrive from all over the island to enjoy the Bahamian cooking here, they know a good thing when they taste it. The guava duff, conch salad and tropical cocktails are recommended. If you come for lunch bring your swimsuit and towel and flake out on the beach afterwards.

Amici *($$$; Radisson Cable Beach, ☎327-6000)* at the Radisson Cable Beach is an elegant Italian eatery with an open but intimate decor. Marble floors and wooden individual gazebos create an attractive dining environment. Fresh pastas highlight the menu, the veal parmesan is excellent. Reservations recommended.

The Forge *($$$; Radisson Cable Beach, ☎327-6000)* is a new Japanese Steak House at the Marriott. Each table has its own grill and your meal is prepared right before your eyes in a flash of knives and flames. The minimalist decor will transport you to a far-off land. All in all a fine dining experience. Reservations recommended.

East of Downtown Nassau

Tamarind Hill Bar & Restaurant *($-$$; Village Rd., ☎393-1306)* is a neighbourhood spot set up inside a bright old Bahamian home with a funky tropical decor and outdoor dining. The menu lists local fare liked cracked conch, grouper fingers, plus sandwiches, salads, quiches and a huge selection of burgers. More discerning palates will even find a few innovative and zesty offerings on the menu.

The Poop Deck *($-$$$; in Nassau Yacht Haven, East Bay St., ☎393-8175)* has a great location over the water. The Bahamian cooking here is authentic and very tasty. Try the stuffed crab or spicy grouper and be sure to save room at the end for some sweet and sticky guava duff.

The Sun and... *($$-$$$$; Lakeview Rd. off Shirley St., ☎393-1205)* serves acclaimed French and Italian cuisine créative. The menu (in French and English) offers quite an impressive selection of dishes, from poached Atlantic salmon served with fresh fruit in season topped with asparagus and sorrel vinaigrette, or grilled and herbed grouper or snapper with grilled scampi topped with salsa, or the classic two small filets topped with goose liver served with a Madeira truffle sauce. Allow time to finish your meal with one of the soufflés. The restaurant has a delightfully cosy ambiance, set as it is in a converted house.

Paradise Island

There are few independent restaurants on Paradise Island, but a whole array of hotel restaurants. Among the local establishments, the following two stand out:

The **Island Restaurant** *($; Paradise Beach Dr., ☎363-3153)* is a local family-run joint. The food is real Bahamian, plus a few standard American favourites. The home-made breakfasts are reasonable here.

Swank's Pizza *($-$$; Paradise Island Shopping Centre, ☎363-2765)* serves the cheapest pizzas on the island, and they are quite good. You can also get decent breakfasts here.

Here is a rundown of the hotel restaurant offerings, some of which are particularly exceptional:

Paradise Paradise's **Club Paradise** *($$-$$$; ☎363-3000)* serves up juicy steaks, ribs and fresh seafood in a thatched-roof building right on the beach. The generous portions and good value for you money make this a good choice.

The **Columbus Tavern Restaurant** *($$-$$$; Paradise Island Dr., ☎363-2534)* is another reasonable choice, this time overlooking the Paradise Harbour Club. The menu here is a bit more extensive with choices like beef Wellington and lobster thermidor among the continental and Bahamian offerings. The decor is bright with lots of brass lanterns and a fine view of the harbour. Reservations recommended

The Club Land 'Or's **Blue Lagoon** *($$-$$$$; Club Land 'Or, Paradise Dr., ☎326-2400)* offers a quiet and elegant change of pace from the glitzy casino across the lake. The menu lists a good selection of French and Italian dishes, some with a Bahamian twist. The fish dishes are wonderfully fresh and savoury.

The Ocean Club's **Courtyard Terrace** *($$$-$$$$; ☎363-3000)* enjoys a stunning seaside location surrounded by palm trees and flowers. Tables are set in a stone courtyard with a fountain. The cuisine is continental, from steak tartare to Chateaubriand. Certainly one of the island's most sophisticated dining rooms. Reservations are recommended.

The buffet at Club Med's **Porcupine Club** *($$$$; Club Med, ☎323-2640)* is an elaborate event and very tasty. Each night there is a different international theme. Non-guests can join the party on Friday and Saturday nights. The dinner show is included.

There are nine restaurants to choose from at **Atlantis** *(☎363-3000)*! Among these, **Seagrapes** *($$)* lays out a huge buffet for breakfast, lunch and dinner. It is all-you-can-eat at the salad bar. This is a good deal if you're really hungry. For more elaborate fine dining, try one of the following five restaurants: The **Boat House** *($$-$$$)* grills up steaks and seafood on the individual hibachis at each table, the decor is upscale. **Water's Edge** *($$$)* serves up healthy Mediterranean specialties from Italy, Spain, Greece and North Africa; there is a buffet each morning. **Bahamian Club** *($$$)* is a cosy steakhouse complete with overstuffed wing chairs and lots of hardwood trim. **Mama Loo's** *($$$)* has an exotic decor and tasty Chinese food, with the odd Bahamian dish thrown in there. **Villa d'Este** *($$$$)* is a splendid Italian restaurant with a classic but contemporary decor of Italianate columns and frescoes highlighted by sexy halogen lights. A superb roasted garlic focaccia is but an introduction to the delicious food. **Cafe Martinique** *($$$$)* is Atlantis' signature restaurant and one of the best in The Bahamas. Wall-to-wall etched glass and candlelit terraces create a romantic atmosphere that once figured in the James Bond movie *Thunderball*. The menu is French, and starts with a choice of soufflés, these things take time you know!

Among the restaurants at the **Radisson Grand Hotel** *(☎363-3500)*, **Julie's Ristorante Italiano** *($$)* is a moderately-priced Italian eatery with a deli setting. Nothing fancy, just a simple meal out. The **Rotisserie** *($$-$$$)* has a very attractive and very simply decorated dining room, best seen at night when the moon is reflected off the ocean. The food is continental and a bit predictable. Thick and juicy steaks are guaranteed, however.

ENTERTAINMENT

Casinos

The **Crystal Palace Casino** *(every day 10am to 4am, some slots open 24 hours a day; at the Nassau Marriott Cable Beach, ☎327-6200)* is a glitzy gambling palace with 800 slot machines, nine roulette wheels, plus tables for blackjack, Caribbean stud poker, baccarat and more.

The **Atlantis Paradise Island Casino** *(10am to 4am, slots are open 24 hours a day; Atlantis, ☎363-3000)* also has 800 slot machines, plus all the tables you could imagine to try your luck at. Guests can participate in complimentary gaming lessons every day at 3pm. Proper dress is required.

Cabarets, Comedy and Theatres

Most hotels put on some sort of native show or musical revue. Among the best ones are:

Jubilation at the Palace Theatre *(Crystal Palace Casino, Cable Beach, ☎327-6200)* is a Vegas-style musical review that pulls out all the stops. Families should note that all shows (except on Tuesdays and Sundays) contain "tasteful cultural nudity". There are dinner and cocktail shows. Reservations recommended.

The **Drumbeat Club** *(West Bay St., ☎322-4233)* puts on a terrific show with everything from a female impersonator to Junkanoo costumes and music.

The **King and Knights Club** *(Forte Nassau Beach Hotel, ☎327-7711)* has native dancing, including limbo and fire

Annual Events

January
New Year's Day Junkanoo Parade starts at 2am.
Annual Nassau Classic Car Festival, Cable Beach; this was a popular event in the 1950s and 1960s, which was revived in 1997.

April
The Snipe Winter Sailing Championship is raced by traditional locally made boats in Montagu Bay. For information ☎393-0145.

June
Goombay Summer Festival features Junkanoo parade and rake 'n' scrape bands.
Caribbean Muzik Fest highlights the musical sounds of the island, from rake 'n' scrape to soca. For information ☎322-7500.

August
Emancipation Day (first Monday in August) is marked by a Junkanoo rush-out in Fox Hill at 4am.
Fox Hill Day (one week later) is marked by gospel concerts and a big cook-out in the afternoon.

October
The Cricket Festival matches teams from all over the Bahamas, and gives the uninitiated another chance to try and figure out the rules of this popular sport. For information ☎326-4720.
Great Bahamas Seafood Festival is a culinary extravaganza of Bahamian cooking, including music and cooking contests. For information ☎302-2072.

September
Bahamas Atlantic Superboat Challenge is a major event in the racing calendar. The course passes under the Paradise Island Bridge with boats reaching speeds of up to 180 kilometres per hour. For information call ☎322-7500.

November
Guy Fawkes Day gives Bahamians the chance to parade the streets after dark, burning an effigy of the malfeasant involved in a plot to blow up the British Parliament.

December
Boxing Day (Dec 26) Junkanoo Parade starts at 2am.

Other Events to watch for include:

The **Changing of the Guard** at Government House occurs every other Wednesday at 10am and includes a performance by The Royal Bahamas Police Force Band all decked out in their leopard-skin tunics and pith helmets. To confirm dates call ☎322-1875.

The **Opening of the Supreme Court** occurs four times a year, in January, April, July and October. The white-wigged Chief Justice takes the opportunity to inspect the Royal Bahamas Police Force Guard of Honour in Rawson Square.

The **People-to-People Tea Party** is hosted by the Governor-General's wife at Government House. Call ☎326-5371, 328-7810 or 326-9772 for information.

dancing every night at 8:30pm and 10:30pm, except Monday. The $16 entrance includes one drink.

Jokers Wild Comedy Club *(Atlantis Paradise Island Casino, ☎363-3000)* is New Providence's only comedy club with international headline acts. Cocktail shows are presented Tuesdays to Sundays at 9:30pm, admission is $20.

Sunsation! At Atlantis *(Atlantis Paradise Island Casino, ☎363-3000)* is this resort's version of the tropical musical revue. Feathered and sequined costumes, some pretty skimpy but still alright for children's eyes, dance and music recreate the colourful excitement of Junkanoo. This is a dinner show put on every night at 7pm except Monday. Reservations recommended.

Dundas Centre for the Performing Arts *(Mackey St., ☎393-3728)* stages a variety of plays, musicals and ballets throughout the year

Bars and Nightclubs

Most hotels have their own nightclubs and lounges. Other options in town include:

Planet Hollywood *(Bay Street at East St., ☎325-STAR)* has the requisite rock memorabilia and over-the-top decor, in this case a huge wave threatens to crash over the bar.

The **Green Shutters Restaurant** is Nassau's best and most authentic English pub, with over 200 years of history. Besides the beer of The Bahamas you can get several English brews on tap.

The **Drop-Off Pub** *(Bay St. opposite Planet Hollywood, ☎322-3444)* is a local joint that serves bar food and snacks all night. The latest pop music is played and there are live bands occasionally. There is a dance floor and a big-screen television to keep everyone happy. This is the coolest dance spot right downtown.

The latest trendy place to be seen is the **601** *(601 Bay St., ☎322-3041)*, the new home of Baha Men, winners of the Tokyo Song of the Year contest in 1996. They perform here when not on tour. Other local bands also perform regularly. Proper dress is required (ie. jacket for men) and under-25s are not allowed in. There is a large dance floor. Sunday is jazz night and Thursday is Ladies' Night. Admission is $20.

Club Waterloo *(West Bay St., ☎393-7324)* is a loud, strobe-lit dance bar with its own crane for bungee-jumping. This full-on experience is popular with younger crowds and spring-break vacationers. Admission is $25.

Jazz is the specialty of the **Silk Cotton Club** *(Market St. near Bay St., ☎356-0955)* on Fridays and Saturday nights from 10am to 2pm.

Culture Club *(Bay and Nassau streets behind the Astoria Hotel, ☎356-6299)* is a happening dance club with a lofty warehouse-like ambiance. This used to be *the* hangout of the popular Baha Men group, though they still perform here on occasion. Admission is charged but usually includes one drink. Thursday is Ladies' Night.

The Zoo *(West Bay St., east of Cable Beach, ☎322-7195)* attracts crowds of young revellers with fancy laser shows, nightly promotions and all the latest tunes from reggae to hip hop and house music. Admission is an unbelievable $40 on Thursday to Sunday and $20 the rest of the week. It is free if you are staying at Breezes, Sandals or Club Med, or if you have just come from dinner at Cafe Johnny Canoe. Happy hour is from 8pm to 10pm.

Rock 'n 'Roll Cafe *(beside Nassau Beach Hotel, Cable Beach, ☎327-7639)* plays loud music into the night. There is a small dance floor. Very popular with visitors, locals and glitterati of all ages. Good selection of beers and cocktails. Happy hour starts at 4pm.

Johnny Canoe's *(next to Nassau Beach Hotel, Cable Beach, ☎327-3373)* is known mostly as a restaurant, though the live entertainment keeps things hopping as the night wears on.

The best of the true-true Bahamian hangouts has to be **Same Ol' Place** *(Thompson Blvd.)* in Over-the-Hill where real rake 'n' scrape gets everyone jumping 'n' dancing and you'll be welcomed like a long-lost cousin.

SHOPPING

Nassau

Bay Street is legendary for its duty-free offerings: china, perfume, crystal, linens, jewellery, watches, leather goods, liquor. Nassau also has two large shopping malls, the biggest is the Mall at Marathon *(Marathon and Robinson Roads)*; the Towne Centre Mall is another, this one at Blue Hill Road and Independence Drive.

Boutique Cartier *(284 Bay St., ☎322-4391)* sells fine jewellery, watches, handbags, silk scarves and other luxury items, all signed Cartier.

Fendi *(Bay and Charlotte streets, ☎322-6300)* sells its watches, perfumes and signature leather bags, and belts.

Coin of the Realm *(Charlotte St., ☎322-4286)*, run by a Bahamian family, sells rare and modern stamps, collectable coins from The Bahamas and conch pearls.

Cole's of Nassau *(Parliament St., ☎322-8393 and the Mall at Marathon, ☎393-3542)* sells upscale women's sportswear, swimwear and designer clothes. Labels include Laurel, Mondi, Adrienne Vittadini and Betsey Johnson.

Colombian Emeralds *(Bay St., ☎326-1661 or 322-8870)* has two locations on Bay Street, one near Rawson Square and the other facing the Straw Market. Precious gems dazzle in this upscale jewellery shop.

The **Discount Warehouse** *(Bay St., ☎325-1522)* also stocks precious gems alongside semi-precious ones. Gold chains and jewellery are also available. Major savings can be had here.

John Bull *(Bay St., ☎322-4252)* sells all manner of duty-free items, from jewellery to cameras and sunglasses. There are other locations on Paradise Island *(☎363-3956)* and Woodes Rogers Walk *(☎322-8846)*.

Little Switzerland *(Bay St., ☎322-8324)* sells duty-free porcelain and china.

There is also a fine selection of jewellery, perfumes and watches.

GNC (General Nutrition Centre) *(Harbour Bay Shopping Centre, ☎394-3950; Mall At Marathon, ☎394-2180)* sells vitamins, minerals, homeopathic medicines and a few health-food items.

The **Island Shops** *(Bay St., ☎322-1011)* sells souvenirs, resort wear, perfumes and delicious Bacardi Rum Cake. Upstairs, the **Island Book Shop** *(☎322-4183)* has one of the best selections of books on The Bahamas, these cover just about any topic from art history to Bahamian slang.

Caripelago Company Limited Gallery *(Bay St., ☎326-3568, Cable Beach ☎327-4749)* sells beautiful handmade arts and crafts, paintings and sculptures. Stop in here to admire these wonderful pieces even if you aren't buying.

Stogies Cigars Atlantic Tobacco Co. *(Charlotte St.,* ☎356-5103) has some of the finest stogies in town, they also have a great gift shop just up the street.

Graycliff *(West Hill St., ☎322-2796)* probably has the best selection of cigars, and you can even see them being made. There are plans to open a cigar factory here, staffed by Cuban cigar rollers.

Marlborough Antiques *(Marlborough St., ☎328-0502)* is a fascinating and pricey store. With everything from old model ships to fine furniture, it is just as good for browsing as shopping.

Charlotte's Gallery *(Charlotte St., ☎322-6310)* exhibits beautiful pieces by Bahamian artists, you can also find pottery and other creative souvenirs here. A different local artist is featured each month.

Island Tings *(Bay St., ☎326-1024)* has the best selection of Bahamian-made souvenirs and art, from music, to Androsia fabric, Abaco ceramics, wood carvings, Christmas decorations, bush medicines, jewellery, good books, and no cheesy t-shirts!

The **Green Lizard** *(West Bay St., ☎356-5013)* has an equally impressive selection of Bahamian-made crafts and pieces of art.

The **Plait Lady** *(Bay St. at Victoria Ave., ☎356-5584)* sells handmade straw items from all over The Bahamas. You'll see the different styles and materials used in each island. All of the items on sale here are genuinely Bahamian.

Nassau's Straw Market *(between Bay St. and Woodes Rogers Walk and Frederick and George streets)* is the place everyone should do a bit of shopping. In operation since the 1930s, this historic market is a real slice of life in The Bahamas. The vendors spend their days here, weaving and decorating hats, baskets and bags. You'll also find handmade shell jewellery, carvings along with loads of t-shirts, towels, and other souvenirs. Try to get introduced to the person who made something you're interested in and beware of Asian-made knock-offs. Bargaining is part of the tradition, but don't bother if you aren't really shopping.

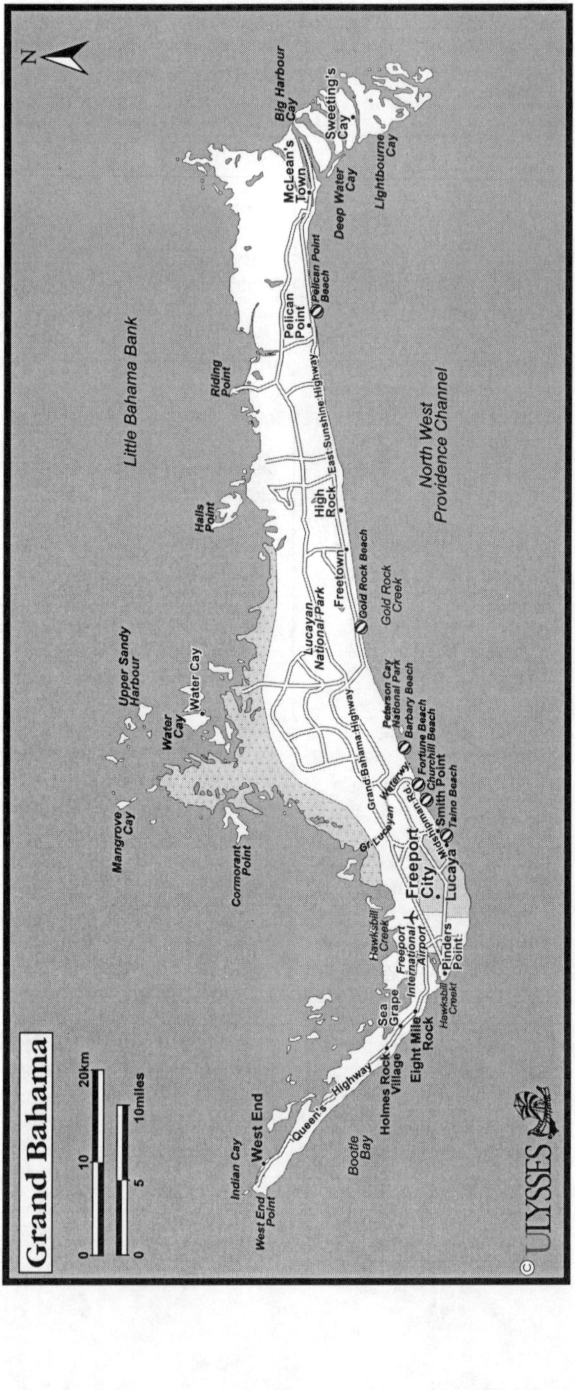

Grand Bahama
0
10
20km
0
5
10miles
N
Little Bahama Bank
North West Providence Channel
West End Point
Indian Cay
West End
Bootle Bay
Queen's Highway
Holmes Rock Village
Eight Mile Rock
Sea Grape
Hawksbill Creek
Freeport International Airport
Pinders Point
Freeport City
Lucaya
Cormorant Point
Mangrove Cay
Water Cay
Water Cay
Upper Sandy Harbour
Gr. Lucayan Waterway
Grand Bahama Highway
Midshipman Rd.
Taino Beach
Smith Point
Churchill Beach
Fortune Beach
Barbary Beach
Peterson Cay National Park
Gold Rock Creek
Gold Rock Beach
Lucayan National Park
Freetown
Halls Point
High Rock
East Sunshine Highway
Riding Point
Pelican Point
Pelican Point Beach
Deep Water Cay
McLean's Town
Lightbourne Cay
Sweeting's Cay
Big Harbour Cay
© ULYSSES

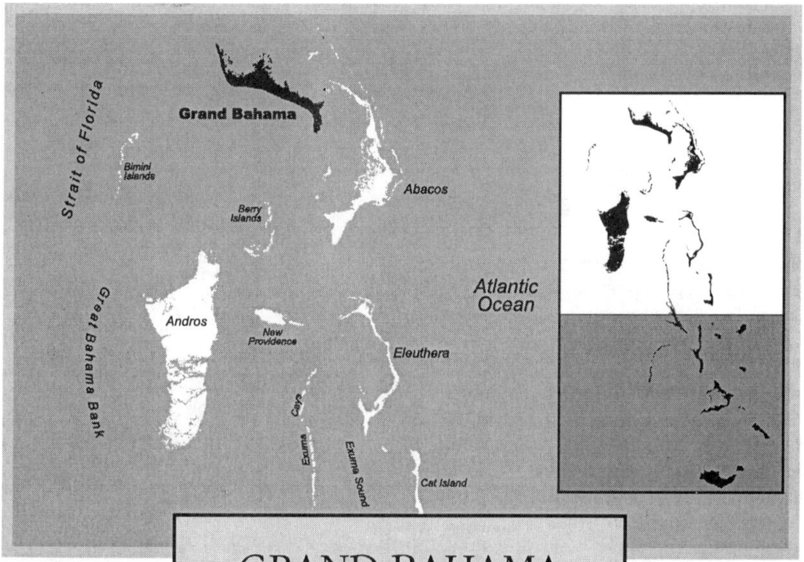

GRAND BAHAMA

Grand Bahama ★★ has been called the Las Vegas of The Bahamas and has been harangued for its lack of soul and its hordes of unsophisticated tourists. And while all of this is entirely bang on, Grand Bahama is so much more than that: it boasts stunning and solitary beaches, excellent facilities and there are still parts of it that are true-true Bahamian. It certainly won't appeal to everyone, but it definitely offers up all the ingredients of a perfect holiday, you just have to look a little harder to find them.

Lying about 175 kilometres to the northwest of Nassau, Grand Bahama is only 80 kilometres east of the Florida coast. For that reason, most of its visitors are American tourists who hop over for long weekends, or even just for the day on cruises out of West Palm Beach – it is that close. The duty-free shopping and casinos are what draw these folks across the Gulf Stream. Unfortuantely, they rarely venture beyond the charmless Freeport and Port Lucaya areas. If they did, they might actually feel they had come to another country. One whose white-sand beaches, spectacular diving and snorkelling and endearing people have so much more to offer than a 50% savings on French perfume or a pile of quarters from a slot machine.

Grand Bahama is 153 kilometres long and 27 kilometres wide at its widest point. Most of the island's interior is covered with casuarinas, Cuban pine and plametto and thatch palm. The northern coast is a tangle of mangrove swamps and shallows. Superb bonefishing flats surround the handful of cays trailing off the eastern end. The south shore is virtually one long stretch of fine white sand and swaying casuarinas. Wild orchids, heaps of curly-tailed lizards, hermit crabs, dolphins, sharks and, if you're lucky, green turtles will greet you on your tramps through Grand Bahama's "outback".

A Short History

Archaeological evidence of Lucayan settlement has been found on Grand Bahama, notably in the discovery of a burial site in a cave in Lucayan National Park. The Lucayans had already been wiped out, however, by the time Juan Ponce de León passed through in 1513 on his infamous and unsuccessful search for the Fountain of Youth. Pirates were the next to haunt these shores, keeping watch over the neighbouring sea routes in the 17th and 18th centuries. Finally in 1806, permanent settlers arrived.

Wrecking vessels were based here and took advantage of the good wrecking grounds near Sandy Cay, while other settlers were drawn to the sponge-rich shallows along the north shore. The rest farmed and fished to survive. And so the modest fishing villages grew until the settlement of West End hit the jackpot with Prohibition in the United States. From 1919 to 1938, rum-runners operated out of West End, which was transformed into one giant liquor warehouse.

West End's reputation as a tropical getaway for well-heeled Floridians made quite an impression on Englishman Billy Butlin who visited in the 1940s and came up with the idea for Butlin's Vacation Village. Set for completion in 1950, the project was only halfway through its first phase when investors started pulling out. That first wing later became the popular Grand Bahama Hotel, and more recently the Jack Tar Village, which closed in 1990.

The Abaco Lumber Company arrived in 1944. In 1946, it was purchased, along with timber rights to Grand Bahama, by an American industrialist named Wallace Groves. He set about modernizing the operation and eventually dreamed up his plan for Grand Bahama: the development of a free port and a major industrial city. He was able to convince the Bahamian government that it was a good idea, and in 1955 the Hawksbill Creek Agreement was signed in which the Grand Bahama Port Authority was contracted to dredge a deepwater harbour at shallow Hawksbill Creek, and the government agreed to create a tax-free zone.

Groves promptly sold his timber mill, which eventually fell into the hands of Owens-Illinois, and he became president of the Grand Bahama Port Authority. Everything was on schedule with the port, the airport and the oil-bunkering storage complex. Inland waterways were dug along the southern shore and foreigners were offered tax breaks and other incentives as encouragement to build dream vacation homes here. Nevertheless, developers still hadn't found a good enough reason for people to choose Grand Bahama, and the project was stalling.

It was decided that only tourism could save the day. In 1960 the Port Authority was granted another 50,000 acres on the condition that a hotel be built. Three years later it was granted an exemption from the law against organized gambling so that a casino could be built to give people a reason to visit, and a few months later the Lucayan Beach Resort & Casino opened.

Things were peachy on Grand Bahama and getting better until the Progressive Liberal Party of Lynden Pindling was elected and immediately came to blows with the Port Authority. The main bone of contention was that the Port Authority employed mostly white foreigners who didn't need permits and who could come and go as they pleased. The government unilaterally amended the Agreement and began requiring work permits for all foreigners, which lead to an exodus of expat residents and of foreign capital. Business slowed to a standstill in many cases and remained that way for nearly two decades until the Free National Movement was elected in 1992 and the Hawksbill Creek Agreement was renewed.

The tax-free zone of Grand Bahama, encompassing Freeport/Lucaya and some 500 square kilometres, is still overseen by Grand Bahama Port Authority. It is once again on the rise, perhaps most notably where tourism is concerned. The redevelopment plan announced in 1997 involving the government-run Grand Bahama Beach Hotel and Lucayan Beach Resort & Casino along with the Grand Lucaya Resort & Casino project, which will integrate existing hotels with new hotels, a golf course and a marina, is the largest single investment in Grand Bahama's history. It will surely transform the island's tourist scene - developers, merchants and tourist industry types certainly expect and hope that it will.

FINDING YOUR WAY AROUND

By Plane

There is one airport on the island, the **Freeport International Airport** *(☎352-6020)*, located about three kilometres north of downtown Freeport. It is served by Bahamasair *(☎1-800-222-4262)* with daily flights from Nassau and Miami. Major carriers from the United States include: American Eagle *(☎1-800-433-7300)* (an American Airlines partner), Comair *(☎1-800-354-9822)* (a Delta Airlines partner) and Gulfstream International *(☎1-800-545-1300)*. British Airways has direct flights from London.

The departure tax of $18 must be paid in cash (Bahamian or US dollars) when checking in for your return flight.

By Boat

By Mailboat: All departures are from Potter's Cay (under the Paradise Island Bridge) in Nassau and all fares are one-way. The *Marcella III* departs Wednesdays at 4pm for Freeport. Travel time: approx. 12 hours. Fare: $45.

By Cruise Ship: Freeport's cruise ship dock is west of Freeport at Hawksbill Creek. It is an unattractive place with a small straw market, but will soon be jazzed up with a bigger market to cater to the cruise ship crowd.

Marinas

The shoreline around Freeport and Port Lucaya is riddled with man-made canals and marinas. Visiting boaters will find electricity, water, fuel and supplies at the following marinas, reservations are recommended:

Port Lucaya Marina: ☎373-9090, ⇛373-5884.
Lucaya Marina: ☎373-8888, ⇛373-7630.
Running Mon Marina: ☎352-6834.

Ferries

A small ferry runs every hour from the Taino Beach Resort & Marina to Port Lucaya, and returns ten minutes later. The one-way fare is $2.

By Taxi

Grand Bahama Taxi Union, ☎352-7101.
Freeport Taxi, ☎352-6666.

Taxis are available at the airport and the cruise ship dock. Expect to $8 for a taxi between the airport and Freeport, $15 between the airport and Port Lucaya, $15 between the cruise ship dock and Freeport and $20 between the cruise ship dock and Port Lucaya.

Taxis with white license plates only operate in the free zone. Others can be hired on an hourly basis. This can be a good way to see the rest of the island. Expect to pay between $25 and $35 per hour.

By Car, Scooter and Dune Buggy

Car rentals can be reserved in advance and picked up at the airport. Beware of a local company called Budge Rent-A-Car, which is not affiliated with the North American chain.

Avis: Freeport International Airport, ☎352-7666; port Lucaya ☎373-1102.
Courtesy Rental: ☎352-5212.
Hertz, Freeport International Airport, ☎353-9277.
Sears Rent-A-Car: Atlantik Beach Hotel, ☎373-4938; International Airport, ☎352-8841.
Star Rent-A-Car: Old Airport Road, ☎352-5953.
Dollar Rent-A-Car: International Airport, ☎352-9308; Radisson Xanadu, ☎352-6782; Atlantik Beach. ☎373-9139; Royal Islander ☎351-6000.

Scooters are available from the Honda Cycle Shop *(☎352-7035)*, in front of the Bahamas Princess Tower, for $40 for a full day.

You can also rent a dune buggie to toot around the island in. Bahama Buggies *(☎352-8750)* near the International Bazaar rents them for $50 per day (from 9am to 5pm), $65 for 24 hours or $300 per week.

By Bus

There are private minibuses between the International Bazaar and downtown Freeport. The fare is $1 one-way. There are a few departures from the Winn Dixie Plaza in town to Port Lucaya, West End and McLean's Town.

Courtesy shuttles run from the Bahamas Princess Resort and the Country Club to Taino Beach and Xanadu Beach.

PRACTICAL INFORMATION

Freeport

Tourist Information: Grand Bahama Island Tourism Board, International Bazaar, ☎352-8044.
Bahamas Ministry of Tourism, in the Charles Hayward Library, East Mall Dr. at Pioneers Way, ☎352-8044.
Bahamas Tourist Office, International Bazaar, ☎352-8044.

What-to-do in Freeport/Lucaya Grand Bahama and *Island Magazine* are two pocket-sized magazines with information on dining, shopping and the latest entertainment offerings. They are available at tourist offices and in hotel lobbies.

Banks: The following banks are all located in downtown Freeport on or near East Mall Drive: Royal Bank of Canada *(☎352-6631)*, Bank of the

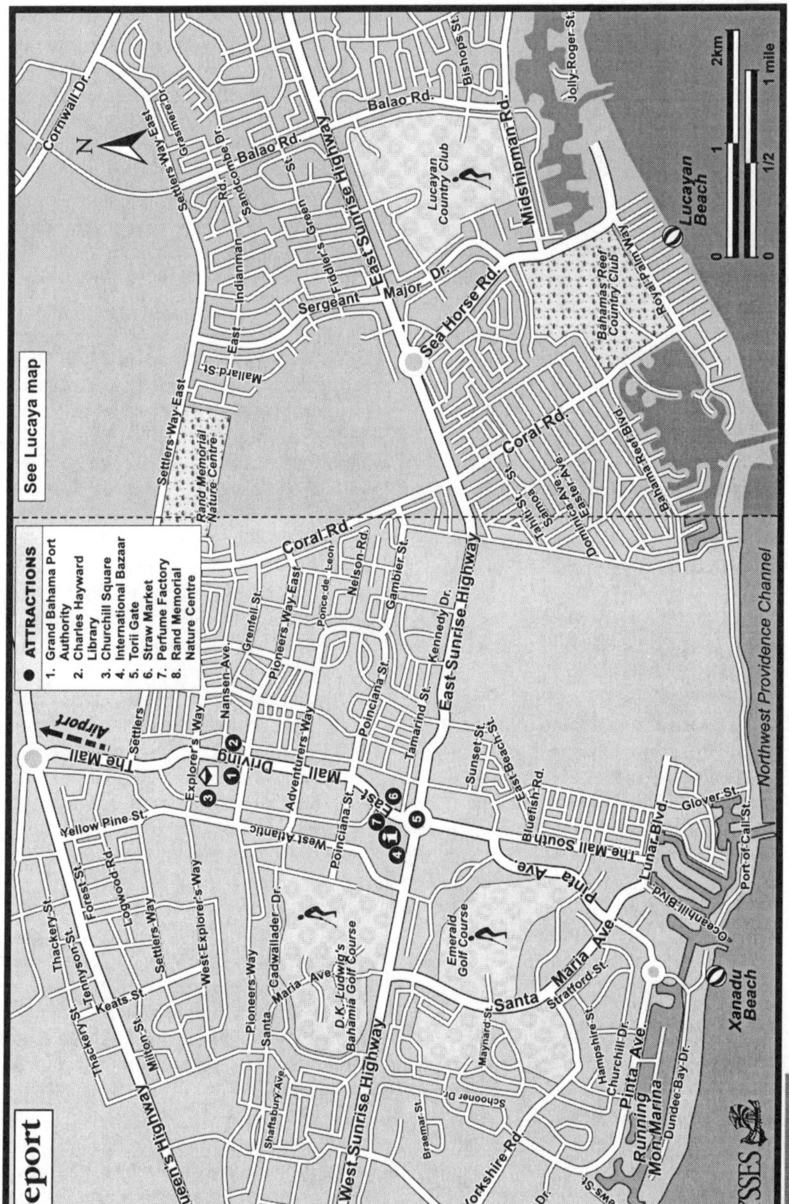
Freeport
See Lucaya map
ATTRACTIONS
1. Grand Bahama Port Authority
2. Charles Hayward Library
3. Churchill Square
4. International Bazaar
5. Torii Gate
6. Straw Market
7. Perfume Factory
8. Rand Memorial Nature Centre
Airport
N
Queen's Highway
West Sunrise Highway
East Sunrise Highway
The Mall
The Mall South
East Mall Drive
Settlers Way
Settlers Way East
Explorer's Way
West Explorer's Way
Pioneers Way
Pioneers Way East
Adventurers Way
Coral Rd.
Sea Horse Rd.
Midshipman Rd.
Balao Rd.
Sergeant Major Dr.
Cornwall Dr.
Grasmere Dr.
Sandcombe Dr.
Indianman Rd.
East St.
Mallard St.
Fiddler's Green
Bishops St.
Jolly Roger St.
Royal Palm Way
Bahama Reef Blvd.
Tahiti St.
Samoa St.
Dominica Ave.
Easter Ave.
Nansen Ave.
Grenfell St.
Ponce de Leon
Nelson Rd.
Gambier St.
Kennedy Dr.
Poinciana St.
Poinciana Dr.
Tamarind St.
Sunset St.
East Beach St.
Bluefish Rd.
Glover St.
Lunar Blvd.
Port of Call St.
Oceanhill Blvd.
Pinta Ave.
Santa Maria Ave.
Stratford St.
Maynard St.
Hampshire St.
Churchill Dr.
Dundee Bay Dr.
Running Mon Marina
St Andrews St.
Aberdeen Dr.
Yorkshire Rd.
Braemar St.
Schooner Dr.
Shaftsbury Ave.
Cadwallader Dr.
West Atlantic
Yellow Pine St.
Forest St.
Logwood Rd.
Thackery St.
Tennyson St.
Keats St.
Milton St.
Lucayan Country Club
Bahamas Reef Country Club
Rand Memorial Nature Centre
D.K. Ludwig's Bahamia Golf Course
Emerald Golf Course
Lucayan Beach
Xanadu Beach
Northwest Providence Channel
0 1 2km
0 1/2 1 mile
© ULYSSES

Bahamas *(☎352-7483)* and Barclays Bank *(☎352-8391)*.

Police: ☎919 or 348-3444.

BaTelCo: Pioneers Way.

Post Office: Explorers Way near East Mall Dr., ☎352-9371.

Hospital: Rand Memorial Hospital on East Atlantic Drive, ☎352-6735.
Lucayan Medical Centre, Adventurers Way, ☎352-7288.
Ambulance ☎352-2689.

Weather: ☎915.

Guided Tours: There are many tour operators in Freeport and Lucaya offering tours to Lucayan National Park and to West End, among other places. H. Forbes Charter Services *(☎352-9311)* probably has the largest selection of tours, including the popular "Super Combination Tour" and a "Grand Bahama Day Trip". Other recommended tours are the "Village Beat" and "Freeport Heritage" tours offered by Inter-Island Adventures *(☎352-9063)*, along with East End Adventures' *($110 per person, family rates available, ☎373-6662)* all-day trip by 4X4 vehicle inland to blue holes, caves, deserted beaches, fishing villages, plus a home-cooked Bahamian meal and a boat trip to Sweeting's Cay.

★ EXPLORING

Freeport ★

Freeport's downtown area lies about one kilometre north of the International Bazaar and is uninspired and spread out. Nothing of the real Bahamas remains amongst the shopping malls and fast-food restaurants. Nevertheless, the newer **Grand Bahama Port Authority** and **Charles Hayward Library** near the intersection of Pioneers Way and East Mall Drive are attractive colonial-style buildings. There is also a bronze bust of Sir Winston Churchill in **Churchill Square**, a decent place to rest your feet. The only good reason to venture downtown is to take care of any banking and shopping. The Winn Dixie Mall has a grocery store, pharmacy and other shops.

The **International Bazaar** ★ is Freeport's centrepiece and worth a browse through despite the fact that it is a tacky shadow of its former self. The Japanese **Torii Gate**, standing in the middle of Ranfurley Circle at the intersection of East Mall Drive and East Sunrise Highway, marks the entrance. The market is like a shopper's world fair with French, Greek, Indian, African and Spanish sections - in all some 25 countries are represented. Everything here is duty free, so there is no denying the great bargains to be found, especially for perfumes, jewellery and more T-shirts and kitschy souvenirs than you can imagine. There are more shops and kiosks behind the market in a big parking lot, as well as across the street from the International Bazaar.

Freeport's **Straw Market** ★ is beside the International Bazaar and has a good selection of handmade bags, hats and baskets. Watch out for the cheaper Asian-made knock-offs. Hair-braiders with their boxes full of coloured beads work the crowds here charging about $2 per braid.

Perfume Factory *(every day 10am to 6pm; across the street from the straw market, behind the International Bazaar, ☎352-9391)* is located in a pretty plum-and-white replica of an old Bahamian mansion. Tours of the factory offer a look at the production process of Fragrance of the Bahamas perfumes,

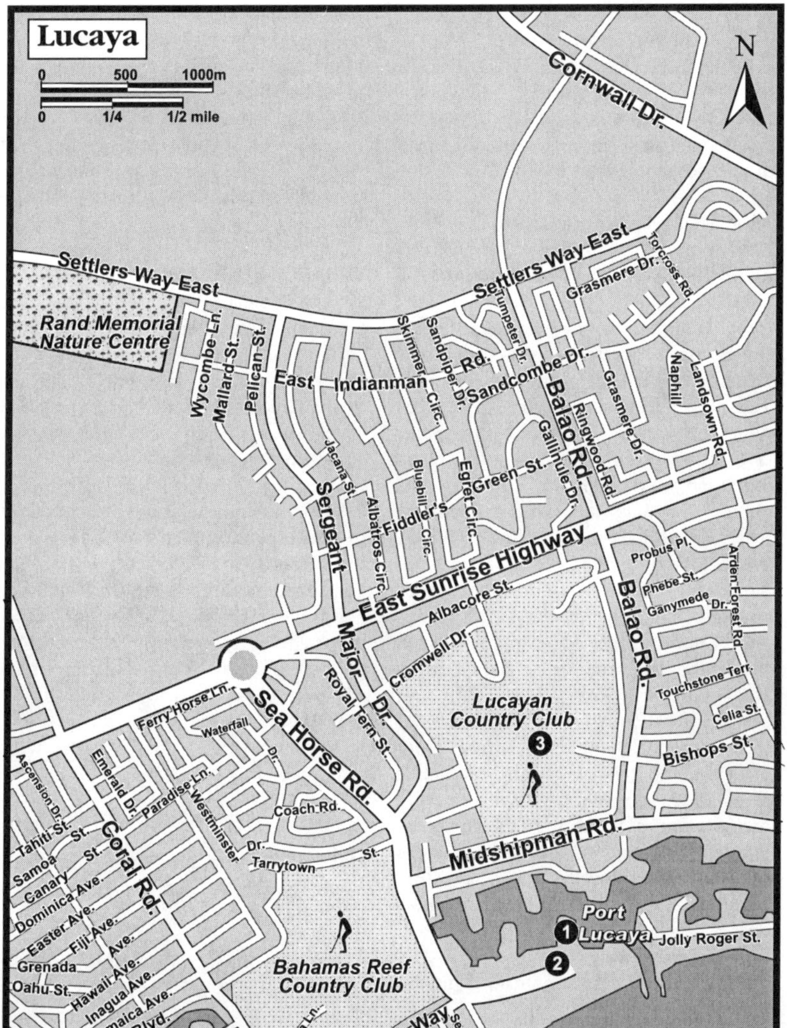
Lucaya
0 500 1000m
0 1/4 1/2 mile
N
Cornwall Dr.
Settlers Way East
Rand Memorial Nature Centre
Torcross Rd.
Grasmere Dr.
Tumpeter Dr.
Wycombe Ln.
Mallard St.
Pelican St.
East Indianman Rd.
Skimmer Circ.
Sandpiper Dr.
Sandcombe Dr.
Balao Rd.
Gallinule Dr.
Ringwood Rd.
Grasmere Dr.
Naphill
Landsown Rd.
Jacana St.
Sergeant Major Dr.
Albatros Circ.
Bluebill Circ.
Egret Circ.
Green St.
Fiddler's
East Sunrise Highway
Albacore St.
Cromwell Dr.
Probus Pl.
Phebe St.
Ganymede Dr.
Arden Forest Rd.
Touchstone Terr.
Celia St.
Bishops St.
Royal Tern St.
Sea Horse Rd.
Lucayan Country Club
Ferry Horse Ln.
Waterfall
Dr.
Ascension Dr.
Emerald Dr.
Paradise Ln.
Westminster Dr.
Coach Rd.
Tarrytown St.
Midshipman Rd.
Tahiti St.
Samoa St.
Canary
Coral Rd.
Dominica Ave.
Easter Ave.
Fiji Ave.
Grenada Ave.
Oahu St.
Hawaii Ave.
Inagua Ave.
Jamaica Ave.
Bahama Reef Blvd.
Port Lucaya
Jolly Roger St.
Bahamas Reef Country Club
Indiana Ln.
Royal Palm Way
Sea Grape St.
Sea View St.
Sea Scape St.
Sea Bisquit St.
Sea Fan St.
Lucayan Beach
ATTRACTIONS
1. Port Lucaya Market Place
2. UNEXSO
3. Balancing Boulders of Lucaya
© ULYSSES

GRAND BAHAMA

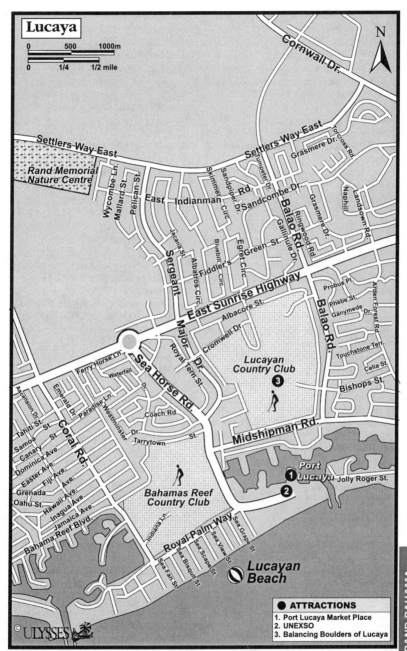

which was started in 1969 by American clothing manufacturer, Albert Whisnant, whose other credits include the development of seersucker. Visitors can also create their own perfume from the fragrant oils for $20, or choose one of the popular house blends.

Rand Memorial Nature Centre ★★ *($5; Mon to Fri 9am to 4pm, Sat 9am to 1pm; East Settlers Way, ☎352-5438)*, about three kilometres east of the centre of Freeport, is the headquarters of the Bahamas National Trust on Grand Bahama. There are trails through this 100-acre pineland sanctuary, parts of which are covered with virgin coppice. Over one hundred native plants including bush medicines and some 21 orchids are highlighted along the way. A freshwater pond is home to a flock of West Indian flamingoes, the national bird of The Bahamas, and many other species that frequent the area, including Cuban emerald hummingbirds, Antillean peewees, great blue herons and kingfishers. Scurrying and slithering about in the underbrush are raccoons, tree frogs, harmless brown-racer snakes and curly-tailed lizards. A replica of a Lucayan village was recently added and the gift shop has some great souvenirs. There are daily guided walks Mondays to Fridays at 10am and 2pm and Saturdays at 10am; the first Saturday of every month there is a guided bird-watching tour, and the third Saturday of every month there is a guided wildflower tour.

Lucaya ★★

Lucaya's biggest attractions are its beach and marketplace. The **Port Lucaya Marketplace** ★ has many of the same duty-free shops as the International Bazaar, plus a good-sized straw market. The boardwalks and pretty pink trellised buildings are more attractive than the Bazaar, and the location overlooking the marina is pleasant. The bandstand in **Count Basie Square** ★ (he used to have a home on Grand Bahama) is the scene of music performances most evenings, anything from rake-'n'-scrape Junkanoo music, to steel-drum performances and gospel choirs.

UNEXSO ★★★, the Underwater Explorers Society, is located at the eastern edge of the marina. Non-divers can participate in the fascinating and fun **Dolphin Close Encounter** *($29, ☎373-1244)* and wade in waist-deep in a sheltered lagoon with semi-wild Atlantic bottlenose dolphins.

While in Lucaya, take time to check out the **Balancing Boulders of Lucaya** ★ at the Lucaya Golf & Country Club. The best time to see this magical rock garden and waterfalls is after dark when the multicoloured floodlights transform it. It is at the 18th hole of the golf course and visible from the club's Arawak Dining Room (see p 136).

East of Freeport/Lucaya

Head east of Freeport on the East Sunrise Highway to reach the Hydroflora Gardens.

Hydroflora Gardens ★ *($3 or $5 with guided tour; Mon to Sat 9am to 5pm; East Beach Dr., off Sunrise Hwy., ☎352-6052)* is a botanical garden with flowers, fruit trees and shrubs of The Bahamas. Special areas highlight bush medicines and bromeliads. Call ahead if you want the guided tour.

The highway curves south at the Grand Lucayan Waterway and towards the Garden of the Groves.

4pm, Sat and Sun 10am to 4pm; at the intersection of Midshipman Rd. and Magellan Dr., ☎373-5668) was created by Freeport developer Wallace Groves and his wife Georgette. Lush with over 5000 species of plants and shrubs, both exotic and indigenous, the garden is also full of tropical birds. There is also a 400-foot-long Fern Gully, waterfalls, a small chapel, a citrus grove and a banana plantation.

Taino Beach ★★, **Churchill Beach** and **Fortune Beach** extend east of Port Lucaya. Of the three, Taino is the prettiest and has the most action.

Eastern Grand Bahama

The Grand Bahama Highway runs the length of the island and along the northern edge of Freepot/Lucaya. An excursion in this direction includes the fabulous Lucayan National Park and a handful of typical Bahamian settlements ending with McLean's Town. This is a full-day trip that covers about 70 kilometres in each direction, the road itself runs inland for most of the trip and isn't very picturesque, though side roads run south to the coast.

Peterson Cay National Park ★

Peterson Cay National Park lies one mile offshore from Barbary Beach, about 25 kilometres east of Freeport. Most people head out here for a picnic and a day of snorkelling, which is fabulous. There is usually a fair number of people, locals and visitors alike, here on weekends. You'll need your own boat to get out there.

Banana Blossom

Lucayan National Park ★★★

Lucayan National Park *(Bahamas National Trust, ☎352-5438)* about 20 kilometres east of Freeport/Lucaya, covers 40 acres. The two very distinct sections of the park are divided by the Grand Bahama Highway. There are no facilities here. The park is a great place to spend the day and have a picnic. If you plan on visiting, bring insect repellant and check the tides, the tourist office has the latter. Stunning Gold Rock Beach is best seen at low tide.

To the north of the highway, trails run through a bush-covered limestone plateau. Bromeliads and orchids can be seen along these, along with several bushes and trees used in traditional bush medicine, including love vine which is used in love potions and dandruff cures. A short distance into the woods, you'll come to two caves which were discovered when their limestone roofs collapsed. Four Lucayan skeletons were found in **Burial Mound Cave** in

1986. A wooden walkway leads partway into water-filled **Ben's Cave**, which is part of the longest known underwater cave system in the world. A lense of freshwater floats on top of heavier salt water further down in the cave. Grouper and snapper that live in the cave have adapted to the freshwater and can be seen from the platform. Experienced divers can enter the cave with UNEXSO (see p 128).

Two trails lead south of the highway through three distinct ecosystems. The **Creek Trail** and the **Mangrove Swamp Trail** form a loop that can be walked in 15 minutes. The first one is a transition zone of hardwoods like mahogany, cedar and poisonwood. You'll then enter an area thick with red mangroves. Boardwalks carry you over Gold Rock Creek, a freshwater creek that was used by Lucayans and home to snappers and barracudas. The creek is part of the underground water system of the aforementioned caves. Herons can be seen in the shallows, which are best explored by kayak (see p 129). The last ecosystem is a whiteland coppice that gives way to **Gold Rock Beach ★★★** with its fringe of coco plums, seagrape trees, spider lilies and casuarinas. Watch out for the hermit crabs lumbering along the path. At low tide, wide Gold Rock Beach's rippled sands and turquoise surf are quite a sight.

East to McLean's Town

The final fifty or so kilometres are uneventful with a few meagre settlements, namely **Freetown** and **High Rock**, which has the pretty Emmanuel Baptist Church. Beach connoisseurs must not miss **Pelican Point Beach ★★**, a stunning stretch of white sand. **McLean's Town** is worth a visit on Columbus Day in October when things really get cracking – literally! The Conch Cracking Contest is a mad dash to remove 25 conchs from their shells. Activities and games are also part of the festivities.

You can ask around for a local guide to take you to pretty **Sweeting's Cay** and **Lightbourne Cay**. Probably the best way to see these idyllic corners of the Bahamas is with East End Adventures (see p 122). **Deep Water Cay**, also accessible from here, is home to an exclusive resort frequented by fishers and yachties (see p 133).

Western Grand Bahama

To West End

The funky settlement of West End lies about 45 kilometres west of downtown Freeport, along the Queen's Highway. On the way you'll pass the cruise-ship dock and the Freeport Harbour Channel, the man-made channel that grew from tiny Hawksbill Creek, named for the hawksbill turtles that once came ashore to nest here. **Eight Mile** is an unattractive place best whizzed through. Holmes isn't much better, though it does have the very popular Buccaneer Club (see p 136).

During Prohibition in the United States, between 1919 and 1933, **West End ★★★** was one giant liquor warehouse. The boom continued with the construction of the Grand Bahama Resort & Country Club. This was the centre of tourism on the island until the hotels and casinos arrived in Freeport. The resort closed down, but reopened in the seventies as a Jack Tar Village, once again drawing moneyed vacationers to the western part of Grand Bahama. The resort closed down once again in 1990 and lies idle today, though its marina is still open. As a result, the main attraction of West End these days is its tumbledown, authentic fishing village ambiance, dominoes and its famous snack bar, the Star Club (see p 136). There is also the picturesque **Catholic Mary Magdalene Church** ★, which is worth a peak.

BEACHES

Xanadu Beach ★ is the closest beach to downtown Freeport. It has fine white sand and its waters get deep quickly. The only hotel on the beach is the Xanadu Beach Resort & Marina. There is a market with crafts and t-shirts. Jet-skis can be rented here, and banana-boat rides and parasailing can be arranged. A courtesy shuttle runs between the Bahamas Princess Resort & Casino and the beach.

Taino Beach ★★ is one of the prettiest on the island. Its fine white sand goes on forever. There is a pier, a crafts market and a handful of eateries in the middle. Its southern end is much wilder, while to the north is the small settlement of Smith's Point.

Churchill Beach and **Fortune Beach** run into each other and together form a quiet and picturesque stretch of golden sand. **Barbary Beach** ★★ is a secluded and little visited stretch of sand beyond the Grand Lucayan Waterway.

The best beach by far is **Gold Rock Beach** ★★★ in Lucayan National Park. At low tide the rippled stretch of white sand is superb. Be sure to check the tides (at the tourist office) to avoid missing the beach at its best. The water is fairly shallow and good for swimming.

Pelican Point Beach ★★ is another impressive sight, it is a way's out but a must if you are heading to McLean's Town.

OUTDOOR ACTIVITIES

Golf

Bahamas Princess Emerald Golf Course *(☎352-9661)* is a challenging par-72, 18-hole golf course designed by Dick Wilson. It is noted for its abundance of water hazards and bunkers and rolling fairways. Green fees are $75 for 18 holes, $50 for nine, carts cost $45, club rental is $20.

Bahamas Princess Ruby Golf Course *(☎352-9661)* is the other championship course of the Bahamas Princess Resort. It was designed by Joe Lee and is 6,750 yards long. Green fees and costs are the same as the Emerald course.

Fortune Hills Golf & Country Club *(East Sunrise Hwy., ☎373-4500)* is a semi-private, Joe-Lee-designed course. Eighteen holes were planned but only nine were completed. Green fees are $28 and include cart rental. Golf club rental is $9.

Lucaya Golf & Country Club *(☎373-1066 or 1-800-622-6770)*, designed by Dick Wilson, at the Clarion Atlantik Beach Resort, is rated one of the top-three golf courses in the Caribbean. The signature 18th hole features the Balancing Boulders of Lucaya, a rock garden and waterfall that is worth a look even if you aren't a golfer (you can see it from the Arawak Dining Room, see p 136). Green fees are $70 for 18 holes including cart rental.

Pirates of the Bahamas Beach Theme Park *(Jolly Roger Dr., ☎373-8456)* has the only professional mini-golf course in Grand Bahama.

Scuba Diving and Snorkelling

Grand Bahama offers spectacular diving and snorkelling. The most popular dive is to the wreck of the *Theo*, a 230-foot steel freighter haunted by turtles, horse-eyed jacks and spotted and green moray eels. Ben's Cave is another big draw for experienced divers. Reputed to be the most extensive underwater cave system in the world, the caverns have stalactites and stalagmites. You must get a permit from UNEXSO before entering the caverns. Two Spanish treasures were discovered off Grand Bahama several years ago: the millions of dollars worth of silver coins were recovered but the sunken galleons are still there for divers to explore. Snorkelling is good and tropical fish abundant on Deadman's Reef and Treasure Reef.

Xanadu Undersea Adventures *(☎352-3811 or 1-800-327-8150)* offers an introductory "learn to dive" course for $79. Two single-tank dives cost $55. They also run night dives and a shark dive.

UNEXSO *(Port Lucaya, ☎373-1244 or 1-800-992-DIVE)*, or Underwater Explorers Society, is the premier dive operation on Grand Bahama, and in The Bahamas for that matter. They are mostly known for their shark and dolphin experiences. The **shark dive** is a once in a lifetime kind of thing, where a group of divers descends with three professional divers: two with sticks keep uncooperative sharks in line and another in a chain-mail suit hand feeds these intimidating creatures. Reservations are recommended, the cost is a $40 add-on to whichever regular dive you're chosen. The **Dolphin Encounter** with Atlantic bottlenose dolphins is much tamer, but just as memorable. Non-divers can go for the "Dolphin Close Encounter" and wade in a sheltered lagoon with dolphins for $29, divers can opt for the full-day "Dolphin Assistant Trainer" for $159 or the add-on "Dolphin Dive" for $109 on top of a two-dive package. Of course, UNEXSO also offers a wide range of dive and snorkel packages and instruction. A one-tank dive is $35, a two-tank dive is $65. A three-hour introductory "learn-to-dive" course is $89. Snorkelling trips cost $18, including equipment rental.

Fishing

All types of sport fishing are possible in Grand Bahama's water, from deep-sea fishing in the Gulf stream and the Northwest Providence Channel to bonefishing on the flats to the north and east of the island. A whole slew of charters and fishing trips can be arranged in the island's marinas. Rates run from $35 to $60 for a half-day of deep-sea fishing to $350 to charter a whole boat for a half day.

The Deep Water Cay Club is known for its bonefishing packages (see p 133).

Cruises

The following cruises and a whole slew of other ones can be arranged through your hotel's tour desk.

The ***Mermaid Kitty*** *(Port Lucaya dock, ☎373-5880)* is a giant glass-bottomed boat that offers 90-minute cruises for $18.

The **Deepstar Submarine** *(Sea Horse Plaza, Sea Horse Rd., ☎373-8665)* offers non-divers an even closer look at the deep blue sea. This COMEX submarine is almost entirely windowed and goes down 30 metres. The trip costs $53.

Cafes and colourful parasols line Freeport's International Bazaar where you can buy duty-free goods from around the world along with local crafts. *(A.V.)*

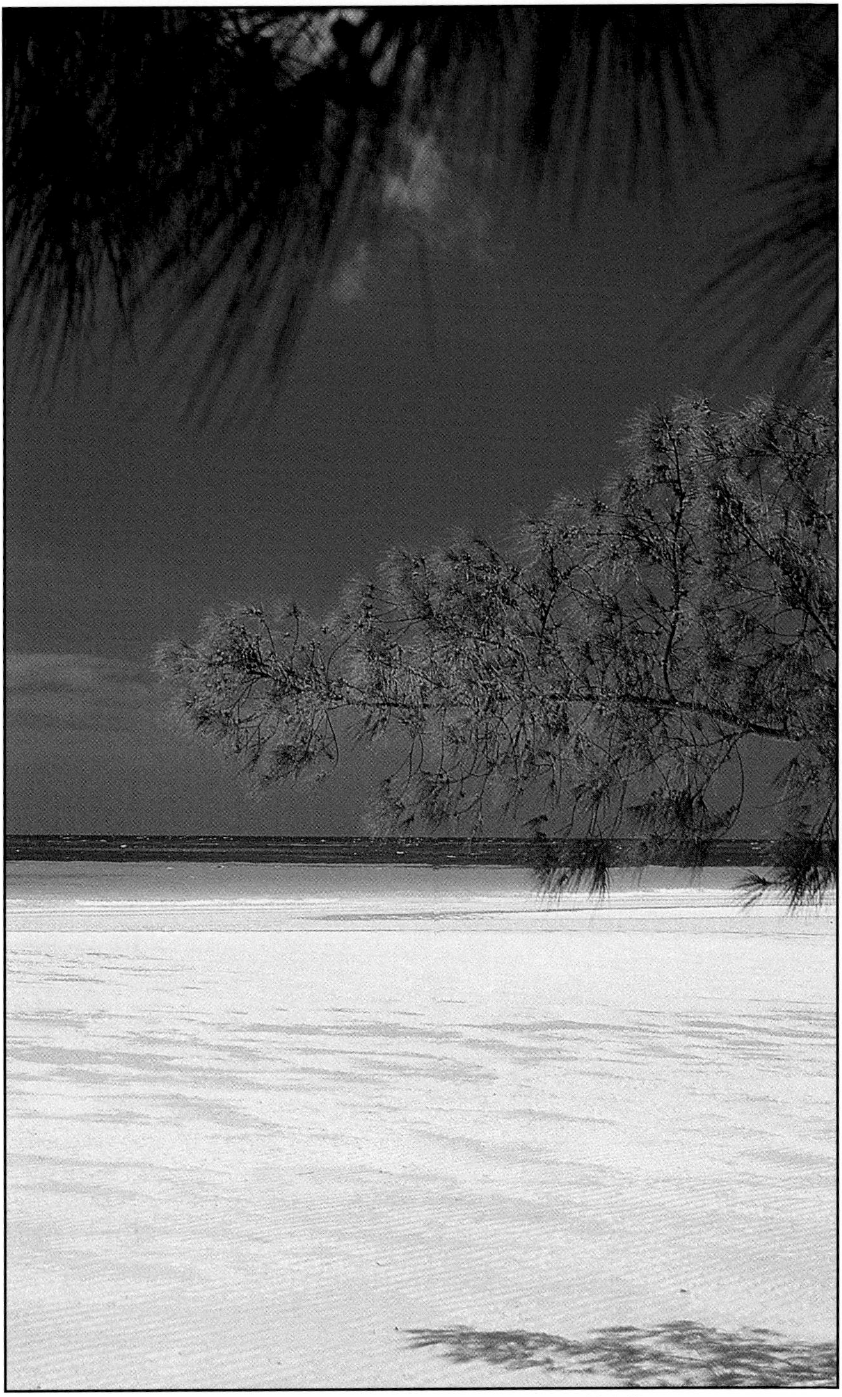

The rippled sand and turquoise waters of idyllic
Gold Rock Beach on Grand Bahama. - *J. M.*

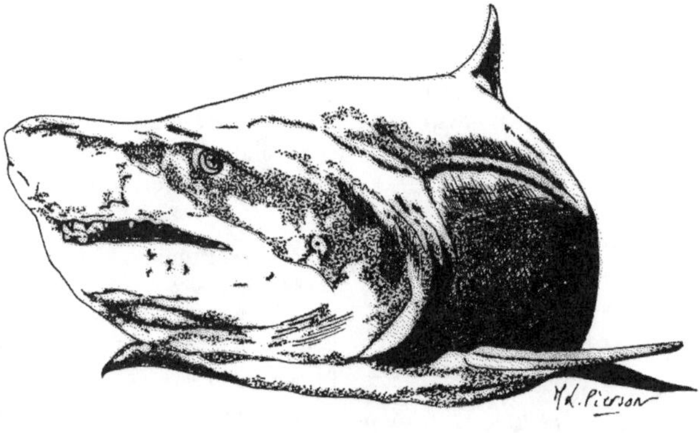

Shark

Paradise Watersports *(☎373-7863)* offers a variety of cruises including "The Bahama Mama Sunset Booze Cruise" with a Bahamian buffet dinner and cocktails under the stars for $25, and "Robinson Crusoe's Beach Party Cruise" with snorkelling and a beach buffet and party for $40.

Kayaking

Kayak Nature Tours *(☎373-2485)* offers two day-long eco-tours. The first, in Lucayan National Park, follows the inland mangrove creeks and features a guided walk, Lucayan caves and a picnic on Gold Rock Beach. Non-kayakers can also do this tour. The other explores the island's north shore and features a picnic on a secluded cay. Cost is $75, or $55 for non-kayakers. Picnic lunch is included.

Horseback Riding

Pinetree Stables *(North Beachway Dr., ☎373-3600)* has trails along the beach and through pine forests. Two-hour rides depart three times a day and cost $35.

Fitness Clubs

Besides hotel gyms at the Bahamas Princess Country Club and the Clarion Atlantic, there is the **YMCA Fitness Centre** *(at intersection of East Atlantic Dr. and Settler's Way, ☎352-7074)* with a weight room and aerobics classes.

Bicycling

Grand Bahama is nice and flat. A bicycle can make getting between downtown Freeport and the casino much easier. You can also bike down to Xanadu Beach or over to Fortune Beach. Simple bikes can be rented from **Honda Cycle Shop** *(☎352-7035)* near the Bahamas Princess Casino for $20 for a full day. The **Lucayan Beach Resort** *(☎373-7777)* rents them for $15 per day.

ACCOMMODATIONS

Freeport

Sun Club Resort *($70; 42 rooms; ☎352-3462, ⇒352-5785 PO Box F-401808, Freeport)* is a decent budget choice that is surprisingly quiet despite its roadside location to the north of downtown Freeport. A free shuttle runs throughout the day to the International Bazaar and Taino Beach. There is a medium-sized pool and a tennis court. Rooms are spacious and perfectly acceptable, some have small kitchenettes.

Castaways Resort *($72; 130 rooms, ≡, ℜ, pb, ≈; near the International Bazaar, ☎352-6682, ⇒352-5087, mailing address: PO Box F-402629, Freeport)* is a reasonable option right next to the Princess Casino and International Bazaar. The rooms have seen better days and are a bit stuffy with a motel-like decor. The rooms overlooking the decent-sized pool are the most attractive. They have a free shuttle to Xanadu Beach.

The Royal Islander *($90; 100 rooms, ≡, pb, ≈; ☎351-6000 or 1-800-899-7797, ⇒351-3545, mailing address: PO Box F-402544, Freeport)* is another motel-like option near the International Bazaar. The decor is fairly standard but nonetheless attractive. Most rooms face the courtyard and pool.

Taino Beach Resort *($95; 68 rooms, ≡, ≈, pb, ℜ, K; 5 Jolly Roger Dr., ☎373-4677, ⇒373-4421, mailing address: PO Box F-43819, Freeport)* has efficiency units that appeal to families and honeymooners alike. Its beachside location at the western end of Taino Beach is another plus. There is a medium-sized pool and a whole array of water sports on offer.

The Running Mon Marina & Resort *($109, low $89; 32 rooms, ≡, ℜ, ⊛, ≈, pb, ℝ; 208 Kelly Ct., Freeport, ☎352-6834, ⇒352-6835, mailing address: PO Box F-402663, Freeport)* is a fairly recent addition to Freeport. Built in 1991, it faces the marina at the south end of The Mall. Rooms are quiet, spacious and have attractive furnishings. There is a dive shop on site and free transportation is offered to Xanadu Beach, the Princess Casino and the Port Lucaya marketplace.

Bahamian Princess Country Club *($120, low $95; 565 rooms, ≡, ≈, K, ⊘; ☎352-6721, ⇒352-6842, mailing address: PO Box F-40207, Freeport)* is part of the same complex as the one below and favoured by families and golfers. It is much more lively than its sister hotel across the street. The complex is spread over a large area; nine wings radiate out from the large pool, the centre of all the action. Rooms are spacious and come in a variety of incarnations, not all of which have kitchenettes. A three-night package here goes for $292.

Xanadu Beach Resort & Marina *($120; 137 rooms, ≡, pb, sat tv, ℜ, ≈; ☎352-6783, ⇒352-5799, mailing address: PO Box F-42438, Freeport, Bahamas)* is the closest beach-side hotel to downtown Freeport. This is the only property on Xanadu Beach and it sits amid the marina overlooking the eponymous beach. Once the favourite

Ulysses' Favourites

Accommodations

Best Value for Your Money:

Sun Club Resort (see p 130), Xanadu Beach Resort & Marina (see p 130), and Silver Sands Hotel (see p 131).

Best Resort for Tennis Buffs:

Bahamas Princess Resort & Casino (see p 131).

Best Resort for Golfers:

Clarion Atlantik Beach & Golf Resort (see p 132).

Best Resort for Families:

Bahamas Princess Resort & Casino (see p 131), Bahamian Princess Country Club (see p 130) and Sun Club Resort (see p 130).

Best Resort for Honeymooners:

Xanadu Beach Resort & Marina (see p 130).

Best Overall Decor:

Lucayan Beach Resort & Casino (see p 132).

haunt of rich big-wigs (eccentric American millionaire Howard Hughes lived out his last two years sealed off from the world on the 12th and 13th floors), the hotel now caters to a more middle-class clientele. The rooms, each with its own balcony, have an attractive decor. There is a dive shop on site.

Bahamas Princess Resort & Casino *($140, low $115; 400 rooms, ≡, pb, ≈, ℜ, sat tv; ☎352-6721 or 1-800-223-1818, ⇛352-2542, mailing address: PO Box F-40207, Freeport)* is the ritziest place to stay in Grand Bahama. From the domed entrance and Moorish tower to the grand lobby, everything about the place seems to be done in excess. There are a large pool with waterfall, tennis courts, the Princess Casino right next door and two golf courses. The rooms are spacious, comfortable and attractive, though not as luxurious and elegant as they are made out to be; suites are quite lavish. There are three-night packages for $336 (high-season) as well as a "Princess Pizzazz" add-on which includes unlimited golf, three meals and more.

Lucaya

Silver Sands Hotel *($95; 144 rooms, ≡, ℜ, K, ≈, pb; Royal Palm Way, ☎373-5700, ⇛373-1039, mailing ad-*

dress: PO Box F-402385, Freeport, Bahamas) offers similar but superior accommodations to the Coral Beach. It caters to families who appreciate its good value. The studio apartments and smaller standard rooms are both modern and spacious with balconies overlooking the pool, marina or gardens. Silver Point Beach is a short walk away and Lucaya Beach is about one kilometre to the east. There are two tennis courts.

Coral Beach Hotel *($98; 10 rooms, ≡, sat tv, K, pb; Royal Palm Way, ☎373-2468, ⇄373-5140, mailing address: PO Box F-402468, Freeport, Bahamas)* began life as a condominium complex. The property is quiet and attractively landscaped, but facilities are limited and in need of refurbishment.

Port Lucaya Resort & Yacht Club *($120; 160 rooms, ≡, pb, sat tv, ≈, ⊛, ℜ; ☎373-6618, ⇄373-6652, Bell Channel Bay Rd., Port Lucaya, mailing address: PO Box F-422452, Freeport)* is a marina-side collection of pastel-coloured, two-story units around an Olympic-sized pool. The decor features the classic but attractive cool-tile floors and wicker furniture. The popular Port Lucaya Marketplace is just next door, which can make some rooms a bit noisy, try to get one on the other side of the complex if you prefer some peace and quiet.

Grand Bahama Beach Hotel *($130; 500 rooms, ≡, sat tv, pb, ℜ, ≈; Port Lucaya, ☎373-1333 or 1-800-622-6770, ⇄373-8662, mailing address: PO Box F-402496, Freeport)* just received a major overhaul that in the next five years will make one big resort called the Grand Lucaya Resort & Casino out of this, the Lucayan Beach Resort & Casino and the Clarion Atlantik Beach Hotel. The whole place will be refurbished and a new luxury hotel will go up between this hotel and the Clarion. The rooms are attractive, this place will only get better as the upgrade continues, be sure to check on its progress before reserving.

Clarion Atlantik Beach & Golf Resort *($140, bkfst incl.; 175 rooms, ≡, pb, sat tv, ℜ, ≈, ⊘, ⊛; Port Lucaya, ☎373-1444 or 1-800-848-3315 in Canada or 1-800-622-6770 in the US, ⇄373-7481, mailing address: PO Box F-402500, Freeport, Bahamas)* just got a major facelift. It faces Lucaya Beach, a big plus on Grand Bahama, and boasts one of the best golf courses on the island complete with its own fantastical rock garden called the Balancing Boulders of Lucaya. Rooms overlook either the beach or the yacht harbour and are pleasantly appointed. There are standard rooms, suites (with kitchenettes) and apartments. The pool is Olympic-sized. Golf packages available.

Pelican Bay at Lucaya *($150; 48 rooms, ≡, ≈, ⊛, sat tv, pb, K; Port Lucaya, mailing address: PO Box F-42654, Freeport, ☎373-9550, ⇄373-9551)* is a brand-new boutique-hotel whose rooms boast attractive and luxurious extras like private trellised balconies with their own hot-tubs. Rooms are set in smaller outbuildings and each is elegantly decorated and near the water.

Lucayan Beach Resort & Casino *($155 to $200, MAP$35; 243 rooms, pb, ≡, sat tv, ℜ, ≈; Lucaya, ☎373-7777 or 1-800-772-1227, ⇄373-6916, mailing address: PO Box F-40336, Freeport)* recently received a $1.4 million facelift making it one one of the shnazziest places to stay on Grand Bahama. The signature candy-striped lighthouse is still the centrepiece, though now a beautiful marble floor anchors the lobby. Rooms have been completely refurbished and now sport an elegant decor of white-washed oak furniture and marble bathrooms. In-room safes have also been added. There are garden-view and ocean-view rooms with sliding-glass doors and private balconies. This place offers both a fine white-sand beach and a refurbished 20,000-square-foot casino. There are also tennis courts and a large beach-side pool.

Eastern Grand Bahama

Club Fortuna Beach *($250-$290; 204 rooms; ⊘, ≡, pb, ≈, ℜ; Fortune Beach, ☎373-4000 or 1-800-742-4276, ⇒373-5555, mailing address: PO Box F-402398, Freeport)* is a secluded, all-inclusive, Italian-owned resort complex on Fortune Beach east of Freeport and Lucaya. It caters to a European clientele, some of whom sunbathe topless on the palapa-dotted beach and who probably appreciate its Club-Med-like ambiance. Rooms are uninspired and set in two-story buildings along the beach, with the majority of them facing the sand. Guests may tire of the food, which does not get rave reviews. Activities include windsurfing, kayaking, snorkelling and tennis.

Deep Water Cay Club *($950 for 3 nights, all-incl.; 9 rooms; ≈, ℜ, ℝ, pb, ≡; Deep Water Cay, mailing address: 1100 Lee Wagener Blvd., Suite 352, Fort Lauderdale, FL 33315, ☎353-3073 or 954-359-0488, ⇒954-359-9488)* is an attractive and little-known spot at the far eastern edge of Grand Bahama Island. Many guests come for the bonefishing, and the club offers attractive packages. The accommodations are in timber-framed cottages. The clubhouse, where meals are taken at one seating, is like an attractive mountain lodge. There is a small saltwater pool. Three-night minimum.

Western Grand Bahama

Castaways Estate & Beach Resort *($75; ≡, pb, K, ℜ; Paradise Cove, mailing address: PO Box F-42629, Freeport)* has a handful of efficiency apartments and cottages. For now there is a simple snack-bar, but a full restaurant and lounge are planned. The rooms are appealing and spacious. The two-bedroom apartments can sleep six people. This place makes a nice change of pace from the casinos and shop of Freeport/Lucaya. Deadman's Reef just offshore is great for snorkelling.

RESTAURANTS

Freeport

Les Fountains *($-$$; East Sunrise Hwy., ☎373-9553)* is a 24-hour eatery that is especially appreciated by visitors and locals for its grand breakfast buffet. Fresh fruit, bacon, eggs, pancakes and sausages should give you that morning jump start you're seeking.

Geneva's Place *($-$$; East Mall Dr. at Kipling Lane, ☎352-5085)* has good Bahamian dishes many of them featuring conch in its many incarnations from cracked (tenderized and deep fried) to conch chowder (a hearty and spicy soup), conch fritters (conch and vegetables in deep-fried dumplings) and stewed conch. Steamed grouper is another good choice. End you meal with the sticky-sweet guava duff.

The restaurant offerings at the Grand Bahama Princess Resort, Casino and Country Club are extensive. The **Lemon**

Peel *($-$$; Tower)* and **The Patio** *($-$$; Country Club)* serve three meals a day, but are busiest at breakfast when they have a big buffet with fresh fruits, muffins as well as pancakes and the like on the menu. See below for the more refined dining options at these locations.

The **Pepper Pot** *($-$$; East Sunrise Hwy. at Coral Rd., ☎373-7655)* is a popular take-away with some vegetarian dishes along with pork chops, ribs and the traditional favourites of Bahamian cuisine. You can get good sandwiches here for lunch and delicious fresh-baked carrot cake.

The **Sir Winston Churchill Pub** *($-$$; beside the straw market; ☎352-8866)* has a few typical pub offerings, and a lot of pizza along with sandwiches. A good quick lunch spot.

Three restaurants share one roof on Ranfurley Circle across from the International Bazaar. Real meat-and-potatoes pub favourites like shepherd's pie and fish and chips are available at **The Prince of Wales Lounge** *($-$$; Ranfurley Circle, ☎352-5110)*. The **Islander's Roost** *($$; Ranfurley Circle, ☎352-5110)* serves up island-seasoned beef, chicken and fish dishes. The decor is an attractive rendition of the British West Indies. **Silvano's** *($$; Ranfurley Circle, ☎352-5110)* has an equally appealing, elegant Italian decor and great home-made pasta dishes. The veal parmesan is well done.

Cafe Michel's *($-$$$; International Bazaar, ☎352-2191)* tries to recreate a Parisian sidewalk bistro and does a passable job at it at least with the decor. The only thing French about the food is the coffee and even that is pushing it. Nevertheless, the American and Bahamian menu offerings, from salads and sandwiches at lunch to steaks and seafood platters for dinner, are tasty and the terrace is pleasant. Decent big breakfasts are available here.

The **Plaka** *($$; International Bazaar, ☎352-5932)* cooks up savoury and spicy Greek favourites like moussaka and souvlaki. Good for lunch or dinner.

Guanahani's *($$-$$$; Princess Country Club, ☎352-6721)* is known for its barbecued offerings. Chicken, beef and fish get their's over the coals with tasty results. The hickory-smoked ribs and lobster are recommended, as is just about everything else on the large menu. The restaurant overlooks the pool and has an elegant, but staid decor.

The **Japanese Steak House** *($$-$$$; International Bazaar, ☎352-9521)* also does a better job with the decor than the food. Waitresses wear kimonos and the small tables at the rear are neat. However, the kobe steak and shrimp teryaki are quite flavourful and make a nice change from grouper and peas 'n' rice.

Morgan's Bluff *($$-$$$; Princess Tower, ☎352-9661)* is a casual seafood restaurant with an amusing pirate decor that children get a kick out of. The cracked conch is good here, very tender and with lots of deep-fried crispy bits. The lobster and clams are a bit more sophisticated and well prepared.

Ruby Swiss *($$-$$$; beside Bahamas Princess Tower, ☎352-8507)* serves steaks and seafood in an attractive dining room complete with an antique Victorian bar. The grouper filet with herbed butter is recommended as is the blackened red fish. Delicious fresh-baked buns are served with meals. The lunch menu has similar tasty offerings, plus a few big sandwiches and salads, at much more reasonable prices. The

Ulysses' Favourites

Restaurants

Best True-true Bahamian Cooking:

Geneva's Place (see p 133), Fatman's Nephew (see p 136), Buccaneer Club (see p 136) and Star Club (see p 136).

Finest Dining:

Ruby Swiss (see p 134), The Crown Room (see p 135), Luciano's (see p 136), Arawak Dining Room (see p 136), Stoned Crab (see p 136) and Pier One (see p 137).

Funkiest Ambiance:

The Brass Helmet (see p 135) and Buccaneer Club (see p 136).

dessert specialty is the Viennese strudel. There is live music with dinner; reservations are recommended.

La Trattoria *($$-$$$; at the Princess Tower, ☎352-9661)* has an attractive Italian decor and good fresh pastas and pizzas. You can combine any sauce and pasta you like. The Alfredo and simple tomato sauces are both delicious. Garlic bread is complimentary. For dessert, try the apple pie pizza topped with ice cream. These are made upon order so take time, but are worth the wait.

The **Rib Room** *($$$; Princess Country Club, ☎352-6721)*, like Guanahani's above, is known for its meats. In this case huge prime steaks and roast beef. The decor is a cross between an English pub and hunting lodge. There are also a few good seafood offerings.

The **Crown Room** *($$$-$$$$; Princess Casino, ☎352-6721)* is right near the slots and tables of the casino. It has an art-deco cruise-ship decor and jazz background music. The continental cuisine is fairly authentic and successful, and pricey too! Rack of lamb, veal and lobster are among the menu offerings.

Lucaya

The **Brass Helmet** *($; Port Lucaya Marketplace, ☎373-2032)* is a funky spot upstairs from UNEXSO. The namesake diving gear adorns the place along with a big shark head. The Bahamian fare and seafood is tasty and very reasonably priced.

Zorba's *($-$$; Port Lucaya Marketplace, ☎373-5192)* does a fine job with souvlaki, moussaka and Greek salads with plump black olives and goat's cheese. The prices are very reasonable, servings generous and ambiance pleasant.

Pisces Restaurant *($$; Port Lucaya Marketplace, ☎373-5192)* has a lengthy and reasonably priced menu with everything from pizza, to burgers, conch, grouper, curries and steaks.

Scorpio's *($$; Port Lucaya Marketplace ☎373-8503)* serves a full menu of Bahamian specialties with conch, lobster and grouper, as well as good grilled steak and chicken. There is another location in downtown Freeport.

Fatman's Nephew *($$-$$$; Port Lucaya Marketplace, ☎373-8520)* is an authentic Bahamian eatery that recently moved to the marketplace and has since taken off. Tables overlook the marina, or you can eat inside. Bahamian favourites figure prominently on the menu, but invariably the fresh catch of the day turns out to be the most popular choice.

Luciano's *($$-$$$; Port Lucaya Marketplace, ☎373-9100)*, the fanciest place in the market, has a contemporary pink and grey decor highlighted by trendy halogen spotlights. The menu is heavy with seafood suggestions with Italian and French flavourings, but the veal Luciano is the restaurant's signature dish.

The **Arawak Dining Room** *($$$; Lucayan Golf & Country Club; ☎373-1066)* is an elegant hotel- restaurant serving continental and Bahamian fare. One of the highlights of a meal here is certainly the caesar salads and creme brulee prepared right before your eyes. The ambiance is best in the evening when the fantastical Balancing Boulders of Lucaya out on the golf course are lit up with multicoloured spotlights. The Sunday brunch is a fine spread.

Brittania Pub *($$$; Bell Channel, Lucaya, ☎373-5919)* draws patrons from the surrounding hotels and residential areas with its pub-like atmosphere and its Greek, yes Greek, food. Of course the Bahamian conch, grouper and lobster creations are available too.

East of Freeport/Lucaya

Taino Beach has a handful of snack bars and lively restaurants. The most popular is **Kaptain Kenny's** *($-$$; Taino Beach, ☎373-8689)*, a big wooden beach-side place with a breezy patio and long bar. The decor is a combination of driftwood, sea glass and sea charts of the islands. Good burgers, made to order, are available as well as typical Bahamian finger food like grouper fingers and conch fritters. There is another Kaptain Kenny's in Freeport, but this one beats it hands down. The beach parties and bonfires are lots of fun.

The **Stoned Crab** *($$-$$$; Taino Beach, ☎373-1442)* is a more elegant option on Taino Beach and is very quiet at midday but come evening draws out wealthy ex-pats and yachties. Place of honour on the menu is given to the many crab dishes. Snow crab claws and crab and avocado cocktail are two tasty offerings. Other fish and seafood dishes are also well prepared, along with a few meat and chicken dishes. The house cocktail is the appropriately named "Stoned Crab".

Western Grand Bahama

Star Club *($$; West End, ☎346-6207)* epitomizes the rising and falling fortunes of West End. This was the first hotel on Grand Bahama and put up its share of famous visitors back in the 1940s. There aren't any rooms for rent here now, just memories and simple Bahamian fare. Come for the stories not the food.

The **Buccaneer Club** *($$$; closed Mon, Holmes Rock, ☎349-3794)* is in a timber building surrounded by a stone wall with a beer-garden feel complemented by copper doors with brass portholes, palm trees, crystal chandeliers, pine trim and polished driftwood. They open at 5pm, when Bahamian classics sidle up to German favourites like wiener schnitzel. Shrimp, lobster and rack of lamb round out the menu offerings. Reservations recommended. The twice weekly beach parties are a great way to see this one-of-a-kind place.

Pier One *($$$; Freeport Harbour, ☎352-6674)* has a great location in a timber building on stilts on a point of land near the cruise-ship dock. Waves crash below as these huge vessels steam in and out of the port. And for those who were too chicken to do the shark dive, the restaurant is also an easy alternative: every night at 6:30pm and 8:30pm the staff dumps a bucket of chum down to the sharks circling down below and the seagulls circling overhead. The last and final reason to come here is for the exceptional seafood. Delicious pan-fried grouper or lemon pan-fried shark are tasty selections. A fresh catch-of-the-day is always featured. Lunch fare is salads, clam chowder and the like. The classic Bahamian cocktails are all on offer.

ENTERTAINMENT

Casinos

The **Princess Casino** *(free admission; every day 9am to 4am; ☎352-7811)* has a curious Moorish decor and lots of flashing lights. There are over 400 slot machines, plus blackjack tables, roulette wheels, baccarat, craps and Caribbean stud poker. No bathing suites or bare feet are permitted.

The **Lucayan Beach Casino** *(free admission; every day 9am to 3am, ☎352-7811)* was the first casino of Grand Bahama. It has just been updated with brand new slot machines. Gamblers can still try their luck at blackjack, roulette, baccarat and craps as well as the newly added Caribbean stud poker.

Theatres and Cabarets

The **Regency Theatre** *(☎352-5533)* west of the Bahamas Princess Resort, stages theatre productions by the Freeport Players' Guild between September and June, and the Grand Bahama Players *(☎373-2299)*. Other theatrical shows are put on by Freeport Friends of the Arts *(☎373-1528)*.

The Princess Casino's Las Vegas-style "**Nightlife**" *($25; Tue to Sun 8:30pm and 10:45pm)* show has dancing girls, some of them briefly topless, and lots of feathers and bright colours.

Many hotels and restaurants have "native" shows, complete with limbo dancing and fire-eating. Reservations are recommended, some of these include dinner. One of the best is at the **Yellow Bird Show Club** *($20 incl. 2 drinks; Mon to Sat 9pm; International Bazaar, ☎373-7368)*. Other similar shows happen at the **Bahamas Princess Country Club** *(Wed, Fri and Sat 6:30pm and 7:30pm, ☎352-7811)*, at the **Bahama Princess Tower** *(Sun to Fri 9pm, ☎352-6721)* and at the **Lucayan Beach Resort** *($29 incl. 2 drinks, $30 incl. buffet dinner; Wed and Sat 8pm and 10pm, ☎373-7777)*. **Joker's Wild Supper & Show Club** *(Midshiipman Rd., Lucaya, ☎373-7765)* combines native dancing and limbo with comedy.

Annual Events

January
Junkanoo Parade starts at 5am in downtown Freeport.
Noisy revelry and colourful costumes mark this must-see event.

March
Freeport Rugby Club Annual Easter Rugby Festival

October
Annual Grand Bahama Triathlon
Columbus Day Conch Cracking Contest, McLean's Town

November
Annual Grand Bahama Conchman Triathlon

Bars and Nightclubs

Kaptain Kenny's at Taino Beach *(☎373-8689)* and in the International Bazaar *(☎351-4759)* are popular drinking holes with the younger student crowd. The bazaar location has drinking contests, and beach parties are the thing at Taino Beach.

The twice-weekly beach parties at the **Buccaneer Club** *($45; Holmes Rock, ☎349-3794)* are among the best of their kind on the island. The German beer-hall is a scream.

The **Bavarian Beer Garden** *(International Bazaar, ☎352-5050)* has at least a dozen imported beers on offer and piped-in oom-pah-pah music; the beer-hall ambiance isn't as much of a success as at the Buccaneer.

SHOPPING

Freeport

Duty-free is the key word here. The **International Bazaar** offers all sorts of imported items, along with reams of T-shirts and souvenirs. For fine jewellery, **Colombian Emeralds International** *(☎352-5464)* is an elegant shop with emerald pieces and other precious stones. Good selection of watches. **John Bull** *(☎352-7515)* has all sorts of big-ticket items like jewellery, watches, gloves, leather goods and cameras. **Fendi** *(☎352-7908)* and **Gucci** *(☎352-4580)* sell their trademark leather goods and Italian fashions. Bahamian fragrances are available at **The Perfume Factory** *(☎352-9391)*, while **Les Parisiennes** *(☎352-5380)* stocks the classics of French perfume. **Far East Traders** *(☎352-9280)* has Oriental hand-embroidered silks and linens. **Bahamas Coin and Stamp** *(☎352-8989)* sells old Bahamian and Spanish coins, they've also got some beautiful postcards and maps of the Bahamas.

Freeport's **Straw Market** is located beside the International Bazaar. There are stalls and kiosks behind the market as well. Handmade baskets, hats and bags can be procured here. Avoid the cheaper made-in-Asia knock-offs. And you can have your hair braided with multicoloured beads too. Braids are generally $2 each, six for $10 and nine for $15.

LMR Drugs *(☎352-7327)* is a well-stocked pharmacy in the Mini Mall, also downtown.

Ernie's Studio *(behind the Winn Dixie Mall, ☎352-8818)* will take care of all your photographic needs.

The **Freeport Book Centre** *(14 West Mall Dr., ☎352-3759)* has the best selection of books on Bahamian culture and history. The latest paperbacks are here too.

Lucaya

The **Port Lucaya Marketplace** has close to 100 stores. **Coconits by Androsia** *(☎373-8387)* sells the signature Androsia batik resort wear from the island of Andros. These cotton and rayon dresses, shirts, shorts and bathing suits make great souvenirs. The **UNEXSO Dive Shop** *(☎373-1244)* rents and sells a huge array of diving gear, just in case you forgot anything. **The Nautique Shoppe** *(☎373-1522)* sells attractive and quality resort-wear and some lovely art. The **Jeweler's Warehouse** *(☎373-8400)* is a diamond-loving bargain-hunter's dream. You can pay up to 50% less than in North America or Europe for good quality gems complete with appraisal certificates.

Lucaya's **Straw Market** is near the water at the northwestern corner of the market. You can peruse and bargain for these handmade baskets, bags and hats. Cheaper, Asian-made items are sold here alongside the hand-made goods; be sure you check that its actually made in The Bahamas before buying.

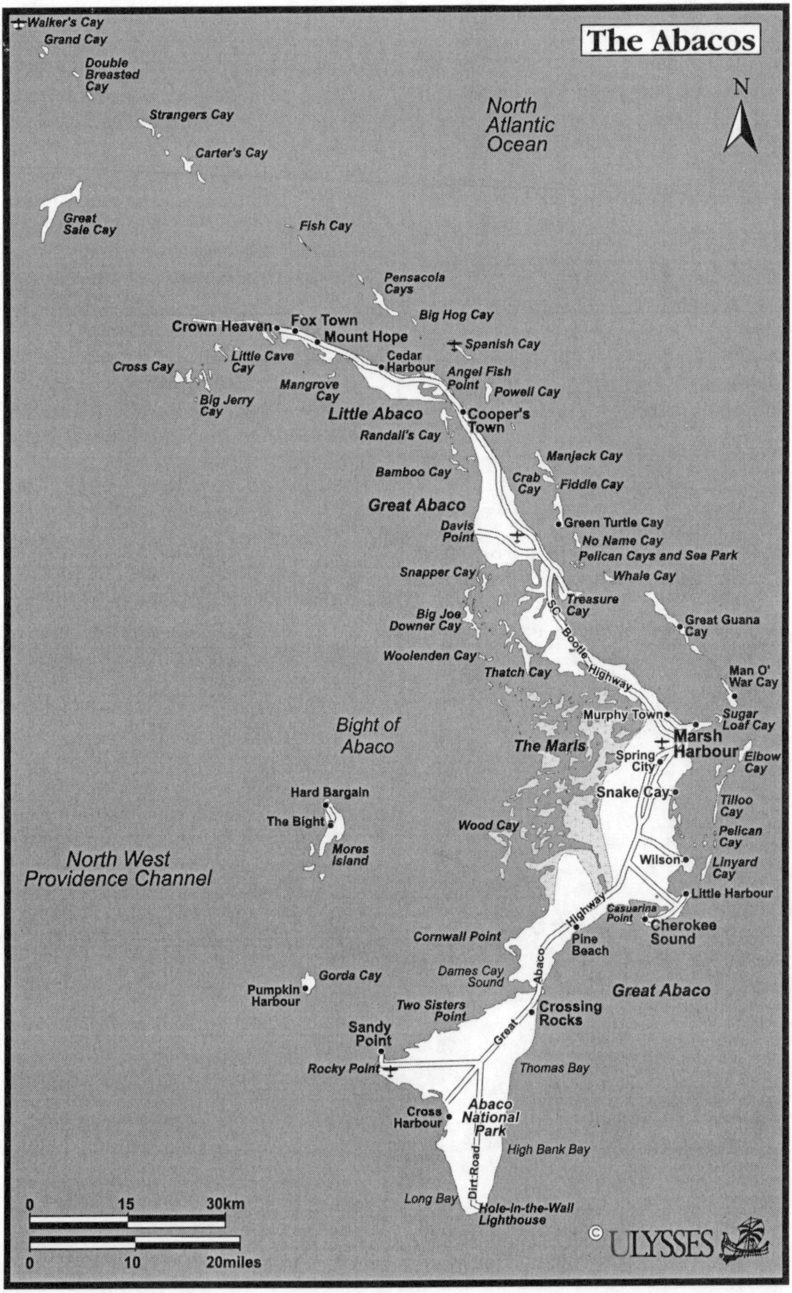
The Abacos
N
North Atlantic Ocean
Walker's Cay
Grand Cay
Double Breasted Cay
Strangers Cay
Carter's Cay
Great Sale Cay
Fish Cay
Pensacola Cays
Big Hog Cay
Crown Heaven
Fox Town
Mount Hope
Spanish Cay
Cross Cay
Little Cave Cay
Cedar Harbour
Angel Fish Point
Mangrove Cay
Powell Cay
Big Jerry Cay
Little Abaco
Cooper's Town
Randall's Cay
Manjack Cay
Bamboo Cay
Crab Cay
Fiddle Cay
Great Abaco
Green Turtle Cay
Davis Point
No Name Cay
Pelican Cays and Sea Park
Snapper Cay
Whale Cay
Treasure Cay
Big Joe Downer Cay
Great Guana Cay
S.C. Bootle Highway
Woolenden Cay
Thatch Cay
Man O' War Cay
Murphy Town
Sugar Loaf Cay
Bight of Abaco
The Marls
Marsh Harbour
Spring City
Elbow Cay
Snake Cay
Tilloo Cay
Hard Bargain
The Bight
Wood Cay
Pelican Cay
Mores Island
Wilson
Linyard Cay
North West Providence Channel
Little Harbour
Casuarina Point
Cherokee Sound
Great Abaco Highway
Cornwall Point
Pine Beach
Dames Cay Sound
Gorda Cay
Pumpkin Harbour
Great Abaco
Two Sisters Point
Crossing Rocks
Sandy Point
Rocky Point
Thomas Bay
Cross Harbour
Abaco National Park
High Bank Bay
Dirt Road
Long Bay
Hole-in-the-Wall Lighthouse
0 15 30km
0 10 20miles
© ULYSSES

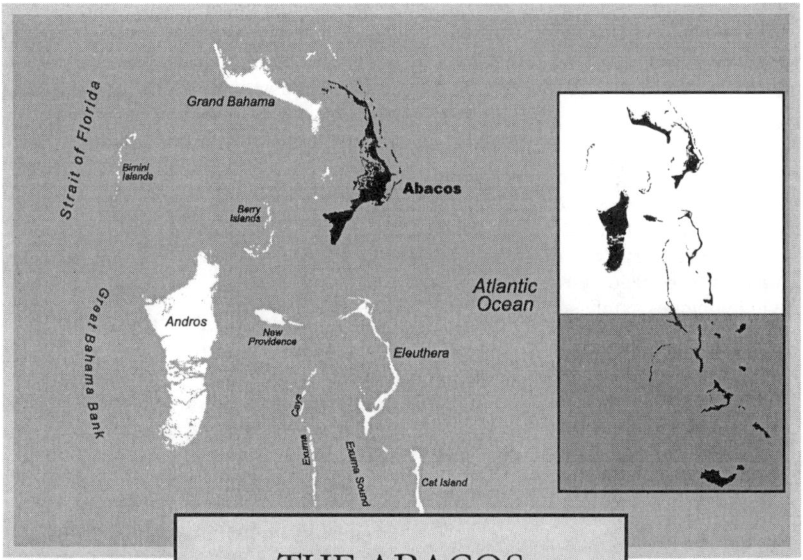

THE ABACOS

There are actually only two Abacos ★★★: Great Abaco, the second largest island in The Bahamas and referred to as the mainland by Abaconians, and Little Abaco, dangling off Great Abaco's northern end. Together they form a 200-kilometre-long boomerang - the rest of the Abacos trail along the east coast between the multi-hued Sea of Abaco and the deep-blue Atlantic Ocean. These cays have names of their own, including Walker's Cay, Spanish Cay, Green Turtle Cay, No Name Cay, Treasure Cay, Great Guana Cay, Man O' War Cay, Elbow Cay, Tilloo Cay and Pelican Cays.

The "top of the Bahamas," as they are known, has gotten a lot of mileage out of also calling itself the "sailing capital of the World" and it is true that nowhere else do yachties island-hop as well as in the Abacos. It is hard to imagine something better than sailing protected turquoise waters and weighing anchor off quaint Loyalist cays. In fact, it does get better with endless choices for divers and fishers, and four national parks to keep nature enthusiasts happy. Escapists remember: Marsh Harbour is a service centre and Treasure Cay is a big resort... the Abacos' real treasures are out in the Sea of Abaco and in the remote corners of the mainland.

The Abacos start 170 kilometres north of Nassau, and continue for 200 kilometres to the tip of Little Abaco. A handful of Abaco's cays dot the sea still farther north, ending with Walker's Cay, which is about 60 kilometres from the tip of Little Abaco. The other cays are within a few kilometres of the mainland, which is mostly forested with pine and low brush. The centre of the west coast is known as the Marls, a tangle of mangrove creeks and swamps giving way to the Bight of Acklins, where bonefishing is awesome.

A Short History

The Lucayans called these islands Habacoa. Once the Spanish had shipped all the Lucayans off the islands, they left them alone, save for Ponce de Leon who passed through on his search for the Fountain of Youth. And nothing remains of the failed French settlement of Lucayonique, established in 1625.

More than a century and a half later, in 1783, Loyalists fleeing the newly independent United States arrived with their slaves and repopulated the islands. The first settled at at Carleton, named for Sir Guy Carleton, commander-in-chief of British forces in the US, while others went to Cherokee Sound. Farming was difficult; the majority of those that stayed eventually made their way to the outlying cays. An estimated 2,000 Loyalists came. They joined or were later joined by a scattering of Old Inhabitants, who drifted here from Harbour Island and taught the Loyalists how to farm the difficult lands. By 1788, the population stood at 196 whites and 198 slaves. Despite this, an isolated island life kept their traditions alive. Even their names were preserved: you'll notice the Lowes and Sawyers on Green Turtle Cay, the Alburys on Man O' War Cay and the Bethels and Malones on Elbow Cay; Russels, Currys and Roberts are also numerous. Some farmed the mainland, as the Harbour Islanders did, but most Loyalists became wreckers who came to the aid of ships damaged by treacherous offshore reefs, and then legally claimed any goods they could salvage. Wrecking was so profitable, however, that some wreckers led ships off course with dummy lights and even went so far as to sabotage the lighthouses that threatened their livelihood – the first light only went up in 1836.

Boatbuilding was a more sound business, and Elbow Cay and Man O' War Cay became and remain the undisputed boatbuilding capitals of The Bahamas. Green Turtle, for its part, became the largest and wealthiest settlement, with many inhabitants also farming the mainland, as Harbour Islanders did on Eleuthera. Green Turtle's distinctive cottages became so popular, that prefab models were exported to the United States. By the start of the 20th century, steam ships, hurricanes and the demise of the sponging industry spelled trouble for Abaco's boatbuilders.

The Americans moved in then, creating the Bahamas Timber Company and gaining a license to the Caribbean pine forests of Abaco, Andros and Grand Bahama. The company operated under various different names until 1943, by which time the population had doubled, logging roads crisscrossed the island and Marsh Harbour had become something of a frontier boomtown. In 1956, another American company, Owens-Illinois, arrived and made its fortune with pulpwood. They had ambitious plans for Abaco. They tried, but could not turn a profit with citrus and other fruits and vegetables. Then someone suggested sugar cane. They set about pulverizing the rock, tilling the soil and importing piles of fertilizer. The Bahamas had never seen anything like it. Only two sugar crops were harvested, however, and the third was abandoned. Owens-Illinois left in the 1970s.

The descendants of Abacos' Loyalists remained loyal right up until the end. In 1972, a group actually considered revolution when their petition to the Queen to separate from the rest of The Bahamas and remain a British crown colony was denied. An allegiance to the Queen is not the only holdover from their Loyalist past. Residents of Green Turtle Cay, Great Guana Cay,

Man O' War Cay and Elbow Cay, the four Loyalist Cays, have a special way of speaking. There is some cockney in there, along with a slightly garbled Elizabethan lilt. Also, a history of intermarriage has created a population whose members all bear a striking resemblance to each other: everywhere you look, tanned freckled-faces, blond hair and blue eyes stare back at you. For all these similarities, however, the cays are each very distinct, right down to their religious affiliations.

FINDING YOUR WAY AROUND

By Plane

There are three airports in The Abacos: Marsh Harbour, Treasure Cay and Walker's Cay. There are also airstrips at Sandy Point and one on Spanish Cay. Marsh Harbour, Treasure Cay, Walker's Cay and Green Turtle Cay are official points of entry. You must clear customs here first if arriving internationally.

The **Marsh Harbour Airport** is the biggest airport in the Abacos. It is located about three-and-a-half kilometres from town. **Bahamasair** has *(☎1-800-222-4262 or 327-5505 in Nassau)* daily flights from Nassau as well as several flights a week from West Palm Beach and Miami. **American Eagle** *(☎367-2231 in Marsh Harbour)* has daily flights from Miami. **Gulfstream International** *(☎367-3415 in Marsh Harbour)* flies from points in Florida, Georgia and Alabama. **US Airways Express** *(☎367-2231 in Marsh Harbour)* flies from Orlando and West Palm Beach. **Island Express** *(☎367-3597)* has flights from Fort Lauderdale, West Palm Beach and Miami.

The **Treasure Cay Airport** is about 25 kilometres north of the resort. The above airlines all serve the airport, some with direct flights, otherwise they touch down here after dropping off passengers in Marsh Harbour.

The airstrip on **Walker's Cay** is served by Pan Am Air Bridge *(☎347-3024 or 1-800-424-2557)* from Fort Lauderdale. Please note: no carry-on luggage is allowed.

By Boat

By Mailboat: All departures are from Potter's Cay (under the Paradise Island Bridge) in Nassau and all fares are one way. The *Mia Dean* departs Tuesdays at 8pm for Marsh Harbour, Hope Town (Elbow Cay), Treasure Cay and Green Turtle Cay. Travel time: 12 hours. Fare: $45. The *Champion II* departs Tuesdays at 8pm for Sandy Point and Bullock Harbour. Travel time: 11 hours. Fare: $25.

Marinas

The Abacos being the "sailing capital of the world" there are several full-service marinas. Here are a few of the major ones:

In Marsh Harbour: **Boat Harbour Marina** at the Abaco Beach Resort *(☎367-2736 or 1-800-468-4799, ⇄367-2819)*; **Conch Inn Marina** *(☎367-4000, ⇄367-4004)*, **Mangoes Marina** *(☎367-4255, ⇄367-3336)* and the **Marsh Harbour Marina** *(☎367-2700)*.

At Treasure Cay: **Treasure Cay Marina** *(☎365-8250 or 1-800-327-1584, ⇄365-8362)*.

On Green Turtle Cay: **Black Sound Marina** *(☎365-4221, ⇄365-4046)*;

Green Turtle Club *(☎365-4271, ≠365-4272)*; **Other Shore Club and Marina** *(☎365-4195)*.

On Man O' War Cay: **Man O' War Marina** *(☎365-6008)*.

On Elbow Cay: **Lighthouse Marina** *(☎366-0154, ≠366-0171)*; **Hope Town Hideaways** *(☎366-0224, ≠366-0434)*; **Sea Spray Marina** *(☎366-0065)*.

Ferries

Ferries and water taxis link the string of cays and Great Abaco.

Albury's Ferry Service *(☎367-3147)* makes the runs from Marsh Harbour to Man O' War Cay, Hope Town (Elbow Cay) and Great Guana Cay. The fare is $8 one way or $12 for a round trip. You can also arrange special charters to Hope Town, Great Guana Cay and Green Turtle Cay. The Marsh Harbour ferry dock is at the east end of Bay Street; it has a snack bar and waiting room. The schedule is as follows:

Man O' War Cay to Marsh Harbour: every day 8am and 1:30pm; Marsh Harbour to Man O' War Cay: every day 10:30am and 4pm.

Hope Town to Marsh Harbour: every day 8am, 11:30am, 1:30pm and 4pm; Marsh Harbour to Hope Town: every day 10:30am, 12:15pm and 4pm.

Great Guana Cay to Marsh Harbour: Mon to Fri 8:15am; Marsh Harbour to Great Guana Cay: Mon to Fri 3:30pm.

Abaco Island Transport (AIT) *(☎365-6010)* departs from Marsh Harbour for Great Guana Cay every day at 9am, noon, 4pm and 6pm, with an extra run on Wednesdays at 11am. The return trip is one hour later. The ferry departs from Conch Inn Marina, the fare is $6 one way. AIT also operates a ferry to Green Turtle Cay. Ferries depart Green Turtle Cay every day at 1:30pm and 3pm for the Green Turtle Ferry Dock, located three kilometres south of Treasure Cay Airport. They make the return trip to Green Turtle Cay at 2:30pm and 4pm. Fare is $8 one way.

Boat Rentals

With so many islands to explore, it can be practical and lots of fun to rent your own motorboat to toot around in (see p 158 for sailboat charters). Rates run between $65 to $90 per day for 5- to 6-metre launches. Try the following places: **Sea Horse Rentals** *(☎367-2513, Marsh Harbour)*, **Rich's Boat Rentals** *(☎367-2742, Marsh Harbou)*, **C&C Boat Rentals** *(☎365-8582, Treasure Cay)*, **Dave's Dive Shop & Boat Rentals** *(☎366-0029, Hope Town)* and **Dames Boat Rental** *(☎365-4205, Green Turtle Cay)*.

By Taxi

Taxis meet incoming flights at Marsh Harbour and Treasure Cay airports. In many cases you'll also have to take a water taxi to get to your final destination. They charge on average $1.50 per mile (about $2.50 per kilometre). Here are some sample fares:

Marsh Harbour Airport to town: $10
Marsh Harbour Airport to ferry dock: $12
Marsh Harbour hotels to ferry dock: $4
Treasure Cay Airport to Treasure Cay Resort: $7
Treasure Cay Airport to government dock in Cooper's Town (free ferry to Spanish Cay): $30
Treasure Cay Airport to Little Abaco: $60 Water taxi from Treasure Cay Airport to Green Turtle Cay: $6

By Car, Scooter and Golf Cart

You'll only need to rent a car for exploring Great and Little Abaco, the length of which are traversed by the Great Abaco Highway, south of Marsh Harbour and the SC Bootle Highway to the north. There are **gas stations** in Marsh Harbour, just south of the Treasure cay Airport and in Cooper's Town. Scooters, golf carts and even bicycles will suffice for exploring the cays. Many establishments rent all of the above. Rates are about $70 per day for a mid-size car, $35 per day for a scooter, $10 per day for a bicycle ($35 per week), $35 per day for a golf cart.

In Marsh Harbour, try the following establishments: **H&L Rentals** *(☎367-2840 or 367-2854)*, **A&A Rentals** *(☎367-2148)* and **Reliable Rentals** *(☎367-4234)* for cars and scooters; **Sea Horse Rentals** *(☎367-2513)* and **R&L Rent-a-Ride** *(☎367-2744)* for bicycles.

In Treasure Cay: **Triple J** *(☎367-2163)* rents cars, **Cash's Resort Carts** *(☎365-8465)* rents carts.

On Green Turtle Cay: **Cay Rentals** *(☎365-4406)*.

In Hope Town, Elbow Cay: **Hope Town Cart Rentals** *(☎366-0064)*, **Island Car Rentals** *(☎366-0448)*.

? PRACTICAL INFORMATION

Marsh Harbour

Bahamas Ministry of Tourism open Monday to Friday 9am to 5:30pm, Queen Elizabeth Dr., ☎367-3067.

Banks are open Mondays to Thursdays from 9:30am to 3pm and Fridays until 5pm, all three banks below are within a few blocks of each other on Don Mackey Boulevard: Barclays Bank *(☎367-2152)*, Canadian Imperial Bank of Commerce (CIBC), with automatic teller machine, *(☎367-2166)*, Royal Bank of Canada, *(☎367-2420)*.

Police and Emergencies: Dundas Town Road, ☎367-2560 or 367-2594; for emergencies ☎919 (also see clinics below); air and sea rescue ☎366-0280.

BaTelCo: Queen Elizabeth Dr.

Post Office: Don Mackey Blvd., ☎367-2571.

Clinic: Government Clinic, Don Mackey Blvd., ☎367-2510 or 367-4010; private Abaco Medical Clinic, ☎367-4240, 24-hour emergencies 367-3159; private Blue Ridge Clinic, ☎367-2295.

Travel Agency: Travel Spot, Memorial Plaza, ☎367-2817 or 367-2567.

Treasure Cay

Bank: Royal Bank of Canada, open Tue and Thu 10am to 2pm, ☎365-8119.

Clinic: Treasure Cay Clinic, ☎367-3350.

Northern Great Abaco and Little Abaco

Clinic: Government clinic, Cooper's Town, ☎365-0019.

Green Turtle Cay

Bank: Barclays Bank, open Tue and Thu 10am to 1pm, ☎365-4144.

Post Office: on Parliament St., ☎365-4242.

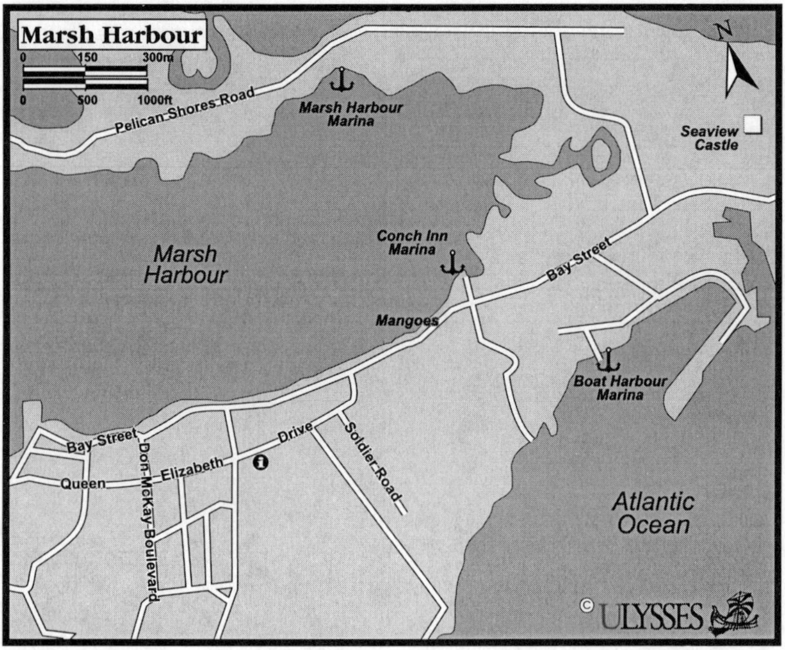

BaTelCo: Hill St., at eastern edge of town.

Clinic: Government clinic with nurse and doctor on Thursdays or Fridays, ☎365-4028.

Man O' War Cay

Banks: There are two banks in town: the CIBC, open on Thursdays from 10am to 2pm, and the Royal Bank of Canada, open on Fridays from 9am to 1pm.

Elbow Cay

Tourist Information: brochures available in the light blue building on Bay Street.

Bank: CIBC, open Wednesdays 10am to 2pm, ☎366-0296.

Clinic: near the government dock.

Southern Great Abaco

Clinics: There are government clinics in Sandy Point *(☎366-4010)* and on More Island *(☎366-6105)*.

EXPLORING

Marsh Harbour

Marsh Harbour is the largest settlement in the Abacos. It has marinas, dive shops, hotels, restaurants and shops galore and so makes a good base for exploring the rest of the island. Otherwise there isn't much to see, hardly any beaches to speak of, none of the New-England fishing-village quaintness

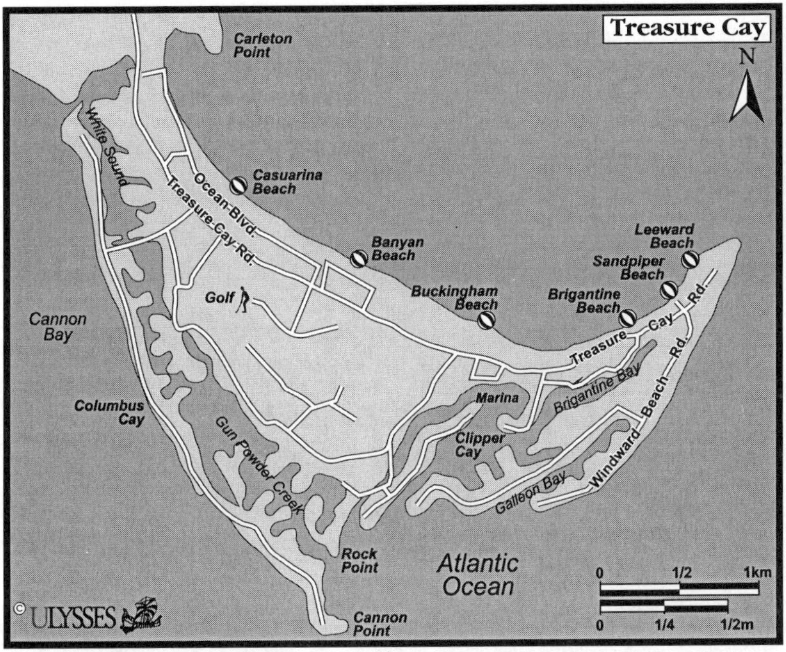

you've come to the Abacos for. Thus it is not worth spending much time here, except perhaps if you have your own boat, are suffering from cabin fever, need a shower or want to go shopping. It's a bit more like Florida than The Bahamas.

The town surrounds a sheltered harbour on the Sea of Abaco about halfway up Great Abaco. The Abaco cays are easily accessible via water-taxis from here. The best way to explore the town is with a bicycle (or car if you are planning to do the rest of the island as well).

Seaview Castle ★ *(up the hill, east of town, ☎367-2315)* is the only attraction per se in Marsh Harbour. This yellow turreted castle was built by Evans Cottman, the "Out-Island Doctor", who moved to The Bahamas from Indiana to provide medical care to Out Islanders. He married a girl from Marsh Harbour and lived with her for a few years on Crooked Island before returning and building his "Castle in the Air". He lived here and continued his runs to the Out Islands until his death in 1976. His daughter still lives in the castle, where she runs the Castle Cafe (see p 166) and Seaview Gift Shop. Cottman's two books *The Out-Island Doctor* and *My Castle in the Air* are both available at the shop.

If you have a bicycle, take a ride down Pelican Shores Road. Sumptuous homes and beautifully landscaped properties line the road. The beach is accessible at various spots along the way. Another easy ride is east along Bay Street towards the ferry dock to Man O' War and Elbow Cays, then to Eastern Shores. More swish beach houses line the road before it peters out into a dirt road leading to Parrot Point. The beach along here is the best in the area. Sugar Loaf Cay to the south has its own collection of expensive manses.

Treasure Cay

The resort-cum-city of Treasure Cay occupies a crescent-shaped peninsula about 27 kilometres north of Marsh Harbour. Before the hotel and marina, there wasn't anything around here, unless you go right back to 1783, when the Loyalists established their first settlement at **Carleton Point** at the western edge of the peninsula. At the time, Carleton Creek separated Treasure Cay, then called Lovel's Island, from the mainland. The Loyalists did not stay long, preferring the cays to the mainland; the ruins of the settlement can be visited easily. The resort first opened in the 1950s, and as it grew, landfill made a peninsula out of the cay. Today it boasts one of the ten best **beaches ★★★** in the world according to *National Geographic Traveler* magazine. This fine sweep of white sand sloping gently into shallow turquoise waters is actually six beaches called, from east to west: Casuarina, Banyan, Buckingham, Brigantine, Sandpiper and Leeward.

Northern Great Abaco and Little Abaco

Beyond Treasure Cay, there is one more town on the map before you cross a short bridge to Little Abaco, where there are a few more towns before the road fizzles out. This part of the Abacos has an almost entirely black population and is real Bahamian. The SC Bootle Highway runs past rolling hills, beaches lined by wispy casuarinas, and forests of Caribbean pine on its way to **Cooper's Town**. Sizeable groves of valencia oranges also grow here, but you'll be hard pressed to spot them from the road. The ferry for Spanish Cay (see below) departs from the government dock.

A short bridge connects Angel Fish Point, the end of Great Abaco, to **Little Abaco ★**. The four towns on the map here are the modest but quaint settlements of **Cedar Harbour**, **Mount Hope**, **Fox Town** and **Crown Haven**. Drive as far as you can, to the dock in Crown Haven, where lobster and conch fishermen haul in their catches.

The Northern Cays

Spanish Cay ★★

Most people who stay here arrive by private boat or plane or via the free water taxi from Cooper's Town (by prior arrangement with the inn).

Spanish Cay, named for two sunken Spanish galleons in the surrounding waters, was until the 1960s the private getaway of HRH Queen Elizabeth II. It was then purchased by a rich Texan named Clint Murchison who transformed the mostly scrub-covered, five-kilometre-long island by importing some 800 palm trees that today have spawned a veritable forest of more than 5,000. The Inn at Spanish Cay (see p 162) is the only outfit on the island which has five beaches. Well-kept properties surround a handful of upscale vacation homes and the guest accommodations of the inn.

Grand Cay ★

If you want a change from uninhabited Walker's Cay, except visitors and local wildlife, head to Grand Cay. The Island Bay Hotel & Restaurant is run by Roosevelt Curry who'll bring you over to the island if you have dinner at his restaurant (see p 168), otherwise it will cost you about $5. You can also lounge on pretty Wells Beach or go bonefishing.

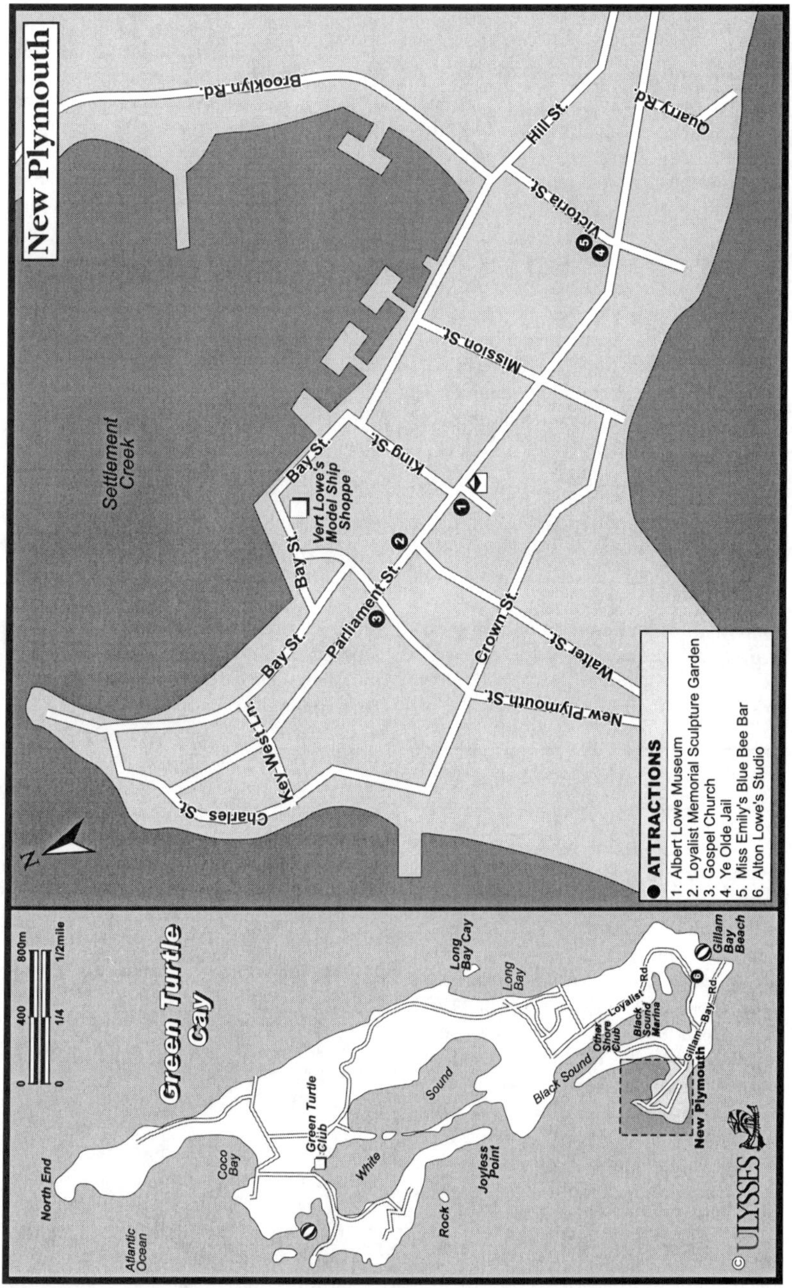
New Plymouth
Settlement Creek
Brooklyn Rd.
Hill St.
Quarry Rd.
Victoria St.
Mission St.
King St.
Bay St.
Vert Lowe's Model Ship Shoppe
Parliament St.
Crown St.
Walter St.
New Plymouth St.
Key West Ln.
Charles St.
N
ATTRACTIONS
1. Albert Lowe Museum
2. Loyalist Memorial Sculpture Garden
3. Gospel Church
4. Ye Olde Jail
5. Miss Emily's Blue Bee Bar
6. Alton Lowe's Studio
Green Turtle Cay
0 400 800m
0 1/4 1/2mile
North End
Atlantic Ocean
Coco Bay
Green Turtle Club
White Sound
Rock
Joyless Point
Long Bay Cay
Long Bay
Black Sound
Other Shore Club
Black Sound Marina
Loyalist Rd.
Gillam Bay Rd.
Gillam Bay Beach
New Plymouth
© ULYSSES

Walker's Cay ★

Rocky little Walker's Cay is the northernmost of the Abaco Cays. The biggest attraction on the island is the Walker's Cay Hotel and Marina. The only permanent residents are sooty terns, frigate birds and curly-tailed iguanas. All the employees of the hotel commute here from Grand Cay. Most guests at the hotel come for the diving or for the huge fishing tournaments. Once you've had your fill of the small crescent-shaped beach, you can explore the tiny surrounding islands of Seal Cay and Sit Down Cay. The hotel can arrange transportation and box lunches.

A lot of fascinating **research** into shark behaviour and coral reproduction goes on at Walker's Cay. Qualified divers can volunteer to help with these two projects through **Oceanographic Expeditions** *(mailing address: 4418 St. Anne St., New Orleans, LA 70119, ☎/≠504-488-1573)*

Green Turtle Cay ★★★

The 15-minute boat ride from Treasure Cay to Green Turtle Cay is like a trip back 200 years to Loyalists times, when New Plymouth's first tidy rows of clapboard houses and white picket fences were built. The 500 Loyalists from New York who arrived in 1783 prospered and multiplied to some 1,800, and their's became the second-largest town in The Bahamas. The grand churches and beautiful homes were the envy of all those who came, and the timber-framed structures with their high-pitched rooves and wide clapboards defined a new architectural style. The settlement lies at the southwestern tip of five-and-a-half-kilometre long Green Turtle Cay, on a small peninsula formed by Settlement Creek, itself bisecting a slightly larger peninsula formed by Black Sound. You'll only need a half-hour to walk all of its picture-perfect streets, make that an hour or two if you want to get in its few sights. The rest of the island is covered by gentle hills, forest and scrub and the homes of more recent arrivals, who incidentally cannot buy any property in town because Loyalists' descendants still hold all the land.

New Plymouth ★★★

The ferry dock will drop you on Bay Street facing Settlement Creek. Most of what there is to see is one block inland along Parliament Street. Here you'll see the tiny pink **post office** and across the street the **Albert Lowe Museum ★★★** *($3; Mon to Say, 10am to 4pm; ☎365-4094)*, dedicated to the history of the Abacos. Gideon Lowe was among those first Loyalists, and this museum exists thanks to the efforts of his many descendants, including one of The Bahamas' best-known artists, Alton Lowe. Old photographs, documents and artefacts occupy simply-furnished period rooms and give some sense of life in the Out Islands in days gone by, while the outstanding model ships, many the work of Albert Lowe, Alton's father, remind visitors that boat-building was the backbone of the island's economy. Several of Alton's paintings also adorn the walls. The restored Loyalist home that houses the museum dates from 1826, and you can also tour the old stone kitchen and pretty back garden.

Another Loyalist home has been restored next door, and it now houses the New Plymouth Club & Inn (see p 163). A half-block further along Parliament Street is the **Loyalist Memorial Sculpture Garden ★**. Laid out in the shape of the Union Jack, the garden features bronze busts of 25 Loyalists and slaves from each Bahamian island; two women, one black and one white, form the centrepiece along with a plaque recounting the struggles of both blacks and whites to settle the Bahamas. The garden was dedicated on the bicentennial of New Plymouth.

The bright yellow **Gospel Church** is still a very important part of the community. Keep walking to the end of Parliament Street at the mailboat dock, the scene of much excitement each week. Charles Street curves around the point and meets Bay Street. An alley off Bay just past New Plymouth is home to Vert Lowe's Model Ship Shoppe, where another of Albert Lowe's sons creates his works of art. The shop and studio are in his old garage where you can admire the precision of his work.

Continue your stroll eastward either along Bay or back down on Parliament. **Ye Olde Jail**, on Parliament between Mission and Victoria Streets, doesn't have any doors and is amusing proof that Green Turtle is crime free. **Miss Emily's Blue Bee Bar** next door and its legendary Goombay Smash are local institutions worth looking into at any time of the day (see p 171). And a stone's throw from here is the final resting place of the original Loyalists. The 200-year-old cemetery is still tidied and prettied up by the descendants of the dearly departed.

Finally, about one kilometre out of town on the main road is **Alton Lowe's Studio ★**. You won't see the artist at work here; though he is devoted to preserving his island's history, he only lives here part of the year. You can admire many of his works, however. A white gate south of the road leads to the studio and cultural centre.

Due east of New Plymouth along Gillam Bay Road is awesome **Gillam Bay Beach ★★★**, go there!

The Rest of the Island

White Sound is about three kilometres north of New Plymouth and home to "White Sound Society", Green Turtle's wealthiest expats. The area is fairly built up, including the luxurious Green Turtle Club and Marina and Bluff House Beach Hotel. **Coco Bay** to the north has a pretty beach and more expat beach homes, but the mood is decidedly more laid back.

Exploring a Deserted Island

A fun way to spend a day is exploring the deserted islands around Green Turtle Cay. If you rent your own boat, you can snorkel, picnic, gather shells or enjoy the privacy of Fiddle Cay and Manjack Cay to the north, Lon Bay Cay to the east or No Name Cay to the south. Or, you can get **Brendal's Dive Shop** *(☎365-4411)* to take you on a day trip to Manjack or No Name for $65.

Great Guana Cay ★★

Great Guana Cay is the longest of the Abaco Cays and geography has blessed it with a fabulous, uninterrupted, 10-kilometre-long sugary **beach ★★★** backed by grassy sand dunes and wheepy casuarinas and shadowed by an offshore reef. Once the least developed of the Loyalist Cays, it is now experiencing a construction boom as spectacular homes rise in the north. The tiny settlement lies about one-third of the way up the island and faces the half-moon-shaped, palm-fringed Kidd's Cove, which is a favourite haunt of wild dolphins. There are less than 30 houses here, mostly of the small clapboard variety, a quaint one-room schoolhouse and an Anglican church with a devout congregation. The road leading up the hill and over the rise to popular Nipper's Restaurant (see p 169) passes the old **graveyard**, which is worth a look.

Man O' War Cay ★★

Man O' War Cay is the least touristy of the Loyalists Cays and perhaps the most fascinating. A conservative, almost Puritanical world view still prevails here: no alcohol is sold on the island (you can bring your own), there is no crime, and revealing clothing and skimpy bathing suits are frowned upon - locals, though shy, will even go so far as to tell you to cover up! The Protestant work ethic is also alive and well here - it is obvious in the industrious buzz from the boat yards and sheds along the water and in the tidy lawns fronting the New England-style, timber-frame cottages and more recent bungalows of the town. A rough road runs the length of the island, covered with hardwood forest and inhabited by a variety of birds.

Most of the residents, all white and almost all Alburys, still make a living as boatbuilders and carpenters, employing Haitians who commute from Great Abaco every day. Only one boatyard makes traditional boats like they used to, however; most everyone having switched to faster fiberglass. **Joe Albury's Studio** ★★ *(☎365-6082)*, facing the harbour, is located behind Joe's Emporium (see p 172). Joe is Man O' War's premier boatbuilder and he can often be found at work in his shed. He still crafts wooden sailboats the way his great-great-great-uncle did 150 years ago: without any plans and with madeira, cedar and mahogany, brass and bronze. Months of work go into each boat, which is truly a work of art.

Sail-making is, of course, an integral part of boatbuilding. Over 40 years ago, Selima Albury started making "ditty bags" with the leftover material from her husband's sail-making business and kept the business going when synthetic sails became more popular than the heavy eight-ounce cotton duck that was once *de rigueur* on traditional Bahamian dinghies. **Albury's Sail Shop** ★ *(Mon to Sat 7am to 5pm; at the northern end of the harbourfront, ☎365-6014)* doesn't make sails anymore. Instead, Salima's daughter Lois, along with her daughter and granddaughter, produce more than 30 different styles of bags (see also p 172). Be sure to allow time for a chat with the ladies.

Elbow Cay ★★★

Eight-kilometre-long Elbow Cay is the most accessible of the Loyalist Cays, lying a short 40-minute ferry ride from Marsh Harbour. This is one reason why it receives the most visitors, though the biggest is certainly the superb tableau created by the candy-striped lighthouse, the protected harbour and the colourful gingerbread cottages of Hope Town. It is the best of New England, the Caribbean and never-never-land all wrapped up in one island.

New England and Charleston Loyalists settled Hope Town in 1785 and were later joined by Harbour Islanders. They survived on subsistence farming, fishing and wrecking, but mostly boatbuilding. Hope Town had the most prosperous boatbuilding industry in the Abacos, fostered by the need for blockade runners during the US Civil War and swift schooners for the shipping of pineapples, citrus fruits, sisal and most

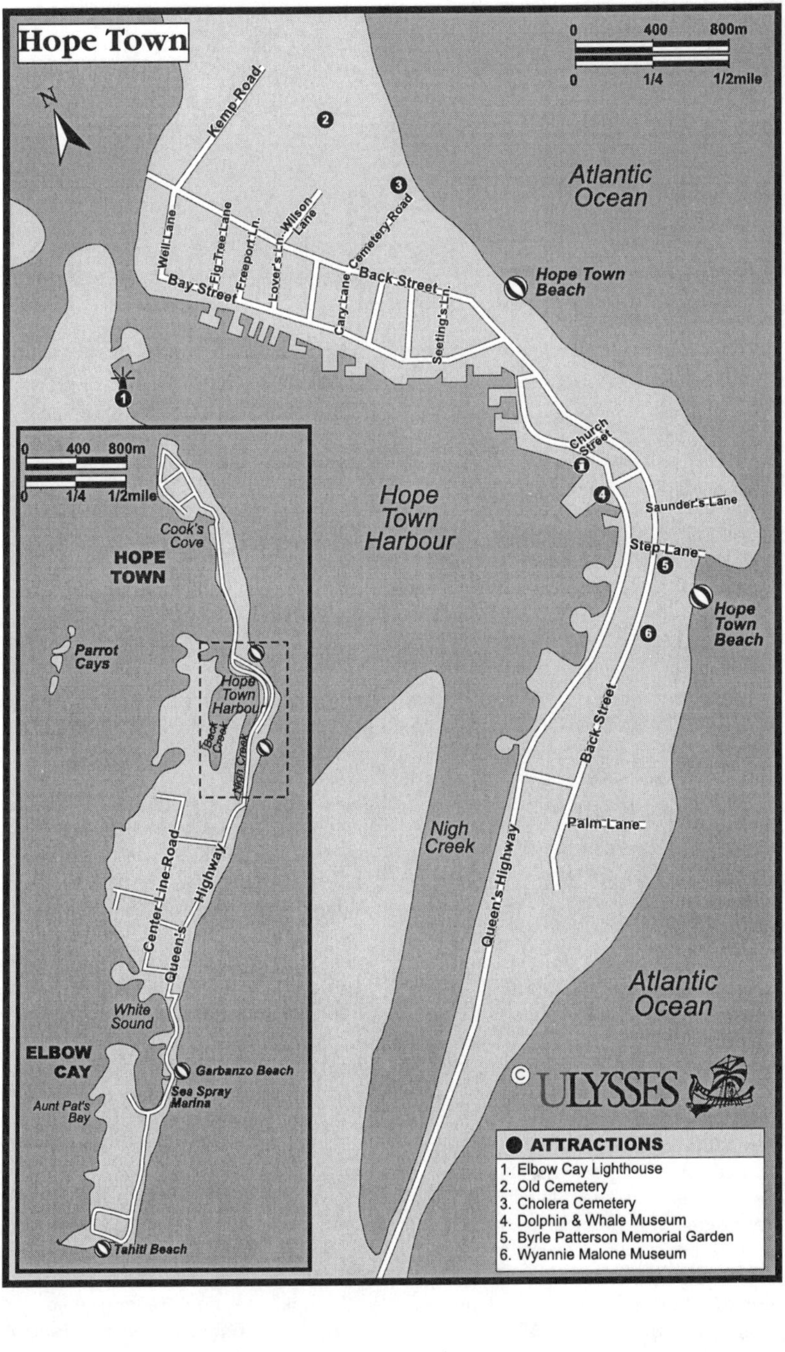
Hope Town
N
0 400 800m
0 1/4 1/2mile
Kemp Road
Well Lane
Fig Tree Lane
Freeport Ln.
Lover's Ln.
Wilson Lane
Cemetery Road
Bay Street
Back Street
Cary Lane
Seeting's Ln.
Atlantic Ocean
Hope Town Beach
Church Street
Saunder's Lane
Step Lane
Hope Town Harbour
Nigh Creek
Queen's Highway
Back Street
Palm Lane
Atlantic Ocean
Cook's Cove
HOPE TOWN
Parrot Cays
Hope Town Harbour
Back Creek
Nigh Creek
Center Line Road
Queen's Highway
White Sound
ELBOW CAY
Garbanzo Beach
Sea Spray Marina
Aunt Pat's Bay
Tahiti Beach
© ULYSSES
ATTRACTIONS
1. Elbow Cay Lighthouse
2. Old Cemetery
3. Cholera Cemetery
4. Dolphin & Whale Museum
5. Byrle Patterson Memorial Garden
6. Wyannie Malone Museum

Hope Town Lighthouse

importantly, sponges. By the 1930s, however, steam was replacing sail and disease and hurricanes destroyed both the sponging and in turn the boatbuilding industry.

Hope Town ★★★

The biggest attraction in Hope Town is the red-and-white-striped **Hope Town Lighthouse ★★★**. Rising 36 metres to the west of the entrance into Hope Town's Harbour, the light is accessible by boat from town, you can flag down a passing boat from the lower public dock (the one facing the light). Construction started in 1838 but was interrupted by residents who saw the light as a threat to their livelihood. They sabotaged the process by refusing to supply the construction crew with fresh water and by sinking boats loaded with construction material. The light was finally operational in 1863. You can climb up to the top of the light to see the original Fresnel lense and, of course, the magnificent view.

Back at the lower public dock, you can explore the two narrow streets running the length of Hope Town – most everyone calls them "Up Along" and "Down Along," but their official names are Back Street and Bay Street. Both are lined with white picket fences or stone walls and shaded with hibiscus bushes and brilliant branches of orange and fuschia bougainvillea. Most of the timber-framed clapboard cottages sport fresh coats of white paint and colourful shutters, but a few show their age and wisdom with weather-beaten silvered clapboards.

Stick to Back Street for now. Wilson Lane runs to the **Old Cemetery**, where crumbling stone tombs at the top of the hill mark the final resting places of many of the original Loyalists. Back on

Back Street, take another short walk up narrow Cemetery Road to the **Cholera Cemetery**, created in 1850 when an epidemic claimed the lives of one third of Hope Town's population.

Down in the centre of town is the small untended tourist information office and next to it the **Dolphin and Whale Museum** *(free admission)*. One small room contains a few bones and maps, as well as information to help you identify local dolphins and eleven species of whales that have been spotted in these waters in the last few years.

The **Byrle Patterson Memorial Garden ★** is a peaceful spot shaded by pine and covered with a carpet of pine needles. There are benches and a gazebo. Some steps lead down to windswept Hope Town Beach.

The final stop is the **Wyannie Malone Museum ★★** *($1; Sun to Fri 11am to 3pm, Sat 10:30am to 2:30pm; hours fluctuate; ☎366-0033)*. Wyannie Malone came to Hope Town as a widow with four children. The museum pays tribute to her and to the history of the cay's settlement. Old artefacts relate the life of the wreckers and original boatbuilders, there are also family trees plus interesting details on the Lucayans. The outhouse, kitchen and bedrooms have been restored to the time of the Loyalists.

The Rest of the Island

The Queen's Highway takes you south out of town. It runs first inland, where it is called Centre Line Road, and then back towards the Atlantic Coast where there is a nude beach. You'll then pass over a narrow isthmus; to the east is **Garbanzo Beach** and to the west is mangrove-fringed **White Sound** and the Sea Spray Resort and Marina. Continuing south on the main road, you'll soon reach the entrance to a private estate. The sign states that there is no access to Tahiti Beach, which is simply not true, the road through is public property so carry on. **Tahiti Beach ★★★** lives up to its name and is a must-see!

Pelican Cays Land and Sea Park ★★★

A sister park to Exuma Land and Sea Park, Pelican Cays Land and Sea Park protects the half-dozen Pelican Cays to the south of Elbow Cay. These are the nesting grounds of a variety of terns. Beautiful undersea caves and pristine coral reefs that harbour over 150 species including spotted eagle rays are also protected. The snorkelling is spectacular. The best way to visit the park is with Bahamas Naturalist Expeditions that organizes several day trips (see p 158).

Southern Great Abaco

Back on the "mainland", the Great Abaco Highway runs due south of Marsh Harbour through woodlands, palms and low scrub. To the west are the **Marls**, a tangle of mangrove creeks and shallow flats where young fish, invertebrates, ducks, egret and herons thrive. The shallow **Bight of Abaco** has great bonefishing.

Little Harbour and Cherokee Sound occupy opposite ends of a hammerhead-shaped peninsula about 25 kilometres south of Marsh Harbour. To get there, drive south of Marsh Harbour on the Great Abaco Highway. Turn left on Dirt Road, which should be paved. A beat-up old sign points to your left to Little Harbour, and a few hundred metres further, another sign points the way to Cherokee Sound.

Little Harbour

This beach and harbour are protected by the Bahamas National Trust. An old lighthouse stands guard over the beach and a handful of beach houses; you can climb to the top of it for an expansive view. At the northern end of the beach is Little Harbour's main event, the renowned **Bronze Art Foundry** ★★★ *(Mon to Sat 10am to noon and 2pm to 4pm; ☎367-2720)*, which was started by Canadian-born artist, Randolph Johnston. Johnston arrived in The Bahamas in 1951 with his wife Margot Broxton and their three sons. They settled here and lived a Swiss-Family-Robinson existence for a while, before Johnston built his own electric generator and foundry. Johnston gained an international reputation over the years and his work can be seen in prestigious galleries and public spaces in The Bahamas. He died in 1992 and his son Peter took over the foundry. There is a guided tour, which includes many original works. The **gallery** *(Mon to Sat 11am to 4pm; ☎366-2250)* sells exquisite paintings and sculptures by leading artists. Johnston's extraordinary autobiography, *An Artist on His Island*, is available here.

Cherokee Sound

Cherokee Sound was one of the first places settled by Loyalists who arrived in 1783. Isolation has preserved the old ways; in fact, electricity only arrived in 1996. The population is deeply religious and churches are filled to capacity most evenings. The biggest money-maker here is lobstering; local men still dive for them. Mangroves dot the shore line and untouched barrier reefs lie offshore.

Casuarina Point

Nature enthusiasts can birdwatch and hike through vast mangrove swamps in **Different of Abaco Nature Park** ★★ *(☎366-2150)*, part of the eco-resort of the same name. It lies south of the small fishing village of Casuarina Point. There are lots of creatures to see, and lots of mosquitoes too, so bring repellent. Guided treks are organized or you can rent a canoe.

South to Sandy Point

The highway continues south through the forlorn settlement of **Crossing Rocks** before cutting west to Sandy Point, another modest little fishing hamlet.

Offshore are Gorda Cay and More's Island, which couldn't be more different. **Gorda Cay**, about 13 kilometres out, is now part of the Walt Disney empire. Two Disney cruise ships stop here regularly. **More's Island** is another 20 kilometres out and is the only inhabited island off the west coast of Great Abaco, with two fishing settlements: **Hard Bargain** and **The Bight**.

Abaco National Park ★★★

About 15 kilometres south of Crossing Rocks, on the Great Abaco Highway, there is a sign that points people down a rough track to the park. You can drive through the park all the way to Hole-in-the-Wall Lighthouse, but the best way to see both is with Bahamas Naturalist Expeditions (see p 158).

Abaco National Park protects 80 square kilometres of forest preserve, a prime habitat for the endangered Bahama parrot, sometimes called the Abaco parrot, which is a ground-nesting species. The vegetation of the park in-

Pelican

cludes casuarinas, flowering plants, orchids, bromeliads and mangrove swamps. Among the other fascinating creatures you can spot in caves and along trails and beaches are atala butterflies, rare red egrets, pelicans, hummingbirds, spoonbills, blue herons and wild boars.

Hole-In-The-Wall Lighthouse ★★ is named for a natural perforation in the rock upon which it stands. This is the southernmost tip of the Abacos and quite a windswept and desolate spot to be. You can climb up to the top of the red-and-white-striped lighthouse, which now houses a field station and ecolodge run by Bahamas Naturalist Expeditions (see p 158).

OUTDOOR ACTIVITIES

Fishing

Deep-sea fishing and bonefishing can be arranged at all the marinas in Marsh Harbour (see p 143), at the Treasure Cay Marina (see p 143) and at Walker's Cay (see p 162). Reservations are recommended for deep-sea fishing charters and guides.

On Elbow Cay contact **Wild Pigeon Charters** *(☎366-0266)* for bonefishing. The premier bonefishing place on the mainland is the Different of Abaco Bonefishing Lodge (see p 165) which offers packages.

Surfing

Garbanzo Beach on Elbow Cay has some good waves. Surfboards can be rented at **Creative Native** *(☎366-0309)* in Hope Town.

Sailing

The Abacos are very popular cruising grounds, with piles of marinas, protected anchorages and deserted cays. Marsh Harbour is the supply centre of the Abacos with the most extensive facilities. Bareboat charters can be arranged here.

The **Moorings** *(office at Conch Inn Marina, ☎367-4000, ⇨367-4004 in Marsh Harbour, for bookings ☎813-535-1446 or 1-800-535-7289)* has bareboat and skippered charters (customized Beneteaus, Jeanneaus and Robertson & Caines) ranging in price from $435 to $910 per day in the high season. Weekend and weekly rates are also available.

Lighthouse Charters *(Hope Town, ☎366-0172)* offers skippered catamaran charters for $280 for a full day or $160 for a half day (for 1 to 4 people; extra person: max 8, $70). A light lunch and snorkelling gear are included. Bareboat charters are also available.

Adventure Excursions

Bahamas Naturalist Expeditions *(PO Box AB20714, Marsh Harbour, ☎367-4505)* arranges a variety of fun day tours including nature walks ($85) and birdwatching excursions ($95) in Abaco National Park, tours of the Marls with dolphins, exploring mangrove creeks, snorkelling in a blue hole ($95), snorkelling and walking in Pelican Cays Land and Sea Park ($50 half-day, $95 full day) and a wild dolphin tour ($95). Groups are small and prices include snacks, beverages and a beach picnic. They also offer sunset, half-day and full-day kayaking tours from $35 to $85.

Less demanding tours of the islands, including Abaco National Park, are offered by **Sand Dollar Tours** *(Marsh Harbour, ☎367-2189)*.

Golf

The **Treasure Cay Golf Course** *(☎365-8578 or 1-800-327-1584)*, the only course in the Abacos, is an 18-hole, par-72, 6,985-yard course. It has a traditional Dick Wilson design with narrow fairways. Green fees for guests of the resort are $35, plus $5 for a cart. Non-guests are welcome, but pay slightly more.

Scuba Diving and Snorkelling

The Abacos offer a huge variety of different diving locales. Here are just a few of the favourites: the wreck of the *San Jacinto* (off Green Turtle Cay), an old steamship that sank in 1865, is now home to moray eels; the wreck of the *Adirondacks* (off Man O' War Cay) sits in a mere 10 metres of water and has well-preserved cannons; Sandy Cay has huge elkhorn coral; the Shark Rodeo (off Walker's Cay) is a chance to witness up close and personal a shark feeding frenzy; others sites have inspired names like The Cathedral, Grouper Alley and Coral Condos. The waters off Walker's Cay offer spectacular visibility great for underwater photography. The following dive shops operate in the Abacos:

Dive Abaco *(at the Conch Inn Marina, Marsh Harbour, ☎367-2787 or 1-800-247-5338, mailing address: PO Box AB20555, Marsh Harbour, Abaco, Bahamas)* organizes packages at the Lofty Fig Villas, the Conch Inn and Abaco Towns by the Sea. This small outfit has many years of experience and caters to small groups. Retail dive shop on site. Rental equipment available

Great Abaco Beach Undersea Adventures *(at the Great Abaco Beach Hotel, Marsh Harbour, ☎367-4662 or 1-800-327-8150, mailing address: PO Box 21766, Fort Lauderdale, FL 33335)* has certification courses, night dives and multilingual guides.

Spanish Cay Diving & Watersports *(at the Inn at Spanish Cay, ☎365-0083, mailing address: PO Box 882, Cooper's Town, Abaco, Bahamas)* has a small retail dive shop plus equipment rental. Private instruction is available.

Brendal's Dive Shop *(at Green Turtle Club, ☎365-4411 or 1-800-780-9941, mailing address: PO Box 270, Green Turtle Cay, Abaco, Bahamas)* organizes packages with the Green Turtle Club, Coco Bay Cottages and Bluff House. They offer introductory resort courses for $85, certification courses as well as snorkeliing ($30), sailing, glass-bottomed boat and deserted island excursions. A two-day dive package is $130. There is a retail dive shop on site. Diving equipment and camera rentals are available.

Dave's Dive Shop and Boat Rentals *(Elbow Cay, ☎366-0029)* has daily dives for $50 for one tank, as well as snorkelling trips for $30.

Man O' War Dive Shop *(Man O' War Cay, ☎365-6013)* caters to more self-sufficient divers. It doesn't organize dives, but has air fills and rents some diving and snorkelling equipment.

Sea Below Dive Shop *(on Walker's Cay, ☎353-1252 or 1-800-925-5377)* has a retail dive shop as well as equipment rental, including underwater cameras. A one-tank dive is $40 and snorkel trips are $20.

Diver's Down at Treasure Cay *(☎365-8465 or 1-800-327-1584, mailing address: 2301 South Federal Hwy., Fort Lauderdale, FL 33316)* has one-tank dives for $50 and snorkelling trips for $35 and offer certification courses and equipment rentals.

ACCOMMODATIONS

Many of the quaint Loyalist cottages and luxurious villas in the Abacos are available for rent. Generally, the minimum rental period is one week, though this is not set in stone. **Abaco Vacation Rentals** *(mailing address: 40 Stone Hill Rd., Westminster MA, 01473, ☎978-874-5995 or 1-800-633-9197, ⇌978-874-6308)* has an extensive collection of listings.

Marsh Harbour

D's Guest House *($75; 8 rooms, pb, ℝ, ≡; Crockette Dr. at Forrest Dr., PO Box AB20655, Marsh Harbour, ☎367-3980)*, on the western edge of town, is a bit out of the way but is a charming place that is popular with travelling Bahamians. Rooms are modern and clean and equipped with refrigerators and microwaves.

Island Breezes *($82; 8 rooms, K, ≡, sat tv, ⊗, pb; PO Box AB20030, Marsh Harbour, ☎367-3776, ⇌367-4179)* is a very decent, budget motel. Rooms have either one king-sized or two double beds. They are a bit dark, but spacious and clean. There is no pool, but guests can swim at the Conch Inn across the street.

The Conch Inn Hotel & Marina *($85; 9 rooms, ≡, pb, sat tv, ℜ; Bay St., PO Box AB20469, Marsh Harbour, ☎367-4000, ⇄367-4004)* is a small place with bright and pretty rooms with cool tile floors and one double and one single bed. You might think the adjacent marina isn't the most desirable situation, but most guests are scuba divers or boaters who take advantage of its supply store and laundry facilities. Each room has a pretty patio facing the water or a leafy garden with a freshwater pool nearby.

If you must stay near the airport, there is always the new and perfectly decent **Marsh Harbour Airport Hotel** *($85; 7 rooms, pb, tv, ≡; Marsh Harbour, ☎367-3658)*. The rooms are modern, comfortable and very functional.

Lofty Fig Villas *($98, low $80; 6 rooms, ≈, ≡, K, pb; P.O. Box AB-20437, Marsh Harbour, ☎367-2681 or 367-3372)* is owned and run by the congenial Sid Dawes from Montreal. The six spacious, bright and pleasantly decorated efficiency villas are set in an open and flowery yard around the pool. Each unit has a queen-sized bed and a pull-out couch. Maid service is provided every day except Sunday. The gazebo and barbecue area is a good place to meet and greet your fellow guests.

Abaco Towns-By-The-Sea *($140 garden-view, $160 ocean-view, $200 beachfront; 128 rooms, pb, ≡, ≈, K, ℜ; PO Box AB20486, Marsh Harbour, ☎367-2227/1, ⇄367-3927)* is an economical self-catering option considering each unit sleeps six people. It is also one of the few places in Marsh Harbour that is close to the beach, this one is lagoon-like and facing the Sea of Abaco. Units are in white stucco townhouses set amidst hibiscus and fruit trees at the end of a quiet road a few minute's walk from town. There are garden view, ocean view and beachfront units, each with an equipped kitchen, two bedrooms, two bathrooms and outdoor grill. Guests have the use of tennis courts, a Sunfish and a windsurfer. Maid service is $15 extra per day.

Pelican Beach Villas *($160, low $130; 11 rooms, ≡, sat tv, ⊗, K, pb; Pelican Shores Rd., PO Box AB20304, Marsh Harbour, ☎367-3600, 1-800-642-7268, ⇄367-3603 or 912-642-7268)* is a more secluded self-catering option. Casuarinas and hammocks sway along the short sand and limestone beach facing the Sea of Abaco, and there is some good snorkelling on Mermaid Reef. Each cottage is just a few steps from the water and has two bedrooms, a pull-out couch, two bathrooms, an equipped kitchen, a patio and a barbecue. Many guests rent motorboats for sightseeing and there is a dock in the creek behind the cottages. There is no restaurant, but the Jib Room is not far (see p 167). The location far outweighs the decor and is a reason to choose this pricey establishment.

Abaco Beach Resort *($185, low $145; 80 rooms, pb, ≡, ℝ, ℜ, sat tv, ⊘, ☎, ≈; PO Box AB20511, Marsh Harbour, ☎367-2158, 1-800-468-4799 ⇄367-2819)*, also known as the Great Abaco Beach Hotel, is the nicest place to stay in Marsh Harbour. It was started by a Canadian World War II pilot. There are many different types of rooms to chose from: the six villas have two bedrooms, private patios, equipped kitchens and living rooms; the 80 guest rooms were recently completely redone and now have cool limestone tile floors, elegant dark-wood, West-Indian-style

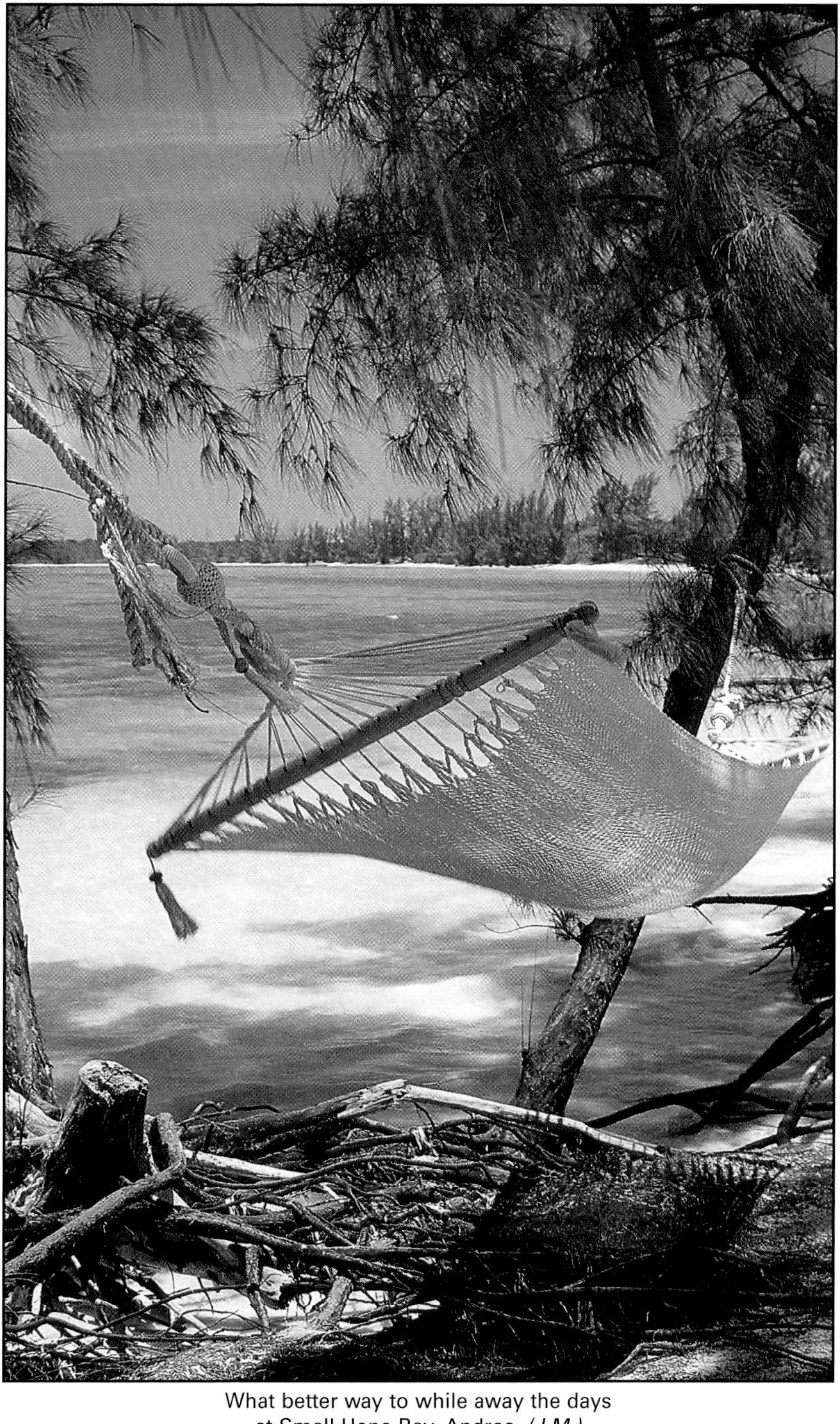

What better way to while away the days
at Small Hope Bay, Andros. *(J.M.)*

Slavery-era hut at the water's edge in Knowles, Cat Island. *(J.M.)*

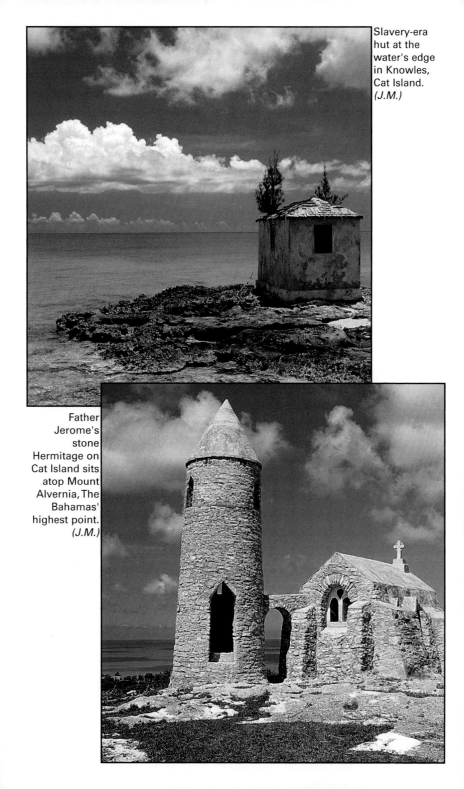

Father Jerome's stone Hermitage on Cat Island sits atop Mount Alvernia, The Bahamas' highest point. *(J.M.)*

Ulysses' Favourites

Accommodations

Best All-inclusive Resort:

Treasure Cay Beach Hotel Resort & Marina (see p 161).

Best Resort for Honeymooners:

Bluff House (see p 162) and Green Turtle Club (see p 163).

Best Escapist Paradise:

Guana Beach (see p 164) and Hope Town Hideaways (see p 165).

Best Eco-Resort:

Different of Abaco Nature Park & Bonefish Club (see p 165).

Best Overall Decor:

Abaco Beach Resort (see p 160), Bluff House Club (see p 162), and New Plymouth Inn (see p 163).

Restaurants

Finest Dining:

Angler's Restaurant (see p 167), New Plymouth Club & Inn (see p 168) and Green Turtle Club (see p 169).

Best True-true Bahamian Cooking:

Mother Merle's Fishnet (see p 167), Rooster's Rest (see p 168), Rudy's Place (see p 170) and Green Turtle Club (see p 169).

furniture, large attractive bathrooms and sunny balconies and minibars. They have either two beds, or one bed and a couch and desk. The resort has two pools, one of which has a hopping swim-up bar. The small beach is a bit too close to the marina. Other services and facilities include a good restaurant, gift shop, supply shop, two tennis courts and coin-laundry machines.

Treasure Cay

Treasure Cay Beach Hotel Resort & Marina *(room $130, low $95, suite $190, low $130, house for 4 $385, low $315, MAP $39, AP $49; 96 rooms, pb, ≡, ⊗, sat tv, ≈, ℜ, K; PO Box AB22183, Treasure Cay, Abaco, ☎365-8578, 1-800-327-1584 or*

954-525-7711, ⇄365-8362 or 954-525-1699, mailing address: 2301 South Federal Hwy., Fort Lauderdale, FL 33316) occupies the whole peninsula. It is one of the biggest and best resorts in the Out Islands. Guest accommodations, either rooms, villas, condominiums or the so-called "Treasure Houses", are spread over the whole peninsula along with some 80 privately-owned condominiums. Most rooms overlook the marina. Most units, except standard rooms, have kitchens. The decor is elegant and attractive throughout and most striking in the bright 2-bedroom houses which sport large decks. There are pools throughout the well-maintained grounds. The resort caters to the whims of golfers, boaters, divers and fishers, as well as it does to those who just want to lounge on the spectacular beach.

Northern Great Abaco and Little Abaco

Fox Town

Tangelo Hotel *($65; 12 rooms, ≡, ⊗, tv, pb; PO Box 820, Fox Town, Little Abaco, ☎365-2222, ⇄365-2200)* has the only decent beds on Little Abaco. The decor is sparse, but just about everything you need is here. Warmth of welcome is a big plus.

The Northern Cays

Spanish Cay

The Inn at Spanish Cay *($180; 12 rooms, pb, ≡, ℜ, K; c/o P.O. Box 882, Cooper's Town, Abaco, ☎365-0083, 365-0466)* is discreetly luxurious on a small private island. Accommodations are in five garden suites or seven apartments with one, two or three bedrooms. Beaches surround the place, which also has four tennis courts. The decor varies from room to room, but the wicker and floral theme is fairly standard.

Walker's Cay

Walker's Cay Hotel & Marina *($140, low $100, MAP $37.50; 71 rooms, ≡, ≈, pb, ℜ; c/o 700 SW 34th St., Ft. Laudersale, FL 33315 ☎353-1252 or 1-800-925-5377, ⇄353-1339 or 954-359-1414)* attracts serious divers and sport-fishers. The rooms have not been kept up, especially the rather dull standard rooms. The pool-side and ocean-view rooms are worth the extra money. You can also rent one- or two-bedroom suites or villas ($275 to $435), as well as the three-bedroom Harbour House ($475). Ask about any package deals they have going when you reserve, as these are usually quite attractive.

Grand Cay

Island Bay Restaurant and Hotel *($50; 20 rooms, tv, pb, ≡; c/o Walker's Cay Hotel, Walker's Cay, ☎353-1200)* is the only option on this isolated northern cay. The rooms are very simple but go with the territory.

Green Turtle Cay

Bluff House Club *(room $115, upper suite $235, 3-bedroom villa $550, MAP $36; 20 rooms, K, ≈, ≡, ⊗, pb, ℜ; Green Turtle Cay, ☎365-4247, ⇄365-4248)* offers casual elegance atop a bluff overlooking a fine-pink-sand beach and the Sea of Abaco. Paths and stairs between palm and pine trees connect the rooms, which range from standard rooms to villas (with one, two or three bedrooms), terraced suites (with king-size beds) and the more secluded and visually-pleasing "tree-houses". All the rooms have private balconies and a smart contemporary decor with tasteful florals and check patterns. There is a tennis court (equipment is included) and free snorkelling gear. Other activities are available by special arrangement. The resort gets a lot of repeat visitors

New Plymouth Inn *($120; 9 rooms, pb, ⊗, ≡, ≈, ℜ; Green Turtle Cay, ☎365-4161, ⇒365-4138 or 908-735-4140)* is set in a lovingly restored, 150-year-old colonial inn that houses a beautiful second-floor gallery with lacy fretwork and single dormer window. Bougainvillea and oleander bloom in the cloistered garden, where old fashioned lampposts and benches evoke Loyalist times. The rooms are small, but have an authentic period decor. There is a small patio and pool. The elegant restaurant comes highly recommended.

Coco Bay Cottages *($150 to $200; 4 rooms, K, ⊗, pb; PO Box AB22795, Green Turtle Cay, ☎365-4464, ⇒365-4301)* face either shell-lined Coco Bay and the Sea of Abaco, or the Atlantic Ocean and beautiful snorkelling reefs, just a stone's throw across the island. There are four spacious cottages with large wrap-around wooden decks, high beamed ceilings and ceiling fans, two bedrooms, equipped kitchens, chess boards and a tropical pastel decor. Guests are invited to take their pick from the tropical fruit trees that dot the property. Minimum 3-night stay.

The **Green Turtle Club** *($184, low $125; 34 rooms, pb, ≡, ≈, ℜ; PO Box AB22792, Green Turtle Cay, ☎365-4271 or 1-800-688-4752, ⇒365-4272)*, is the only four-star establishment in the Abacos. It has British elegance and Cape Cod charm from the very clubby lounge to the stunning rooms. Guests lodge in hillside bungalows or harbourside rooms. The less expensive rooms have an attractive and casual white decor with colourful tropical prints, while the suites are elegantly appointed with imported draperies and rugs, oak floors and a West-Indian colonial feel. This is also a yacht club, with place of honour going to members' villas and yachts. The dining room is open to non-guests. Most guests are divers or boaters; these types of excursions as well as sport-fishing are offered.

Linton's Beach & Harbour Cottages *($190, low $150; 5 rooms, pb, ⊗, K; Green Turtle Cay, ☎365-4003, 1-800-688-4752/615-269-5682 from the US, ⇒615-353-1882 from the US)* is a secluded oceanfront retreat surrounded by sand, palms and casuarinas. There are two cottages to choose from, both equally attractive. Each has a patio and two bedrooms. The ocean breezes keep things cool and relatively bug free. Bicycles are included for the short trip to New Plymouth. There is also a dock on Black Sound.

Two swish vacation rentals are available through **Abaco Vacation Rentals** (see p 159). Other interesting options on Green Turtle Cay are **Deck House** *($800 per week; ☎513-821-9471)* a cottage and guest house that includes a motor boat, and **Treehouse** *($800 per week; ☎365-4258 or 1-800-942-9304 ext. 20510)*, leafy octagonal cottages for six.

Great Guana Cay

The newest spot on the island is the cosy **Dolphin Beach Resort** *(rooms $125 to $160, cottages $170 to $190, bkfst incl.; 19 rooms, ≡, ⊗, pb, ℝ, K, ≈; Great Guana Cay, ☎365-5137 or*

1-800-222-2646, ⇄1-800-678-7479) bed and breakfast. Rooms and cottages have an appealing contemporary decor with Scandia teak furniture, futons, bright colours and sun throughout. Boardwalks connect the cottages which are laid out amidst tropical foliage, just a few metres from the white-sand Atlantic beach. There are a simple patio and medium-sized pool and tennis courts. A full continental breakfast is included, and a shop prepares meals like salads and sandwiches. Only cottages have full kitchens, rooms have refrigerators, microwaves and coffee makers. The town is an easy walk away.

The **Guana Beach Resort** *($140, low $125, MAP $35; 16 rooms, pb, ≈, ℜ, K, ≡, ⊗; PO Box AB20474, Marsh Harbour, ☎367-3590, 1-800-227-3366, ⇄954-747-9130)* is civilized but barefoot. The rooms have a casual tropical decor, with either one king-sized bed or two doubles. Each one has a full kitchen. The resort is set in the middle of a long peninsula with its own marina and Kidd's Cove on one side and an untouched, 11-kilometre-long, white-sand beach on the other. There is a good Bahamian restaurant. Snorkelling equipment and water transfers are included. Bicycles can be rented. Renovation and expansion plans are in the works. Two-bedroom suites are $210 or $190 in the low season.

Guana Seaside Village *($160, low $120; 10 rooms, K, ≡, ⊗, ℜ, K; ☎365-5146 or 1-800-242-0942, mailing address PO Box 2838, Jupiter FL 33468)* is a new addition to Great Guana Cay. It is about two kilometres north of the village facing the Sea of Abaco. Only two of the rooms take advantage of the location. Among the others are two with kitchenettes. Sportfishing and bonefishing can be arranged. The hotel has only been in operation since 1996 and is still growing.

Man O' War Cay

Schooner's Landing *($175, low $150; 4 rooms, pb, ≡, ⊗, tv, K; ☎365-6072, ⇄365-6285)* is a sea-side complex with four terracotta-roofed townhouses. Each has two bedrooms, 2 full baths, full kitchen and comfortable wicker-clad living room. There is a television but no satellite hook-up, hence the VCR. Most guests take full advantage of the kitchens and outdoor barbecues. A sandy beach is a short walk beyond the surf pounding against the sea-wall in front of the units. There is a three-night minimum.

Elbow Cay

Abaco Inn *($90, low $120, MAP $35; 12 rooms, pb, ≈, ⊗, ≡; Hopetown, Elbow Cay, ☎366-0133, 1-800-468-8799, ⇄366-0113)* is an elegant but informal and unpretentious place about two-and-a-half kilometres south of Hope Town on the narrowest point of Elbow Cay. To the east are the crashing waves of the Atlantic Ocean and to the west, the calmer ripples of the Sea of Abaco. Between the shingled-cottages spread over the sandy property are seagrapes, palms and hammocks. Each room has a beamed sloped ceiling, simple furniture and a breezy patio. There is a picturesque gazebo near the saltwater pool. The limestone shore is good for romantic strolls. The lively bar is surely the best on the island. Free bikes, snorkel gear and welcome cocktail. Ocean-view cabins are $10 to $15 more.

Sea Spray Resort Villas & Marina *($700 per week for 1-bedroom; 10 rooms, pb, ≈, ℜ, ≡; White Sound, Elbow Cay,*

☎366-0065, ⇌366-0383) is a collection of one- and two-bedroom villas south of Hope Town. The villas are fully equipped with kitchens and living rooms, but there is also a clubhouse with a restaurant plus daily maid service to remind you that you are on vacation. The Alburys, who own the place, are full of information on what to see and do in the Abacos. There is free transportation to Hope Town.

Hope Town Harbour Lodge *($110 to $145; 20 rooms, ≡, ⊗, ≈, ℜ; plus Butterfly House; Hope Town, Elbow Cay, ☎366-0095, 1-800-316-7844, ⇌366-0286)* is a colourful place, both inside and out. There are rooms in the main harbour-side house or across the road in pool-side and beach-side cottages. Not all the rooms have air conditioning, but they all have fans. The friendly staff can arrange boat rentals and water sports. The lodge also has historic Butterfly House for rent. It costs $1,250 per week and sleeps six people.

Club Soleil Resort *($115; 6 rooms, pb, ℜ, ℝ, ≈; Hopetown, Elbow Cay, ☎366-0003, ⇌366-0254)* is a touch of the Spanish Mediterranean in The Bahamas. It is on the western side of Hope Town Harbour and is only accessible by boat, be sure to call ahead to arrange a pick-up if you haven't got your own boat. The rooms have a balcony, a TV and VCR, coffee-maker, refrigerator and two double beds. They overlook the harbour or the enticing wooden-decked pool and have a fairly standard decor.

Hope Town Hideaways *($140, $910 per week; 8 rooms, pb, K, ≈, ≡; 1 Purple Porpoise Pl., PO Box AB-20419, Hope Town, Elbow Cay, ☎366-0224, ⇌366-0434)* are idyllic, white-trimmed, pink villas on an 11-acre property near Club Soleil. They offer great views of the lighthouse, harbour and Hope Town. Each is beautifully furnished, has a complete kitchen, two bedrooms with separate bathrooms and entrances, two day beds (maximum occupancy is 6), a porch swing, TV and VCR. Some even have their own private pool. There is housekeeping service, and hosts Chris and Peggy Thompson will gladly help you organize fishing, diving, snorkelling and eco-excursions.

Turtle Hill *($225 per night, $1,200 per week; pb, ≡, ⊗, K, ≈; Hope Town, Elbow Cay, ☎/⇌366-0557)* is a new cluster of vacation cottages with a big pool, pristine beach and flowery property. The cottages are elegantly decorated and sleep up to six. Maid service and a golf cart are included. The owners of this place also have a "Tres Jolie" cottage in town which rents for $600 per week.

Many of the historic Loyalist cottages that line Hope Town's streets are for rent. For a list of 30 houses in and around town, contact **Tanny Key Hope Town Vacation Rentals** *(Back St., ☎366-0053, ⇌366-0051)*. Weekly rates range from $450 for a one-bedroom to $1,300 for a three-bedroom. You can also try **Hope Town Villas** *($150 per night, $850 per week; pb, K, ≡; General Delivery, Hope Town, Elbow Cay, ☎366-0030, ⇌366-0377)*, two restored Loyalist cottages right in Hope Town. **Abaco Vacation Rentals** (see p 159) has a good selection as well.

Southern Great Abaco

Casuarina Point

Different of Abaco Nature Park & Bonefish Club *($125 all-incl.; 8 rooms, 14 huts, ≡, ⊗, pb, sb, ℜ; PO Box AB20092, Marsh Harbour, ☎366-2150* *or 1-800-688-4752, ⇌327-8152)* is a family-run bonefishing lodge, eco-resort and nature park (see p 156). The setting is very natural, just as owner Nettie Symonette intends it to be. Not everyone appreciates this, though fishers and nature-types seem to love it. Rooms are attractively rustic with hardwood floors, simple furnishings and a screened-in porch facing a saltwater marsh with birds, wild boars, iguanas and lots of mosquitoes. You can also opt for the even more rustic thatched huts with fans and shared bathrooms. Meals are served in the rustic but elegant dining room (see p 170). The gift shop is worth some browsing time (see p 172). Bonefishing trips are organized with local guides, but you might have to bring some of your own equipment (see p 157).

Sandy Point

Oeisha's Resort *($65; 8 rooms, ≡, pb, ℜ; ☎366-4139, ⇌365-6285)* is more a motel than a resort with a handful of forgettable rooms. The restaurant can get noisy as the night wears on.

Pete & Gay Guest House *($65; 10 rooms, ≡, tv, ℜ; ☎366-4045)* is next to the dock. Rooms are quieter and have televisions.

Hole-in-the-Wall

Hole in the Wall Lighthouse now houses a eco-lodge with bare-bones dormitory accommodations and a shared kitchen. Bahamas Naturalist Expeditions *(☎367-4505)* uses it as a field station and as a base for their excursions into Abaco National Park.

RESTAURANTS

Marsh Harbour

The **Castle Cafe** *($; east of downtown, ☎367-2315)* set in Evans Cottman's castle (see p 147) with a grand view over Marsh Harbour is open for lunch. The breezy terrace is a pretty spot in which to enjoy the home-made daily soup or large selection of sandwiches. There are sweet desserts and lots of cold drinks, including the house special, the Castle Creeper.

The **Flour House Bakery** *($; Bay St.)* prepares excellent cakes, rolls and a variety of breads. Another recommended bakery in town is **Lovely's Bakery** *($; Queen Elizabeth Dr., ☎367-2710)*, which turns out divine fresh-baked pies and sweets; they also prepare pizzas and snacks.

Sapodilly's Harbourside Bar & Grill *($-$$; East Bay St., ☎367-3498)* is a funky spot known for its burgers, from standard hamburgers to tasty grouper burgers. The catch of the day is always fresh and good. There is dancing as the night wears on.

Sharkee's Island Pizza *($-$$; across from the Conch Inn, ☎367-3535)* serves good pizzas and Billy's famous ice cream in-house, but also has free delivery around Marsh Harbour.

The **Tiki Hut** *($-$$; Bay St., ☎367-2575)*, located on a floating octagonal platform in the marina, has a novel location and surprisingly good food. The Grilled grouper is tasty and is served with good peas 'n' rice and fresh steamed vegetables. Other choices include baked pork chops and chicken alfredo.

The **Jib Room** *($$; Pelican Shores Rd., ☎367-2700)* has a popular cookout twice a week with ribs and lobster on Wednesdays and steaks on Saturdays. On Thursdays, a more refined sit-down meal is served. This place is frequented mostly by boaters and residents of the homes along Pelican Shores Road.

Mother Merle's Fishnet *($$; Dundas Town, ☎367-2770)*, located in a suburb of Marsh Harbour called Dundas Town, is the best of the local eateries serving true Bahamian cooking. The menu is quite exhaustive, including conch chowder, barbecued chicken and fresh lobster and grouper. The atmosphere is homey and unpretentious.

Angler's Restaurant *($$-$$$; at the Abaco Beach Resort, ☎367-2871)*. Start your day here with cinnamon French toast made with fresh Bahamian bread or, if you prefer, standard bacon and eggs. The lunch and dinner menus change daily, but always have a popular fresh catch of the day among the original creations like papaya soup. There is a buffet on Thursdays. The decor is airy and nautical, overlooking the marina.

The **Conch Inn Cafe** *($$-$$$; at the Conch Inn, ☎367-2319)* is a relaxed but sophisticated spot that serves three meals a day. The breakfasts are hearty and filling. The lunch and dinner menu has the standard burgers and conch, as well as some more original selections, including some vegetarian dishes. The fresh catch of the day is usually the most popular dish.

Mangoes *($$-$$$; Bay St., ☎367-2366)* is another favourite for a more elegant evening out. The huge grate-room interior overlooking the marina is attractive and the menu lists Bahamian favourites with sophisticated international flavours plus the traditional stand-bys like steaks and lobster.

Wally's *($$-$$$; East Bay St., ☎367-2074)* is one of the most popular and attractive restaurants in Marsh Harbour. Patrons are seated in pretty white wicker chairs either inside or out on the large terrace of a lovely pink colonial villa. The menu lists tasty morsels like rum marinated grilled shrimp and grilled tarragon chicken, conch cakes and key lime pie. It's best to arrive early, when both the food and the staff are likely to be fresher. Wear mosquito repellent in the evenings. Reservations are recommended.

Treasure Cay

For some authentic Bahamian cooking, follow the locals to **Touch of Class** *($-$$; SC Bootle Hwy., south of the turn-off for Treasure Cay)*.

The Spinnaker *($$-$$$; Treasure Cay Hotel, ☎365-8535)* is a fairly fancy spot. It caters mostly to guests on the meal plans at Treasure Cay Hotel. The menu has a decidedly international flavour and is quite successful. There is usually some live dinner entertainment.

Northern Great Abaco and Little Abaco

Cooper's Town

If there is action in Cooper's Town, it is likely to be at the **Conch Trawl Inn & Shipwreck Bar** *($)* with its quirky decor of marine bric-a-brac and menu of Bahamian and seafood dishes.

The Northern Cays

Spanish Cay

The **Inn at Spanish Cay** has two dining rooms, the **Wrecker's Raw Bar** *($$$)* and the **Point House** *($-$$)*. Contrary to what might presume, the former is the more elegant of the two, serving lunch and dinner in an attractive octagonal-shaped building on stilts with views of all sides. The menu lists fresh seafood dishes, as well as meat and chicken. The latter serves good breakfasts and lunches.

Grand Cay

The **Island Bay Restaurant & Motel** *($-$$; ☎353-1200)* is run by Roosevelt Curry, who will bring you over to Grand Cay for free if you eat at his restaurant. Not a bad deal, since the native fare is pretty good.

Walker's Cay

Walker's Cay Hotel & Marina has two dining establishments, which, like the rooms, are only adequate. The **Conch Pearl** *($$)* serves continental and Bahamian cuisine and is open for breakfast and dinner. There is a decent outdoor terrace. The **Lobster Trap** has a more predictable menu of burgers, pizzas and cracked conch.

Green Turtle Cay

New Plymouth

Laura's Kitchen *($; King St., ☎365-4287)* serves good Bahamian home-cooking that pleases both visitors and locals alike. Sandwiches, cracked conch and other quick dishes are prepared at lunch, while the evening menu changes daily, but may include grouper, chicken or pork chops. Reservations are a good idea for dinner.

Fresh breads and cakes can be bought at **McIntosh Restaurant & Bakery** *($; Parliament St.)*. This is the best choice for a hearty breakfast. They also have quick and simple lunches and dinners; the cuisine is Bahamian.

Rooster's Rest Pub and Restaurant *($$; closed Sun; Gillam Bay Rd., ☎365-4066)* doesn't stand on ceremony, serving real Bahamian favourites is a modest locale. For lunch there are burgers and conch. Among the dinner selections are finger-licking-good ribs and fried grouper, all served with generous servings of peas 'n' rice and potato salad. Reservations are recommended for dinner.

The **New Plymouth Club & Inn** *($$$; ☎365-4161)* serves the most elegant meals in town. Reservations are required by 5pm for the evening meal which commences at 7:30pm. The menu changes daily, but includes two or three main dish choices, which might be fresh Bahamian lobster or a succulent roast beef. The meal is served on the candlelit verandah where night blossoms add to the romantic mood. Timing is key at breakfast, which is only served between 8am and 9am; lunch runs from 11:30am to 1:30pm. Quite a spread is laid out for Sunday brunch.

White Sound

The **Bluff House Restaurant** *($$$; ☎365-4247)* also prepares elegant candlelit dinners. A short but excellent wine list complements the comparably large menu with Bahamian, continental and American dishes. There is live music on Tuesdays and a much more informal beach barbecue on Thursdays. Reservations required for evening meals. Breakfast and lunch are served as well.

The **Green Turtle Club** *($$$; ☎365-4271)* is a member of the Chaîne des Rôtisseurs gourmet society. An elegant candle-lit dining room is the setting for its four-course evening meals. The menu changes daily and always offers a choice of three or four main dishes. Breakfast and lunch are served on the patio overlooking the harbour. Reservations for dinner must be made by 5pm.

Great Guana Cay

Facing the island's famous beach, **Nipper's** *($-$$)* is the place to be on Great Guana. Colourful picnic tables are set on a big breezy deck. The menu consists of burgers and seafood platters. On Sundays there is a big pig-roast. As the night wears on, the place transforms into the island's favourite drinking hole.

In keeping with the barefoot ambiance, the dining room at the **Guana Beach Resort** *($$; ☎365-5133)* is pretty laid-back. Unfortunately, the kitchen seems to slack off a bit and the menu offerings are nothing to write home about. The mood is definitely festive though during the Wednesday conch nights and the Friday beach barbecue.

Man O' War Cay

Most places here are closed Sundays. Breakfast is another challenge, your best bet is to plan ahead with fresh bread from Albury's Bakery.

Ena's Place *($; Mon, Tue and Thu until 6pm, Wed, Fri and Sat until 9pm, closed Sun; ☎365-6187)* has a shady patio with tables and chairs, though many locals get their orders to go. Ena serves home-made Bahamian favourites, that are best finished off with the even-better, home-made pies and sweets. You can also get ice cream cones here.

Sheila's Deli *($10; ☎365-6118)* is the local take-out place serving a different home-cooked and very Bahamian meal each evening. Sheila serves while supplies last, so don't arrive any later than 6pm.

Elbow Cay

Hope Town

Munchie's Restaurant *($; Back St., ☎366-0423)* serves real Bahamian lunches including simple sandwiches, cracked conch and fries, peas 'n' rice and macaroni salad. There are also burgers and pizzas, all served on the small shaded terrace.

Harbour's Edge Bar & Restaurant *($-$$$; ☎366-0087)*, open for lunch and dinner, is a small spot with a pool table and a wide outdoor deck near the Upper Public Dock. Many patrons arrive by water, tying their boats up to the deck. The menu has burgers, pizzas, salads, steaks, fresh fish and conch in all its forms – not too original but in generous portions and quite tasty. There is a band here on Saturdays.

The **Hope Town Harbour Lodge** *(☎366-0095)* has two dining possibilities. The **Reef Bar and Grill** *($)* is open for lunch, happy hour and dinner, with tasty snack foods, burgers, conch salad and the like. The **Lodge Restaurant** *($-$$$)* is open for breakfast, lunch and dinner. The cuisine is inventive but comfortable. There is a popular Sunday brunch (reservations required).

The Rest of the Island

Abaco Inn *($-$$$; ☎366-0133)* serves three meals a day. You might start with French toast or waffles in the morning, fresh and wonderfully seasoned salads at lunchtime and, for dinner, inventive seafood dishes prepared with fresh tuna, lobster or red snapper perhaps; there is also a meat or chicken choice on this menu, which changes daily. Reservations are required for dinner, and a free pick-up is offered.

The **Club Soleil** *($$-$$$; ☎366-0003)* will also come and pick you up by boat if you call ahead. Lunch is the typical cracked conch and burger scenario, while dinner is a more elaborate affair where seafood is always the preferred and freshest choice.

Rudy's Place *($$$; Centre Line Rd., ☎366-0062)* serves authentic Bahamian home-made soups, Bahamian bread lamb chops, grouper and tasty salads. Rudy also prepares a few Bahamian dishes with an international twist. The three-course menu changes daily. You must call ahead to reserve; there is free transportation to and from the restaurant.

Southern Great Abaco

Casuarina Point

The best dining experience south of Marsh Harbour is at **Different of Abaco** *($$; ☎366-2150)* where Nettie Symonette's dining room is a work in progress. The walls are covered with a fascinating collection of ancient artefacts and implements. The timber-framed room is surrounded by a wide wooden deck. The menu is very Bahamian, but surprising nonetheless, with dishes like wild boar plus a few seafood selections.

Little Harbour

And the funkiest dining experience south of Marsh Harbour is at **Pete's Pub** *($-$$)*, a beach-side open-air spot. The menu is whatever's on the barbecue that night. This is also a popular drinking hole.

ENTERTAINMENT

Many of the restaurants in the Abacos double as bars as the evening wears on, so check the restaurants section; listed below are the annual events and places that stand out.

Marsh Harbour

Wally's *(☎367-2074)* has live music and dancing on Wednesdays and Saturdays.

The **Jib Room** *(☎367-2700)* hops with a band on the restaurant's cookout nights: Wednesday and Sunday.

Sapodilly's *(☎367-3498)* has a pool table.

Treasure Cay

Treasure Cay's best-known watering hole is the **Tipsy Seagull**, with a cocktail party each Friday.

Annual Events

January
Green turtle Cay's Junkanoo is one of the liveliest and most popular in The Bahamas with fabulous costumes and a parade through the streets.

April
Treasure Cay Billfish championship.

May
Green Turtle Fishing Tournament.
Treasure Cay Invitational (fishing tournament).
Annual Bahamian Arts & Crafts Festival at Treasure Cay.

July
Regatta Week draws sailors and crews from up and down the eastern seaboard. The festivities follow the races from Green Turtle Cay to Great Guana Cay, to Man O' War Cay, to Elbow Cay and finally to Marsh Harbour.

August
Great Abaco Triathlon in Marsh Harbour.

December
Junkanoo (Boxing Day, Dec. 26) see above.
Plymouth Historical Weekend, on Green Turtle Cay, celebrates Loyalist heritage with activities and barbecues.

Green Turtle Cay

Miss Emily's Blue Bee Bar is renowned for its legendary Goombay Smash. The secret recipe was created by the late Miss Emilie and is now guarded by her daughter Violet. These sweet cocktails are so easy to drink – it can be dangerous! The place hops all day long, but the rum really gets flowing as the sun sets.

Rooster's Rest Pub and Restaurant *(☎365-4066)* hosts the local rake 'n' scrape band the "Gully Roosters" on Friday and Saturday nights. Call ahead for a pick-up.

The outdoor **Garden Theatre** *(☎365-4094)* stages a variety of shows throughout the year from music to comedy.

If you missed Junkanoo (Boxing Day and New Year's Day), head over to the **Bluff House**, where they have a weekly Junkanoo party on the beach.

Elbow Cay

Harbour's Edge Bar *(☎366-0087)* has a pool table and live music on Saturdays. **Cap'n Jack's Bar** *(☎366-0247)* hosts a live band on Wednesdays and Fridays and has a big-screen TV.

SHOPPING

Marsh Harbour

For a sweet dessert or cool afternoon delight, search out **Billy's Ice Cream**. It is home-made from fresh local fruits and is too die for. One place that sells it, along with lots of souvenirs, is **Tropical Treasures and Treats** *(☎367-4822)*.

The **Juliette Art Gallery** *(Royal Harbour Village, near the entrance to Abaco Beach Hotel, ☎367-4551)* has a fine collection, in all price ranges, of originals and prints by renowned Bahamian artists, including Amos Ferguson.

Also in the Royal Harbour Village are the **Sand Dollar Shoppe** *(☎367-4405)* with jewellery made by Abaco Gold, and **Cultural Illusions** *(☎367-4648)* upstairs with Androsia batik, straw goods and other fantastic souvenris.

Barefoot Gifts *(Bay St., ☎367-3596)* has fashionable resort wear, as well as souvenir T-shirts and island music. **Island Gallery** *(☎366-0354)* next door has a good selection of Abaco ceramics and other gifts.

Duty-free jewellery, fine china and the like are available at **Little Switzerland** *(across from Royal Harbour Village)* and **John Bull** *(Bay St.)*.

Darville Straw Industry *(Bay St., ☎367-2649)* has a good selection of hand-made straw work.

Treasure Cay

Abaco Ceramics *(☎365-8489)* sells its handmade platters, butter dishes, vases and the like throughout The Bahamas, but here you can see them being made.

Green Turtle Cay

Ocean Blue Gallery *(☎365-4234)* has many works by leading Bahamian artists, occasionally including paintings by Alton Lowe. Lowe's paintings are also sold at the Albert Lowe Museum (see p 150).

The **Sand Dollar Shoppe** *(☎365-4221)* also has a location in New Plymouth with gifts and beautiful "Abaco Gold" jewellery.

Vert Lowe's Model Ship Shoppe (see p 151) sells the most unique and most expensive souvenirs on the island.

Elbow Cay

Ebb Tide *(Back St.)* has Androsia batiks, books, art and other souvenirs.

Locally made wood carvings can be bought and admired at **Water's Edge Studio** on Bay Street.

Man O' War Cay

Albury Sail Shop sells a variety of canvas bags and clothing (see p 152).

Joe's Emporium has a quirky collection of original souvenirs from natural sponges to hand-crafted boat models and furniture (see p 152).

Southern Great Abaco

Casuarina Point

The gift shop at **Different of Abaco** *(☎366-2150)* has some original souvenir ideas, including bush medicines and teas.

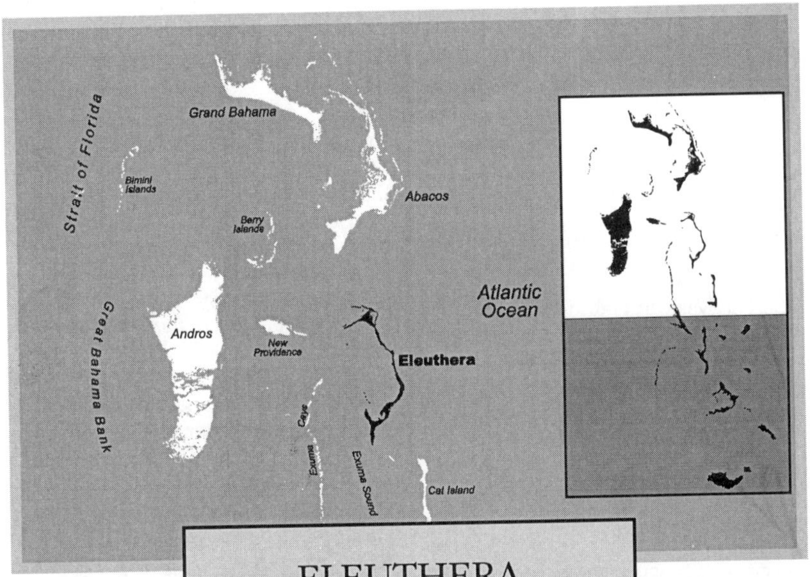

ELEUTHERA

Eleuthera ★★★ has been the prime destination of new arrivals and visitors for as long as it has been known as a tourist's paradise. The fortunes of this thin island, with its magnificent coastline and bountiful land, have risen and fallen throughout its storied history, from the arrival of the Eleutheran Adventurers to visits by royals and celebrities.

Brochures and locals go on about Eleuthera's magnificent beaches, and with reason. This island has some of The Bahamas' best beaches, perhaps even *the* best. There are of course those indescribable pink sands, but there are also the choice waves of Surfer' Beach, the unique rock formations of Lighthouse Beach or the calm, casuarina-lined crescents of sand on the Caribbean shore. Beaches have been the only constant in Eleutheran tourism. The island's deluxe resorts haven't fared as well: some have been claimed by squatters and hurricanes while rumours of renovations surround others that lie dormant. Nevertheless, one of the most spectacular places to stay in The Bahamas is here, at the Pink Sands.

And if beachcombing is not your thing, Harbour Island and Spanish Wells are both blessed with picturesque architecture, sweet Eleutheran pineapples are still to be had by a lucky few, fringing reefs and the notorious Devil's Backbone offer diverse underwater adventures and the feisty tarpons are plentiful off Tarpum Bay.

A 175-kilometre-long crescent on the eastern edge of The Bahamas, Eleuthera is but three kilometres wide on average, a bow-shot as they say. At its northern tip, the island widens into a triangle of land with historic and pretty Harbour Island off one face and quaint Spanish Wells off the top point. The triangle meets the rest of the island at a spaghetti-thin isthmus known as

Glass Window which separates the rough seas of the Atlantic from the calm waters to the west. Green hilly terrain runs the length of the island and across its t-shaped southern end.

A Short History

The Lucayans of Eleuthera called their island Cigatoo. Columbus made quick work of them, however, and the island remained uninhabited for the next 150 years or so. In 1644, a group of Bermudians who faced hostility for withdrawing from the Church of England decided to try and settle somewhere in The Bahamas, which had been claimed by the English in 1629. They made two unsuccessful attempts at finding suitable land in the chain in 1644 and 1645, and then Captain William Sayle took an interest in their cause. Hastened by the severe persecution that these Independents faced, Sayle set off to England and gained the support of prominent men close to Cromwell. Sayle became part of a group of 26 men who called themselves "The Company of Adventurers for the Plantation of the Islands of Eleutheria". They renamed The Bahamas "Eleutheria", based on the Greek word for freedom, and drew up what is today considered the first constitution of The Bahamas, the *Articles and Orders*, which called for religious freedom and for the creation of the first republic in the New World with a governor, council and senate.

In 1648, about 70 settlers set sail from Bermuda aboard a ship called the *William* and a smaller boat built especially for shallow waters. They were within sight of Eleutheria when the *William* was wrecked on an outlying reef taking one man and all the provisions and supplies down with it. The settlers scrambled ashore and, according to the story, took refuge in a cave near the shore (see p 182).

The settlers scraped by just barely, and were twice saved by the generosity of settlers from similar religious backgrounds in Virginia and then New England. Of the original group, many including Sayle found the going too rough and returned to Bermuda in 1657. Others arrived, however, or were sent there as happened with troublesome slaves and freed blacks from Bermuda and the mainland colonies. Settlements were established on Harbour Island and Spanish Wells and along the shore. These suffered greatly at the hands of the Spanish and pirates starting in 1684. The original settlers who survived this period became known as the Old Inhabitants when they were joined in the 1780s by people who wished to remain loyal to the British crown following the declaration of independence by the newly formed United States. The Old Inhabitants were a resilient group and kept to themselves, and still do for that matter. They looked down on the slavery-practising Loyalists.

Eleuthera's soil had always proven fertile for the growing of fruits and vegetables, and by the middle of the 19th century, the island was known for its tomatoes, oranges and, in particular, its pineapples. Ships carried the produce from Governor's Harbour to New York, making the former a commercial hub. Pineapples reached their peak in 1900, when seven million dozen pineapples were exported. In the 1930s major dairy and poultry farms were established at Hatchet Bay, though nothing much remains of them now. The island is still the fruit and vegetable basket of The Bahamas, though pineapples don't fill as many baskets as they used to. Onions, citrus fruits, tomatoes, mangoes and papayas are the most common crops nowadays.

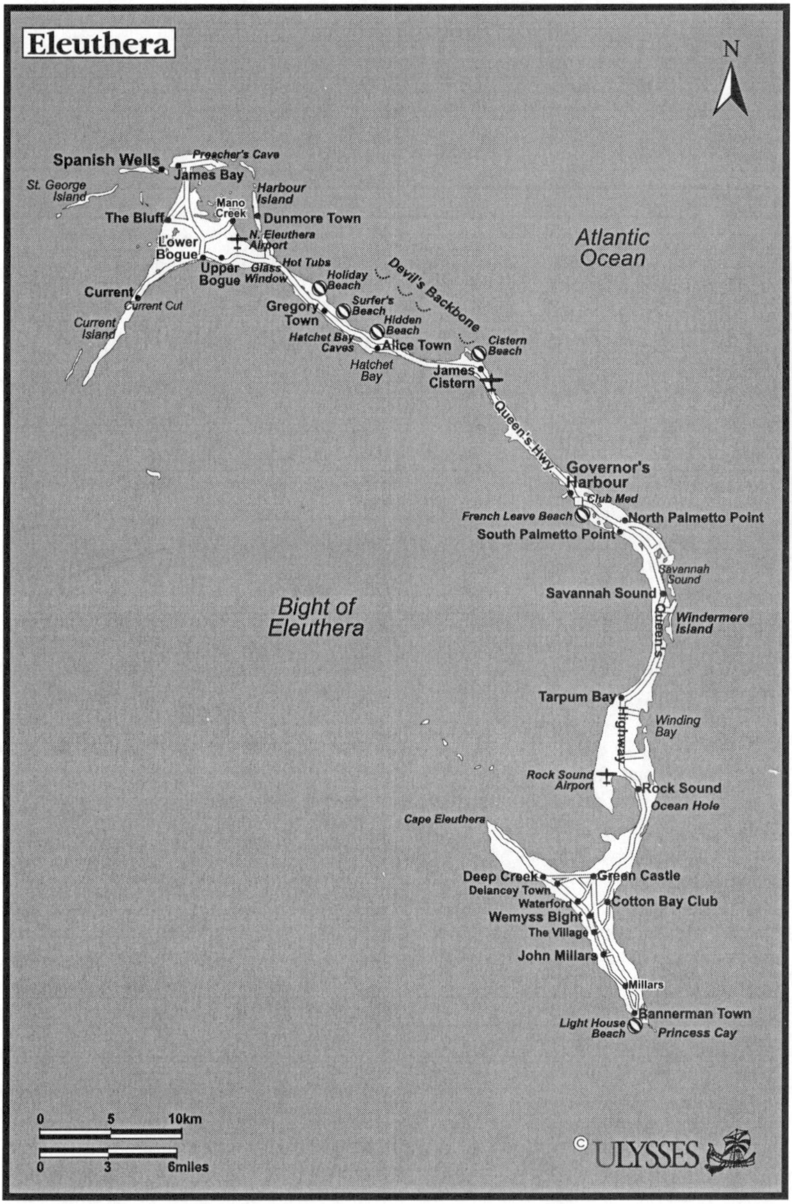
Eleuthera
N
Atlantic Ocean
Spanish Wells
Preacher's Cave
James Bay
St. George Island
Harbour Island
Mano Creek
Dunmore Town
The Bluff
N. Eleuthera Airport
Lower Bogue
Upper Bogue
Glass Window
Hot Tubs
Holiday Beach
Devil's Backbone
Current
Current Cut
Current Island
Gregory Town
Surfer's Beach
Hidden Beach
Hatchet Bay Caves
Alice Town
Hatchet Bay
Cistern Beach
James Cistern
Queen's Hwy.
Governor's Harbour
Club Med
French Leave Beach
North Palmetto Point
South Palmetto Point
Savannah Sound
Savannah Sound
Windermere Island
Queen's
Bight of Eleuthera
Tarpum Bay
Highway
Winding Bay
Rock Sound Airport
Rock Sound
Ocean Hole
Cape Eleuthera
Deep Creek
Green Castle
Delancey Town
Waterford
Cotton Bay Club
Wemyss Bight
The Village
John Millars
Millars
Bannerman Town
Light House Beach
Princess Cay
0 5 10km
0 3 6miles
© ULYSSES

Eleutheran Pineapples

The Eleutheran sugar-loaf pineapple reached its peak in 1900, when seven million dozen pineapples were exported. Smaller and softer than the pineapples usually sold in supermarkets today, the sugarloaf is so sweet you can almost eat the core. Its seedlings are said to have spawned similar crops in Hawaii. Ultimately, it was the Hawaiian pineapple, or rather American import duties put in place to protect it, that spelled disaster for the Eleutheran pineapple industry. Growing conditions and the fruit's fragility combined for a very labour-intensive crop, plus the fruit often spoiled before it reached market. These days you can be hard pressed to find a fresh, locally grown pineapple. The fruit is grown in nutrient-rich potholes on the island, has an 18-month maturation period and must be picked by hand. All of which represents far too much work for the average modern Eleutheran.

However, the biggest money-maker on Eleuthera is, you guessed it, tourism. The island is actually the third largest tourist centre in The Bahamas after New Providence and Grand Bahama. In the 1980s, sophisticated and exclusive places like the Windermere Island Club, the Cotton Bay Club and the Winding Bay Club, all closed at last check, attracted royalty, glitterati and socialites the likes of which Eleutherans can only imagine now. In 1992, Hurricane Andrew roared across the northern part of the island taking a few hotels with it, among them the Pink Sands on Harbour Island. Thankfully, this place has rebuilt itself, and it is now the best place to stay on the island, perhaps in the whole chain, just ask the celebrities who are once again flocking to this playground of the rich and famous.

FINDING YOUR WAY AROUND

By Plane

Eleuthera has three airports; all three are ports of entry. The **North Eleuthera Airport** is about three kilometres from the ferry to Harbour Island. Bahamasair offers daily flights from Nassau and twice-weekly flights from Miami. Gulfstream International has daily flights from Fort Lauderdale and Miami. US Airways Express also flies from Fort Lauderdale. Sandpiper Airlines *(☎333-2640)* provide daily flights from Nassau. The Pink Sands Hotel on Harbour Island offers its own charters from Florida and Nassau two to three times a week.

The **Governor's Harbour Airport** is located about 12 kilometres north of the town of Governor's Harbour. Bahamasair has daily flights from Nassau and twice-weekly flights from Miami. American Eagle, a partner of American Airlines, offers daily and weekend service from Miami to Governor's Harbour. Club Med has its own charter service (contact your travel agent) and a bus that brings guests from the airport to the Club.

The **Rock Sound Airport** is four kilometres north of Rock Sound. Bahamasair offers daily flights from Nassau, while American Eagle has daily flights from Miami. The Venta Club Eleuthera (see p 193) also uses this airport for its bi-weekly charters from Italy.

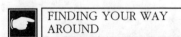

By Boat and Water Taxi

The Harbour Island Club as well as Valentine's Yacht Club, both on Harbour Island, have fully equipped marinas. The Spanish Wells Yacht Haven Marina is equally equipped.

The water taxi to Harbour Island is $5 per person one way, or $8 if you are alone. There are always boats waiting around at both the Government Dock on Harbour Island and the dock east of North Eleuthera Airport. The water taxi from James Bay to Spanish Wells costs $5 per person one way, or $10 if you are alone. Someone in the blue building by the dock in Spanish Wells will call a boat for you if there isn't one around.

Have your hotel arrange night taxis.

A charter boat from Spanish Wells to Harbour Island is $50 one way.

By Mailboat: All departures are from Potter's Cay (under the Paradise Island Bridge) in Nassau and all fares are one way. The *Current Pride* departs Thursdays at 7am for Current, The Bluff and Hatchet Bay. Travel time: 5 hours. Fare: $20. The *Eleuthera Express* departs Mondays at 7pm for Governor's Harbour. Travel time: 5 1/2 hours. Fare: $20. The *Captain Fox* departs Fridays at noon for Hatchet Bay. Travel time: 6 hours. Fare: $20. The *Bahamas Daybreak III* departs Mondays at 5pm and Thursdays at 7am for Rock Sound, Davis Harbour and South Eleuthera. Travel time: 5 hours. Fare $25. The *Eleuthera Express* departs Thursdays at 7am for Spanish Wells. Travel time: 5 hours. Fare: $25. The *Spanish Rose* departs Thursdays at 7am for Spanish Wells. Travel time: 5 hours. Fare: $20.

By Taxi

Taxis meet flights at North Eleuthera, Governor's Harbour and Rock Sound Airports. Here are some fares from North Eleuthera: $4 per person to the ferry to Harbour Island, $5 per person for the ferry, $3 to your hotel once on Harbour Island; $27 to Cove Eleuthera for two; $10 for a Pinders taxi to the ferry to Spanish Wells ($25 if not Pinders taxi). Taxi fares from Governor's Harbour: $42 to Cove Eleuthera for two; $20 to Club Med for two; Taxi fares from Rock Sound: $20 to Tarpum Bay for two.

On Harbour Island taxis cost between $4 and $6 per trip.

By Car

Car rentals can be arranged through your hotel, and the cars are often delivered to you. Pay special attention to insurance rules. Renters must often assume full responsibility for damage to the vehicle.

In North Eleuthera try **Wendell Bullard Car Rental** *(☎335-1165).*

In Gregory Town try the **Hilltop Garage** *(about $60 per day; ☎335-5028)*.

In Governor's Harbour try the **Highway Service Station** *(Queen's Highway, ☎332-2077)* at the southern end of town, **Pinder Car Rental** *(☎332-2568)* or **Winsett Cooper Car Rental** *(☎332-1592)*

By Golf Cart

Golf carts are the preferred mode of transportation on Harbour Island. As it stands, however, the island is so small and taxis are inexpensive, that you may decide you don't need one. If you do, the following places rent them for between $35 and $45 a day:

Ross's Garage, Colebrooke St., Harbour Island, ☎333-2122.
Sunshine Rentals, Colebrooke St., Harbour Island, ☎333-2509.
Big M, Princess St., Harbour Island, ☎333-2043.

PRACTICAL INFORMATION

Harbour Island

Bahamas Ministry of Tourism: Bay Street, Dunmore Town, ☎333-2621, ⇄333-2622.

Police: Administration Building, Goal Lane, ☎333-2111 or 333-2919.

Bank: Royal Bank of Canada, open Mon to Thu 9am to 3pm, Fri until 5pm, Murray Street, ☎333-2250.

BaTelCo: Open Mon to Fri 9am to 4:30pm, Colebrook St., ☎333-2175.

Post Office: Open Mon to Fri 9am to 5:30pm, Administration Building, Goal Lane, ☎333-2315.

Clinic: Open Mon to Fri, 9am to 5pm, Church Street, ☎333-2227.

Spanish Wells

Bank: Royal Bank of Canada, open Mon 9am to 3pm, Tue to Thu until 1pm, Fri until 5pm, ☎333-4131.

Police: ☎333-4030.

BaTelCo is located four blocks west of the Commissioner's Office; however, public phones are at the Commissioner's Office.

Post Office: Commissioner's Office.

Clinic: Main Street at Adventurer's Ave.

Gregory Town

The **post office** *(Tue and Fri,; ☎335-5180)*, **police station** *(every day, ☎335-5322)*, **clinic** *(Tue and Fri; ☎335-5108)* and **BaTelCo** *(Mon to Fri 8am to 5pm)* are all in the same building on Seaview Drive on the bay.

Governor's Harbour

Bahamas Ministry of Tourism: On Queen's Highway at Haynes Ave., ☎332-2142, ⇄332-2480.

Banks: Barclay's Bank, at the corner of Colebrook Lane and Queen's Highway; Royal Bank of Canada, Queen's Highway at Birdie Lane. Both banks are open Mon to Thu 9am to 3pm and Fri until 5pm.

Police: On Queen's Highway, just past Haynes, ☎332-2111.

BaTelCo: Haynes Ave at Pine Street.

Post Office: Open Mon to Fri 9am to 4:30pm, Administration Building, Haynes Ave. on the waterfront, ☎332-2060.

Clinic: Levi Medical Centre, Queen's Highway at the northern end of town, ☎332-2774.

Rock Sound

Bank: Barclay's Bank, open Mon to Thu 9am to 1pm, Fri 3pm to 5pm, Queen's Highway.

Police: ☎332-2244.

Clinic: Mon to Fri 9am to 1pm.

EXPLORING

Harbour Island ★★★

Harbour Island, or Briland as locals call it, is just under three quarters of a kilometre wide and five kilometres long. It lies about two kilometres off the northern end of Eleuthera. It was settled at the time of the Eleutheran Adventurers, in fact Captain William Sayle was probably headed for its excellent harbour when his ship was wrecked. After 1783 it attracted many Loyalists, and by the 19th century had the second highest population in The Bahamas.

The settlement, called Dunmore Town, was named for Governor Lord Dunmore who had a summer residence there. The island was small but populous, and so Loyalists were given farmland on Eleuthera instead. This land is still farmed by Brilanders who were shipbuilders, however, for the most part – the largest ship ever built in The Bahamas came out of Harbour Island. Many of the roads leading to the harbour today were once shipyards. As in the rest of The Bahamas, Harbour Island prospered during the US Civil War and US Prohibition. But the end of the Second World War signalled the end of shipbuilding and the island's quaint houses began to crumble. Tourism saved these as it did the island's economy. Many of the historic old houses now belong to non-residents and are rented out to vacationers, while a handful of resorts line the marvellous pink sand beach that runs along the island's eastern shore.

All of Dunmore Town can very easily be explored on foot, and perhaps the best way to see it is to stroll about aimlessly, all the while making sure to take in the few sights described below.

The Government Dock is as good a place as any to start. The **Ministry of Tourism** is located just north of the dock on Bay Street. Heading south on Bay Street, you will quickly come to the **Hill Steps** heading up Hill Street. These were hand-carved by prisoners. Continue south past Valentine's to the end of the road to the **Roundheads**, an English battery built in the 17th century that lies amidst the vegetation.

Backtrack up Bay Street and take one of the first two streets to the right up Dunmore Street and turn left.

On your right at Hill Street is **Blessed Sacrament Catholic Church** and right nearby is striking **St. John's Anglican Church** ★ built in 1768 and most likely the oldest church in The Bahamas. Three blocks further at Chapel Road is the pale yellow **Wesley Methodist Church** ★★. Its maritime decor is a tribute to Harbour Island's seafaring heritage. The triangular parcel of land at King and Dunmore Streets is occupied by a monument to Dr. Albert Johnson, The Bahamas' first real doctor.

From this intersection make your way back to Bay Street. If you continue along Dunmore Street you'll pass many of the island's grocery stores and fruit stands. King Street has an Androsia shop (see p 198). Either way, cut down Princess Street, which has a few pretty shops, notably the Princess Street Gallery. If you head north on Bay

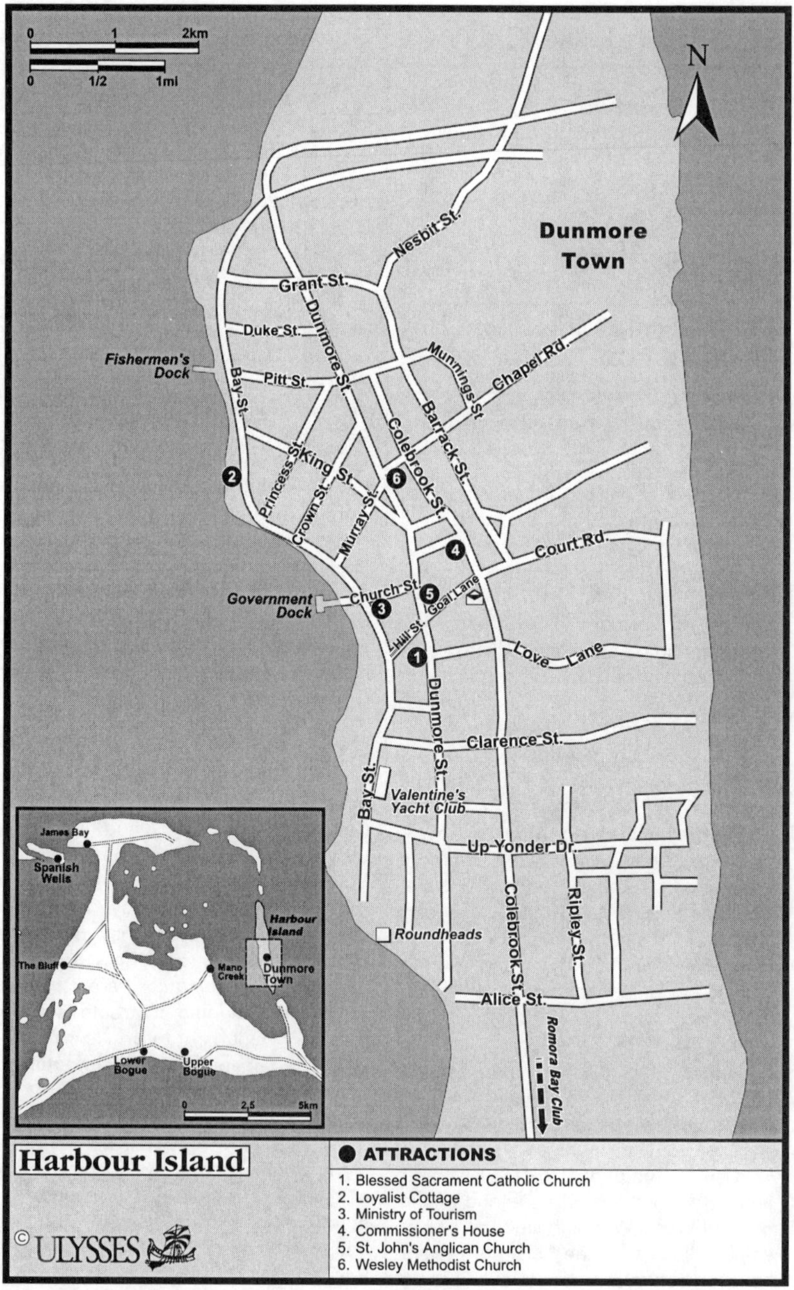
0 1 2km
0 1/2 1mi
N
Dunmore Town
Nesbit St.
Grant St.
Duke St.
Dunmore St.
Munnings St.
Chapel Rd.
Fishermen's Dock
Pitt St.
Bay St.
Barrack St.
Colebrook St.
Princess St.
King St.
Crown St.
Murray St.
Court Rd.
Government Dock
Church St.
Goal Lane
Hill St.
Love Lane
Clarence St.
Valentine's Yacht Club
Up Yonder Dr.
Roundheads
Ripley St.
Alice St.
Romora Bay Club
James Bay
Spanish Wells
Harbour Island
The Bluff
Mano Creek
Dunmore Town
Lower Bogue
Upper Bogue
0 2.5 5km
Harbour Island
ATTRACTIONS
1. Blessed Sacrament Catholic Church
2. Loyalist Cottage
3. Ministry of Tourism
4. Commissioner's House
5. St. John's Anglican Church
6. Wesley Methodist Church
© ULYSSES

Street, you'll pass the abandoned **Higgs Sugar Mill** *(not open to visitors)*, which thrived in the late 1800s when even rhum was produced on Harbour Island. Bay Street peters out eventually at a rocky stretch of shoreline. Heading back south along Bay, lovely wooden cottages line the harbour. Bougainvillea and palms poke through the picket fences surrounding these typically New England houses, some rustic with weathered-wood clapboards, others gleaming with a fresh coat of white paint and purple or pink trim. One of the oldest and finest is the turquoise-shuttered **Loyalist Cottage** ★★★ *(not open to visitors)*, built in 1797, between King and Princess Streets.

If you must hit the beach (and you must), head west across the island. If you aren't staying in one of the hotels along the beach, three paths lead to the famous **Pink Sands Beach** ★★★ (see p 186). There is one at the end of Clarence Street and another at the end of Court Road. By taking the latter, you will pass the stately **Commissioner's House**, the site of Lord Dunmore's summer residence. The other access is at the end of Chapel Road. It runs past a large and well-kept old cemetery, and then between the Pink Sands and Coral Sands resorts.

Spanish Wells ★★

Before the Eleutheran Adventurers settled on St. George's Cay, the Spanish had left their mark. They exterminated the native islanders and then sunk a freshwater well, hence the name Spanish Wells. Ship logs of the time noted this as the last place to take on fresh water before heading east across the ocean. Ponce de Leon is among those who made use of it.

Since English settlement of The Bahamas began, Spanish Wells has the highest concentration of pioneer blood in the chain. Half of the present blond-haired and blue-eyed residents are Pinders and are directly descended from those first settlers. Few Loyalists settled here because of the islanders' strong opposition to slavery. The population has stuck it out through Spanish raids, American attacks and hurricanes, all of which explain what has been termed the "clannishness" of the islanders.

Spanish Wells has been called the "Island of Worker Bees" and indeed there is a certain eerie orderliness to the place, the streets are clean and usually empty because everyone is at work. Lobstering is very profitable and most of the boys and men are involved and gone for long periods of time. The strong fishing tradition makes for good fishing guides. The cottages are smaller and less ornamental than those on Harbour Island, but picture-perfect. The population is deeply religious and the island has several churches.

Tourism is not the major industry here and the people are not overly welcoming. There is not much to do in town except stroll about and marvel at the quaintness of the place. There really is nothing like it elsewhere in The Bahamas. A few blocks west of the **Gospel Church** is the **Spanish Wells Museum** *(free admission; Mon to Sat, 10am to noon and 1pm to 3pm)* that claims to relate the island's history but is rarely open when it says it will be. Across the street from the museum is a small quilt shop. The designs on one of these quilts have been passed down the generations directly from the original settlers – just like the genes, the accent and the name Pinder.

North Eleuthera

What we will call North Eleuthera includes the settlements of James Bay, Current and The Bogues. **Preacher's Cave** ★★ lies about three kilometres east of the settlement of **James Bay**, the departure point of the ferry to Spanish Wells. Following the wreck of the *William*, the Eleutheran Adventurers took shelter in this lofty cave. A hole in the ceiling of the cave, which is 10 metres high, provided enough light, and a boulder at the far end was later fashioned into a pulpit for church services. Try to imagine conditions 350 years ago when the settlers had nothing but their faith in God to sustain them and you will understand why Bahamians look to this brave group with pride.

Current lies at the southwestern tip of the triangular parcel of land at the northern end of Eleuthera. It claims to be the oldest settlement on the island and its mostly white population is believed to be descended from native Americans from Cape Cod. This is a simple no-frills place, known for its basketry and its supreme dive site, the Current Cut (see p 187). **Upper and Lower Bogue** were settled by freed slaves about 150 years ago.

The Queen's Highway runs east from Lower Bogue to the Glass Window, about 12 kilometres away.

The **Glass Window** ★★★ marks the narrowest point on Eleuthera where, to the east, the deep blue waters of the ocean churn and crash against rocks and, to the west, are the calm turquoise waters of the Bight of Eleuthera (many mistake it for the Caribbean Sea). At the turn of the century, a natural bridge spanned this small gap between the northern and southern parts of Eleuthera, but was washed out in 1918. A bridge was then built only to be knocked seven feet off its mark by a huge wave called a "rage" in 1991. All this to say that when people warn you to be careful when crossing the bridge or when taking pictures, they mean it, not only are rogue waves a problem, but the cliff edges are not stable.

South of the Glass Window, some big rocks known as the Cow and Bull mark the entrance to the **Hot Tubs** on the eastern shore. Four- to five-foot-deep depressions in the rocky shoreline fill up with water and are warmed by the sun. These hot pools are a real treat on cooler winter days! Further south still, a sign indicates the road on the right-hand side to Gaulding's Cay Beach (see p 186)

Gregory Town ★★

Gregory Town is a collection of colourful weathered clapboard cottages nestled into the hillside that slopes down toward a perfect little cove. This is a quiet place most of the year. In early June, however, it hosts the Annual Eleuthera Pineapple Festival (see p 197). Traditionally the centre of pineapple farming on the island, the industry is on the decline these days. The festival is still a ton of fun, even if it isn't overflowing with pineapples. Many other vegetables are still grown locally.

Even if it isn't festival time, this little hamlet is definitely worth a stop for several reasons, not the least of which is **Thompson's Bakery**, up the hill on Sugar Hill Street, just follow your nose. Yummy donuts, breads, johnnycake, potato bread, cassava bread, pizzas and, best of all, pineapple tarts and pies can be purchased for a tasty snack or picnic lunch. Near the bakery you can still see an old beehive oven. A fire was made in the oven and, when it was good and hot, the coals were brushed out. Wet rags were placed on the outside to keep the heat and moisture in. Two little gift shops are also worth a turn, **Island Made** on the Queen's Highway and **Rebecca's Beach Shop** around the corner.

The **Gregory Town Plantation and Distillery**, where pineapple rhum is made, can be visited.

Hatchet Bay

Heading south of Gregory Town you will soon reach the settlement of Hatchet Bay, which has a good protected harbour and full-service marina. Before you get there though, a strange sight appears in the fields on both sides of the road, the **Hatchet Bay Silos**, which locals like to joke have been used by aliens. These were in fact built in the 1930s as part of a large-scale dairy and chicken farm. An Angus cattle farm also once thrived in the area. Now the silos make for good stories and help mark the way to the **Hatchet Bay Cave ★★**, a series of passageways through the hillside. A farm road runs south from the highway (right) about six-and-a-half kilometres southeast of Gregory Town, after the ivy-covered silo (the third set of silos). Take the road to the end, and to your left is the cave entrance. You can hire a local guide in Gregory Town or go yourself with a flashlight, some grubby clothes and a good pair of shoes. The first chamber has a few harmless bats and some graffiti (some from the 19th century). A ladder is in place to reach the next chamber, which is in better shape with some fantastic stalactites and stalagmites (do not touch, the oils on your hand will discolour them). It takes at least 45 minutes to explore the cave.

The highway passes several opulent old homes, now derelict and lived in by squatters, that stand as a testament to the wealth and prosperity once enjoyed in this area. The road passes through Alice Town and then rounds the shore as it passes through James Cistern. The Governor's Harbour Airport, once a US Navy Base, will be on your right.

Governor's Harbour ★

Governor's Harbour, about halfway down the island, is the seat of government for Eleuthera. The original settlement, which dates back to the time of the Eleutheran Adventurers, was on **Cupid's Cay**, accessible by a bridge reputed to be over 150 years old. **Wesley Methodist Church**, also 150 years old, with its blue shutters and bell tower, stands next to the bridge. The ruins of a pineapple plantation can be seen, and the rest of the area is in a semi-derelict state. The dock receives cruise ships on occasion, but the activity is not as bustling as it was in the mid-19th-century when this was a commercial centre. The cargo shops unloaded sought-after goods in Governor's Harbour before loading up with pineapples and other produce and heading to New York. The latest fashions were seen in Governor's Harbour before they even made it to Nassau.

Back on the mainland, so to speak, just opposite Cupid's Cay is the impressive green-shuttered and buttressed **Hayne's Library ★**, built in 1897. **St. Patrick's Anglican Church ★** and its fenced-in cemetery are beside. The impressive pink Commissioner's Office tells of the money that once changed hands in this town, as do the merchants' homes on the hillside at the end of the bay. Pine

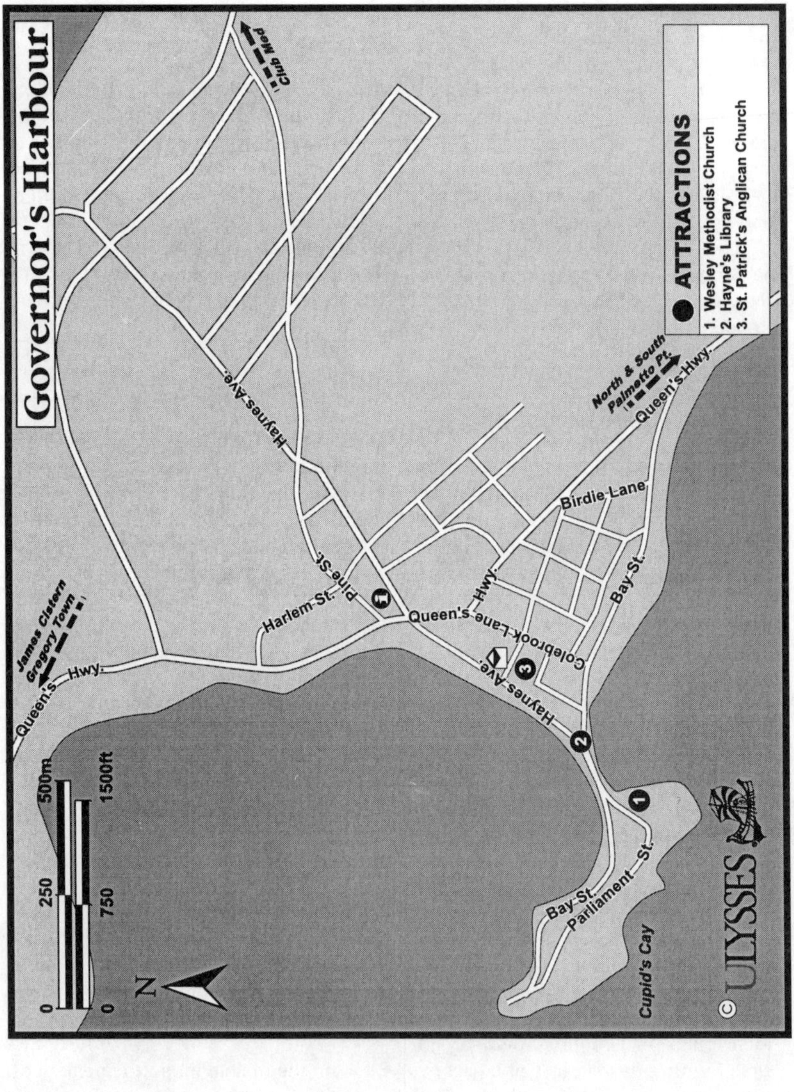
Governor's Harbour
ATTRACTIONS
1. Wesley Methodist Church
2. Hayne's Library
3. St. Patrick's Anglican Church
Club Med
Haynes Ave.
North & South Palmetto Pt.
Queen's Hwy.
Birdie Lane
Bay St.
Pine St.
Harlem St.
Queen's Hwy.
Colebrook Lane
Haynes Ave.
James Cistern
Gregory Town
Queen's Hwy.
Bay St.
Parliament St.
Cupid's Cay
0
250
500m
0
750
1500ft
N
© ULYSSES

Street and Haynes Avenue are both lined with some real treasures.

Eleuthera's first hotel was a collection of holiday cottages called French Leave which opened in 1947 on the present-day site of Clud Med, hence the name of the **beach** ★★ to this day. This pink-sand beach is over the hill on the Atlantic side of the island and much prettier than the sandy shoreline near town.

North and South Palmetto

There are two ways to reach North Palmetto Point, the Queen's Highway along the southern shore, or the much prettier Old Queen's Highway, which is still driveable along the Atlantic shore. The latter follows the stunning beach of North Palmetto Point. If you're hungry stop at Mate & Jenny's in South Palmetto Point for pizza (see p 197).

Windermere Island

Technically, this stunner of a beach is closed to tourists. A road south of Savannah Sound leads to a gate beyond which is the former playground of royals and celebrities, the chic Windermere Island Club, which remains closed. The rest of the island is made up of opulent private homes. If you are lucky you will succeed in sweet-talking the guard into letting you look around and enjoy the spectacular **beach** ★★ where a pregnant and bathing-suit clad Princess Diana was once photographed.

Tarpum Bay ★★

Tarpum Bay is a lovely little spot with real island charm, goats wandering through the streets, inexpensive and simple places to stay and friendly locals.

The picturesque and colourful town has been captured perfectly by artist **Mal Flanders**, whose studio and gallery just south of town are open to visitors. This one-time columnist from the United States has lived here for over 25 years. His brightly-coloured pieces are a cross between naive and comic-book styles. They go between $30 and $600.

Tarpum Bay is also home to the very eccentric, bearded, Irish, calypso-singing artist Peter MacMillan-Hughes. The **MacMillan-Hughes Art Gallery** ★★ *($1; ☎334-4091)* is open every day, except when the artist is out of town, which is fairly often. MacMillan-Hughes always wears purple and has surrounded himself with it in the white limestone castle he built for himself in Tarpum Bay. The best part of the tours he offers of the castle that also serves as his gallery is undoubtedly him. He paints and sculpts in bronze and his patrons include Prince Charles.

Rock Sound

The road heads due south from here towards Rock Sound. It passes through an eerie forest of banyan trees, keep an eye out for the really huge one about 100 metres south of the old sign for the Rock Sound Club.

Rock Sound was once called Wreck Sound because of the profits to be made from wrecking. In the 1980s this place boomed thanks to the nearby Winding Bay Club, Rock Sound Club and Cotton Bay Club, now all closed – all signs that there was money here at one point in the not so distant past. These days, however, things are very slow indeed.

There is a fascinating sight about two kilometres inland. The **Ocean Hole ★★** is a 100-metre-wide tidal blue hole. It looks like a lake, until you notice that the water level is not constant and that there are tropical fish swimming in it. This bottomless lake has been explored by Jacques Cousteau. It leads ultimately to the sea and is affected by ocean swells and tides. The colourful parrot fish like to be fed so bring some bread or French fries. This is a popular swimming hole with steps that descend right down to the surface.

South to Lighthouse Beach

About 10 kilometres south of Rock Sound is the old **Cotton Bay Club**, once a retreat for millionaires, with its gardens and shuttered pink cottages. The resort closed in 1995 and at press time remained so despite reports that millions of dollars were to be invested in it by a group of Colombians. The superb championship golf course is still open (see p 187).

South of Cotton Bay the Queen's Highway splits at Wemyss Bight. One road heads northwest to magnificent **Cape Eleuthera**. The once snazzy Cape Eleuthera Resort and Yacht Club boasted a championship golf course and an exclusive guest book. The marina and the scenery are all that remain.

The other road heads southeast from Wemyss Bight through a handful of remote settlements and ends at Bannerman Town. A cruise ship dock of all things harbours liners at the fancifully named Princess Cay, west of Bannerman Town. A very rough track heads north of Bannerman Town to the **East Point Lighthouse**, restored in the 1980s, and beyond that to deserted **Lighthouse Beach ★★★** (see p 187).

BEACHES

Eleuthera understandably boasts The Bahamas' most beautiful beaches, and unique rock formations, pounding surf and pink sand have something to do with the island's spectacular shores.

The obvious starting point is on Harbour Island's five-kilometre-long **Pink Sands Beach ★★★**. The rose hue of the fine sand is somewhere between blush champagne and the brilliant coral pink of a perfect sunrise, the best time of day, by the way, to see it. If you aren't staying at one of the beachfront hotels, the beach is accessible by paths and steps at the end of Chapel Road, Court Road and Clarence Street. Lined by a short bluff of green vegetation, the pink sand slopes gently, getting darker as it runs into a rolling but very manageable surf. Facing due east, it is protected by outlying reefs and is great for swimming and frolicking.

Heading south, the next notable stretch of sand is **Gaulding Cay Beach ★** *(5 1/2 km north of Gregory Town, left, west, on 2nd dirt road)*. Lined with wheepy casuarinas, this calm beach is usually deserted. Just north of Gregory Town, a road to the right (east) at a white wall leads over the hill to **Holiday Beach** on the Atlantic shore. About five kilometres south of Gregory Town is **Surfer's Beach ★★★**. A very rough road called Ocean Boulevard runs east over the hill, down and to the right then through sea grape trees to the beach. This place has an almost mythic significance to surfers (see p 187).

Continuing south is **James Cistern Beach**, another good surfing and/or snorkelling beach, depending on the conditions. Again, a very rough track leads across the island to the beach.

The first paved road north of the Rainbow Inn leads to beautiful **Hidden Beach**, so named because at high tide it is completely hidden. Check on the tides before venturing here.

French Leave Beach ★★ is so named because the Club Med that fronts it is built on the old site of the first hotel on Eleuthera, called French Leave. This pink beach remains completely natural with no houses or construction to mar its beauty. The Old Queen's Highway along the Atlantic shore is drivable between Governor's Harbour and North Palmetto Point, and it passes some beautiful coastline and beaches.

Just south of Savannah Sound, a road leads to **Windermere Island** ★★, the former sandy playground of the rich and famous. Theoretically, the club is still closed and the gate is guarded, so you will have to sweet talk your way in.

The final beach of note is the most remote and spectacular – **Lighthouse Beach** ★★★. If you have your own wheels (preferably 4WD) and the time, go. At the southernmost point of the island, the road deteriorates and the last five kilometres or so are rough going. Running for almost ten kilometres north of the lighthouse is the beach. It is clean, deserted and marked by awesome rock formations that can only be likened to swirled icing.

OUTDOORS

Scuba Diving and Snorkelling

Eleuthera is known for two dive sites in particular. The first is called Current Cut, a narrow opening between Current Island and Eleuthera where divers ride a three- to eight-knot tidal current through schools of fish. The other site lies on Devil's Backbone, the fringing reef off Eleuthera's northernmost shore that has claimed many ships including the historic *William*. Three wrecks from different periods of history can be seen in one dive, these include a train wreck that slid off a barge in 1865, of all things.

The main diving operations are located on Harbour Island. **Valentine's Dive Centre** *(☎333-2309)* at Valentine's Yacht Club and Marina has complete facilities including courses for all levels. A two-tank dive is $55. Packages with accommodations and diving are available. The **Romora Bay Club Dive Shop** *(☎333-2323)* also offers courses, from short resort classes to certification. A two-tank dive is $50. Both dive shops rent underwater still and video cameras and scuba and snorkelling equipment.

Surfing

Surfers from Australia and Hawaii flock to **Surfer's Beach** south of Gregory Town for what is reputed to be the "second-best wave in the world". An American who goes by the name Surfer Pete, who now lives in Gregory Town with his wife Rebecca, might be hanging around here or at Rebecca's Beach Shop in town. He repairs surfboards and rents them for $2. Waves are at their peak at low tide with a southwestern wind. When the wind is right, the waves at **James Cistern Beach** can top three metres.

Golf

The only place to golf on Eleuthera is the fabulous **Cotton Bay Club**. The hotel has been closed since 1995, but the championship, 18-hole, par-72, Robert Trent Jones Jr. course has been kept up. Green fees are $70; there are no golf carts but there are caddies ($20). Club rental is $15 per bag.

Fishing

The **Romora Bay Club** *(☎333-2323, Harbour Island)* organizes deep-sea fishing trips. Be sure to reserve at least two days ahead of time.

On Spanish Wells your hotel should be able to put you in touch with **Al Broadstreet** who takes people deep-sea fishing for $350 a day.

ACCOMMODATIONS

Harbour Island

Tingum Village Hotel *($75, low $65, MAP $35; 12 rooms, ≡, ℜ, ⊗, pb; Colebrook St., P.O. Box 61, Harbour Island, ☎/⇄333-2161)*, run by Ma Ruby, is a decent, inexpensive option for Harbour Island. Rooms are spacious and cool with tile floors. There is also a three-bedroom cottage with kitchenette ($175). Ma Ruby's Restaurant is an equally good, casual choice (see p 194).

Valentine's Yacht Club & Inn *($120, low $95, MAP $35; 26 rooms, pb, ≡, ⊗, ⊛, ≈; Bay St., PO Box 1, Harbour Island, ☎242-333-2080, 242-333-2142, ⇄242-333-2135)* is the hotel of choice for scuba divers and boaters. They have the best-equipped dive shop on the island. The small rooms are nothing special, though guests do have the use of a tennis court, bicycles to explore the island, and there is a shuttle to the pink-sand beach on the other side of the island. Bonefishing and deep-sea fishing are also offered.

The Landing *($125, low $100; pb, ℜ, ⊗, ≡; 6 rooms; Bay St., PO Box 190, Harbour Island, ☎333-2707, ⇄333-2650)* is located in a charming but creaky old house that will be appreciated by some and not by others. Overlooking the Government Dock, it has the look and feel of a B&B except that breakfast is not included, a shame since the restaurant is quite good (see p 194). The rooms are large, bare and a bit noisy, with no televisions or telephones. The Landing also includes the cottage and building (suites $150) next door. Boat, golf cart rentals and bicycle rentals, fishing, scuba diving, tennis and babysitting can all be arranged.

The **Coral Sands Hotel** *($165, low $120, MAP $40 per person; closed early Sep to mid-Nov; 33 rooms, pb, ≡, ℜ; Chapel St., General Post Office, Harbour Island, ☎333-2350, 333-2320 or 1-800-468-2799, ⇄333-2368)* is run by the remarkable Brett and Sharon King. Brett was an American flying ace before he became an actor and the one-time love interest of Elizabeth Taylor before he arrived in Harbour Island with his stylish wife Sharon to run this hotel. Facing the island's famous pink sand beach, the Coral Sands is a two-story, pale-yellow building. Each room has a private balcony and typical island decor. They do not have televisions, but there is a game room with satellite television, pool table and books. There are suites for up to four people, as well as a cottage and house both with kitchenette and set back from the beach. Guests can borrow sailboats, rowboats, surfriders, kayaks and snorkelling equipment. Scuba diving and fishing can be arranged.

The **Runaway Hill Club** *($220, low $170, MAP $50 per person; 10 rooms, pb, ≡, ⊗, ℜ, ≈; Colebrook St., PO Box EL-27031, Harbour Island, ☎333-2150, ⇄333-2420)* was once a private home

Ulysses' Favourites

Accommodations

Best Value for Your Money:

Tingum Village Hotel (see p 188), The Cove Eleuthera (see p 191), Laughing Bird Apartments (see p 192) and Cartwright's Oceanfront Cottages (see p 193).

Warmest Welcome:

Coral Sands Hotel (see p 188), Pink Sands (see p 190) and The Cove Eleuthera (see p 191).

Best Resort for Families:

Club Med Eleuthera (see p 192) and Coral Sands Hotel (see p 188).

Best Resort for Honeymooners:

Dunmore Beach Club (see p 190) and Pink Sands (see p 190).

Best Overall Decor:

Pink Sands (see p 190) and Ocean View Club (see p 190).

Restaurants

Best True-true Bahamian Cooking:

Angela's Starfish Restaurant (see p 194), Elvina's Restaurant and Bar (see p 196) and Sammy's Place (see p 197).

Best Dining Experience:

Angela's Starfish Restaurant (see p 194), The Landing (see p 194), Club House Restaurant at Pink Sands (see p 195) and The Cove Eleuthera (see p 196).

Funkiest Ambiance:

Ma Ruby's (see p 194), Mate and Jenny's Pizza (see p 197).

and the decor makes it feel so. Each room is unique, and personal touches in the lounge, dining area and bar contribute to this place's standing as one of the loveliest on the island. There are a small pool and terraced patios for suntanning and lounging and, of course, a pink-sand beach at your feet.

Non-guests can dine here with reservations. No children under 16.

Ocean View Club *($300 MAP; 9 rooms; Goal Lane, PO Box 134, Harbour Island, ☎333-2276, ⇒333-2459)* is a very exclusive establishment with a devote following of mostly European customers, read friends of the owner. If you feel worthy and the proprietress, Philippa Simmons, accepts you into her little clique (she has been said to send people away) you'll enjoy the exquisite decor featuring French antiques, Provençale fabrics and an oversized outdoor chess board. Not for everyone, obviously!

The **Romora Bay Club** *($340, low$200, bkfst and lunch incl.; 33 rooms, tv, ≡, ℜ; Colebrook St., PO Box EL-27146, Harbour Island, ☎333-2325, ⇒333-2500)* is one of the few Harbour Island hotels that doesn't face the famous pink-sand beach. However, this doesn't seem to bother the guests, most of whom are divers, and swimming is still in clear waters. The rooms are all decorated differently, generally with a cool and modern feel. Each has a private patio, VCR and CD player. Accommodations are also offered in bungalows. The main building houses the recommended Ludo's Restaurant, Parrot Bar and Sloppy Joe's Bar (see p 195). There are a dive shop and tennis courts on site. Fishing, snorkelling, sailing, kayaking, horseback riding and picnics, including their very own "X-rated" honeymoon picnic to a deserted island, can all be arranged. Weekly diving and honeymoon packages available. Rates include a dive lesson and one dive.

The **Dunmore Beach Club**'s *($395, low $345, all-inclusive; 12 cottages, pb, ℜ, ≡, ⊗; Barrack St., PO Box 27122, Harbour Island, ☎333-2200, ⇒333-2429)* accommodations are set in small white-washed cottages laid out along twisting flowery lanes spread over eight acres. The decor features a lot of white wicker and tropical florals and is cosy and bright. Bathrooms are small. Most cottages have one queen-size bed, some also have a small sitting room or extra room for small children. It is private at your convenience, or you can enjoy the socializing going on at the clubhouse. You'll think you are in a New England summer house, with the wicker furniture, bookshelves, fireplace and beach views. The adjoining dining room features a delicious table d'hote in the evenings and is quite formal; non-guests can dine here with reservations (see p 195). Tennis court on site.

Pink Sands Hotel *($500, low $320, MAP; 25 cottages, pb, ≡, ⊗, ☎, sat tv, ≈, ℜ, ⊘; Chapel St., PO Box 27187, Harbour Island, ☎333-2030, 1-800-OUTPOST or 800-614-790 in the UK, ⇒333-2060)* is where we all wish to stay when going to Harbour Island. It is reason enough to choose The Bahamas for that matter. The place was almost washed away by Hurricane Andrew in 1992: phase I of the rebuilding is complete and phase II is ongoing. The one- and two-bedroom cottages come in garden-view and ocean-view varieties and each features an Italian marble floor, stylized Adirondack chairs, comfy bathrobes, quiet central air conditioning, a CD player with a selection of CDs, a walk-in closet, a wet bar, toaster and coffee machine, its own private patio with teak furniture, and the list goes on... The amenities are numerous but the best part is the refreshing decor featuring elegant bathrooms, airy architecture and colourful batik prints created especially for the hotel, and who can forget the pink sand! There are also three tennis courts, conference facilities, a library and two restaurants with the best dining on the island (see p 195; non-guests need reservations). Service is impeccable and unpretentious. All the standard activities can be arranged.

Finally, another option on Harbour Island is to rent one of the picturesque cottages that line its streets. Contact **Island Real Estate** *(Geraldine Albury, PO Box 27045, Harbour Island, ☎333-2316 or 333-2278, ⇄333-2354)* or **Tip Top Real Estate** *(SE Albury, PO Box 2, Harbour Island, ☎333-2251)*. Rates range from $500 to $3000 per week, with or without maid service, for one- to five-bedroom cottages and villas.

Spanish Wells

Before Hurricane Andrew in 1992, the **Adventurers Resort** *($75-$150; 9 rooms, 8 apartments, pb, ≡ ⊗; PO Box EL-27498, Spanish Wells, ☎/⇄333-4883, ☎333-4143)* was known as the Spanish Wells Harbour Club. The new facilities are simple but pleasant. The resort faces a tiny white-sand beach with a few palapas.

Spanish Wells Yacht Haven *($85, low $75; 5 rooms, pb, K, ≡, sat tv, ℜ, ≈; PO Box EL-27427, Spanish Wells, ⇄333-4649)* with its full-service marina caters mostly to boaters, though it does have five functional rooms for other visitors that venture to Spanish Wells. Two of the rooms have kitchenettes. There is also a small pool.

Gregory Town

Surfer's Haven *($30; pb, ⊗; near Surfer's Beach; ☎332-2181 or 335-0349)* is actually about three kilometres south of Gregory Town. The three simple rooms of this guesthouse are a great low-budget option with a homey feel. Guests can use the kitchen.

Cambridge Villas *($80, low $65, MAP $30; 25 rooms, ≡, pb, ℜ, ≈; PO Box EL-1548, Gregory Town, ☎335-5080 or 1-800-688-4752, ⇄335-5308)* on the way into Gregory Town offers standard rooms and equipped apartments. The decor and service leave a bit to be desired, the pool is fairly large, which is appreciated when you consider the distance to the beach (free transportation is offered). All sorts of activities can be arranged and there is a popular bar with a pool table and live music on occasion. Charter flights can be arranged with the hotel's own private plane.

Cove Eleuthera *($99-$119, low $79-$99, MAP $33; 24 rooms, pb, ≡, ⊗, ℜ, ≈; 5 km south of Glass Window, 3 km north of Gregory Town, PO Box EL-1548, Gregory Town, ☎335-5142, 1-800-552-5960 or 954-974-3913, ⇄335-5338 or 954-970-8124)* is a secluded and relaxing spot with six square cottages, each containing four smallish rooms that may not be the nicest or most luxurious on Eleuthera but are a sure bet nonetheless. Fresh flowers will appear every day in your room and you'll enjoy fine meals and the good company of your hospitable hosts, Ann and George Mullin. Ann will lead you to her giant map of Eleuthera in the lounge and point out *all* the must-sees up and down the island. The lounge, called Cozy Cafe Cruise, also has piles of books and movies to pass the time. The property fronts two peaceful coves with a calm little beach and a rocky point. Rooms have two double beds and private patios; bathrooms have shower stalls instead of tubs. Sea kayaks, snorkelling gear and bicycles are complimentary. There are two tennis courts and a small pool. Scuba diving, fishing and Jean-Michel Cousteau's Out Island Snorkeling Adventures can be arranged. The restaurant is recommended (see p 196).

Hatchet Bay

Rainbow Inn *($105, 3-bedroom villa $175, MAP $30; 4 rooms; K, ℝ, ℜ, ≈, pb, ≡, ⊗; PO Box EL-25053, Hatchet Bay, Governor's Harbour, ☎/⇨335-0294 or ☎1-800-688-4752 or 0181-876-1296 in the UK; closed Sep to mid-Nov)* provides accommodations in octagonal villas with screened-in porches and room for up to two, three or four people. Some units have complete kitchens, others just kitchenettes. Scuba diving can be arranged and the inn also offers Jean-Michel Cousteau's Out Island Snorkeling Adventures. There are tennis courts, a salt-water pool, and just down a short hill from the inn, a pink-sand beach. Good sunsets can be had from the restaurant (see p 196).

Governor's Harbour

Richard & Carmen's Tuck-A-Way Motel *($52-65, low $50-60; 10 rooms, sat tv, ≡, K; PO Box EL-25045, Governor's Harbour, ☎332-2591, ⇨332-2755)* is a cute little no-frills motel in a residential part of Governor's Harbour. The rooms are dark and small. Some have their own kitchenette or you can use the common kitchen. A few-blocks walk and you've reached the water at the town's edge, otherwise it is about ten minutes to the much nicer pink-sand beach on the north shore.

The **Laughing Bird Apartments** *($80; 6 rooms, K, pb, ≡; PO Box EL-25076, Governor's Harbour, ☎332-2012 or 332-1029, ⇨332-2358)* provide a comfortable and simple self-catering option in Governor's Harbour. Each studio sleeps two (some have king-size beds), has a small kitchenette and a private patio overlooking the beach; note that the much better pink-sand beach is on the other side of the island, about a ten-minute walk away. The lovely English couple that runs the place also has a small gift shop on the premises. They also have larger apartments closer to the centre of town.

Buccaneer Club *($99 low $88; 5 rooms, pb, ≡, tv, ≈; PO Box EL-86, Governor's Harbour, ☎332-2000, ⇨332-2888)* has existed in Governor's Harbour for many years but not in its current form. The five guest rooms now occupy a renovated hilltop Bahamian farmhouse. The rooms feature modern and uninteresting decor but are comfortable, with two double beds and new and spotless bathrooms. The small freshwater pool was unfortunately not so spotless. Across the lawn is the club's popular restaurant and bar, worth checking out even if you aren't staying here (see p 196).

The **Duck Inn** *($150 for 2, $250 for 4; 3 houses, pb, ≡, ⊗, K; Governor's Harbour, ☎332-2608, ⇨332-2160)* combines three historic homes all built around 1850. Newly renovated and decorated with monasterial antiques and island colours, they surround exotic fruit trees and an exquisite orchid garden with waterfalls and 400 varieties of plants. This is easily one of the prettiest self-catering possibilities on the island; guests also have the use of a barbecue.

Club Med Eleuthera *($133-$235 per person, all-incl.; 288 rooms, ≈, pb, ≡; mailing address: French Leave, PO Box EL-80, Governor's Harbour, ☎332-2270/1 or 1-800-CLUBMED, ⇨332-2271)* is a family village, with its own circus and baby, petit, mini and kids clubs, plus just about every outdoor activity you can imagine, including tennis, sailing, scuba diving and snorkelling. Diving is geared towards beginners with complete courses. Singles

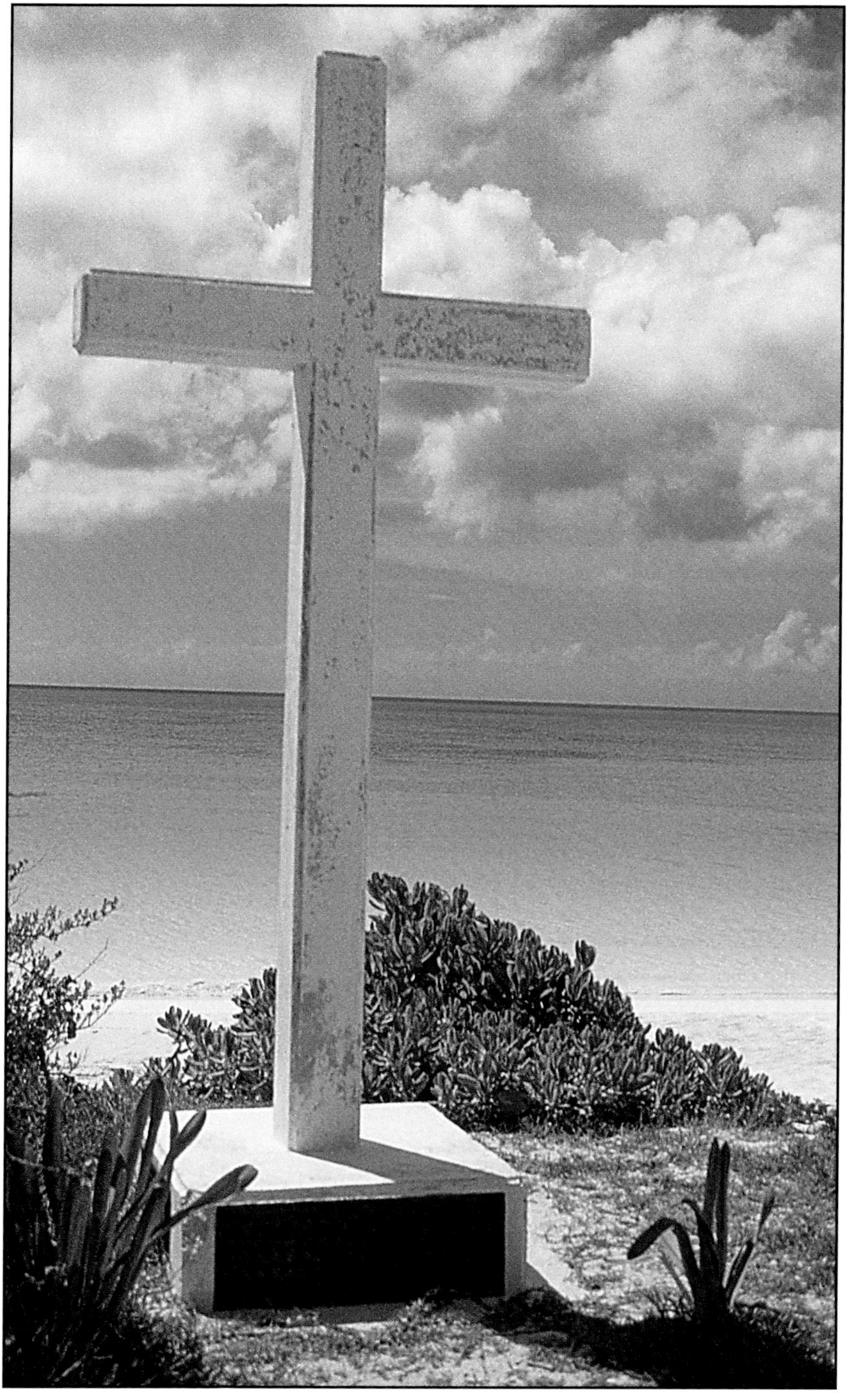

One of the many monuments marking Columbus' supposed landfall on San Salvador. *(J.M.)*

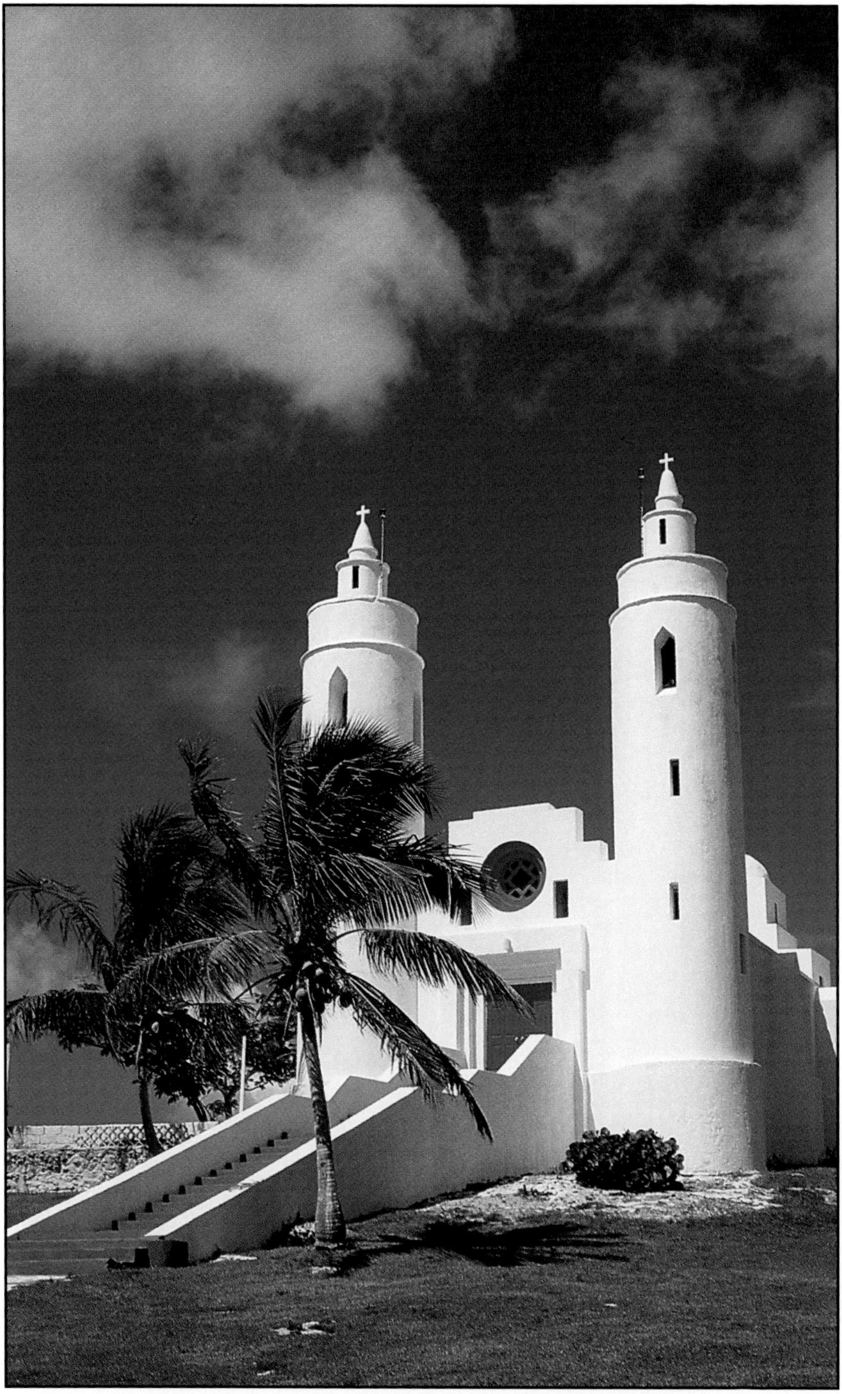

St. Peter and Paul's Catholic Church, Clarence Town, Long Island, one of Father Jerome's architectural masterpieces. *(J.M.)*

and couples are also welcome, but remember there are a lot of children. This is not the place to get away from it all, indeed the group meals and bikini and sarong dress code encourage a get-to-know-ya atmosphere. All meals and drinks (except those taken outside meal times) are included. Most of the guests are European in the summer, with more North Americans in the winter, and the GOs come from the world over. Rooms are located in long two- or three-story buildings facing the large pool and stage area, the garden or the pink-sand beach. Each room has bamboo furniture, a safe, and there is laundry service and a self-serve laundromat. Non-guests can come for lunch and an afternoon by the pool for $30, you must call ahead. The Club has its own bank and a resident doctor. Excursions and car rentals can be arranged.

North and South Palmetto Point

Palmetto Shores Vacation Villas *($90; 15 rooms; PO Box EL-25131, South Palmetto Point, ☎/⇌332-1305)* are strewn over a beachfront property, a few minutes outside of South Palm. The accommodations are simple (not quite villas), but very affordable. A three-bedroom place is only $20 more than a one-bedroom. There are tennis courts and a pretty stretch of beach.

Unique Village *($110, low $90, 4-person villa $180, low $160; MAP $35 per person, AP $50 per person; 10 rooms, ≡, sat tv, K, pb, ℜ; PO Box EL-187, North Palmetto Point, ☎332-1288, ⇌332-1838)* offers an attractive setup, with a secluded location and spacious rooms with kitchens, tile floors, wicker furniture, and balconies overlooking the beach; newer units have French doors opening out onto the balconies. There are hammocks slung between the trees and steps lead down to the pink-sand beach. Snorkelling equipment is available for free, and the hotel can arrange scuba diving and fishing. The two-story building includes a comfortable dining lounge and bar.

Tarpum Bay

Hilton's Haven *($55, low $50, MAP $34; 10 rooms, ℜ, ≡, ⊗, pb; General Post Office, Tarpum Bay, ☎334-4231, 334-4125 or 1-800-688-4752)* is a small place in the centre of Tarpum Springs. The rooms have seen better days, but each has its own balcony and each is inexpensive and clean. The best thing about the place is the hostess and owner, Mary Hilton. The on-site restaurant and bar are a also pretty popular with locals. Fishing guides and car rentals can be arranged.

Venta Club Eleuthera *($80-$120 all-inclusive; pb, sat tv, ≈, ⊘, ≡, ⊗; 108 rooms; Winding Bay, ☎332-4054, ⇌334-4057, www.ivv.it)* sometimes simply called Club Eleuthera, former Winding Bay Club, 24 one-story bungalows for a taste of the Italian Riviera in The Bahamas. Some of the staff don't even speak English, though some speak French; pool-side aerobics, snorkelling masks available, sunfish, windsurfing, kayaks, bicycles, tennis and, of course, soccer. Scuba diving and deepwater fishing are extra, excursions to other points on the island are organized, there are mangroves to explore, and the rooms are a bit cramped. All in all, an exclusive resort run by and for Italians.

Cartwright's Oceanfront Cottages *($90; 5 rooms; K, pb; General Post Office, Tarpum Bay, ☎334-4215)* offers not only the hospitality of Iris Cartwright but also great snorkelling and swimming just 50 feet from your door, spectacular sunsets from your patio and pretty Tarpum Bay a short walk away. Car rentals can be arranged to explore the island. The cottages are tastefully decorated and fully equipped; maid service is included.

Rock Sound

The only decent hotel left in Rock Sound these days is just north of town and may not even be open anymore so double check: **Edwina's Place** *($70; 9 rooms, pb, ≡; PO Box EL-30, Rock Sound, ☎334-2094, ⇒334-2280)* is run by Edwina Burrows, who cooks and does all the cleaning herself. The motel-style rooms are dated to be sure but are spick and span.

RESTAURANTS

Harbour Island

Want something easy and quick but pig's feet stew is not your bag? Try **Island Pizza** *($-$$; Dunmore St.)*. With the usual and not so usual toppings. There are a few tables or you can get it to go.

Ma Ruby's *($-$$; Colebrook St., ☎333-2161)*, at Tignum Village, is famous for her hamburgers, which rank among Jimmy Buffet's favourites but not mine. Go for the Ma's own reputed conch burger instead. The native fare, conch fritter, grouper fingers and the like are all tasty, and the place has a fun feel and decor.

For real afternoon tea with all the fixings, stop in to **Miss Mae's Tea Room and Snack Bar** *($-$$; Dunmore St.)*.

There are a handful of takeaways in town. For those days when you don't feel like washing the salt out of your hair, the **Three Sisters** *($-$$; Love Lane)* and **T&D Takeaway** *($-$$; Munning St., ☎333-2616)* are the answer. Now this is real Bahamian cooking: cracked conch, of course, conch salad, mutton souse, peas 'n' rice and pig's feet stew, yum!

At **Angela's Starfish Restaurant** *($$-$$$; Dunmore St., ☎333-2253)*, Angela Johnson is the Bahama-Mama and the patrons have all come home for dinner. Sunday dinner here is a big event when the table and folding chairs on the front yard fill up with locals and visitors alike. Breakfast is just as popular, so reservations are recommended all day long.

The **Harbour Lounge** *($$-$$$; closed Mon; Bay St., ☎333-2031)* is just as colourful outside as it is inside, and outside things become that much more brilliant as the sun sets. The menu features tasty Bahamian favourites that come in large portions as well as a few innovative dishes like grilled marinated mahi-mahi and curried pumpkin soup.

Valentine's Yacht Club *($$-$$$; Bay St., ☎333-2142)* is home to the island's pub, **The Inn**. The fare is Bahamian with a selection of grouper dishes, pork chops and lamb. Dishes are tasty, if a little heavy, and the servings are large. The boaters and divers that frequent the yacht club make up the majority of the clientele, not exactly a sedate crowd.

The Landing Restaurant *($$$; Bay St., ☎333-2707)* occupies the first floor of the main house of the hotel. With large casement windows open on three sides, breezes flow through the pretty pale yellow dining room decorated with local art. You can eat in the garden at the back or on the verandah, where you'll catch the sunset. The menu lists Bahamian favourites like cracked conch and grouper as well as dishes with French and Italian flavourings like risotto with shrimp, fettucine with saffron and conch and frogs legs. Cap off your meal with delicious profiteroles or tartuffo. The selection of specialty coffees are good and strong. Also open for lunch and breakfast with pancakes, French toast and fruit plates.

The **Romora Bay Club** *(Colebrook St., ☎333-2325)* has two dining possibilities. First there is **Sloppy Joe's Bar** *($)* with burgers, club sandwiches and hot (conch chowder) and cold (gazpacho) soups. Cocktails as the sun goes down are best taken from the large verandah overlooking the water. The second option at the Romora is **Ludo's** *($$$)* where chef Ludocic Jarland prepares Bahamian and French dishes. The fine wine list is sure to contain the perfect accompaniment.

Coral Sands Hotel *(Chapel St., ☎333-2305)* serves unpretentious Bahamian and American dishes in its **Beach Bar Sun Deck** *($-$$)*, where the toasted lobster sandwich is the favourite at lunch, and the **Mediterranean Cafe** *($$$)* for dinner. The best choice on the menu is invariably the fresh catch of the day, usually grouper, prepared in a variety of ways. There is an extensive wine list. Non-guests must have reservations and can order between 7pm and 8pm.

The dining room at the **Dunmore Beach Club** *($$$$; Barrack St., ☎333-2200)* is open to non-guests with reservations. Meals are served in one sitting at 8pm and men must have a jacket in winter. The table d'hote ($45) changes daily but always features excellent Bahamian, continental or Asian cuisine. The cosy and attractive dining room is reason enough to dine here.

When you dine at the **Runaway Hill Club** *($$$$; Colebrooke St., ☎333-2241)* it almost feels like you've been invited to a friend's for dinner. There is a set menu each evening with a few choices for the main dish, usually fish and beef. The London broil and lobster bisque are both particularly good. Local catches are prepared in a handful of original ways. The ambiance is casual, but elegant, men are requested to wear a jacket.

The **Pink Sands Hotel** *(Chapel St., ☎333-2030)* has two restaurants, The Blue Bar and The Club House Restaurant. The **Blue Bar** *($-$$)*, with its festive blue-tiled decor, overlooks the namesake pink-sand beach and is fun for afternoon drinks or for lunch, with an innovative take on native dishes. The **Club House Restaurant** *($$$$)* offers guests and a few lucky non-guests the best dining on the island. Non-guests must make reservations and these are only taken if there is enough room, which unfortunately is not always the case. In good weather, dinner is taken outside on teak tables in a fragrant and dense tropical garden. The four-course menu ($65) is a breath of fresh air, having included tasty offerings like swordfish carpaccio with pink grapefruit and white wine vinaigrette, tandoori seared mutton snapper with cucumber, mint, cilantro and sour cream relish and barbecue jerked pork with tropical fruit salsa and straw potatoes. It changes daily and always includes a choice of meat, fish or pasta. Wines are selected for each meal and you can finish with dessert or a cheese plate.

Spanish Wells

A few blocks over from the Spanish Wells Yacht Haven is **Jack's Outback** *($-$$; Harbourfront)*, the island's own diner complete with diner fare like cheesburgers, fries and chocolate sundaes and, of course, the requisite conch, grouper and lobster dishes.

North Eleuthera

The **Calypso Cafe** *(next to the North Eleuthera Airport, ☎335-1353)* caters mostly to travellers. They are open for breakfast and lunch when they serve sandwiches, salads and burgers. Dinner is by reservation only. Be sure to ask for one of their fresh fruit smoothies (alcoholic or not).

Gregory Town

In Gregory Town proper, **Elvina's Restaurant and Bar** *($; at the southern end of town; ☎335-5032)* serves native Bahamian dishes, as well as a mean Jamaican jerked chicken and pork.

The Cove Eleuthera *($$-$$$$; 5 km south of the Glass Window, 3 km north of Gregory Town, ☎333-5142)* has a large, inviting and relaxing dining room with plants here and there and fresh flowers on each table. Slides of underwater scenes are projected throughout dinner and occasionally there is live music. The Cove's cooks are some of the best from the island and prepare delightful homemade soups, a delicious grouper filet as well as lamb chops, grilled marinated chicken and, of course, cracked conch. On Saturdays there is a roast beef buffet. For dessert, it is a tough choice between Rosemary's pineapple apple crisp, Ann's lime pie and Mercia's coconut pie. Reservations for groups of four or more are appreciated. Breakfast *($)* and lunch *($-$$)* are also served.

Hatchet Bay

The restaurant of the **Rainbow Inn** *($$-$$$; ☎335-0294)* has lots of ambience, decorated with stuff pulled from the sea and maritime bric-a-brac like old brass lanterns, sea glass and burgees. Thick dark-wood tables are set around the perimeter of the octagonal building so that each one is by a window, some of which offer great views of the sea and sunsets. Krabby Ken, the owner, is usually brooding in a corner when he isn't checking on his guests. The menu is a tad uninspired but reliable. There is live music on occasion.

Governor's Harbour

The restaurant and bar at the **Buccaneer Club** *($$; closed Wed; Haynes Ave., ☎332-2000)* is a bland room that is saved by a colourful Mal Flanders mural behind the bar. The atmosphere is friendly, with live music some nights, and the menu has typical native fare and American dishes that come in hefty servings. The grouper fingers are finger-licking good here.

Picchio *($$-$$$; Pine St., ☎332-2455)* occupies a pretty gabled gingerbread house up the hill behind the tourist office. They serve decent Italian cuisine. Call ahead for reservations.

You can join the evening party at **Club Med** *($$$; ☎332-2270)*, if there is room. Dinner includes the show put on by the Gos and is a huge buffet with continental and Bahamian dishes, and seating is at eight-person tables. This is not the place for a quiet dinner for two. An afternoon by pool with lunch is the same price as the dinner and the show. You must call ahead to enter the club, but strangely, reservations are not taken.

North and South Palmetto

Mate and Jenny's Pizza *($-$$; South Palmetto Point, ☎332-1504)* is a gem. For some, the yummy pizzas with their thin and crispy crusts, are the raison d'etre of this place, for others it is the cocktails, cold beer and pool table. The pizza comes with the standard pepperoni and cheese or the more original conch. They also serve the local specialties like cracked conch and broiled grouper. Flags from around the world and snapshots cover the walls.

Unique Village *($$-$$$; North Palmetto Point, ☎322-1838)* has the most complete menu in the area. Happy hour is from 5pm to 7pm when the dinner menu has big steaks, a surprisingly light cracked conch, and the fresh catch of the day among other choices. There is live music on Thursdays and, on Sundays at midday, a barbecue. Breakfast is also recommended with true Bahamian dishes like stewed fish as well as boring old bacon and eggs. Lunch consists of burgers, conch chowder, and lots of salads.

Tarpum Bay

Shine's Famous Seafood *($; small blue-shingled house by the bay)* is famous for its johnnycakes at breakfast and sandwiches, burgers and the like the rest of the day.

Hilton's Haven *($-$$; ☎334-4231 or 334-4125)* has a small restaurant and bar with a simple menu of home-made native dishes for breakfast, lunch and dinner. At dinner, the pork chops, roast beef, fresh grouper and peas 'n' rice are all tasty and affordable. Mary Hilton's pies and cold drinks are also appreciated by customers.

Rock Sound

Among the many local spots, **Sammy's Place** *($-$$; ☎334-2121)* has all the elements of a successful island eatery: namely gossip, rum punches, cold Kaliks, cracked conch, conch fritters, conch chowder, Creole grouper, lobster, johnnycakes, omelettes and stewed fish.

ENTERTAINMENT

Harbour Island

SeaGrapes *(Colebrook St., ☎333-2439)* has live funky music and some serious dancing from Wednesdays to Saturdays. Wednesday is ladies' nights.

The **Vic Hum Club** *(Barrack St. at Munning St., ☎333-2161)* is *the* dance bar on the island. The inspired decor, including a giant coconut behind the bar and checkerboard dance floor, have hosted basketball games, international model shoots, big name performers and, of course, the nightly parade of revellers.

Gusty's *(Coconut Grove, ☎333-2165)* owes much of its popularity to sightings of and even jam sessions by blues legend Jimmy Buffett. The rest of the time it is a dance bar.

Gregory Town

Gregory Town's annual **Eleuthera Pineapple Festival** in early June celebrates this sweet fruit and just keeps getting bigger and bigger, drawing more and more tourists. Fun activities like a teen beauty pageant, a "pineapple-on-a-rope'' eating contest, a pineapple recipe contest and a "pineathelon" race are highlights of the festival. There are refreshing Gregory Town Specials (with pineapple rum or coconut water) and tons of food to keep you going. The Junkanoo Rushout on Saturday ends the festival with a bang.

Governor's Harbour

The **Globe Princess Theater** *(Queen's Highway)* shows recent movies every night at 8pm for $5.

The local joint of choice these days in Governor's Harbour is **Ronnie's Hideaway** *(on Cupid's Cay)* with dancing from 10pm onwards, pool and a game on the big-screen television all night long. Club Med has a shuttle.

Another popular spot is **The Blue Room Restaurant and Bar** *(Pinder's Lane)* with oldies but goodies on Friday and Saturday nights.

SHOPPING

Harbour Island

The **Princess Street Gallery** *(Princess St. between Bay and King streets)* sells originals and prints of many top Bahamian artists, including resident islander Eddie Minnis, as well as pretty decorative items made on Harbour Island.

Briland Androsia *(King St. between Princess and Crown streets)* sells pretty batik items hand-made on Andros. There are dresses, shorts and even bathing suits.

Miss Mae's *(Dunmore St.)* has beautiful household items, colourful prints and cards and other souvenirs.

The **Island Trading Company**, the gift shop at the Pink Sands Hotel, sells the unique batik prints used in the hotel's rooms and many other swish items.

Gregory Town

Island Made is run by Pamela Thompson a Floridian who has been in The Bahamas for 20 years. She combs the beaches for driftwood and shells to use in her island creations. She also sells local straw work, t-shirts and Androsia.

Rebecca's Beach Shop *(☎335-5436)* sells everything for a perfect day at the beach. Rebecca is married to an American known here as Surfer Pete, who can usually be found at Surfer's Beach.

Follow your nose up the hill to the **Thompson Bakery** *(☎335-5053)* where superb fresh bread and divine pineapple tarts (a must), pies, pizzas and sandwiches are available to go.

Governor's Harbour

Norma's Gift Shop *(Queen's Hwy., ☎332-2002)* has a large selection of souvenirs, beachwear, t-shirts, batik dresses, jewellery and perfume. **Brenda's Gift Shop** *(Haynes Ave., ☎332-2089)* has the same.

Rock Sound

Rock Sound has a fair-sized shopping centre with the very well-stocked North American-style **Rock Sound Super Market.**

For nice souvenirs, the **Almond Tree Shop** *(☎334-2385)* is a pretty gift boutique with handmade arts and crafts. **Goombay Gifts** *(☎334-2191)* has T-shirts and straw-work.

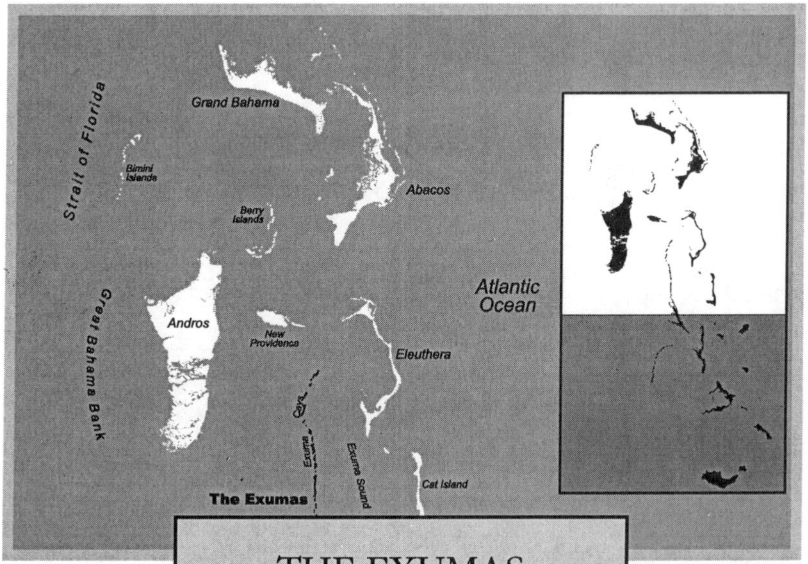

THE EXUMAS

Geographically, the islands of the Exumas ★★★ lie more or less at the centre of The Bahamas, about 65 kilometres southeast of Nassau. In the hearts and minds of most Bahamians sailors, they are also at the heart of The Bahamas. As home to the Family Island Regatta, the biggest truly Bahamian boat races, these 365 islands and cays, extending over 150 kilometres from Sail Rocks in the north to Little Exuma in the south, are very special indeed.

When American astronauts looked down at the Earth, they remarked upon the beauty of these islands trailing off in a sweeping arc, fringed with white beaches and surrounded by translucent waters full of swirls running from pale turquoise to sapphire blue to deep indigo. Be sure to get a window seat on your way here so that you can get some sense of the sight they beheld.

Tourism has not marred the serene existence of most of the Exumas. The majority of Exumans still make a living from the land and the sea. What draws visitors are the exceptional cruising waters and idyllic deserted islands. Diving and snorkelling are superb throughout the chain, but especially in Exuma Cays Land and Sea Park, the first national park to protect a submerged area. There are teeming bonefishing flats to the southwest of the island and deep-sea fishing in Exuma Sound.

A Short History

The Lucayans called these islands Yumey. Columbus never visited them but was told about them or may have even spotted them from Long Island, for they show up on maps from the time. After the capture and enslavement of the Exumas' Lucayans, the islands remained empty until a few Nassauvians drifted over, seeking respite from the pirates of New Providence. They were kept busy with salt raking and some wrecking. It wasn't until the arrival of the Loyalists and their slaves from the Carolinas, Georgia and Florida in 1783 that anything permanent was established; cotton plantations were then built at Rolle Town, Steventon, Ramsey and Mount Thompson, with the largest one at Rolleville. Lord Denys Rolle, originally from Devonshire, England, arrived on a ship called the *Peace & Plenty* with 140 slaves. Eventually more than 400 slaves worked the 7000-acre plantation.

For several years on Great Exuma, everyone got around by boat, there was a road but it was in poor condition and there was no town. Finally in 1793, land was purchased and George Town was laid out. The Loyalists' fortunes turned soon after this. Most of them were merchants with little farming experience, add to that the ravages of the chenille bug, and by 1802 the cotton plantations had failed. Those that could sell their lands did, other simply abandoned them. The Rolle plantation had since been inherited by Lord Denys' son, Lord John. It remained in his hands until Emancipation, when he turned it over to his slaves. In 1896 it became a commonage estate, where former Rolle slaves and their descendents, who all took the Rolle surname, could build and farm.

From that point on, Exumans lived mostly from farming and from the sea. Salt raking and sponging peaked and declined in the early 1900s. George Town experienced a small boom during the Second World War, when the Americans constructed a small seaplane base from which they monitored coastal traffic in the Crooked Island Passage. In 1953, the first annual Family Island Regatta was held here and soon Royals like the King of Greece and Jackie Onassis started coming to enjoy the party in George Town and the virgin beauty of the islands. Despite all this attention, mass tourism has yet to hit the Exumas. So far there are no megaresorts, though Ritz Carlton has the plans drawn up and their sights fixed on Ocean Bight.

FINDING YOUR WAY AROUND

By Plane

There is one major airport in the Exumas, **George Town Airport**, which is 16 kilometres north of George Town in Moss Town. **Bahamasair** *(☎345-0035 in Moss Town or 327-5505)* has daily flights from Nassau and twice-weekly flights from Miami. **American Eagle** *(☎327-5124 in Nassau)* has daily flights from Miami.

There is also an airstrip on Staniel Cay for charters and private planes. All arrivals must clear customs at the airport, however. Island Express *(☎954-359-0380)* has flights from Fort Lauderdale.

By Boat

By Mailboat: All departures are from Potter's Cay (under the Paradise Island Bridge) in Nassau and all fares are one way. The *Grand Master* departs Tuesdays at 2pm for George Town. Travel time: 12 hours. Fare: $35. The *Ettienne & Cephas* departs Tuesday at 2pm and puts in at Staniel Cay, Black Point, Little Farmer's Cay and Barraterre on its way to Ragged Island. Travel time: 12 hours (of total 21). Fare: $30.

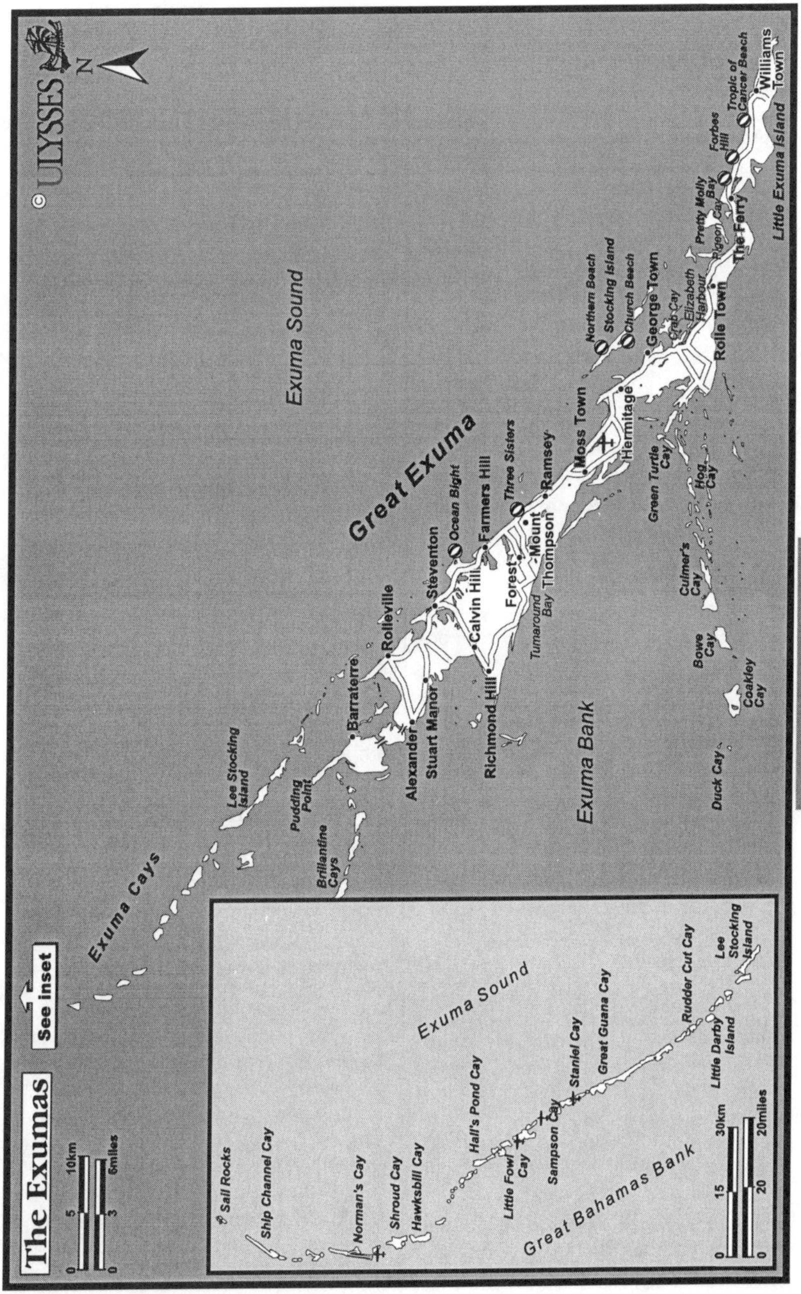
The Exumas
0 5 10km
0 3 6miles
© ULYSSES
N
See inset
Exuma Cays
Exuma Sound
Great Exuma
Exuma Bank
Lee Stocking Island
Pudding Point
Brillantine Cays
Barraterre
Rolleville
Steveton
Alexander
Stuart Manor
Richmond Hill
Calvin Hill
Ocean Bight
Farmers Hill
Forest
Mount Thompson
Tumaround Bay
Three Sisters
Ramsey
Moss Town
Hermitage
Northern Beach
Stocking Island
Church Beach
George Town
Crab Cay
Elizabeth Harbour
Rolle Town
Pigeon Cay
Pretty Molly Bay
The Ferry
Forbes Hill
Tropic of Cancer Beach
Williams Town
Little Exuma Island
Green Turtle Cay
Hog Cay
Culmer's Cay
Bowe Cay
Coakley Cay
Duck Cay
Sail Rocks
Ship Channel Cay
Norman's Cay
Shroud Cay
Hawksbill Cay
Hall's Pond Cay
Little Fowl Cay
Sampson Cay
Staniel Cay
Great Guana Cay
Little Darby Island
Rudder Cut Cay
Lee Stocking Island
Great Bahamas Bank
0 15 30km
0 20 20miles

Marinas

There are a handful of equipped marinas in the Exumas:

George Town Dock ☎336-2578.

Happy People Marina, Staniel Cay, ☎355-2008.

Staniel Cay Yacht Club, ☎355-2024.

Sampson Cay Colony, ☎355-2034.

Ferries

The Club Peace & Plenty has a ferry service to Stocking Island, departing the club at 10am and 1pm, and returning at 12:45pm and 3:45pm. Another ferry runs from the Peace & Plenty Beach Inn at 10am and 12:30pm, returning at 1pm and 4pm. It is free for Peace & Plenty guests and $5 for non-guests.

Boat Rentals

Exuma Dive Centre *(☎336-2390)* rents 17-foot motorboats for $75 per day or $375 per week. A $100 security deposit is required for daily rentals, $150 for weekly rentals.

By Car and Scooter

The Queen's Highway runs the length of northeastern coast of Great Exuma, a few roads run southwest. A small bridge connects Great and Little Exuma. Bridges also connect Great Exuma and the two Barraterre Cays.

Exuma Transport *(☎336-2101)* and **Thompson's Car Rental** *(☎336-2442)* both rent cars in George Town for $60 per day.

Scooters can be rented from **Exuma Dive Centre** *(☎336-2390)* in George Town for $40 per day, with a $25 deposit.

By Bus

There is limited public transportation provided by a minibus that runs northwest from George Town to Moss Town at 2:45pm and 6:35pm, and southeast to Williams Town at 8am, noon and 5:30pm. The fare is $3 per trip.

Guided Tours

Christina Rolle runs a small tour company called **Island Tours** *(☎358-4014)*. She gives two tours of the island, one to Little Exuma and the other to Barraterre. The price is $15 per person, but if there are less than six people it may cost more.

Seaside Tours *(George Town; ☎336-2091)* offers daily tours of northern and southern Great Exuma, as well as trips to see the ruins on Crab Cay.

PRACTICAL INFORMATION

Great Exuma

George Town

Tourist Information: Bahamas Ministry of Tourism, open Mon to Fri 9am to 5:30pm, east of the Club Peace & Plenty, facing the Anglican Church, ☎336-2431.

Bank: Scotiabank, south of the channel in Lake Victoria, open Mon to Fri 9:30am to 1pm, Fri also 3pm to 5pm, ☎336-2651.

Police: in the Government Building, beside Club Peace & Plenty, ☎336-2666.

BaTelCo: at the southern end of town.

Post Office: in the Government Building.

Clinic: Government Clinic, beside the Anglican Church, ☎336-2088. Private clinic northwest of town, ☎336-2220.

Travel Agency: H.L. Young, above the Scotiabank, ☎336-2703.

★ EXPLORING

Great Exuma

George Town ★★

George Town is the capital of the Exumas, and the largest settlement on the islands. It lies along one circular road that runs around inland Lake Victoria. A narrow channel leads into the lake from small Kidd's Cove which overlooks Elizabeth Harbour, protected by beautiful Stocking Island, an 11-kilometre-long barrier island, which is a quick boat ride away (see p 203). Elizabeth island, Guana Cay and Crab Cay also lie offshore and can be visited. This huge harbour was once used by pirates, and in more recent years by British war ships.

There are a handful of historic buildings in George Town. Pretty white **St. Andrew's Anglican Church** ★ and its **cemetery** are up the hill to the west of the town centre. The church dates from 1887 and it is the third on this site overlooking the lake; the first one was consecrated in 1802 shortly after the founding of George Town. Heading back towards town, try and pick out the **old sponge warehouse** and **slave kitchen** (you'll have to go inside to the pub for this one) from the present pink facade of the Club Peace & Plenty Hotel. Next door is the grand columned neoclassical **Government Building** ★, also pink. It houses the post office, police station, law courts and jail. The government dock is straight ahead. The weekly mail boat arrives here and stirs things up in this otherwise quiet town, unless of course you are here during the Family Island Regatta (see p 214).

Continuing around the lake, you'll pass a curious monument to the famous regatta. ***Patsy***, the first wooden dinghy to win the regatta, lies in Regatta Park. The **Straw Market** is here as well. Next you'll enter the commercial part of George Town where the bank, grocery store and marina are located.

Stocking Island ★★★

Stocking Island is a sliver of paradise just ten minutes from George Town by boat. A ferry (see p 202) runs from the Club Peace & Plenty to what they like to call Hamburger Beach because of the snack bar, but what is really called Church Beach. Facing Elizabeth Harbour, it is protected and good for swimming with small children. Snorkelling equipment, sailboats and kayaks can be rented here. There is also a path across the island to the much wilder and awesome northern **beach** ★★★ with crashing surf, shells, white sand and high grassy bluffs. Another path leads up to the **Salt Beacon**, erected to guide ships coming for salt. There is good snorkelling and diving in Gaviotta Bay, which is actually three blue holes that offer excellent shelter for boats during hurricanes. One of these is a stromatolite reef, a growing limestone reef dating back 3.5 million years. It is more commonly known as Mystery Cave.

Northern Great Exuma

The drive north of George Town is an uneventful ride through a series of tiny settlements, all former plantations, and alongside some fabulous wild beaches. You'll pass through **Hermitage**, **Moss Town** and **Ramsey**, where you can have a good meal at Iva Bowe's place (see p 213). Continuing north at the settlement of **Mount Thompson**, you'll see three rocks just offshore. These are called the **Three Sisters ★★**, legend has it that three sisters who bore children out of wedlock each drowned here. The geological explanation for the rocks has it that their composition is different from the surrounding limestone. Picnics to the rocks are organized from the Three Sisters resort (see p 210).

Just beyond the settlement of **Farmer's Hill** is **Ocean Bight ★★★**, with a spectacular, so-far unspoilt beach. This is the proposed sight for the Ritz Carlton Bahama Club project. The next settlements are **Rocker's Point** and **Steventon**. **Rolleville**, not to be confused with Rolle Town to the south, lies at the end of the road at the northern tip of Great Exuma. One story goes that farm slaves from the Rolle plantation were given land here, while domestic slaves went to Rolle Town. Whether or not this is true, they all eventually took up farming.

Two separate cays lie just north of Great Exuma and **Barraterre** is on the second one. Two bridges lead to this drowsy hilltop hamlet, once part of the McKenzie plantation, hence the proliferation of McKenzies today. There isn't much to see here, things only perk up when the mailboat arrives.

Southern Great Exuma

There is really only one settlement south of George Town: **Rolle Town ★**. This was once the centre of the vast Rolle Estate, which included Rolleville, Mount Thompson, Ramsey and Steventon. It was originally granted to Lord Denys Rolle, who arrived in the Exumas aboard a ship called the *Peace & Plenty* in 1783, and was then passed on to his son, Lord John Rolle. He was the largest slave-holder on the island and after emancipation, he ceded all the lands of the estate to his 300-odd slaves. History has been kind to Lord John, painting him as a great benefactor and forgetting the slave revolts on the plantation in 1829 and the fact that he was compensated by the Crown for his gift. Nevertheless, the lands were turned over to the slaves forever. With all those Rolles, for it was common for slaves to take their masters' name, there was much confusion, and in 1896 the land became a commonage estate where anyone with the surname Rolle could build and plant, and still can. Rolle is still the most common surname in the Exumas, accounting for nearly half the population. Apparently the Rolles themselves know which Rolles they are, however!

The town sits on a hill overlooking excellent and beautiful bonefishing flats (see p 210). Many of the tiny stone and plain clapboard shacks are former slave dwellings that run the test of time with a bright coat of paint every few years. Tucked in behind one of these are three **Loyalist tombs ★★**. The romantic and tragic story that goes with them makes them much more interesting. Back in 1789, Captain Alexander McKay arrived on Great Exuma to establish a plantation on 400 acres he had been granted. In 1791, his young wife Anne joined him. The plantation was already beginning to fail by this time, and in March of 1792

McKay tried to sell his lands. Eight short months later Anne died, probably in childbirth. Obviously grief-stricken, the Captain built a lavish tomb for her, a sure sign of his undying love. Two years later he died and was buried in a smaller tomb next to his wife and child. The fact that the graves lie on the Rolle Estate, suggests that McKay may have been an overseer of the plantation.

The Peace & Plenty Bonefish Lodge (see p 210) is right before the bridge to Little Exuma.

Little Exuma ★

The Ferry is a tiny settlement up the hill on the other side of the bridge and is named for the cable ferry that once linked Little and Great Exuma. The hulk of an old ferry lies half-submerged by the bridge. Gleaming white St. Christopher's Anglican Church is the Fitzgerald family chapel and supposedly the smallest church in The Bahamas.

The **Shark Lady Museum ★★★**, also in The Ferry, is the closest thing the Exumas have to a museum. It is actually the home of Gloria Patience, the "Shark Lady". Now in her seventies, this remarkable lady has wrestled with about 1,800 sharks in her lifetime. She once skippered a sailboat with a topless crew, she was a consultant to *Jaws* author Peter Benchley and she has communed with Jacques Cousteau. She also firmly states, and one tends to believe her, that sharks are not the docile creatures current thinking makes them out to be. A flowery garden and yard crowded with stones and relics fronts her small house called Tara, where she tells her stories and sells shark-bone jewellery and all sorts of quirky collectables and bric-a-brac.

Uninhabited **Pigeon Cay**, lying just offshore, can be visited for a picnic and snorkelling. A wrecked ship lies in shallow water nearby. You can arrange a ride out by asking around in The Ferry.

The road continues southeast past appropriately named **Pretty Molly Bay**. The ghost of pretty Molly, a slave who committed suicide by walking out to sea one night, supposedly haunts this beautiful beach. The defunct Sand Dollar Beach Club is here. The scars of Hurricane Lilly can still be seen in the toppled palms. **Forbes Hill** has a beautiful beach, and a few kilometres south, Tropic of Cancer Beach is another stunning swath of sand.

Williams Town lies alongside a large reddish-coloured salt lake. Most everyone here is a Kelsall, having descended from slaves on the Kelsall Plantation where cotton was farmed and salt was raked. Roger Kelsall came here in 1784 from Georgia with his family. The plantation did not prosper and was eventually taken over by Kelsall's son John who was named Speaker of the Assembly in 1794. The plantation was not his priority and was abandoned in the early 1800s. Despite this, its ruins are among the best preserved in The Bahamas. The main house of the **Hermitage Estate ★★**, called the **Cotton House**, was built in 1784 and lived in until the 1970s – it is now abandoned and being swallowed up by the bush. A simple stone bungalow with a shingled roof, the house overlooks the estate and large salt lagoon, and backs onto the sea. A separate kitchen and storehouse with a large brick chimney and fireplace can also be seen, as well as two adjoining roofless buildings believed to have been slave quarters. Made of cut limestone blocks, they share a chimney and each has a large fireplace.

Norman's Cay

Until the early 1980s, stunning Norman's Cay was a posh getaway for the rich and famous. Then the wrong famous person, a German-Colombian drug-lord by the name of Carlos Lehder, decided to not just move in, but to buy the whole island. The Colombian flag was rung up and Lehder's armed thugs drove out the residents. Soon planes were arriving and taking off daily with their illegal cargoes. An exposé on American television in 1983 revealed that Lyndon Pindling's government was turning a complicitous blind eye. As a result, Lehder was eventually sent to jail, and the scandal-racked Pindling government was ultimately brought down. A few residents have since returned to Norman's Cay, where they like to keep things nice and quiet, but the former Norman's Cay Club never reopened.

On a bluff overlooking the town and the sea stands the **Salt Beacon**, a Tuscan-styled column erected during first half of 19th century to guide ships coming for salt at William's Town.

Exuma Cays

Lee Stocking Island ★★

Lee Stocking Island, about eight kilometres north of Great Exuma, is home to a field station of the **Caribbean Marine Research Center** *(PO Box EX-29001, George Town, Exuma, ☎/⇌345-6039)*. Ongoing studies include finding ways to manage the region's valuable marine species, including mutton snapper, queen conch, spiny lobster and Nassau grouper; protecting coral reef ecosystems; monitoring the effects of global climate change in marine ecosystems and exploring deep-sea environments. A conservation lodge with visitor accommodations is in the works. For now visitors are welcome to visit the island where short tours are given.

Staniel Cay ★★

Staniel Cay has a small local population and a tiny settlement with a twee little straw market. Things remain sleepy most of the year here. Try to time your visit to coincide with the Annual Bonefishing Tournament in early August during Independence Day Weekend, or at New Year's when the island hosts a small regatta. Staniel makes a good base for exploring the surrounding cays, especially Exuma Cays Land and Sea Park (see below).

The coolest thing here has to be **Thunderball Grotto ★★★**, which you might recognize from the James Bond movies *Thunderball* and *Never Say Never Again*, or from the comedy *Splash*. Snorkelling and diving trips are organized down into this cavern, where colourful tropical fish glitter in the shaft of light streaming through holes in the roof. The grotto is northwest off Staniel Cay.

Exuma Cays Land and Sea Park ★★★

Exuma Cays Land and Sea Park was created in 1958. Covering an area of 450 square kilometres, it was the first park to protect a submerged area. The parks runs from Wax Way Cut in the

Bananaquit

north to Conch Cut in the south. There are exceptional anchorages, stunning beaches, walking trails and some of the best snorkelling in The Bahamas. The park ranger station *(access to park is free; Mon to Sat 9am to noon, 1pm to 5pm, Sun 9am to 1pm)* is located on Warderick Wells Cay. The ranger departs from Staniel Cay on a daily run of the park and sometimes takes people with him. Otherwise you'll need your own boat. As such it can be costly to visit the park. Remember that all commercial fishing is banned as is shell-collecting. *Nothing* can be removed, doing so carries very hefty fines.

Among the earthbound highlights are the driftwood-strewn beaches of Shroud Cay, the trails and plantation ruins of Hawksbill Cay and the six-and-a-half kilometres of trails on Warderick Wells Cay. An exceptional variety of species inhabit these islands. Birders chance spotting rare red-legged thrushes, nighthawks, long-tailed tropicbirds, bananaquits, Bahama mockingbirds, terns and herons. On the ground are rare hutias, the only indigenous land mammal in The Bahamas, and both curly- and blue-tailed lizards.

The underwater highlights include shallow reef gardens teeming with conch, spiny lobsters, sea turtles, groupers and all manner of colourful tropical fish. Depths between one and three metres make for excellent snorkelling.

Allan's Cays are not part of the park, but are nonetheless protected by the Bahamas National Trust. They harbour the only population of Bahamian dragons, a rare species of rock iguanas that can grow to up to five feet in length. They lumber about the beach here, quite oblivious to humans.

BEACHES

Most of Exumas snow-white beaches are deserted, pristine and dotted with driftwood, sand dollars and beautiful shells of all kinds.

The best beach in the vicinity of George Town is, hands-down, the beach on the north shore of **Stocking Island ★★★**. Nothing quite prepares you for the sight of the surf crashing onto this deserted stretch of sand when you reach the top of the grassy bluffs that line the beach. The surf can be rough, so swimming is iffy, but what a sight! If you want to swim or have little ones in toe, Peace & Plenty's "Hamburger Beach", actually called **Church Beach** ★, has crystal-clear waters that are almost as calm as a swimming pool's.

North of George Town, there are fine stretches facing the **Three Sisters** ★ and at **Ocean Bight** ★★★. The latter is a protected crescent of sand. Go there before it is changed forever by a proposed resort and casino.

The northern shore of Little Exuma has three terrific beaches. **Pretty Molly Bay** ★★ and **Forbes Hill** ★★ are semi-protected sweeps lined with palms and casuarinas. **Tropic of Cancer Beach** ★★★ is a long beach with great shelling and a steady surf.

OUTDOOR ACTIVITIES

Scuba Diving and Snorkelling

Many of the top dives in the Exumas are blue-hole dives. These include Angelfish Blue Hole, Crab Cay Crevasse and Mystery Cave, a stromatolite reef, which is a growing limestone reef (see p 203). The abundance of coral heads and shallow reefs allows divers to view a wealth of underwater species like lobsters, stingrays and colourful corals.

The best snorkelling in the Exumas, and maybe even the whole Bahamas, is in Exuma Cays Land and Sea Park where the waters and reefs are literally teeming with life. The closest jumping-off point for the park is Staniel Cay (see also p 206 and 209).

Another popular snorkelling and diving locale is the Thunderball Grotto, from the James Bond movie of the same name, just off Staniel Cay (see p 206).

Exuma Dive Centre *(mailing address: PO Box EX-29238, George Town, ☎336-2390)* offers diving and snorkelling trips. A one-tank dive is $50, snorkelling trip $25. They also rent diving equipment and offer full diving instruction, from introductory courses ($90) to full certification.

Exuma Fantasea *(mailing address: PO Box EX-29261, George Town, ☎336-3842)* offers eco-dives led by a marine biologist. They specialize in blue-hole diving, but also offer three dives daily. A one-tank dive is $55; instruction includes resort courses for $90 as well as various certification levels. Snorkelling trips cost $25.

Fishing

For deep-sea fishing excursions, try **Cooper's Charter Services** *(☎336-2711)*. A full day costs $500. There are several skilled private guides in the islands; for recommendations contact the **Exumas Guides Association** *(☎336-2222)*.

The **Peace & Plenty Bonefish Lodge** steals the show as far as bonefishing is concerned in the Exumas. It offers bonefishing and fly-tying courses, plus some of the best guides in The Bahamas. Two people can get a boat, guide and tackle for $290 per day. The lodge also offers various packages including accommodation and fishing (see also p 210).

Birdwatching

The birdwatching opportunities are exceptional in the Exumas, certainly on par with Great Inagua and Great Abaco.

Unfortunately, remote Exuma Cays Land and Sea Park (see p 206) can be complicated and costly to reach. If you haven't got your own boat, consider one of the options below.

Adventure Excursions

Two outfits on Paradise Island organize day-long snorkelling and walking excursions to Exuma Cays Land and Sea Park: **Island World Adventures** *(☎363-3577)* and **Out Island Voyages** *(☎394-0951 or 1-800-241-4591)*, the latter also offers more luxurious four- and seven-day cruises in the Exumas.

Sea-kayaking trips to the chain and to Exuma Cays Land and Sea Park are offered by the following outfits in the United States and Canada: **Ibis Tours** *(☎1-800-525-9411, ⇌954-738-1605)* and **Ecosummer Expeditions** *(mailing address: 1516 Duranleau St., Vancouver BC, V6H 3S4, ☎604-669-7741 or 1-800-465-8884, ⇌604-669-3244)*

ACCOMMODATIONS

Great Exuma

George Town

Two Turtles Inn *($88, low $68, bkfst incl.; 12 rooms, ≡, ⊗, K, sat tv, pb; PO Box EX-29251, George Town, ☎336-2545, ⇌336-2528)* is a no-fuss place right in town. Rooms are dull with old wood panelling, carpeting and louvered windows. Each has one twin and one double bed. Three rooms have kitchenettes.

Regatta Point *($122, low $104; 6 rooms, ⊗, K, pb; PO Box EX-29006, George Town, ☎336-2206, ⇌336-2046)* is a collection of self-catering units on the dangling point beyond the government dock. It is just a short walk from town but very secluded and private. Facing a small beach lined with palm trees, the four standard units are nice and breezy. Two larger units have a slightly more romantic feel. Bicycles can be borrowed free of charge.

Coconut Cove Hotel *($128, low $100, bkfst $8; 11 rooms, pb, sat tv, ≡, ⊗, ℜ, ≈; PO Box EX-29299, George Town, ☎336-2659, ⇌336-2658).* Hosts Tom Chimento and Pamela Predmore decided to share their breezy beachside home a few years ago, transforming it into a cosy and luxurious hotel. The romantic tone is set outside with trellises, a waterfall and footbridge and continues inside with rich mahogany doors and panels. Sliding glass doors line the beach side of the hotel, lead to private balconies for each room and offer great views. Mosquito netting is draped over the king-size beds and there are cosy his and hers bathrobes. The top-of-the-line "Paradise Suite" has a private patio with an outdoor hot tub, plus an oversized marble bathtub and an indoor Jacuzzi. Amenities in each room include an iron and ironing board and a hair dryer. There is a small pool.

Club Peace & Plenty *($140, low $110, MAP $36; 35 rooms, ≡, ≈, ℜ; PO Box EX-29055, George Town, ☎336-2551 or 1-800-525-2210, ⇌336-2093).* Named after the ship that brought Lord Denys Rolle here in 1783, Club Peace & Plenty is the oldest hotel in the Exumas. The lobby, located in the old sponge warehouse, along with new adjoining two-storied buildings that contain the guest rooms, form a U around a small pool facing the harbour. Pink predominates in the recently refurbished rooms, with their shell-filled lamps, colourful underwater-scene bedspreads and coordinated curtains.

Each one has a large balcony overlooking the pool or the harbour (though they remain quite dark). The latter are more private. Children under six are not allowed in winter. The hotel has a free ferry to Stocking Island, plus the use of a Sunfish and a tennis court. It offers Jean-Michel Cousteau's Out Island Snorkeling Adventures. The club has a good restaurant and bar (see p 212).

Peace & Plenty Beach Inn *($150, low $130, MAP $36; 16 rooms, pb, ≡, sat tv, ℜ, ≈, ⊗; PO Box EX-29055, George Town, ☎336-2250, or 1-800-525-2210, ⇌336-2253)* is down the road a ways from the Club Peace & Plenty in a residential part of town called Jolly Hall. As its name suggests, it has a beach, though it isn't much to coo about. Open since 1991, the facilities are modern and well designed. Green predominates in the rooms here, which boast Italian tile floors and are superior to those at the Club; they all face the water with private balconies. There is a small pool, and guests have the use of a Sunfish. The dining room and bar are equally attractive (see p 213). Meal plans here are interchangeable with the Club and there is a free shuttle to George Town.

Flamingo Bay Hotel & Villas *($160; 12 rooms, ≡, ℜ, ⊗, sat tv; PO EX-29090, George Town, ☎/⇌336-2660)* is just south of George Town. Rooms and public areas of this establishment have a comfortable Southwestern decor, with a bit of island styling thrown in. The whole sits overlooking Flamingo Bay.

Stocking Island

Hotel Higgins Landing *($330 to $520 with MAP, AP add $20; 5 cottages, pb, ℜ; Stocking Island, mailing address: PO Box EX-29146, George Town, ☎336-2460, ⇌357-0008)*, the only hotel of Stocking island, is the first solar-powered resort in The Bahamas, and the environmental-friendliness of this charming spot doesn't end here: there are composting toilets, rain water is the only source of water, there are no bathtubs (they use too much water), cross-ventilation is used instead of air-conditioning to keep things cool and there are no electric lights in the dining room. Provided you can afford it, there are plenty of other reasons besides green ones to stay here, however. Rustic but elegant rooms sport antique iron beds, hand-embroidered pillow cases, cool terracotta floor tiles and big balconies with great views, while the dining room is decked out in fine Pennsylvania antiques collected by the gracious hosts. There is an outdoor honour bar and cosy library and book exchange. Guests can explore the almost deserted island or take to the water in a Sunfish, kayak or windsurfer. No children under 18 permitted. No smoking.

Northern Great Exuma

The Palms At Three Sisters Beach Resort *($105, low $75; 14 rooms, ≡, ⊗, sat tv, pb, ℜ; in Mount Thompson, mailing address: PO Box EX-29216, George Town, ☎358-4040, ⇌358-4043)* is a plantation-style hotel surrounded by green grass and faces a beautiful breezy white-sand beach and the Three Sisters Rocks. The 12 rooms are decent, but a bit lacklustre. Each has sliding glass doors leading to a patio. Two cottages are also available. There is a tennis court.

Southern Great Exuma

Peace & Plenty Bonefish Lodge *($376; 8 rooms, ≡, ℜ; mailing address: PO Box EX-29713, George Town, ☎345-5555*

Ulysses' Favourites

Accommodations

Best Value for Your Money:

Regatta Point (see p 209) and Club Peace & Plenty (see p 209).

Best Resort for Honeymooners:

Coconut Cove Hotel (see p 209) and Hotel Higgins Landing (see p 210).

Best Overall Decor:

Hotel Higgins Landing (see p 210).

Restaurants

Best True-true Bahamian Cooking:

Eddie's Edgewater Bar & Restaurant (see p 212), Iva Bowe's Central Highway Inn (see p 213) and Kermit's Hilltop Tavern (see p 213).

Best Dining Experience:

Eddie's Edgewater (see p 212), Club Peace & Plenty (see p 212), Coconut Cove (see p 213) and Higgins Landing (see p 213).

Funkiest Ambiance:

Club Thunderball (see p 214).

or 1-800-525-2210, ⇄345-5556), at the southern end of Great Exuma, has large, tastefully decorated rooms with two queen-sized beds. They are comfortable but fairly standard. The lodge is a separate building, built of local stone and timber. The decor is "lodgey", with a card room and lounge. The lodge is the best of its kind in The Bahamas and seems to charge extra for it; a variety of packages are available, for example three nights including fishing is $1504. See also p 213.

Little Exuma

La Shante Beach Club and Guest House *($85, low $65; 4 rooms, pb, ≡, sat tv, K, ℜ; PO Box EX-29183, Forbes Hill, ☎345-4136)* is a very quiet no-frills hideaway that faces a stunning deserted white-sand beach. The rooms are very bare, with white tiles, pale green walls and white bedspreads. Each has a patio overlooking the surf. Dwight Brice runs the place and will gladly help plan your island excursions and offer free transportation to George Town.

Exuma Cays

Staniel Cay

Happy People Marina *($75; 8 rooms, pb, sb, ≡, ℜ; Staniel Cay, ☎355-2008)* has colourful motel-style waterfront rooms. The restaurant is not right on site (see p 214).

Staniel Cay Yacht Club *($170, low $155, MAP $30; 6 cottages, ≡, pb, ℝ, sat tv; Staniel Cay, ☎355-2024, ⇌355-2044)* is popular with families and fishers. The six colourfully painted and individually decorated cottages include four cottages, one houseboat cottage and one guest house with room for six people. Each one has a balcony to take full advantage of the exceptional waterfront locale. Bicycles and small motorboats can be rented, there is also a full-service marina. Diving and fishing excursions are arranged.

Sampson Cay

Sampson Cay Colony *($125; 4 rooms, pb, ≡, ℜ, K; Sampson Cay, ☎/⇌355-2034)* is run by the Mitchells, Rosie plays hostess and Marcus is a modern-day wrecker with a marine salvage company. They offer two spacious efficiency cottages and two villas; one of the latter is in a curious two-story stone tower of sorts.

Cistern Cay

True escapists with a lot of money to burn can have a whole island to themselves. **Cistern Cay** *(☎326-7875 or 804-288-2823)* has an opulent house that comes complete with chef and fishing guide. A mere $38,000 will get you a week in this paradise!

RESTAURANTS

Great Exuma

George Town

Quick and simple lunches and breakfasts are available at **Sam's Place** *($; at the Exuma Dock, ☎336-2579)* overlooking the harbour. A tasty alternating dinner menu is also offered. Sam opens up at 7:30am.

Towne Cafe & Bakery *($; ☎336-2194)* makes fresh breads, cakes and muffins and also serves an authentic Bahamian breakfast of Johnny cake, grits and souse that will keep you going all morning. You can also get a freshly-squeezed orange juice.

Eddie's Edgewater Bar & Restaurant *($-$$; on the southwestern shore of Lake Victoria, ☎336-2050)* is a tiny place, but turns out some excellent Bahamian cooking. Just as good if not better than the big hotels, plus great ambiance and prices you can live with.

The restaurant at the **Two Turtles Club** *($$; ☎336-2545)* is more interesting than the rooms. The food is standard, but the atmosphere is usually pretty fun, especially on Tuesdays and Fridays when it hosts a barbecue. Not open for breakfast.

The **Club Peace & Plenty** *($$-$$$; ☎336-2551)* has a bright and airy restaurant overlooking the pool. The food is fairly sophisticated, but the menu still lists several Bahamian home-cooking favourites, like grits for breakfast, cracked conch for lunch and steamed grouper for dinner; if you prefer, you can also get French toast, bacon and eggs in morning, and a prime steak or even Cornish hens in the evening. Lunch is also served on the beach on Stocking Island (see p 203).

Coconut Cove Restaurant *($$-$$$; ☎336-2659)* boasts an award-winning chef and exceptional service. The main dining room is an attractive glassed-in, wood-pannelled room, or you can eat outside on a wood patio. The menu selections are Bahamian and Italian, with good desserts coffee. It is open for breakfast, lunch and dinner.

The **Peace & Plenty Beach Inn** *($$-$$$; ☎336-2250)* prepares Bahamian favourites like at the Club, but also lists some continental and French selections on its menu. The dining room is set in an attractive grate room overlooking the water.

Stocking Island

Non-guests are welcome to dine at **Higgins Landing** *($$$$; closed Mon, ☎336-2460)* with reservations; there is a free pick-up in George Town. There is one seating at 6:30pm. The several-course menu changes daily and when I visited offered baked brie, spinach and basil salad with pine nuts, coconut shrimp with curried cream sauce and basmati rice. Fresh bread and fine wines are served with each meal. The dining room, with views of the bay, is a cosy fuss of oak antiques, candles, antique silver flatware and fine china.

Northern Great Exuma

Iva Bowe's Central Highway Inn *($; Ramsey, ☎345-7014)* has a good reputation on the island for the best and most tender cracked conch in the Exumas. She also prepares other tasty Bahamian favourites and serves them up in a modest locale.

Kermit Rolle, Exuma's most enterprising taxi driver, has two popular eateries. **Kermit's Airport Lounge** *($; at the airport, ☎345-0002)* serves burgers and fried fish and is a handy place to wait. The food and ambiance are much better at **Kermit's Hilltop Tavern** *($-$$; Rolleville, ☎345-6006)*, where the menu offers a tasty curried mutton alongside cracked conch, steamed conch and steamed grouper. A few tables are set up on the roof and offer great views of the multi-hued sea.

In Barraterre the best food is at the **Fisherman's Inn** *($-$$; ☎355-5017)*, open for breakfast, lunch and dinner. Seafood predominates and reservations are recommended in the evening.

Southern Great Exuma

Peace & Plenty Bonefish Lodge *($$-$$$; ☎345-5555)* is a member of the Chaîne des Rôtisseurs gourmet society and as such has a fairly sophisticated menu, with an emphasis on the freshest seafoods. The dramatic but elegant stone and timber lodge adds to the dining experience. Reservations recommended.

Little Exuma

Mom's Bakery *($; William's Town ☎345-4062)* bakes up fresh breads, cakes and snacks.

Kelson Point Restaurant & Bar *($-$$; William's Town, ☎345-4043)* is a family-run eatery with sandwiches, cracked conch and conch chowder. A good red snapper platter is served in the evening.

Annual Events

March
The Annual Cruising Regatta is raced by visiting yachts in Elizabeth Habour. For information call Kermit Rolle *(☎345-0002).*

April
The Family Island Regatta, held in George Town, is the biggest and best of its kind in The Bahamas. For four days over 50 traditional Bahamian sloops and work boats are pitted against each other in a series of races to determine the best sailors, crews and boatbuilders in The Bahamas. The festivities and races draw crowds from all over the Bahamas starting a week before the actual races and lasting a few days afterward. There are cookouts, rake 'n' scrape bands, activities and contests. For information call the Ministry of Tourism *(☎336-2430 or 1-800-422-4262 or 1-800-667-3777)* or Chris Kettle *(☎358-4034).* Hotel reservations are an absolute must during the period.

October
Annual Bahamas Bonefish Bonanza

December
George Town's Junkanoo is a particularly noisy and colourful event, complete with the traditional costumed parade.

Exuma Cays

Staniel Cay

The **Royal Entertainer Lodge** *($; ☎355-2008)* at the Happy People Marina is a fun and authentic place. The food is home-cooked Bahamian. There is live music on occasion.

The **Club Thunderball** *($-$$)* is a funky spot overlooking the famous grotto. A pool table and satellite television keep the place full all evening long.

The **Staniel Cay Yacht Club & Marina** *($-$$; ☎355-2011)* has an informal dining room in the clubhouse, serving three meals a day. Box lunches are also available. It caters mostly to cottage guests, visiting sailors are welcome but must have reservations.

ENTERTAINMENT

Great Exuma

George Town

Eddie's Edgewater Bar & Restaurant *(on the southwestern shore of Lake Victoria, ☎336-2050)* rocks on Saturday nights to a live rake 'n' scrape band. It attracts locals and visitors alike.

The **Club Peace & Plenty** *(☎336-2551)* has an attractive pub-lounge with a nautical decor in a converted slave kitchen. Beers on tap and sweet cocktails are served here; when it fills up, the party inevitably spills out onto the pool deck.

Northern Great Exuma

The **Whale's Tail** *(Hooper's Bay, ☎336-2979)* restaurant, in the small settlement of Hooper's Bay about five kilometres north of George Town, becomes the hippest dance club as the night wears on. There is live music on Saturdays.

Kermit's Hilltop Tavern *(Rolleville, ☎345-6006)* has live music and dancing on Saturdays. It is the place to be any night on the week in Northern Great Exuma.

SHOPPING

Great Exuma

George Town

Exuma Markets *(just past the channel into Lake Victoria, ☎336-2033)* is a well-stocked grocery store, with over the counter drugs and newspapers.

The **Straw Market** lines the main street facing the library and school. Straw bags, hats plus t-shirts and souvenirs.

Peace & Plenty Boutique *(facing the Club Peace & Plenty, ☎336-2222)* sells Androsia batik clothing and cloth, a handful of souvenirs and even fly-fishing equipment.

Sandpiper *(next to the above, ☎336-2084)* has a good selection of paperbacks and books on The Bahamas. They also sell pretty souvenirs, arts and crafts, silk-screen-printed t-shirts, and their own line of beachwear.

For duty free items: **Scentuous Perfumes** has perfumes and **John Marshall Liquor** has wine and spirits, both are near the marina.

Little Exuma

The Ferry

The **Shark Lady** (see p 205) sells all sorts of eccentric knick-knacks that she has collected over the years, as well as her own shark's-teeth jewellery. Worth a visit even if you are just browsing.

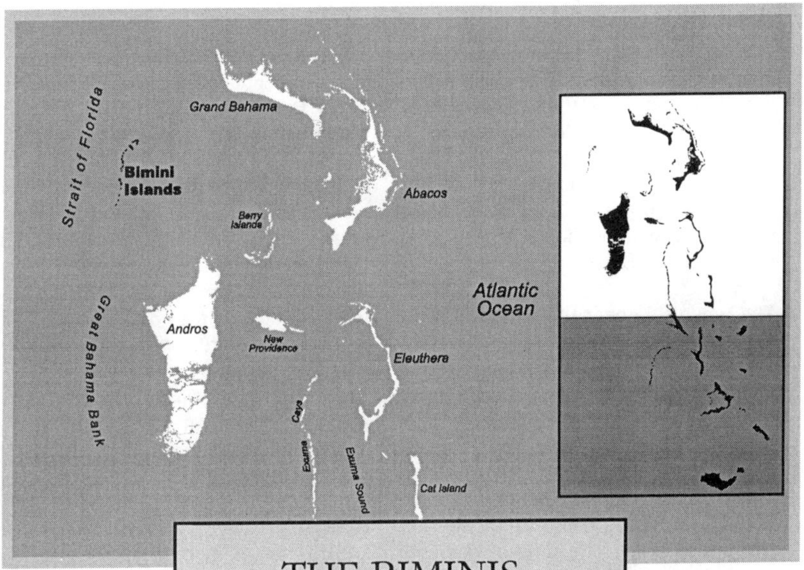

THE BIMINIS

The Biminis ★★ are a brash, salty "manly" and rugged paradise, which is just the way the anglers who worship the place like it. The waters around North and South Bimini are something of a proving ground for real anglers who, it seems, cannot call themselves such until they have cast into these waters. Most everyone who comes here comes for the fish and the chance to add their catch to the more than 50 world records that have been set here.

The Biminis are promoted as the fishing capital of the world, but it is not only this activity that keeps visitors coming. College students and yachties alike are drawn here for the chance to follow in the brazen and drunken footsteps of Ernest Hemingway or perhaps to scuba dive amidst what many believe to be the lost city of Atlantis or to swim with rare wild spotted dolphins.

Located only 80 kilometres from Florida, what many call Bimini, or more properly the Biminis, is actually two islands lying where the Gulf Stream meets the Bahama Bank. North Bimini is the centre of the action. It is shaped like an upside down baited hook, and is only 12 kilometres long and a mere 500 metres wide at its widest point. Alice Town, the main settlement, is at one end and a short ferry ride from broader South Bimini, which is essentially uninhabited, save a few pricey homes and an airstrip. There are two settlements north of Alice Town, and most of North Bimini beyond them is privately owned and covered with incomplete vacation communities or mangrove swamps.

A Short History

Ponce de Léon first came to the New World as part of Columbus' second voyage. In 1513, as Governor of Puerto Rico, he sailed through The Bahamas in search of a fountain that "maketh owld men yonge ageyne" that he had heard about from the Lucayans. He never found the fabled fountain of youth but did stumble upon the Gulf Stream and Florida and won himself the name Don of Florida and Bimini.

The Biminis lie near the maritime highways used by treasure-laden Spanish ships and so became a popular pirate haunt. The most famous among them was Henry Morgan who is said to have buried a treasure stolen from the fortress at Porto Bello in Panamá somewhere in the Biminis. Pirates were so active around the Biminis that the first real settlers had to clear piles of pirate debris from the harbour just to enter it. After the pirates were chased out, wrecking took over; the Biminis' five founding families settled here in 1835 as wreckers. They salvaged the goods of wrecked ships and saved many lives, but it has also been suggested that they also lured a few ships onto the rocks to increase their revenues.

Sponging was the next money-maker in the Biminis, but didn't compare to the boom that came with Prohibition in the United States. As the island closest to the American mainland, Bimini was the export capital. Shipments arrived constantly from Nassau before being shipped off to the Florida Everglades or "Rum Row" off the coast of New Jersey. Prohibition was repealed in 1933, but not before the Biminis had attracted attention as a rough-and-tumble fishing Mecca thanks to Ernest Hemingway, whose novel *Islands in the Stream* is set here. He also wrote *To Have and Have Not* in the Biminis in between barroom brawls and catching prize fish.

In the mid-1930s, Bimini's reputation as the fishing capital of the world was solidified when Bahamian Nevil Norton Stuart transformed a Prohibition-era bar called the Fountain of Youth into the Bimini Big Game Fishing Club. He later added a marina, and soon Judy Garland and Martin Luther King Jr. were stopping by. The airstrip on South Bimini was constructed in 1957. The latest stories about the Biminis (besides the world-record catches) haven't been quite so auspicious. The proximity of the United States have made the Biminis a favourite with drug traffickers. The situation is not as bad as in the mid-1980s, thanks in part to the many undercover U.S. narcotics agents, but a lot of drugs still pass through here.

FINDING YOUR WAY AROUND

From Alice Town to Porgy Bay, two roads run the length of North Bimini. The Queen's Highway to the west and the King's Highway to the east. Beyond that, a road leads to Bimini Bay Hotel. There is a chain here, and you can only continue exploring the rest of the island with permission.

By Plane

Bimini International Airport is on South Bimini. It is served by **Bimini Island Air** *(☎954-938-8991)* and **Island Air Charters** *(☎1-800-444-9904)* from Fort Lauderdale and by **Major's Air Service** *(☎352-5778)* from Freeport. A quick water taxi links South Bimini to North Bimini for $5 per person

Pan Am Air Bridge *(☎347-3024 or 1-800-424-2557)* used to be called Chalk's and is practically an institution; it has been flying seaplanes into North Bimini for years. There are daily flights from Fort Lauderdale, Miami and Nassau to Alice Town. (N.B. no carry-on luggage is allowed on these planes.)

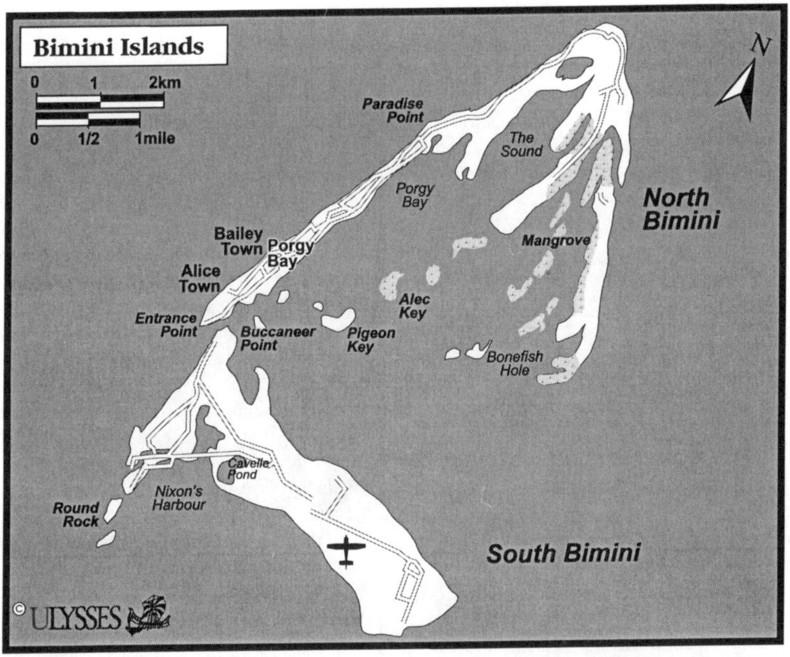

By Taxi

Called the Bimini Bus Service, the island's taxi service is actually a red van that covers the island. A trip from the Pan-Am terminal to your hotel should cost $3.

By Boat

Most people get to The Biminis by boat. Alice Town is the official port of entry. Of the handful of marinas, the Bimini Big Game Fishing Club is the best equipped.

By Mailboat: All departures are from Potter's Cay (under the Paradise Island Bridge) in Nassau and all fares are one way. The *Bimini Mack* serves Alice Town and Cat Cay. Travel time: 12 hours. Fare: $45.

By Golf Cart and Scooter

The place is small enough to cover on foot, but it seems *de rigueur* to have a golf cart, and scooters are fun. The **Compleat Angler Hotel** *(☎347-3122)* rents golf carts for about $65 a day, **Sawyer Scooter Rentals** *(☎347-2555)* and **Bimini Rentals** *(☎347-3400)* both rent scooters.

? PRACTICAL INFORMATION

North Bimini

Tourist Office: Alice Town, ☎347-3529, ⇌347-3530.

Bank: Royal Bank of Canada, open Mon and Fri 9am to 3pm, Tue, Wed and Thu 9am to 1pm, Alice Town, ☎347-3031.

Police: ☎347-3144.

Post Office: in Government Building, open Mon to Fri 9am to 5:30pm, ☎347-3546.

Clinic: Government clinic with doctor and nurse, open Mon to Fri 9am to 2pm, Alice Town, ☎347-3210.

South Bimini

Police: ☎347-3424.

★ EXPLORING

North Bimini ★★

Alice Town is a little rough around the edges. It is generally a very laid-back place, except during tournaments when things get rowdy and people live and breathe fishing. At the southern end of town, a couple of hundred metres south of the Pan-Am seaplane dock is an old cemetery. Another couple of hundred metres in the other direction is the dock for the ferry to South Bimini. The old post office across from the mailboat dock is slated for renovation.

Besides the funky down-home bars, pelicans and smell of baking bread, the only real sight per se in Alice Town is the **Ernest Hemingway Museum ★★★**, in the lounge of the **Compleat Angler Hotel**, built in the 1930s and now part of the Bimini Blue Water Resort. This is a must for anyone following in the footsteps of Papa Hemingway. You can even stay in the room the writer used during his visits between 1935 and 1937. The dark wooden walls are covered with Hemingway photos, paintings and quotes. The exterior of the hotel is made from rum barrels used during Prohibition.

Every eatery seems to have a fishing hall of fame. Among these, take a gander at Captain Bob's (south of the Blue Harbour Marina) collection of photos of record catches. Besides the photos and food, you'll surely get some good advice on where they're biting, plus a few stories on the one that got away or the many legends surrounding the Biminis, from Atlantis to the Fountain of Youth to a place called **Memory Ledge** where supposedly if you lie down you'll remember everything you have ever forgotten.

North of Alice Town are the bedroom communities, if you can really call them that for they all seem to blend together, of Bailey Town and Porgy Bay. Beaches of fine white sand lined with casuarinas run the whole length of the western shore, with the best up at Bimini Bay.

If you have insect repellent, hire a guide to explore the eastern half of North Bimini and the **Healing Hole ★**. This freshwater sulphur spring lies in the middle of a remote mangrove swamp. It is a smelly and muddy adventure, but also a thrilling and reportedly meditative experience. Martin Luther King Jr. found peace and quiet here in 1965.

South Bimini ★

What little of South Bimini has been developed lies south of the dock for the ferry to North Bimini. A road heads south from the dock, a left fork leads to the airstrip, continuing straight the road follows **Tiki Hut Beach**, which is good for snorkelling (see p 221), to **Port-Royal**, a canal community of cushy American-owned weekend houses.

East of Port-Royal is the **Shark Laboratory.** Officially called the Bimini Biological Field Station, it is a research centre run by the University of Miami that studies the lemon shark. You probably won't see any sharks about, but if there is someone around they'll be glad to give you a tour. Students of marine biology can sign up for six- and 10-day courses here by contacting the university.

Make your way back up to the fork to the airstrip and follow it east. A small sign on the left-hand side of the road points the way to the alleged **Fountain of Youth**. This is supposedly the miraculous fountain that Ponce de Léon searched in vane for in 1513. It is a sorry sight and is usually dried up so there is no way to test the waters.

BEACHES

Bimini's beaches are natural stretches of white sand. They aren't raked clean every morning, and invariably there is a handful of shiny cruising boats, their angling lines at the ready, moored just offshore, especially off Alice Town. The Biminis have two beaches of particular note. The first extends north of Alice Town. The sand gets better and better as you head north, peaking at **Bimini Bay Beach ★★**. The southern half of the eastern coast of South Bimini is better known as **Tiki Hut Beach ★**. There is one tiki hut here for shade, otherwise grab your snorkelling gear (see p 222).

OUTDOOR ACTIVITIES

Fishing

This chapter might well have been all about fishing in Bimini. The marinas here are all full-service places bustling with action and ready to supply you with charters, advice, bait, and other supplies. Over 50 world-record catches, including winning swordfish, sailfish, bonito, wahoo, mackerel, tuna, barracuda, shark and grouper (see p 73 for seasons), have been pulled from these waters, sometimes after hours-long fights across kilometres of ocean. Bimini's bonefishing flats are just as renowned. The biggest fish ever caught in Bahamian waters is now hanging on a wall at the Bimini Big Game Fishing Club; it is a 482-kilogram marlin reeled in 1979.

Hotel owners will recommend you bring your own tackle, though some of the marinas do rent and sell some items. You can charter boats and hire captains and guides from the big marinas: **Bimini Big Game Fishing Club** *(☎347-3391 or 1-800-737-1007)*, **Bimini Blue Water Marina** *(☎347-3166)*, **Weech's Bimini Dock** *(☎347-3028)* and the **Bimini Beach Club and Marina** on South Bimini *(☎954-725-0919 in Florida)*. It costs between $275 and $600 for a half day and between $400 and $900 for a full day of deep-sea fishing.

Bonefishing the flats requires the delicate precision of a local guide. These men are the best; they have international reputations and are revered like Olympic athletes. Ansel Saunders *(☎347-3055)* is a world-record holder; there is a handful of other skilled guides, among them Bonefish Cordell *(☎347-2576)* and Bonefish Ebbie *(☎347-2053)*.

The calendar is packed with tournaments. These bring out the best and the worst of Bimini – if you plan on participating, book well ahead:

- January: Mid-Winter Wahoo Tournament
- March: Hemingway Billfish Tournament; Bacardi Rum Billfish Tournament

- April: Bimini Break & Blue Marlin Tournament
- May: Annual Bimini Festival
- July: All Billfish Classic; Jimmy Albury Memorial Blue Marlin Tournament
- August: Native Fishing Tournament
- November: All Wahoo Tournament
- December: Annual Bonefish Willie Bonefishing Tournament; Adam Clayton Powell Memorial Wahoo Tournament

Scuba Diving and Snorkelling

The mysterious lost continent of Atlantis, black coral, sunken ships, airplanes and underwater wildlife that includes eagle rays, octopus and countless species of fish attract a fair number of divers and snorkellers to the Biminis, which lie near the 600-metre underwater cliff on the edge of the Bahama Bank with caverns and magnificent reef creatures and pelagics.

Moselle's Shoal, otherwise known as **Bimini Road**, otherwise known as **Atlantis**, lies in shallow water northwest of Bimini Bay. Enormous limestone blocks with supposed evidence of human engineering, are lined up like a giant highway extending for over 300 metres and are visible to pilots passing overhead. The mystery deepens when you add the fact that some of these blocks disappeared in 1925 (though this seems to be explained by the building of a new limestone jetty in Miami) and the discovery in 1977 of huge sand mounds in the mangrove swamps of east Bimini that are thought to be beacons for extra-terrestrials.

The other renowned dive of the Biminis is the wreck of the ***Sapona***. This Prohibition-era concrete barge was built by Henry Ford and served as a private club and speakeasy until a hurricane sent it down. American navy pilots used it for target practice during the Second World War. It now harbours a wealth of marine life.

The Biminis' hotels offer packages with the islands' only dive shop, **Bill and Nowdla Keefe's Bimini Undersea** *(near the ferry dock; ☎342-3089 or 1-800-348-4644 or 954-653-5572, ⇄347-3079; mailing address: PO Box 693515, Miami, FL 33269)*. They offer PADI and NAUI certification courses. A resort course is $99, a two-dive trip is $69, they also rent underwater still and video cameras and scuba equipment.

Bimini Undersea rents snorkelling gear for $15 and organizes snorkelling trips for $25. Snorkelling sites of Tiki Hut Beach include a drug-running plane downed in the 1980s and reef formations populated by lobsters, octopus, eagle rays and colourful parrotfish.

Kayaking

Bimini Undersea (see above) rents sea kayaks for $30 per day.

Swimming with Dolphins

The Biminis are visited by rare Atlantic spotted dolphins. This species is particularly friendly and you can spend an hour frolicking with these amazing creatures with Wild Dolphin Excursions *($79 for adults)*, courtesy of **Bimini Undersea**'s (see above).

ACCOMMODATIONS

North Bimini

Alice Town

Weech's Bimini Dock *($60; 4 rooms, pb, ≡; PO Box 613, ☎347-3028, ⇄347-3508)* is a no-nonsense but very acceptable low-budget option near the marina.

All My Children Hotel *($65 to $99; 48 rooms, ≡, pb, tv; ☎347-2506)* is not a tribute to the American soap opera, but rather a reference to the owner's many children. The rooms are unremarkable but clean and decent. Not the best choice in Alice Town, but they will do in a pinch.

The **Compleat Angler Hotel** *($68 to $85; 12 rooms, ≡, ≈, pb; PO Box 601, ☎347-3122, 347-3185, ⇄347-3293)* is to be recommended more as an attraction and bar than a place to stay, it is noisy and the wood-panelled rooms have seen better days. Be that as it may, Hemingway buffs and night owls will relish a stay in this historic and weathered hotel. Room No. 1, where the writer penned parts of *To Have and Have Not*, is still available. The manager and bartender, Ossie Brown, can help you organize fishing and diving trips.

Sea Crest Hotel & Marina *($85; 13 rooms, ≡, sat tv; PO Box 654, ☎/⇄347-3071)* offers good value for the money with comfortable accommodations right in the heart of Alice Town. All the rooms have private balconies and those on the third and top floors have lofty cathedral ceilings and good views. There is no restaurant, but Captain Bob's is right across the street.

The **Bimini Blue Water Resort** *($97, cottages $65 to $285; 12 rooms, ≡, pb, ℜ, sat tv, ≈; PO Box 601, ☎347-3166 or 1-800-688-4752, ⇄347-3293)* also has full marina facilities. The accommodations range from standard rooms with private balconies to a three-bedroom, three-bathroom cottage called the Marlin Cottage. Hemingway escaped to the cottage in the 1930s, and it is the main setting of *Island in the Stream*. The main building contains the dining room and bar. Some rooms are in the main building, others are in the newer addition. The former have a certain charming patina of age, the latter don't. The Compleat Angler (see above) is part of the resort.

The **Bimini Big Game Fishing Club, Hotel & Marina** *($149, cottage $178, penthouse $298; 49 rooms, ℜ, ≈, ≡, pb, K, sat tv; PO Box 699, ☎347-3391/3, 1-800-737-1007, ⇄347-3392, US mailing address: PO Box 523238, Miami FL 33152)* offers a whole array of services, including a full-service marina, diving excursions, sport-fishing trips and fish-cleaning. It also sponsors several fishing tournaments throughout the year. Lodging options are the nicest on the island and run the gamut from 35 rooms to 12 equipped cottages and 4 luxurious penthouses. Though the cottages have kitchenettes, cooking is forbidden, there are barbecues outside though. The place is like a self-contained little village and the service is very professional. The pool is fairly small. Interesting fishing and diving packages are available as are boat charters from the marina. This is the hotel of choice during fishing tournaments, so reserve well in advance.

Ulysses' Favourites

Accommodations

Best Value For Your Money:

The Bimini Blue Water Resort (see p 223).

Best Resort for Fishers:

Bimini Big Game Fishing Club, Hotel & Marina (see p 223).

Restaurants

Best True-true Bahamian Cooking:

Red Lion Pub (see p 225) and Sandra's Bar & Restaurant (see p 225).

Finest Dining:

The Gulfstream Restaurant (see p 225).

North of Porgy Bay

The **Bimini Bay Hotel** *($75 to $95; ≈, pb; PO Box 607, ☎/⇄347-2171)* needs an upgrade and may just get it before too long. For now however the Art-Deco hotel offers a variety of time-worn rooms. The hotel has a small pool and boasts a pleasant breezy location not far from the lovely Bimini Bay Beach.

South Bimini

So far, the best place to stay on South Bimini is the **Bimini Beach Club & Marina** *($90; 40 rooms, sat tv, pb, ≡; mailing address: 1410 SE 12th St., Deerfield Beach, FL, 33441, ☎954-725-0919 or 1-888-824-6464)*. This place is frequented by scuba divers instead of fishers, a variety of scuba packages are offered. They also organize sport-fishing trips. Accommodations are in pleasantly decorated rooms. The saltwater pool is of average size. The hotel is located on the south-western tip of the island.

RESTAURANTS

North Bimini

Alice Town

Captain Bob's *($-$$; King's Hwy., ☎347-3260)* is "the" breakfast place in town with hearty helpings of eggs, bacon, sausages and corned-beef hash. They also serve a good selection of fresh seafood dishes.

Fisherman's Paradise *($-$$; south end of town, ☎347-3220)* is a popular local place with good local fare like fish stew, macaroni and cheese and lamb chops.

The Anchorage *($-$$$; at the Bimini Blue Water Resort, ☎347-3166)* has good location overlooking the harbour and offering ocean views. They serve breakfast, lunch and dinner. The decor is not fancy, and neither is the cooking, but both are reliable. Stick to the seafood dishes, they are the freshest.

Big Game Sports Bar & Grill *($$; at the Bimini Big Game Club, ☎347-3391)* has a satellite television and a great view for atmosphere and Bahamian and American dishes to keep fishers happy. The menu is not flashy with ribs, grouper fingers, burgers, conch salad, conch chowder, conch fritters and conch pizza, the house specialty.

The **Red Lion Pub** *($$; no credit cards; King's Hwy., beside Bimini Big Game Club, ☎347-3259)* is famous for its Bahamian home-cooking, in particular the Shrimp Delight, spicy conch-stuffed shrimp, the pies (either banana cream or key lime), plus grouper in foil, steak, barbecued ribs and lamb. This is a friendly easy-going place for a good meal.

The Gulfstream Restaurant *($$$; in the Bimini Big Game Club, ☎347-3391)* offers the finest dining in the Biminis. Patrons can enjoy a drink at the Gulfstream Bar or the Barefoot Bar beforehand (see p 225). There is an attractive decor and usually some live entertainment. The menu lists original dishes using the freshest seafood. There are also beef, lamb and chicken dishes. Heavenly Bahamian bread and good peas 'n' rice accompany each meal. Reservations recommended.

Bailey Town

Sandra's Bar & Restaurant *($; King's Hwy., ☎347-2336)* serves no-nonsense Bahamian meals and snacks, and makes a fun stop for lunch or a cold one when exploring north of Alice Town.

ENTERTAINMENT

North Bimini

Alice Town

We've talked about the **Compleat Angler Hotel** *(11am to 1am; King's Hwy., ☎347-2122)* as a museum and a hotel, but it is perhaps best visited when you are in search of a cold Kalik or Goombay Smash. Hemingway threw back share at the bar more than 50 years ago, and the place has hardly changed. A great calypso band gets the dance floor thumping on weekends throughout the year and on Wednesdays from December to April.

The other bar-cum-attraction in Alice Town is the **End of the World Bar** *(near the Pan-Am Air Bridge dock, ☎347-2094)*, put on the map by a controversial black New York Congressman named Adam Powell Jr. who did a fair share of politicking from here. The place is the size of a shoe box, the floors are covered in sand, the walls are covered with graffiti and undergarments hang from the rafters. You have to see it to believe it! Things really start to move after midnight.

The Bimini Big Game Fishing Club and Hotel has no less than three bars. The **Barefoot Bar** by the pool is open from mid-morning to late afternoon. The **Gulfstream Bar** has its famous rum punches (Bacardi owns the place so that's what is in the punch) and live calypso music. And finally there's the **Sports Bar & Grill** (see p 225).

SHOPPING

North Bimini

Alice Town

The **Straw Market** *(opposite the All My Children Hotel, King's Hwy.)* sells all manner of straw items plus t-shirts and souvenirs.

The **Bimini Big Game Logo Shop** has all the beach and boating clothing you may have forgotten, and souvenirs too.

For quality souvenirs and gifts, check **The Gateway Gallery** *(at the southern end of town)*, which has locally made crafts, or **Island Gems** *(across from the Bimini Big Game Club)*, which sells Androsia, perfume and jewellery.

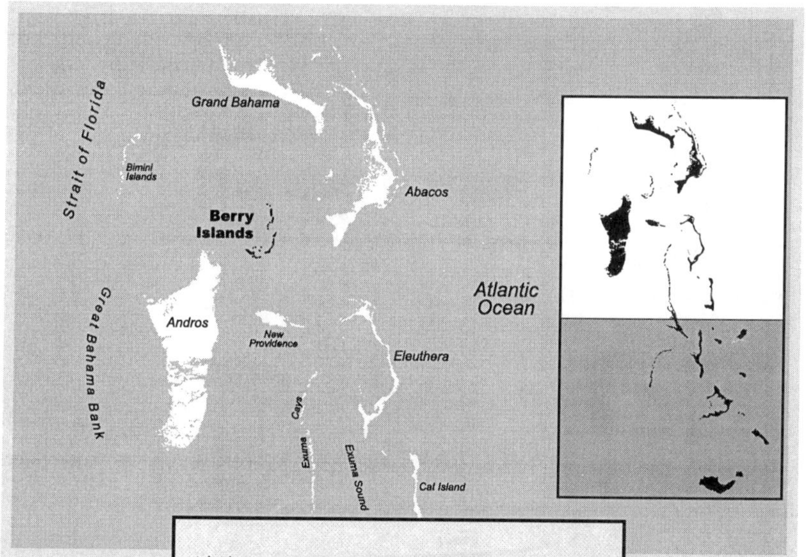

THE BERRY ISLANDS

Yachties, sailors, fishers and rich escapists are the types you are likely to encounter along the deserted beaches of the wispy chain of 30 islands and cays. Some of the Berry Islands ★ are privately owned and one of the two full-service hotels in the chain was a private members-only retreat until just four years ago. Cary Grant, Brigitte Bardot, Jack Nicklaus and the Rockefellers have all escaped to these secluded little paradises at one point or another.

Lying 55 kilometres west of Nassau on the eastern edge of the Bahama Bank and off the northeastern tip of Andros, the main islands of the chain from north to south are: Great Stirrup Cay, Cistern Cay, Great Harbour Cay, Anderson Cay, Haines Cay, Hoffmans Cay, Bond's Cay, Sandy Cay, Whale Cay and Chub Cay. Great Harbour Cay is the largest, measuring 16 kilometres in length by four kilometres in width. Chub Cay is the other island with any tourist facilities. The deep waters of the Northwest Providence Channel to the north and the Tongue of the Ocean account for the great deep-sea fishing.

The islands remained unsettled right up until 1836 when Governor Colebrook decided to resettle Africans that had been rescued from captured slave ships in the Berry Islands. He ordered the construction of town on Great Stirrup Cay and called it Williamstown in honour of King William IV. It was to be a port of entry and had its own customs house. Poor soil conditions doomed the settlement, however, and Williamstown now stands in ruins. Great Stirrup Cay and neighbouring Little Stirrup have since been purchased by the Norwegian Cruise Line and the Royal Caribbean Cruise Line.

Great Harbour Cay and Chub Cay are the only two islands with any tourist industry to speak of. Bond's Cay, in the south, is a private bird sanctuary. The other islands are either inhabited by sponge fishers, privately owned or deserted. Boaters often put in at the latter. Imagine the possibilities: your own deserted island paradise where anything goes...

FINDING YOUR WAY AROUND

By Plane

Private charters serve Berry Islands. **Tropical Diversions Air** *(☎1-800-343-7256 or 954-921-9084)* is affiliated with Great Harbour Cay Club and offers flights from Fort Lauderdale to Great Harbour Cay. Cat Island Air *(on Great Harbour ☎361-8021)* flies from Nassau to Great Harbour. **Island Express** *(☎954-359-0380)* flies from Fort Lauderdale to Chub Cay.

Chub Cay Club and Great Harbour Cay Club both arrange airport pickups

By Boat

Both the Great Harbour Club has and the Chub Cay Club have fully-equipped marinas. Only Great Harbour Club is a port of entry, so if you are arriving internationally you must clear customs here before docking at Chub Cay.

Mailboat: All departures are from Potter's Cay (under the Paradise Island Bridge) in Nassau and all fares are one way. The *Champion II* departs Tuesdays at 7pm.

By Car

Great Harbour Cay

Happy People Rentals at the Great Harbour Cay Marina rent jeeps for $50 a day or $300 for a week. They also rent scooters, boats and snorkelling equipment.

PRACTICAL INFORMATION

There are no banks on the Berry Islands, the two hotels can exchange travellers cheques.

Great Harbour Cay

Police: Bullock's Harbour, ☎367-8344.

Clinic: Government clinic with a nurse, open Mon to Fri 9am to 2pm, ☎367-8400.

EXPLORING

Great Harbour Cay

Following the demise of Williamstown, nothing much happened in the Berry Islands until Douglas Fairbanks Jr. became involved in a plan to develop Great Harbour Cay. Needless to say, he attracted a lot of attention to this remote little island, which became a popular getaway for movie stars and millionaires.

The terrain is hilly, and the eastern shore is two long sweeping arcs of sand. The main settlement is at **Bullock's Harbour**, a ramshackle place with a lot of roosters and a population of sponge fishers. It is located on a small

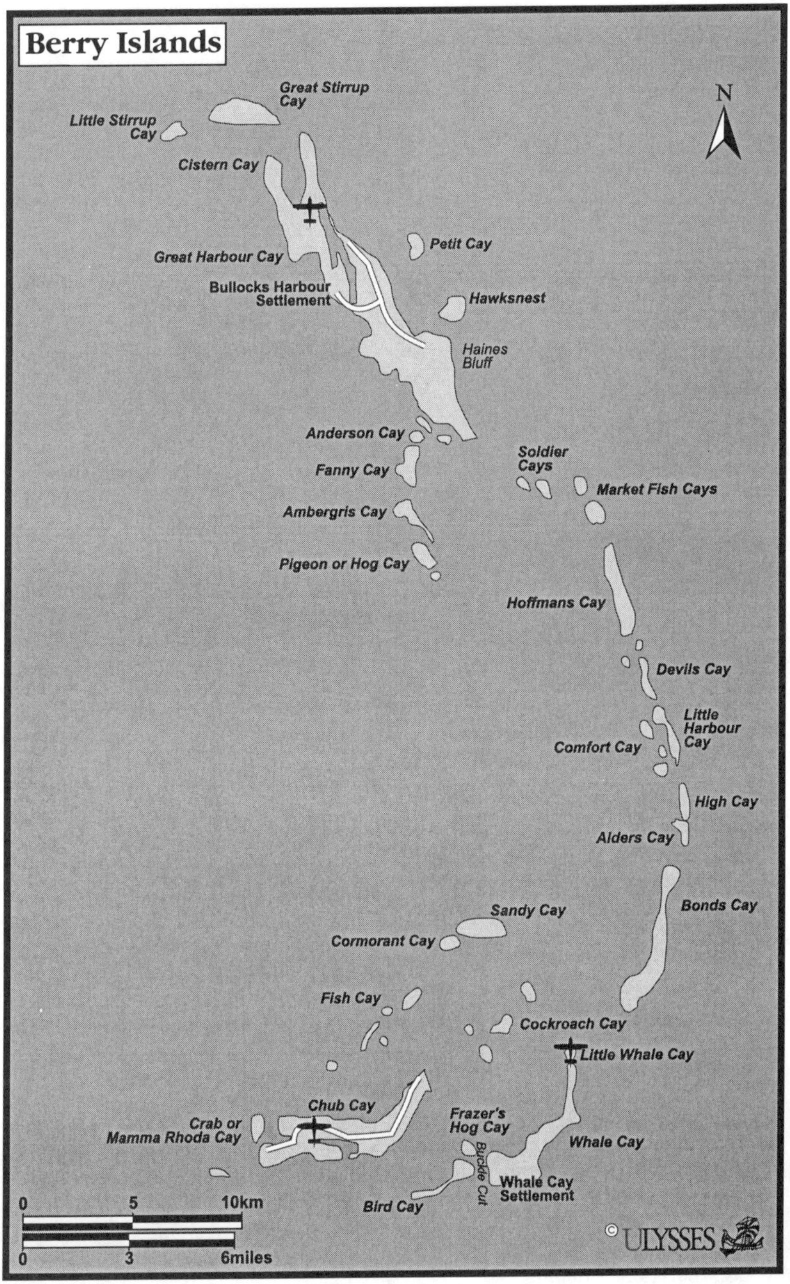
Berry Islands
N
Great Stirrup Cay
Little Stirrup Cay
Cistern Cay
Petit Cay
Great Harbour Cay
Bullocks Harbour Settlement
Hawksnest
Haines Bluff
Anderson Cay
Soldier Cays
Fanny Cay
Market Fish Cays
Ambergris Cay
Pigeon or Hog Cay
Hoffmans Cay
Devils Cay
Little Harbour Cay
Comfort Cay
High Cay
Alders Cay
Bonds Cay
Sandy Cay
Cormorant Cay
Fish Cay
Cockroach Cay
Little Whale Cay
Chub Cay
Frazer's Hog Cay
Crab or Mamma Rhoda Cay
Whale Cay
Buckle Cut
Whale Cay Settlement
Bird Cay
0 5 10km
0 3 6miles
© ULYSSES

Heron

cay facing the Bay of Five Pirates and the Great Harbour Cay Yacht Club and Marina and accessible across a causeway.

The **Great Harbour Cay Yacht Club and Marina** occupies the shore of a narrow bay at the southeastern corner of the Bay of Five Pirates. The townhouses are on the northern and eastern sides of the inlet, facing the marina, on the southern side. Royal Palm Drive crosses the island to the eastern shore where the beach villas face a white-sand beach and the waters of Great Harbour Bay.

The southern part of the island beyond **Shell Beach** is uninhabited. Heading north, along pretty **Sugar Beach** ★ there are a few snazzy beach houses, while to the west, mangrove swamps harbour egrets and herons.

Chub Cay

This is the southernmost island in the chain and doesn't have much going on except the exclusive **Chub Cay Club**. In the 1950s this was the private stomping ground of rich Texas businessmen. They were more interested in the fishing than anything else, and the accommodations they had built were very simple, the same cannot be said about the world-class 90-slip marina, however.

Today the island also boasts a handful of luxurious private homes. Major rebuilding was needed after Hurricane Andrew in 1992, and in 1994 the club opened all its facilities to the public. There are still members, but now you and I can join them. The majority of guests arrive by private yacht and still come for the fishing. Big game fish abound in the deep waters of the nearby Northwest Providence Channel and Tongue of the Ocean. Visitors who arrive by plane can take their pick of the many charter boats at Chub Cay. The waters around Chub Cay also hold many wonders for scuba divers (see below).

OUTDOOR ACTIVITIES

Fishing

The Berry Islands have vast bonefishing flats and superb deep-sea fishing with great catches like billfish, dolphinfish, wahoo and king mackerel; light-tackle catches include grouper, barracuda and snapper. For bonefishing call Percy Darville *(☎367-8119)* who charges $315 for a full day. For deep-sea fishing, Revis Anderson charges $500 for a full day.

Remember that you must have a permit to fish with your own boat (see p 74).

Scuba Diving and Snorkelling

Great Harbour Cay

Sugar Beach, running along the eastern shore is good for snorkelling. Diving trips are organized at the **Great Harbour Marina** *(☎367-8005)*. Snorkelling gear can be rented for $10 per day from **Happy People Rental** (see above).

Chub Cay

A variety of rare corals thrive in the waters of Chub Cay. Chub Cay sits on the edge of the Tongue of the Ocean, making for excellent wall diving, notable dives include Chub Wall and Mamma Rhoda Rock, the latter is protected by the Bahamas National Trust. **Bahama Island Adventures** *(☎1-800-329-1337)*, run by Chub Cay Club, organize the scuba diving.

Golf

Great Harbour Cay

The Great Harbour Cay Club has a nine-hole golf course designed by Joe Lee. Clubs can be rented from Happy People Rentals (see above) for $15.

ACCOMMODATIONS

Great Harbour Cay

The **Great Harbour Cay Club** *($180 and up for townhouse, $90 and up for beach villa; 16 rooms, pb, ≡, K, ℜ, ≈, ⊗, sat tv; Great Harbour Cay, ☎367-8838, 1-800-343-7256 or 954-921-9084, ⇒367-8115)* offers two very different types of accommodations; there are the more secluded and private beach villas on the eastern shore, or the townhouses facing the full-service marina. Both options are fully equipped with kitchens, linens and maid service. The Club takes care of car rentals, sport-fishing charters and snorkelling trips. There is also a golf course.

Chub Cay

The **Chub Cay Club** *($175-$300; 8 rooms, 9 villas, pb, ≡, ℝ, K, sat tv, ≈, ℜ; Chub Cay, Berry Islands, ☎325-1490, ⇒322-5199, mailing address: PO Box 661067, Miami Springs, FL, 33266)* was, until 1994, an exclusive members-only resort. Now anyone can enjoy the big swimming pool and

Ulysses' Favourites

Accommodations

Fishers' Favourite:

Chub Cay Club (see p 231).

Most Well-Rounded Resort:

Great Harbour Cay Yacht Club & Marina (see p 231).

Restaurants

Best True-true Bahamian Cooking:

Coolie May's Take-Away (see p 232).

Finest Dining:

Tamboo Dinner Club (see p 232).

casual yacht club atmosphere. The 90-slip marina and great game fishing are the big draws here as the accommodations are fairly functional, whether you choose the rooms that face the pool or the villas that face a pretty horseshoe-shaped beach for two, four or six people. The latter have kitchens. The club also has two tennis courts and bicycles. Fishing, scuba diving and snorkelling can all be arranged.

RESTAURANTS

Great Harbour Cay

Coolie May's Take-Away *($; near the main intersection, Bullock's Harbour, ☎367-8730)* is open for lunch with a very simple menu. Cooly also runs a catering business and has a vast menu with tasty native dishes and home-made desserts. For an evening meal you must make your choice from the menu by 9am.

The Wharf *($-$$; closed Tue; near the marina, ☎367-8762)* is open from 7am to 11am for huge greasy breakfasts like corned-beef hash and pancakes. It opens up again at 4pm with a big menu for supper. There are standard burgers, pizzas and salads but also fresh seafood dishes. The television is generally always on, which can be distracting and lends the place something of a sports-bar ambiance when there is an important game to catch.

The Tamboo Dinner Club *($$$$; Wed and Sat only, reservations required; at the marina, ☎367-8203)* is the nicest place for dinner on Great Harbour and everybody knows it, so reserve early. Tables are set in an interesting curved, glassed-in room overlooking the harbour. Native dishes, including the freshest seafood, are featured on the four-course menu.

Chub Cay

Harbour House *($$-$$$; Chub Cay Club, ☎325-1490)* serves a good Bahamian fried chicken and stand-bys like burgers and fries. Your best bet is the fish, conch and lobster that are caught fresh every day.

ENTERTAINMENT

Great Harbour Cay

For a very civilized evening, stop in at the elegant lounge of the **Tamboo Dinner Club** *(☎367-8203)* on a Saturday night.

Chub Cay

The **Hilltop Bar** is at the highest point of the island. There is a pool table, a television to watch the game and live music on occasion.

SHOPPING

Great Harbour Cay

A&L General Store (Bullocks Harbour) sells everything from groceries to tools and cosmetics.

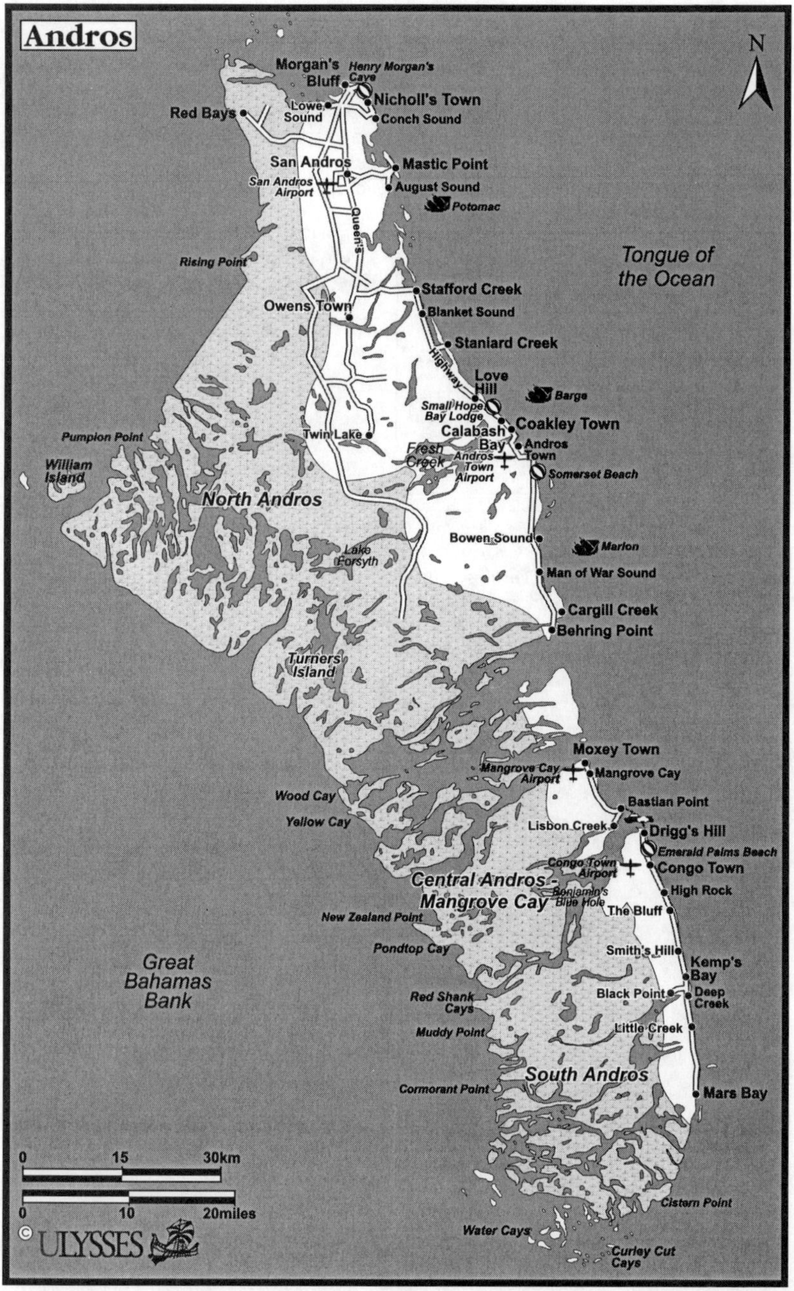
Andros
N
Morgan's Bluff
Henry Morgan's Caye
Nicholl's Town
Lowe Sound
Red Bays
Conch Sound
San Andros
Mastic Point
San Andros Airport
August Sound
Potomac
Queen's
Rising Point
Tongue of the Ocean
Stafford Creek
Owens Town
Blanket Sound
Staniard Creek
Highway
Love Hill
Barge
Small Hope Bay Lodge
Coakley Town
Calabash Bay
Pumpion Point
Twin Lake
Andros Town
Fresh Creek
Andros Town Airport
William Island
Somerset Beach
North Andros
Bowen Sound
Marion
Lake Forsyth
Man of War Sound
Cargill Creek
Behring Point
Turners Island
Moxey Town
Mangrove Cay Airport
Mangrove Cay
Wood Cay
Bastian Point
Yellow Cay
Lisbon Creek
Drigg's Hill
Emerald Palms Beach
Congo Town Airport
Congo Town
Central Andros - Mangrove Cay
High Rock
Benjamin's Blue Hole
The Bluff
New Zealand Point
Pondtop Cay
Smith's Hill
Kemp's Bay
Great Bahamas Bank
Black Point
Deep Creek
Red Shank Cays
Muddy Point
Little Creek
South Andros
Cormorant Point
Mars Bay
0
15
30km
0
10
20miles
Cistern Point
© ULYSSES
Water Cays
Curley Cut Cays

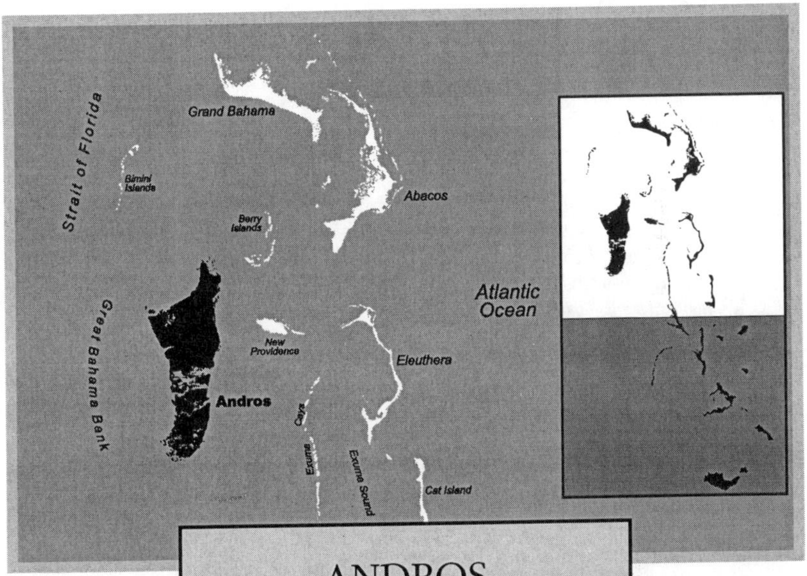

ANDROS

Andros ★★ is the biggest of the Islands of The Bahamas. It is so big, almost 6000 square kilometres, that all the other islands could almost fit into it. Shallow flats and shoals to the west and a formidable barrier reef to the east isolate the island but also account for unrivalled bonefishing and superb scuba diving. Nevertheless, Andros is still one of The Bahamas' last great outposts.

Two wide and shallow bights separate the land mass into three main islands, North Andros, Central Andros or Mangrove Cay, and South Andros. Just off the beautiful breezy beaches of the east coast is the 225-kilometre-long Andros Barrier Reef, the third largest in world and second largest in the western hemisphere. It drops off into a 2,900-metre-deep sea canyon called the Tongue of the Ocean. Superb scuba diving along the reef and over the wall has earned the island international recognition. The mysterious blue holes that dot the interior offer still more exceptional diving opportunities. The western part of the island, for its part, is rather appropriately called "The Mud".

The stone lace structure of the island is one of the oldest on Earth, having remained unscathed by the last ice age. Today it is an impenetrable tangle of palm trees, hardwood and pine forests and mangroves sliced by inland waterways and dotted with blue holes and caverns. Water levels rise and fall with the tides, forever modifying the landscape. Rain water collects in underground tunnels and caves and forms a freshwater lense on top of the salt water. This precious resource is tapped, and provides fresh water for all of Nassau at a rate of seven million gallons a day. The Spanish were so impressed by all the water, and believing the Holy Spirit dwells over water, called the island La Isla del Espirítu Santo, the "Island of the Holy Spirit".

The Chickcharnie

Andros' colourful history has one particularly interesting little creature. The Chickcharnie is described as a three-toed elf with large round yellow eyes and red pupils, feathers, a wiry beard and a loud screeching voice. It supposedly makes its nest in the tallest pine trees by bending the tops of two trees together. Superstitious Androsians once believed, and probably still do though they may not admit to it, that if they felled the trees of a chickcharnie, misery and hardship would befall them, as was the case with Neville Chamberlain and his sisal plantation, don't you know!

There may actually be a logical, though incredible, scientific explanation for the origin of the chickharnie. The now-extinct, three-foot-high flightless barn owl (*Tyto pollens*) once inhabited The Bahamas and Caribbean and bore a striking resemblance, minus the embellishments, to the chickcharnie. Chances are that the species survived on Andros longer than elsewhere and that early settlers would have come upon them.

A dizzying array of creatures dwells in this wild place, huge tracts of which remain unexplored. The most common might well be the mosquito – make sure you bring repellent and long pants! You are sure to see crabs of all sorts scurrying about, especially after rain and between May and September. There are hermit crabs and the more sought-after land crabs, which Androsians hunt down and cook up with delight. In the bush, wild boar still roam about, while overhead, turkey vultures, just called crows here, keep an eye on things. Other winged species include ospreys, herons, cormorants, white-crowned pigeons, the rare red-legged thrush, the great lizard cuckoo and the Bahama woodstar. Orchids and bromeliads also thrive in the bush, and are still faithfully used as medicines and teas by islanders.

A Short History

The Spanish made note of what they called Isla del Espirítu Santo in 1550. Though there is no record of their having visited the island, archaeological evidence does exist to prove that Lucayanas once inhabited it, and since the Spanish are responsible for their genocide, they must have stopped in at some point.

There are various explanations as to the origin of the name. One posits that Sir Edmund Andros, royal governor of New England in 1686, and later of Virginia and Maryland, may have beein given the senseless honour of having a far-off land named for him. Another more likely theory points to the English colony at San Andro on Nicaragua's Mosquito Coast that was uprooted by the Spanish in 1783 and may have ended up on Andros. Records from 1788 indicate the presence of white families and slaves. Still another possibility is that sponge fishermen from the Greek Island of Andros named it after their homeland.

However and whenever it was named, the island did harbour its share of pirates. They monitored shipments from Florida and Cuba from South Andros, and are even reputed to have had a harem and a pasture for stolen Cuban cattle. The notorious Henry Morgan patrolled the seas from his own safe haven at the northern tip of Andros at present-day Morgan's Bluff, legend has it he hid a handsome treasure in Morgan's cave (see p 239).

Andros did not attract Loyalists after the American Revolution like so many other Bahamian islands did. Nevertheless, the island's predominantly black population is descended from slaves. In South Andros they arrived after Emancipation from the Exumas and Long Island. The settlement of Red Bays, the only west coast settlement on Andros, claims Seminole ancestry from natives and black slaves who arrived from Florida in colonial times (see p 240).

Up until the early 20th century, the only economic activities of any scale practised on Andros were sisal plantations and sponging. Neville Chamberlain, future Prime Minister of Great Britain, was manager of his family's sisal plantation for four short years, time for the first crop to mature and prove unprofitable. Sponging was more lucrative. From the mid-19th century on, thousands of men went out on "The Mud" to collect the plentiful and desirable wool sponge. Exports peaked in 1917, but overfishing, a series of devastating hurricanes and then a fungal blight in 1938 led to the closure of the sponge beds and an end to prosperity on Andros.

The Bahamas Lumber Company came in the forties for timber and then in the fifties the Owens-Illinois company set up a pulp mill. They have both left, but their legacy lives on in the island's network of roads. There were a few failed agricultural ventures, and farming today is minimal. One of the largest current employers on the island is the joint American-Bahamian-British Atlantic Undersea Test and Evaluation Centre, or AUTEC, which opened south of Andros Town in 1964 creating jobs and injecting capital into the island's economy. Colombian drug traffickers used the island during the eighties, some more successfully than others as the downed planes littering the mangroves will attest. These days, however, most Androsians make a living as fishers, and a small percentage as spongers.

FINDING YOUR WAY AROUND

By Plane

Andros is served by four airports. The northernmost is the **San Andros Airport** with two daily flights from Nassau on **Bahamasair** *(☎329-2273 in San Andros)* and flights on island Express from Fort Lauderdale. The **Andros Town Airport** is served by the same flights. **Mangrove Cay Airport** is served by seasonal flights from Nassau on **Bahamasair** and daily flights from Nassau on Congo Air *(☎377-5382 in Nassau, 369-0021 on Mangrove Cay)*. **Congo Town Airport** has daily flights from Nassau on **Bahamasair** *(☎369-2632 in South Andros)*, plus daily flights on **Congo Air** *(☎369-2632 in Congo Town)* also from Nassau.

Small Hope Bay Lodge *(☎368-2013 or 1-800-223-6961)* also offers charters from Fort Lauderdale to **Andros Town Airport**.

By Boat

By Mailboat: Andros is served by a veritable fleet of mailboats! All departures are from Potter's Cay (under the Paradise Island Bridge) in Nassau and all fares are one way. The *Lady D* departs Tuesdays at noon for Stafford Creek, Blanket Sound, Staniard Creek, Fresh Creek and Behring Point. Travel time: 5 hours. Fare: $30. The *Lady*

Gloria departs Tuesdays at 10pm for Cargill Creek and Bowen Sound. Travel time: 5 hours. Fare: $30. The *Captain Moxey* departs Mondays at 11pm for Drigg's Hill, Congo Town, The Bluff and Kemp's Bay. Travel time: 7 hours. Fare: $30. The *Mangrove Cay Express* departs Wednesdays at 6pm for Lisbon Creek. Travel time: 5.5 hours. Fare: $30. The *Lisa J II* departs Wednesdays at 3:30pm for Mastic Point, Nicholls Town and Morgan's Bluff. Travel time: 5 hours. Fare: $30. The *Lady Margo* departs Wednesdays at 2am for North Andros. Travel time: 5 hours. Fare: $30. The *Challenger* departs for North Andros. Schedule, travel time and fare vary. The *Delmar L* departs Thursdays at 10pm for South Andros. Travel time: 7.5 hours. Fare: $30.

Marinas

Lighthouse Yacht Club & Marina, Fresh Creek, ☎1-800-825-5099.

Chickcharnie Hotel, Fresh Creek, ☎368-2025.

Ferries

There is a ferry between Lisbon Creek on Mangrove Cay and Drigg's Hill in South Andros. Its scheduled runs at 8am and 4pm are free, though you can get across at other times for a fee.

By Car

One road runs the length of the east coast of the island. Dodging potholes make driving the island a bit of a challenge. From north to south, gas is available in Morgan's Bluff, Love Hill, Coakley Town and The Bluff.

In North Andros, you can rent cars from Basil Martin *(☎329-3169)* in Mastic Point, from Bereth Rent-a-Car *(☎368-2102)* in Coakley Town, and through Emerald Palms By the Sea hotel *(☎369-2661)* in Drigg's Hill. A day's rental will cost between $65 and $85, and a credit card number or $100 cash deposit is usually required.

By Taxi

Taxis meet the incoming flights at the four airports. The fare from Andros Town Airport to Small Hope Bay Lodge is $20, and that from Mangrove Cay airport to town is $6.

? PRACTICAL INFORMATION

The mosquitoes are very hungry here; be prepared, bring repellent!

North Andros

San Andros

Bank: Canadian Imperial Bank of Commerce, open Wednesday 10:30am to 2:30pm.

Clinic: ☎329-2055.

Mastic Point

Clinic: ☎329-1849.

Nicholl's Town

Post Office: ☎329-2034.

Clinic: ☎329-2055.

Staniard Creek

Clinic: ☎368-2626.

Fresh Creek

Tourist Information: Bahamas Ministry of Tourism, Commissioner's Office, ☎368-2010 or 368-2601.

Bank: Royal Bank of Canada, open Wednesday 9:30am to 3:30pm, ☎368-2071.

Clinic: ☎368-2038

Central Andros

Mangrove Cay

Clinic: ☎369-0089

South Andros

Kemp's Bay

Bank: Bank of The Bahamas, open Wednesday 10am to 2:45pm.

Police: ☎369-4733.

Clinic: ☎369-4849.

★ EXPLORING

North Andros

Morgan's Bluff

Morgan's Bluff is the northernmost settlement on Andros and a very lively place each year during the All Andros and Berry Islands Independence Regatta. Islanders fill the parking lot near the small harbour to watch the race and join the activities. If it isn't mid-July when you visit, chances are you might see the giant barge that carries freshwater to Nassau on a daily basis.

The settlement is named for pirate Henry Morgan who supposedly hid his treasure in a nearby cave. You, like many before, can try to find it. **Henry Morgan's Cave ★** is just east of the road; there is a sign. A short clamber through the tree roots leads to a lofty gallery and the cave is on from there. There are a few bats and lots of mosquitoes, you'll need a flashlight.

The road heads southwest to ***Lowe Sound****, a quaint fishing village. Beachfront Nicholl's Town and Conch Sound are east of here.*

Nicholl's Town

Nicholl's Town is the administrative centre for North Andros. It has a picturesque location, along the palm-lined shore. The Georgian-style **Administration Building** is attractive and faces small International Square which is grandly dedicated to the spirit of international friendship and cooperation. This used to be an important diving hub, but since the closure of the Andros Beach Hotel, things have slowed down considerably. The hotel is rumoured to reopening, but at press time it remained closed. Along the beach, east of the hotel, a darker blue circle is discernable in the water just a few metres offshore – a blue hole!

Backtrack to Lowe Sound and head south on the Queen's Highway.

Before you get to San Andros you'll see a sign on your left (east) and the turnoff to **Uncle Charlie's Blue Hole**. A very rough track leads a few hundred metres into the bush to the edge of the hole.

The water level varies in the hole, sometimes you can even see it rising or falling. Legends about the much-feared blue-hole monster "Lusca" surround the hole which has been explored by scuba divers.

Red Bays ★★★

A road runs west from the Queen's Highway, just north of San Andros, to fascinating Red Bays, the only settlement on Andros' west coast. The local Baptist pastor and former prinicpal of the school, Bert Newton, has documented the settlement's history and claims that his ancestors arrived here from Florida in canoes. Runaway slaves who had escaped to Florida, which then belonged to Spain, joined small groups of Seminole natives. When Florida became American, they fled further south where they heard of free land to the east: The Bahamas, where Britain has abolished slavery. Thus these black Seminoles piled into their dug-out canoes and made for Andros. One of the first families was headed by Samuel Lewis. The original Red Bays, where sponges were plentiful, was about 15 kilometres north of here, but hurricanes forced the settlers to higher ground in an area thick with trees that came to be called Lewis Coppice which is the present site of Red Bays. For years, the settlement remained isolated. It was only in 1968 that the road was cleared. The famous watertight **baskets ★★★** made only here are part of the Seminole legacy of these people.

Today, Red Bays is a modest fishing village, where some residents still collect sponges. The shore is littered with them.

*Back on the Queen's Highway you'll pass a few farms, notably a **Mennonite farm**. Here you can buy fresh fruits and vegetables. The pot-holed road continues south through **San Andros** and pine forests before heading east and then south along the shore.*

Staniard Creek

Staniard Creek is reputed to be the prettiest place on the island. The creek itself is a stunningly luminescent pale turquoise; the sunny town, however, leaves a bit to be desired, though it is flowery and has a superb beach.

Just north of here is the **Forfar Field Station** *(☎329-6129)*, a privately run research facility catering to North American high school and college students. This was once a diving lodge run by Charlie Forfar, an avid diver who died trying to set a world record for the deepest dive.

Love Hill and Calabash Bay

A few trails lead from Love Hill into the bush. One goes to **Captain Bill's Blue Hole ★** where local kids go swimming. This is also a good trail for birdwatching and orchid admiring.

To the south is the pretty settlement of Calabash Bay, whose bay is known to some as **Small Hope Bay ★★★**. The oft-retold story goes that Henry Morgan and Blackbeard combined their loot into one huge treasure and hid it here. They did such a good job that they exclaimed there was "small hope" anyone would uncover it.

Fresh Creek

Fresh Creek is the name of the creek that runs between Coakley Town and Andros Town, and is the name used to describe the two together. A wild dolphin has taken a recent liking to the creek and to visitors too, the Small

Hope Bay Lodge ferries guests up the creek to swim with this friendly creature.

Most everything, except the bank and the Androsia Batik Factory, is on the north side of the creek in **Coakley Town**. The town was named for **Coakley House** (see p 246), which was built by a Swedish captain of industry named Axel Wenner-Gren, who also built the Andros Yacht Club across the creek (now the **Lighthouse Yacht Club**) and was one of the first investors in Hog Cay, now Paradise Island. The lighthouse in question lies at the mouth of Fresh Creek.

Andros Town is not really a town per se. Just south of the bridge is the **Androsia Batik Factory ★★★** *(Mon to Sat, 8am to 4pm, ☎352-2255)*, which started as a simple cottage industry in 1972 by Rosi Birch of Small Hope Bay Lodge after a German guest taught her the art of "Batik". Androsia now employs 45 Androsians, is sold throughout The Bahamas and is one of the prettiest souvenirs you'll find here. You can visit the factory and watch the batik-ing process. Sponge cut-outs are dipped in hot wax and applied to cotton and rayon. The fabric is then steeped in big tubs of different-coloured dyes. The wax repels the dye, and after it is melted off in a superheated bath with white hibiscus, seagrapes, turtles, shells and other island motifs left behind. The cloth is line dried by the sun and the tradewinds. It is then transformed into colourful resort wear from golf shirts to bikinis. Unfortunately, they don't print the fabric every day, but you can see the bolts of fabric and check out the factory outlet store, which sells the latest Androsia creations as well as seconds and left-overs from last year.

About two kilometres south of town is **AUTEC**, the Atlantic Undersea Test and Evaluation Center, a joint American-Bahamian-British facility for underwater weapons development. It employs 800 Americans and 100 Androsians. Access is restricted to personnel.

The highway continues south and is a maze of bone-jarring, car-eating potholes. Take it slow. There isn't much to see for about 25 kilometres until you reach Cargill Creek save a few rusting half-submerged cars.

Cargill Creek and Behring Point

This area is prime **bonefishing ★★★** territory. There is a handful of fishing lodges (see p 246) that can show you the best of the region. Cargill Creek faces the creek of the same name and the settlement of Behring Point on the other side. The road fizzles out after Behring Point.

Central Andros

Mangrove Cay

Mangrove Cay is the main island of Central Andros. The Queen's Highway continues south along its eastern shore, but it is in even worse shape than its northern section. **Little Harbour**, at its northeastern tip, is the main settlement. The northern part of town is known as **Moxey Town**. The action here centres around the few local eateries and the dock where the sponges, lobsters and conchs are all hauled in. Mangrove Cay is also bonefishing heaven. A ferry runs from Lisbon Creek to Drigg's Hill on South Andros.

Benjamin's Blue Hole lies in the South Bight of Andros, the waterway that divides Mangrove Cay and South Andros. It was discovered by George Benjamin and its fantastic stalactities

Mangrove Tree

and stalagmites proved that underwater caves were once above ground. Jacques Cousteau came to Andros to document its blue holes and named the underwater cave the "Grotto". Experienced divers can explore it.

South Andros

South Andros is very remote and does not get many visitors despite the fact that it boasts as many spectacular beaches and equally as superb bonefishing as its northern neighbours. There is a substantial resort (Emerald Palms by the Sea, see p 247) with a superb **beach** ★★★ just south of **Drigg's Hill**. The airport is at tiny little **Congo Town. The Bluff** is the administrative centre for South Andros. **Kemp's Bay** for its part, thrives from the schools of grouper just offshore. The road ends at the quaint fishing village of **Mars Bay**, whose harbour is actually a big blue hole that has been explored by divers.

BEACHES

Andros east coast is virtually one long breezy strand of gold and white sand. Unfortunately (and thankfully to some), not all of it is easily accessible. Here are some of its best stretches. **Nicholl's Town** ★ has a pretty palm-fringed, white-sand beach at the northern end of North Andros. **Small Hope Bay** ★★★ is a fine crescent of gold sand. Its northern part is best for swimming and sunbathing. **Somerset Beach** ★, three kilometres south of Andros Town, is good for shelling at low tide. On South Andros, the **Emerald Palms Beach** ★★★ seems endless; it is line with majestic palms trees.

OUTDOOR ACTIVITIES

Fishing

Andros' interior is sliced by inland waterways and fishing flats, while the west coast, is one giant fishing flat. Tarpon and bonefish abound in this fly-fisher's paradise. Each settlement has its local guides who know these flats like the backs of their hands. The small **Andros Bonefishing Guides Association** *(☎329-7372 or 368-4261)* is good for recommendations. In most cases, fishers will need to bring their own gear and tackle. All lodges and guides have a catch and release policy.

There are a handful of excellent bonefishing lodges offering full days (eight hours) of bonefishing with excellent guides at an average cost of $300. These places are listed in the "Accommodations" section of this chapter (see p 246).

Small Hope Bay Lodge *(☎368-2014, ⇌368-2015)* offers all types of sportfishing. Full day of bonefishing is $300, half-day $175; full day of reef fishing is $380, half-day is $220; full day of deep-sea fishing is $480, half-day is $275. Box lunches are included on all full-day trips. They also have a two-night bonefishing and tarpon fishing excursion to the west side.

Scuba Diving and Snorkelling

Andros barrier reef and blue holes offer the best of both worlds for snorkellers and divers. Close to shore, calm, shallow, coral-reef gardens teem with colourful and surprisingly tame fish. Divers can explore a few wrecks, notably the ***Marion***, the **Barge** and the ***Potomac***. Along the edge of the 225-kilometre-long barrier reef, things get more exciting with the classic **Over the Wall** dive. Andros' blue holes present a challenge to even the most experienced divers. These dives might cost a bit more, but it's an experience you'll never forget!

Small Hope Bay Lodge *(☎368-2014)* is the only full dive shop on Andros and is staffed by very enthusiastic dive-masters. Resort courses and snorkelling courses are free for guests of the lodge. Certification courses are also available. There are regularly scheduled day and night dives; a one-tank dive is $45, a two-tank dive is $55. Experienced divers can choose from a list of exciting custom-tailored specialty dives and one-on-one advanced dives to blue holes, caverns and Over the Wall. These are $110.

Birdwatching and Hiking

Andros' bush offers birders the chance to see countless rare species. It is best not to wander off without a guide, however, as the woods are popular with wild-boar hunters. **Small Hope Bay Lodge** *(☎368-2014)* offers several self-guided walks complete with maps and binoculars. These are free for guests.

ACCOMMODATIONS

Many of the smaller hotels on Andros charge less for extended stays. Enquire when reserving.

North Andros

Nicholl's Town

Green Windows Inn *($55; 12 rooms, ≡, tv, ℝ; PO Box 23076, Nicholl's Town, ☎329-2194, ⇌329-2016)* is an inexpen-

Ulysses' Favourites

Accommodations

Warmest Welcome:

Small Hope Bay Lodge (see p 245).

Best Resort for Activities:

Small Hope Bay Lodge (see p 245), Seascape Inn (see p 247) and Emerald Palms By-The-Sea (see p 247).

Most Luxurious Setup:

Kamalame Cove (see p 245).

Restaurants

Best True-true Bahamian Cooking:

Big Josh's Seafood Restaurant & Lounge (see p 248) and Dig Dig's (see p 248).

Best Dining Experience:

Small Hope Bay Lodge (see p 248), Lighthouse Yacht Club (see p 248) and Emerald Palms By-The-Sea (see p 249).

sive and modest spot right in Nicholl's Town. The beach is a short walk away. There are standard rooms with double beds and a shared bathroom, or equipped suites with small kitchenettes and private baths.

The **Andros Beach Hotel** *(☎329-2582)* was still closed as of early 1998 but was rumoured to be re-opening. As this is the only substantial estalbishment in the north, it may be worth checking into.

Conch Sound

Conch Sound Resort Inn *($83; 16 rooms, pb, sat tv, ℝ, ℜ, ≈; PO Box 23029, Conch Sound, ☎329-2060 or 329-2341)* has attractive and comfortable rooms with double beds, or much fancier villas that sleep up to six people. It has a pink leather pull-out couch and oak furniture. There are two bedrooms, a dining room and a fully equipped kitchen. The resort's pool is fairly small. The restaurant is large and family-style. Bonefishing can be arranged.

Staniard Creek

Quality Inn *($50; 11 rooms, pb, sb, ≡, ℜ; Staniard Creek, ☎368-6217)*, also known as Dicky's Place, overlooks Staniard Creek and caters mostly to visiting students at the Forfar research station, but everyone is welcome. Rooms are clean and very modest with one double bed. Upstairs rooms share a bathroom. There is a small adjoining restaurant and bar.

Kamalame Cove *($300 per person all-incl; ≡, ⊗, ≈, K, Staniard Creek, ☎368-6281, ⇌368-6279, mailing address: 13727 SW 152nd St., suite 213, Miami, FL 33177)*. Imagine your dream beach house: tradewinds breeze through open windows and doors, fans hang from cathedral ceilings, mosquito nets draped over king-size beds, hammocks hang between palm trees just steps from your private beach... well, you can have just that at Kamalame Cove. The luxurious main house can sleep up to 10 people, but even if you are only two you must pay for a minimum of six people, a whopping $3000 per night! This includes gourmet cooking, wines, snorkelling and eco-tours. Deep-sea fishing, bonefishing and scuba diving are extra. There is a small free-form pool and a small but pristine private beach. There are also smaller but equally exquisite guesthouses with kitchenettes.

Calabash Bay / Small Hope Bay

Staying at **Small Hope Bay Lodge** *($330, low $300, all-incl; 20 rooms, pb, ⊗, ℜ, ⊛; mailing address: PO Box CB-11817, Nassau, ☎368-2013/4 or 1-800-223-6961, ⇌368-2015)* is like being at camp but with massages, no curfew, good food and, if you want, you can do nothing at all! This is a true favourite! When Canadian Dick Birch built the place in 1960, he started with the central lodge, which is just a bit reminiscent of a typical cabin in the Canadian woods, except that it is built with coral stone and strong Andros pine. It even has a large central fireplace (it does get cool in the winter apparently). Rooms are set in two rows of adjoining beachfront cottages, also built of coral and Andros pine and surrounded by coconut palms, casuarinas and hammocks for lazing. They sport simple wooden furniture and platform beds or waterbeds. Each is brightened with Androsia batik. There is no air conditioning, and no need with the swift breezes coming off the bay. Besides excellent fishing, snorkelling and diving, including free introductory resort course, the Lodge offers nature walks, bike tours and birdwatching on trails. There is an outdoor hot tub, a protected swimming beach, a nude sunbathing solarium and a Laser and windsurfer that guests can use. Children will find lots to keep them busy in the game room. All sorts of packages are available. And the food is delish (see p 248).

Closer to town is the new **Point of View** *(☎368-2750)* fishing lodge. Fourteen individual and modern wood cottages surround the restaurant and fish-shaped pool overlooking the ocean. There is a dock.

Fresh Creek

Landmark Hotel *($65; 15 rooms, ≡, tv, ℜ; Fresh Creek, ☎368-2082)* is a casual place above one of the town's popular eateries and watering holes (see p 249). Rooms have the bare essentials: a bed, closet and bathroom, plus a television and a balcony.

Chickcharnie's Hotel *($75; 13 rooms, ℜ, ≡, tv, pb, sb; Fresh Creek, ☎368-2025)* rents modest, bland rooms with either two twin beds or one double. A long balcony offers nice views of the creek. The restaurant is a local favourite (see p 248).

Andros Lighthouse Yacht Club Marina *($130; 20 rooms, ⊗, ≡, pb, sat tv, ℜ, ≈; Fresh Creek, ☎368-2305, ⇌368-2300)* lies on the south side of Fresh Creek facing town. This is the old Andros Yacht Club, built by Axel Wenner-Gren in the 1940s. It is now run by the government. Rooms have king-sized beds, cool tile floors and are so big that they feel a bit empty. The bathrooms are just as spacious. There are also two-bedroom cottages. The pool, however, is quite small. The restaurant is recommended (see p 248). There are tennis courts and scuba diving and fishing can be arranged.

Coakley House *($350; pb, ≡, K; ☎368-1667 or 1-800-223-6961, ⇌368-2015, mailing address: PO Box 21667, Fort Lauderdale, FL 33335)* is a lovely self-catering place owned and run by the folks at the Small Hope Bay Lodge. Its unique design boasts 35 windows and 7 doors. The house sleeps six very comfortable and has an attractive, and laid-back decor and a great location overlooking the ocean at the mouth of Fresh Creek. Weekly rates are available, as well as all-inclusive rates where all meals and maid and cook service are included, two nights all-inclusive for two people during the high season cost $970 and $770 in the low season.

Cargill Creek

Charlie's Haven *(room $130 per person including all meals; 10 rooms, ≡, ⊗, pb, ℜ; Cargill Creek, ☎368-4087)* was one of the first bonefish lodges in this part of the world, and Charlie Smith is one of the best, as his loyal following will attest. The place just oozes atmosphere, from the photos of great catches to the maritime paraphernalia adorning every corner of the bar. The rooms are small but adequate. A guided boat costs $300 for two people.

Andros Island Bonefishing Club *($158 for room and meals per person, $146 per person double occ.; 12 rooms, pb, ℝ, ℜ, ⊗; Cargill Creek, Andros, ☎368-5167, or 1-800-245-1950, ⇌368-5235, mailing address: c/o Frontiers PO Box 959, Wexford PA, 15090, or c/o Frontiers, 18 Albermarle St., London W1X 3HA, England)* has spacious, simply furnished rooms with two queen-sized beds and plenty of room to stow your fishing gear. The fishing happens on Cargill Creek, which is right in front of the lodge, and on the flats of North Bight; when they aren't out on the flats, fishers congregate at the lodge. There are a couple of couches and a satellite television. The bar is at one end and meals are served here too. There are packages; for example, four nights and three days of fishing cost $1,465 per person or $980 double occupancy.

Cargill Creek Fishing Lodge *($165 for room and meals per person, $150 per person double occ.; 11 rooms, 2 cottages, pb, ≈, ≡, ℜ, ⊗, K; PO Box N-1882, Nassau, ☎368-5129, ⇌368-5046)* lies just downstream from the above club, and also faces the flats of Cargill Creek. Accommodations are in new wooden cottages with beamed ceilings and cool tile floors. A larger cottage with kitchenette and room for six people is also available. There is a also small pool around which barbecues are set up on occasion. The lively bar and restaurant are recommended (see p 248). A day of fishing costs $300 for two people. Four nights and three days of fishing cost $1,560 per person or $1,050 double occupancy

Behring Point

Tranquillity Hill Fishing Lodge *(room $148 per person including all meals; 10 rooms, ≡, sat tv, ℜ, Behring Point, ☎/⇌368-4132)* is a pink and green building. The owners of this place planned to clear the mangrove-lined shore and put in a marina when I visited. Rooms have two double beds and tile floors. They are clean but lack charm. There are three deluxe rooms upstairs with a couch. A full-day on the bonefish flats costs $300 for two people.

Daisy Nottage's Cottages *($100 all-incl.; 15 rooms, sat tv, pb, K, ≡, ⊗, sat tv; Behring Point, ☎368-4293)* are overseen by the remarkable Miss Nottage, a pipe-smoking former midwife and bush- medicine expert, and her cats. She has 10 modern and spotless rooms and five two-bedroom, fully equipped cottages. Meals are served in her small restaurant.

Central Andros

Mangrove Cay

Moxey's Guest House *($50; 8 rooms, ⊗, ≡, ℜ, pb; Little Harbour, Mangrove Cay, ☎369-0023)* along with its adjoining restaurant and bar are popular gathering spots in town. There are six standard and very acceptable rooms plus two suites for up to eight people.

Mangrove Cay Inn *($65; 8 rooms, pb, ⊗, ℜ; Mangrove Cay, ☎369-0069, ⇒369-0014)* is a well-equipped, friendly spot that is well suited to exploring the blue holes south of Little Harbour. Rooms are modern and pink with high-beamed ceilings. The beach is a short walk away. The restaurant is recommended (see p 248).

Helen's Motel Complex *($75; 8 rooms, ≡, ℜ, K, pb; c/o PO Box SS-5268, Nassau, ☎369-0033)* is south of town and near the narrow beach. Rooms are non-descript, with tiled floors. Some have kitchenettes.

Seascape Inn *($90, bkfst incl; 5 rooms, pb, ⊗, ℜ; PO Box 023824, Mangrove Cay, ☎369-0342)* is the newest addition to Mangrove Cay. Accommodations are in five wooden cabins on stilts with breezy wooden balconies. Inside, they are lofty, bright and very homey. The restaurant and bar are also on stilts. Hammocks are slung here and there. All sorts of activities are possible from birdwatching to kayak trips and scuba diving.

South Andros

Drigg's Hill

Emerald Palms By-The-Sea *($100, MAP $40; 20 rooms, pb, ≈, ℜ, ℝ, sat tv; PO Box 800, Drigg's Hill, ☎369-2661, ⇒369-2667)* is an expansive resort run by the government with a relaxed, laid-back ambiance. Facing an eight-kilometre beach, the property is covered with palm trees. There is a decent-sized pool, hammocks and a tennis court. You can play shuffleboard or borrow the Hobie Cat. The rooms have an attractive tropical decor with teak furniture, some have four-poster beds and mosquito netting. Each has a VCR. There is a pretty dining room (see p 249).

Kemp's Bay

Royal Palm Bonefishing Bay Camp *($100 for room only; 5 rooms, pb, K, ≈, ℜ, ≡, ℝ; Johnson Bay at Kemp's Bay, ☎813-249-9908 or 1-800-450-9908, ⇒813-889-9189)* has seen better days, with rough carpeting and bland furniture in its standard rooms. The equipped conch-sided cottage is much nicer with two bedrooms. Packages are also available, three days of bonefishing and four nights accommodations costs $1100 per person.

RESTAURANTS

North Andros

Lowe Sound

Big Josh's Seafood Restaurant & Lounge *($-$$; Lowe Sound, ☎329-7517)* has authentic Bahamian cooking, including tender cracked conch and fresh catch of the day, all prepared by Josh's widow Malvese.

Calabash Bay / Small Hope Bay

Small Hope Bay Lodge *($$-$$$; ☎368-2013)* serves up some of the finest food on Andros, either out on their seaside patio or in the lodge if its cool. Breakfast can be simple or elaborate, depending on your appetite. Lunch is a buffet with a hot entree, cold cuts, vegetables, salads and dessert. Dinner is when the kitchen really shines. It starts with cocktails and conch fritters and continues with a home-made soup, salad bar and choice of meat or fish entree, which might be rack of lamb or fresh lobster. Cakes, pies and fruit salads are offered for dessert. Reservations are required for non-guests.

Fresh Creek

Two local eateries vie for the title of best native cuisine, **Chickcharnie's Hotel** *($-$$; ☎368-2025)* with great views of the creek and **Skinny's Landmark Restaurant** *($-$$; ☎368-2082)* with live entertainment on occasion.

The **Lighthouse Club** *($$-$$$)* has a large elegant dining room facing the marina and creek. Their conch chowder is good and hearty, and steamed grouper is a good choice for an entree. Other Bahamian and American dishes are offered on the large menu.

Cargill Creek and Behring Point

The **Sea View Restaurant** *($; ☎368-4005)* serves good Bahamian breakfasts along with the good-old eggs and bacon. Lunch and dinner are tasty native fare.

The **Andros Island Bonefishing Club** *($-$$$; ☎368-5167)* has a modest dining room that serves very basic cuisine and a few Bahamian dishes. Guests of the place seem to appreciate its simplicity. Reservations are required for non-guests.

The dining room at the **Cargill Creek Fishing Lodge** *($-$$$; ☎368-5129)* is a bit more elaborate with tasty fresh seafood offerings and finger-licking-good spare ribs.

Dig-Dig's *($$-$$$; ☎368-5097)* in a small pink house by the road, is open for lunch and dinner, but you must call ahead so that owners Liz (from Canada) and Alton (from here) know to prepare your meal, and you might even get a choice. Either way, you'll be served the house cocktail (fresh coconut water, sweet condensed milk and gin) and the best Bahamian cooking in this neck of the woods.

Central Andros

Mangrove Cay

Stacey's Restaurant & Lounge *($; ☎369-0161)*, south of Moxey Town, sticks to native fare.

The **Mangrove Cay Inn** *($-$$; ☎369-0069)* has the most elaborate

Annual Events

July
All Andros & Berry Islands Independence Regatta pits traditional Bahamian sailboats against each other. Festivities include live bands, dominoes, crab cracking and a bonefishing tournament.

August
August Monday Regatta, Little Harbour.

November
North Andros Thanksgiving Bonefish Tournament.

menu on Mangrove Cay. There are simple sandwiches plus good cracked conch, grouper, lobster and a few meat and chicken dishes. The restaurant also has sweet cocktails and yummy fruit punch.

South Andros

Drigg's Hill

The **Emerald Palms By the Sea** *($$-$$$; ☎369-2661)* resort has a lovely glassed-in restaurant overlooking the pool deck and the beach. It serves Bahamian and continental fare, with fresh and original seafood selections. There are cookouts and seafood buffets by the pool on occasion. Reservations are recommended for dinner.

ENTERTAINMENT

North Andros

Nicholl's Town

Rumors *(☎329-2398)* is the jazziest place in town with live bands on occasion and dancing.

Morgan's Bluff

Willy's Water Lounge is the jumpiest place come regatta time.

Fresh Creek

Skinny's Lounge downstairs from the Landmark Hotel has live music on weekends.

Cargill Creek

The **Cribside Lounge** is the acclaimed favourite hangout. Rake-'n'-scrape bands perform here regularly.

Central Andros

Mangrove Cay

The **Angler's Bar & Grill** at Moxey's Guest House (see p 247), has a pub-like ambiance and a crowd of locals and visitors.

The **New Happy Three Soca Club** *(☎369-0030)* is a funky dance club in Moxey Town, where the dance of choice is the sensuous soca.

South Andros

Kemp's Bay

Ocean View Restaurant & Bar *(☎369-3796)* and **Big J's On The Bay** *(☎369-1954)* both liven up as the evening progresses.

SHOPPING

North Andros

Red Bays

Henry Wallace carves local woods like horseflesh into magnificent pieces and sells them from his home, ask around for directions. Yvonne Russell is one of the town's top straw weavers using techniques handed-down from Seminole natives to create the famous watertight jugs and baskets; a basket costs $5, a jug $15. She also sells from her home.

Fresh Creek

Androsia Batik Factory *(☎352-2255)* in Andros Town has a large selection of Androsia resort clothing and fabric from this year and last at factory prices.

A **market** is planned for Saturdays in Andros Town and Coakley Town with Red Bays' straw baskets and other souvenirs.

Central Andros

Mangrove Cay

The **Hibiscus Gift Shop** has a good selection of locally made crafts, straw items and jewellery.

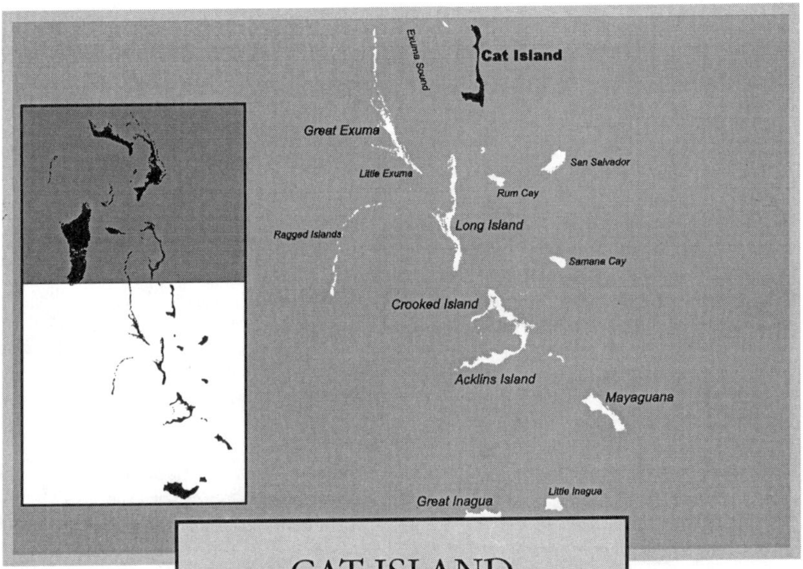

CAT ISLAND

Long and skinny Cat Island's greatest attraction is surely its tradition and history. It has plantation ruins up and down the length of it. Some of its 18 settlements are nothing more than a handful of small square cottages that either have tiny casuarinas growing out of them or are painted bright green and red. Large stone African baking ovens still dot the landscape. There is a medieval-looking hermitage at its (and The Bahamas') highest point.

The natural beauty of Cat Island ★★ is also high up on the reasons-to-come list. There are caves and blue holes to explore, walls to dive, fish to hook, and trails to walk. And of course there are beaches (this is The Bahamas after all!); to the west calm crescents of sand and to the east stretches of pinkish sand between grand cliffs.

It is the sixth largest island of The Bahamas. Shaped like a boot, it is 77 kilometres long and between 1.5 and 7 kilometres wide for most of its length, except at its southern end where the foot is almost 20 kilometres wide. The highest point in The Bahamas, 206-foot-high Mount Alvernia rises up behind New Bight, the capital of the island. The peak of a long-ago submerged mountain chain, Cat is hilly by Bahamian standards. Washed by the North Atlantic, the eastern shore is much steeper and marked by high bluffs and dramatic cliffs, while to the west deserted beaches slope gently into Exuma Sound.

Rich red soil has given the island a lush interior and made it famous for a variety of fruits and vegetables including pineapples. The island is covered with many saltwater and freshwater lakes. The latter are often in fact bottomless blue holes where three to four metres of fresh water sit on salt water. They range in length from one kilometre to about 13 kilometres. Kilometres of

Obeah

Obeah (a word from the Ashanti language of West Africa) is African-based witchcraft that allows the living to placate the spirits of the dead. Cat Islanders believe very strongly in spirits, both good and bad, and take care not to offend them. Many of the houses along the Queen's Highway that seem abandoned are, at least by the living. Often when the last of a generation dies, his house is left for his spirit and a new house is built for the next generation. The practice of Obeah involves bottles of all kinds, filled with dead spiders or liquor depending on the "fix" or spell being employed. You will see them hanging from trees and in graveyards. Few Bahamians will openly discuss Obeah, for it is still officially banned, but they do consult practitioners, the modern-day version of the feared and revered Obeah man of old.

submerged passages connect the holes to the sea and ocean currents, and tides can actually pull items from the lakes and deposit them on Atlantic beaches. The interior is also marshy and swampy in places with vast areas of mangroves, mahogany and cascadilla. Small ponds provide a habitat for endangered freshwater turtles. Land crabs, both black and white, also roam the island. Birdlife also abounds.

A Short History

Two stories explain the island's name: one claims it is named for Arthur Catt, a pirate who hid a treasure of gold here, the other says it is named for the cats released here by the Spanish to keep the rat population under control and discovered by the English when they settled in the 17th century. The island wasn't always called Cat Island either. Up until 1926, it was believed to be the first landfall of Columbus and so was officially called San Salvador (the name was then transferred to Watling's Island, present-day San Salvador). Islanders still hold on to the belief that theirs' was the first island to welcome Columbus. The island did play a pivotal role in Spain's "discovery" of the New World, however. In 1495, the town of Columba was settled. It became a transshipment point for Lucayan slaves on their way to Hispaniola.

As The Bahamas were claimed and then neglected by the European powers, Cat Island remained deserted. Some time around 1670, Bermudian seamen arrived and settled near present-day Port Howe and Hawk's Nest. Cat Island was attacked on numerous occasions by the Spanish and by pirates in 1717 and 1718. Woodes Rogers, the first royal governor, suggested the settlers abandon Cat Island, which they finally did in 1722, but only for four months. Rogers was actually planning to settle on Cat Island when he died in 1729.

Loyalists from the United States were next to arrive in 1783, more than doubling the island's population. They ran profitable cotton and cattle estates. Crop failures and the abolition of the slave trade on British ships in 1807 sent many Loyalists back to the United States. Tension between slaves and slave owners also contributed. Claims of abuse and revolts lead to the burning of the pre-Loyalist Henry Hawkings Armbrister plantation house at New Bight which was built in the 1760s. There was also the serious uprising on the Golden Grove plantation where

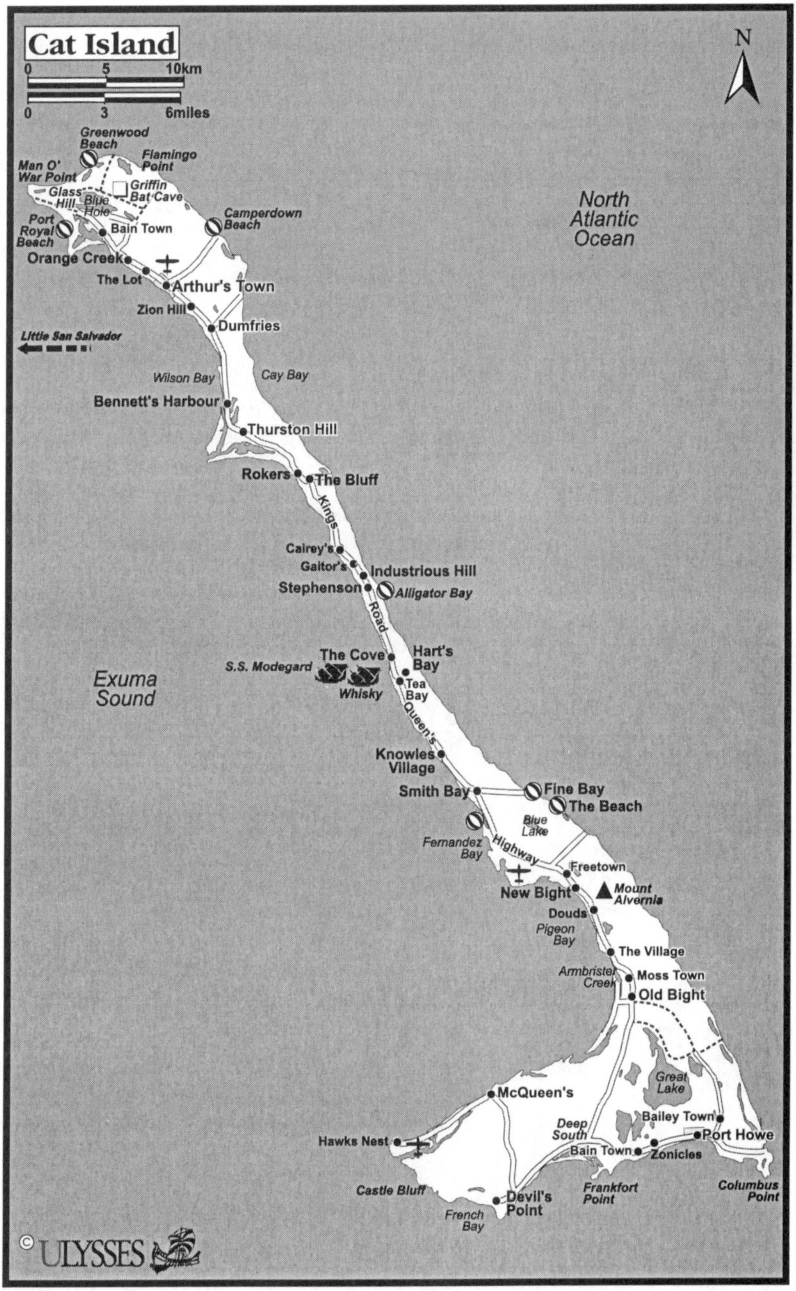

Cat Island
0 5 10km
0 3 6miles
N
Greenwood Beach
Flamingo Point
Man O' War Point
Glass Hill
Blue Hole
Griffin Bat Cave
Port Royal Beach
Bain Town
Camperdown Beach
North Atlantic Ocean
Orange Creek
The Lot
Arthur's Town
Zion Hill
Dumfries
Little San Salvador
Wilson Bay
Cay Bay
Bennett's Harbour
Thurston Hill
Rokers
The Bluff
Kings
Cairey's
Gaitor's
Industrious Hill
Stephenson
Alligator Bay
Road
The Cove
Hart's Bay
S.S. Modegard
Whisky
Tea Bay
Exuma Sound
Queen's
Knowles Village
Smith Bay
Fine Bay
The Beach
Blue Lake
Fernandez Bay
Highway
Freetown
New Bight
Mount Alvernia
Douds
Pigeon Bay
The Village
Armbrister Creek
Moss Town
Old Bight
Great Lake
McQueen's
Bailey Town
Deep South
Port Howe
Hawks Nest
Bain Town
Zonicles
Castle Bluff
Frankfort Point
Columbus Point
Devil's Point
French Bay
© ULYSSES

seven slaves led a revolt. Shots were fired and the seven were sentenced to death. Dick, the ring leader, was the only one to be executed, and he became a martyr of the struggle for freedom. When freedom finally came in 1838, most of the Loyalists abandoned their plantations and the island was left to the former slaves. Cotton still grows wild on Cat Island.

Pineapples and sisal became the major cash crops in the latter part of the 19th century. Production was so great that a railway was built starting just north of Old Bight and ending at the harbour in The Village. Cat Islanders still get by for the most part from agriculture, growing tomatoes and pineapples in potholes where the nutrient rich soil collects, and is then manually fertilized by guano, bat dung collected from the many caves. What they do not consume themselves they sell to local shops. Straw work is the other main occupation.

Cat Island is one of the most traditional Bahamian islands. Of the four islands that were originally settled (the others being New Providence, Eleuthera, Harbour Island), it is the most remote and the least touched by tourism. Electricity only arrived in 1993. Traditional music, dance, bush medicine, legends and *obeah* (Bahamian counterpart to voodoo or santeria) are still a part of every day life on this historic island.

FINDING YOUR WAY AROUND

By Plane

The airport in New Bight is the only port of entry on Cat Island. It is located about three kilometres north of town. It has very few facilities, basically a telephone and toilets. Fernandez Bay, the Bridge Inn and the Greenwood offer complimentary ground transportation. There is also an airport in Arthur's Town and an airstrip at Hawk's Nest, but you must clear customs at New Bight first if you are arriving from another country.

Bahamasair *(the day of the flight: ☎342-2017 for New Bight, 354-2049 for Arthur's Town)* flies from Nassau to New Bight and Arthur's Town two to three times a week. The following charter companies fly into New Bight. Their schedules change often and can depend on demand, the fare is often the same whether you are one or six: **Air Sunshine** *(☎954-434-8900)* from Fort Lauderdale and Sarasota, Florida; **Island Express** from Fort Lauderdale; **Sandpiper Air** from Nassau; **Sunshine Tours** *(☎342-5011 or in Nassau 377-1703, 323-4170)* from Nassau; **Larry Meredith** *(☎342-3018)* on Cat Island and **Fernandez Bay Village** (see p 263 for telephone numbers) also offer charter flights from points in Florida and The Bahamas.

By Boat

The only marina facilities on the island are at Hawk's Nest at the southern tip of the island. Remember this is not a port of entry, you must clear customs and immigration at New Bight if you are coming from abroad. Boats also moor in Fernandez Bay.

By Mailboat: The *North Cat Island Special* leaves Nassau Wednesdays at 1pm and stops at New Bight, Bennett's Harbour and Arthur's Town. Travel time: 40 hours. Fare: $40 one way. The *M/V Seahauler* leaves Nassau Tuesdays at 3pm and stops at New Bight, Old Bight, Smith Bay, Bennett's Harbour and Arthur's Town. Travel time: 17 hours. Fare: $40 one way.

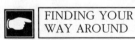

Fernandez Bay Village rents motorboats with or without a captain for $25 to $50 per hour.

By Car

A single road called the Queen's Highway (some sources call it Kings Road) runs the length of the island along the western shore from north to south. Smaller tracks run east to the coast at some points.

Car Rental: Jason Russell at the New Bight Service Station & Car Rental *(New Bight, ☎/⇒342-3014)* in New Bight rents a few big American sedans for $85 per day. So far only cash is accepted, but this may change. There is no insurance per se, renters must accept responsibility for damages.

Gas Stations: You can get gas in New Bight, Orange Creek and west of Port Howe.

By Scooter

The Cookie House (Arthur's Town) can arrange scooter rentals for $20 per day.

PRACTICAL INFORMATION

There are no commercial banks on Cat Island. Hotels accept and exchange (there may be a fee) travellers cheques. Some charge a fee for credit card payments.

There is no tourist office on Cat Island. You should be able to get ample information from your hotel.

Tours: A company called Island Vacations *(☎354-1111, ⇒356-4379)* out of Nassau organizes guided tours of Cat Island. A handful of islanders also offer their own tours; ask for a recommendation at your hotel or contact: Daisy Mae Hunter with Sunshine Tours *(☎342-5011)* in Port Howe or Lincoln Cleare *(☎354-5042)* in Orange Creek.

New Bight and Southern Cat Island

New Bight

The Government Administrative Complex on the Queen's Highway houses the Police *(☎354-3039)* BaTelCo's *(☎342-3060)* offices and the post office.

Northern Cat Island

Smith Bay

The island's doctor on call and main medical clinic *(☎342-3026)* are in Smith Bay, north of New Bight, on the Queen's Highway.

Arthur's Town

Arthur's Town also has a medical clinic *(☎354-4050)* with a nurse on duty, a BaTelCo *(☎354-2060)* and a police station *(☎354-2046)*

EXPLORING

New Bight and Southern Cat Island

Since the capital New Bight is at a halfway point of sorts on the island, we will tour the island in two legs, starting with the southern end and then heading north.

The Hermit of Cat Island

Born in 1876 in Surrey England, John Hawes was many things before he became Father Jerome, the Hermit of Cat Island. He came from a respectable family and was a talented and successful architect when he chose to become an Anglican minister in 1901. He studied and emulated the life of St. Francis of Assissi, dressing like a monk, calling himself Father Jerome and living a modest lifestyle. In 1908 he came to The Bahamas to rebuild hurricane-ravaged churches including two masterpieces, St. Paul's Anglican Church and St. Peter's and St. Paul's Catholic Church, both on Long Island. He drifted about for a few years, breeding fox-terriers and driving mules in Western Canada before realizing that he could only emulate St. Francis' life as a Catholic and that he must convert. In 1911 he was received into the Catholic Church and then studied the priesthood in Rome for three years. The next 24 years were spent as a bush priest in Western Australia where he built many churches and helped introduce the Mission Style to that country. In 1932 and in ill health, Father Jerome asked the Catholic Bishop of Nassau if he could retire as a hermit to Cat Island. In 1939, he began work on his hermitage on Mount Como, which he renamed Alvernia after the site where St. Francis of Assissi walked his stations of the Cross. He lived in a cave amidst snakes, crabs and spiders until it was completed.

This great humanitarian was deeply trusted and respected by islanders. Following the hurricane of 1941, the barefoot hermit toiled for weeks with locals to rebuild; he then explained the principles of stone construction so that future buildings could withstand the winds. Islanders regularly climbed up to his hermitage to ask for help and were never turned down. From here he read and wrote and also designed churches and buildings locally and worldwide, including four churches on Cat Island and St. Augustine's Abbey in Fox Hill. His sermons were popular, despite his futile attempts to eradicate Obeah and convert islanders to Catholicism. Father Jerome died in a Miami hospital in 1956 and was buried, as requested, barefoot and without a casket in a cave on Mount Alvernia.

New Bight ★★

The settlement at New Bight comprises three districts, namely from north to south Freetown, Pigeon Bay and Doud's. Following the abolition of the slave trade on British ships, thousands of Africans were freed from slave ships before actually becoming slaves and resettled in The Bahamas. Freetown was one such settlement. The gleaming-white Catholic **Church of the Holy Redeemer ★** and its convent neighbour were designed by architect and hermit Father Jerome. They are no longer in use.

Pigeon Bay gets its name from the ever-present, white-crowned pigeons of the area. Finally, Doud's was established around the estate of Loyalist Seth Doud.

Mount Como, renamed Alvernia by Father Jerome, rises to the east of New Bight. Seen from down below, Fra Jerome's **Hermitage ★★★** on its summit seems small and far away. A rough track just past the Government administrative Complex and before the Armbrister plantation house (see below) leads to a stone gate and the start of a cleared path up the hill. Jerome built steep stone steps and a station of the Cross alongside the path. A short 15-minute hike leads up to the hermitage, and you will soon realize why it seemed so far away – it is tiny!

No steel, lumber, concrete or materials that can rust or rot away were used in its construction; it is made entirely of native stone in a cross between Mediterranean and medieval styles. The bell tower is only 12 feet high, the chapel with its little altar and single pew is 8 feet by 5 feet, and the guest cell with its simple desk and ledge for sleeping a mere 4 feet by 5 feet. When he began construction of the hermitage in 1939, Father Jerome lived in a cave until rats and crabs chased him out and into a tent. He finally moved in and lived there as a hermit, sleeping on the cloister floor on a straw mat bed until his death. He is buried barefoot and without a casket in a cave about 30 feet below the chapel. There is a brass sundial at the far end of the site. The exceptional, sweeping, 360-degree **view ★★★** is worth the hike in itself, especially at sunrise and sunset; it takes in the Atlantic Ocean on one side and Exuma Sound on the other.

Much of the land in New Bight was part of the **Armbrister Plantation** established in 1780 before the arrival of the Loyalists. One your way down from the Hermitage, take the track to the left which runs right through the front door of the **Henry Hawkins' Estate ★**. It was burnt during a slave revolt but its walls still stand as a reminder of those times. In the 1950s, Frances Armbrister and her son Tony returned to the family's ancestral lands and built Fernandez Bay Village using the ruins of the plantation buildings and slave settlement.

The Village

The Village was once the terminus of Cat Island's railroad, and ruins of the port and tracks can still be seen. It lies at the mouth of Armbrister Creek, a good spot for canoeing (see p 263). Most of the track was ripped up during the Second World War and transformed in to steel, but pieces of it are intact and other pieces have been scavenged by the islands.

A rough track running east before you reach Old Bight seems the most logical route to Port Howe. However, though it appears on many maps, it is not passable, you'll have to take the long way.

Old Bight

Old Bight was once called Davis Settlement, now it encompasses four formerly distinct settlements known as Moss Town, Chair Road, Cotton Bottom and The Swamp. Cotton and cattle plantations once thrived in this area and the hills are covered with plantation ruins.

Old Bight is home to what many say is the most beautiful building on the island, Father Jerome's **Saint Francis of Assissi Catholic Church ★★★** *(for the key see Mrs. Burrows across the road)*. Its construction was thanks in part to donations from Franciscan brothers in Western Australia, where Fra. Jerome spent 24 years of his life. Inside, behind the Gothic facade, there are frescoes and beautifully sculpted angels above the altar. Neither it nor the new church next door are in use.

St. Mary's Emancipation Church ★ is the only monument in The Bahamas to the emancipation of her slaves. It was built in 1889 and donated by the family of Governor Blaney Balfour, who read the Emancipation Proclamation. A beautiful flame tree stands in front of it.

The road continues south from Old Bight and across the island. The Deep South roundabout decorated with 570 conch shells regulates (!) the intersection with the east-west road running along the southern coast.

Devil's Point

Those that still hold to the belief that Cat Island was Columbus' San Salvador claim that this settlement, once called Jenny's Point, is where the trio of Spanish ships made their second anchorage. On a high bluff a navigation light stands on the remains of a fortress from which residents watched for privates and other attackers in Morgan's Bay to the east and French Bay to the west.

Backtrack about one kilometre to the north-running track towards McQueen's.

McQueen's

Established by Loyalist Alexander McQueen in the late 1700s, not much happens in McQueen's these days. It once prospered, however, as the many beautiful ornate chimneys attest. West of McQueen's is Hawk's Nest, site of the only marina on the island, and in the late 1600s the first English settlement on Cat Island, which was destroyed by pirate attacks in 1717.

Back at the roundabout, head east towards Port Howe.

Bain Town

This area is known as the Great Lake District. Bain Town is also graced with one of Father Jerome's churches. **Saint John the Baptist Catholic Church**, like many of the others is no longer used. Rebecca House, owned by the Bains, is another conch-inspired creation. Lucky passers-by are invited in to admire the living room's ceiling made of 966 conch shells.

A few feet behind the church is the entrance to one of the island's most famous caves, called Lotto-Man Hole. An East Indian sailor was marooned on the island and took refuge in the cave, or so the story goes. You are best to explore the cave with the help of a guide. The Mermaid Hole, also to be explored with a guide, is in the area.

Zonicles

The small settlement of Zonicles was named for Loyalist Charles Zonicles. It offers good views of the island's southern coast, called the discovery coast.

Port Howe

The larger settlement of Port Howe is a few kilometres down the road. It was established by Loyalist settlers who first called it Carlyle and then renamed it in honour of Admiral James Howe, Britain's Chief Naval Officer during the Revolution. Before the Loyalists, however, the Spanish established Columba at present-day **Columbus Point**, or so Cat Islanders choose to believe. Later, a handful of watchtowers was established to protect the island from vicious pirate attacks.

In 1783, one thousand acres were given to Andrew Deveaux Jr. as thanks for having liberated Nassau from the Spanish (see p 23). Located next to the primary school is elegant **Deveaux House ★★★** *(on the south side of the road, where it curves north)*. It copied

Clapboard House

the style of contemporary plantation houses in the southern states and its interior was the work of French craftsmen. It had wooden galleries overlooking the sea. Its grandeur, which encouraged settlement in the Out Islands, is still evident even though it is in ruins. The roof and heavy wooden floor beams have survived, but restoration is badly needed before these things are lost. Interestingly the slave quarters are located right next to the house, suggesting a certain level of trust between master and slave. The kitchen, with its large fireplace and chimney, as well as the ablution block, are also still standing.

Bailey Town, which is considered part of Port Howe, is home to the simple **St. Mark's Episcopal Church**, built in the late 19th century. Its buttressed construction is typical of Cat Island buildings. The bell outside still rings in the service. Our Lady of Zion Catholic Church is another pretty site in town.

The road continues north to the Greenwood Inn (see p 264). Just beyond the turnoff for the hotel the road seems to continue and does but over very rough track that should be avoided.

Northern Cat Island

Heading north from New Bight, the first settlement beyond Fernandez Bay Village is Smith Bay.

Smith Bay

Most of the activity in Smith Bay revolves around Hazel's Seaside Bar, the arrival of the mailboat and the medical clinic. There is a stunning African Cotton Tree whose deep-red flowers bloom in February and March. It is also known as the Passion Tree because it bleeds a red liquid at Easter.

There are good beaches on both shores in this area. A road cuts east from Smith Bay to The Beach. This is one of the finest stretches of sand on the rougher Atlantic coast of the island.

Knowles

The road up to Knowles hugs the shore. To your right are countless slave huts in ruins and to your left the calm shore dotted with palms and the occasional overturned boat. The tiny huts built right at the water's edge are old water closets. A few of the buildings on the water side of the road face the sea instead of the road. These were built before the road became the main means of transportation, when people and supplies arrived by water. Houses built facing the road are more recent.

The tiny **Columbus World Centre Museum ★** is run by Knowles' Cat Island's foremost local historian, Eris Moncur, one of the staunchest supporters of Cat Island's claim to the name San Salvador. Moncur will show you around himself.

Tea Bay and The Cove

The **scenery ★★★** grows ever more splendid as you make your way north through Tea Bay, so-named because plantation owners used to take their afternoon tea here. Note the picturesque Baptist Church in the centre of town. The settlement of Hart's Bay, on a hilltop just beyond Tea Bay, is in decline and its many fascinating **ruins ★** are thought to predate the Loyalists.

The Cove also has good ruins, both on land and at sea. Two wrecks are visible off the eastern shore, you can see the path cut through the reef by the *S.S. Modegard* when she ran aground in 1910, the wreck of the *Whisky* dates from the 19th century.

Stephenson and Industrious Hill

The road worsens as you continue north to Stephenson. Another track cuts east to the Atlantic shore and the great beach at **Alligator Bay**.

The Caves at Industrious Hill are worth checking out, but only with a bright flashlight and a guide. These multi chambered caves have provided shelter for Cat Islanders during hurricanes for hundreds of years, but they have also claimed at least one person so be careful.

North to Dumfries

Heading north to Dumfries you will traverse **Rokers** and **The Bluff**, the latter established by Scottish Loyalists in the late 18th century. In the mid-19th century, it was one of the largest settlements on Cat Island, with 150 people at the time.

Pirates and privateers used to hang out in **Bennett's Harbour** and watch for easy prey. The settlement was one of three free towns established by slaves freed from ships after the abolition of the slave trade. The nearby salt ponds produced fifty thousand bushels of salt per year in the 1850s, they are no longer in use today.

Dumfries

Dumfries was established up on the hill behind the present settlement by Loyal-

Blue Hole Legends

Cat Island's blue holes are the stuff of legends. Ferocious man-eating monsters are reputed to lie just beneath the surface in blue holes, just waiting to pounce. The monster in the "Bad Blue Hole" located off Dickies Road near Orange Creek apparently likes to eat horses, so when a horse dies near the hole, locals just dump the body in to it instead of burning it. When a man and his dog disappeared near the hole not too long ago, islanders' knew what had happened! There is also the story of Mermaid Hole inhabited by a beautiful siren and Gaitor's Hole inhabited by a merman that seduced a young island girl one day as she was doing her laundry. When she returned several months later she was pregnant and claimed the merman, with whom she had been living in an underwater love nest, was the father. The girl's father and brother apparently captured and killed the merman, and the legend claims that the lovechild was born with a tail!

ists who originated from Dumfries in Scotland. They brought the name with them to the United States and then after the Revolutionary War to The Bahamas and even to Canada and Jamaica where some of them ended up.

Dumfries is home to Cat Island's famous cave guide, Mr. Gaitor. Seek him out at the Turning Point Bar for a tour of the Great Crown cave north of Dumfries and some fabulous stories.

Arthur's Town

Arthur's Town is the metropolis of northern Cat island. The focus of the city is Sir Roland Symonette Park. The road to the right of the park leads past **St. Andrews Anglican Church**, built in the 1870s, to the airport. To the right is the high school, the second one ever established by the Bahamian government.

Arthur's Town's other claim to fame is that it is the boyhood home of Academy Award winning actor and Bahamian ambassador to Japan, Sydney Poitier. There are no monuments to him, and the house is abandoned.

Beyond the Cookie House Restaurant (see p 266) another road also leads to the airport and then continues east across the island to Camperdown Beach, which is lined with coconut palms and seagrape trees.

Orange Creek to Man O' War Point

Orange Creek is named for the curious natural phenomenon in which the combined elements of the angle of the sun and the waves give the creek a brilliant orange glow. Apparently, it is rare that these elements come together, but you never know. Nevertheless, the sandy shores at the creek mouth and the narrow beaches facing Exuma Sound are pretty. Don't bother wandering up the creek too far where the water hardly moves and is quite foul.

The road continues a short distance past Orange Creek and splits into a few rough tracks. The rest of the island to Man O' War Point is best explored on foot. There are the Griffin Bat Cave and pretty Port Royal Beach to be seen (see below).

BEACHES

Of the countless beaches that trim the island, a handful are worth seeking out. **Fernandez Bay** ★★★ is lined by a wide crescent of fine white sand and weepy casuarinas. The gin-clear water is very calm. Just offshore are two tiny cays. Close by is another more secluded beach called **Skinny Dip** ★. The track running east from Smith Bay leads to the beach at **Fine Bay** ★★, which has big waves and is good for surfing. **Alligator Bay** ★ is another Atlantic beach, this one opposite Stephenson. **Camperdown Beach** ★ and **Port Royal Beach** ★ north of Orange Creek are wild and deserted. The beach at **Greenwood** ★★★ is 13 kilometres long and empty. It has a pretty pinkish hue.

OUTDOOR ACTIVITIES

Scuba Diving and Snorkelling

The rougher Atlantic shore offers wild reefs and pinnacles along its whole length. To the south are stunning fringing reefs, coral patches and sea gardens. There are wall dives, completely submerged blue holes and wrecks to explore. Most hotels can organize a day of diving.

At the **Cat Island Dive Centre** *(☎342-3053)* at the Greenwood Inn, a two-tank dive is $65, a certification course is $370, guided snorkelling trips are $20. They are the most equipped dive shop on the island and are located close to the island's best dive sites.

Cat Island Sea Club *(☎474-4821)* at Fernandez Bay Village offers an introductory resort course for $100, certification for $370 and guided snorkel trips for $25. Snorkel and scuba equipment can be rented. Jean-Michel Cousteau's Out Island Snorkeling Adventures (see p 72) are also offered.

Hawk's Nest Club *(☎357-7257)* has a small dive shop to take advantage of the fine coral near Devil's Point and the good snorkelling in Morgan's Bay. A two-tank dive is $70.

Fishing

Bonefishing flats abound in the creeks and off the western shore of the island. For sportfishing, the best spot is off the southern end of the island between Devil's Point and Columbus Point where wahoo, yellowfin tuna and marlin flourish.

Fernandez Bay Village *(☎342-3043)* organizes bonefishing trips for $150 for a half day and $200 for a full day and sportfishing for $200 and $300.

For bonefishing in Orange Creek, contact Lincoln or Willard Cleare at ☎354-4052.

In Port Howe, The **Greenwood Inn** *(☎342-3053)* charges $140 and $200 for bonefishing and $460 for a day of sportfishing, or you can contact Charles Zonicle *(☎342-5005)* who arranges his own bonefishing trips.

Hawk's Nest Club *(☎357-7257)* is close to some of the best bonefishing. The club rents boats for $350 a day with captain.

Hiking

Besides the obvious climb up Mount Alvernia with its spectacular views, there are many good cleared trails north of Orange Creek leading to the beach, Port Royal Beach to the west,

Man O' War Point and its beach and cave to the north, Blue Hole and Glass Hill also to the north and Griffin Bat Cave to the east. This last cave actually has walls and windows built by slaves. Finally, Pretty Camperdown Beach is only accessible by foot. These trails are worth exploring, and a guide called Willard Cleare *(☎354-4052)* is a good idea.

Another dirt road runs east from Port Howe to Columbus Point past old plantation ruins.

Wildlife Observation

Snorkelling and scuba diving are great ways to see sharks and coral, but there are also plenty of birds to view and freshwater turtles to observe. Armbrister Creek near Old Bight is good for birdwatching and is best explored by canoe, Fernandez Bay Village offers guided trips for $25. The turtles can be spotted in freshwater ponds near Tea Bay and Knowles.

ACCOMMODATIONS

New Bight and Southern Cat Island

New Bight

The **Bridge Inn** *($80, low $70; ℜ, ≈, ⊛, ≡, ⊗, sat tv, pb; 12 rooms; New Bight, Cat Island, ☎342-3013 or 1-800-688-4752, ⇛342-3041)*, run by the Russell family, has clean, motel-style rooms with native-stone walls, beamed ceilings and blue bed spreads. There are shower stalls instead of bath tubs. Not all the rooms have air conditioning (add $40 for double). Guests have the use of a pool and hot tub. There are singles, doubles and triples. The Russells, who own the place, will pick you up at the airport for free and can organize diving, fishing, car rentals, sailing, etc. Located in a clearing just off Queen's Highway, and a short walk to the beach (not visible from the rooms), the setting leaves a bit to be desired. The inn's bar/restaurant does draw quite a rowdy crowd though. A three-night package for two including all meals is $420.

Fernandez Bay Village *($225, low $195 with 2 meals; ℜ, ⊗, K, pb; Fernandez Bay, New Bight, Cat Island, ☎342-3043, ⇛342-3051, US mailing address: 1507 South University Dr., Suite A, Plantation, Florida, 33324, ☎954-474-4821 or 1-800-940-1905, ⇛954-474-4864 in Florida)* is by far the nicest place on Cat Island and reason enough to visit this remote paradise. Hidden between the casuarinas, on fine white sand and just steps from the calm gin-clear waters are nine villas ideal for families or couples. Made of native stone, six of the villas have fully equipped kitchens. There are ceiling fans (no air-conditioning, but you won't need it), private patios, and some even have roofless garden bathrooms. The setting and ambiance are fairly rustic and very relaxed, but classy nonetheless. The staff is friendly and helpful but doesn't wait on you hand and foot; they will, however, happily organize a car or boat rental or a day of diving (dive master on site), snorkelling, fishing, hiking or beachcombing. You can also rig up the resort's Zuma sailboats for a day of sailing or rent a bicycle ($7 a day). The resort has a well-stocked general store, or you can opt for the two-meal (breakfast or lunch and dinner) plan, or even a combination of both, provided you reserve for supper (see p 265). Breakfast and lunch are served in the main house, where you can peruse the books in the library, curl up by the fireplace or even watch a movie. The resort is run by

Ulysses' Favourites

Accommodations

Best Escapist Paradise:

Fernandez Bay Village (see p 263) and Cutlass Bay Club (see p 264).

Best Resort for Divers:

Greenwood Inn (see p 264).

Restaurants

Best True-true Bahamian Cooking:

The Sailing Club (see p 265), The Bridge Inn (see p 265) and Bachelor's Rest (see p 266).

Finest Dining:

Fernandez Bay Village (see p 265).

the Armbrister family, which has owned the land since 1870 when it was a plantation. N.B. Fernandez Bay is on the lee side of the island, so the bugs can be bad – bring some long pants and strong repellent!

Near McQueen's

Hawk's Nest Resort and Marina *($135 per person with 2 meals; 12 rooms; ℜ, ℝ, pb, ⊗, ≡; Cat Island, ☎/⇒357-7257 or 1-800-688-4752)* on the southeastern tip of the island was recently renovated. Ten comfortable guestrooms face palm trees and the beach, and there are also two cottages with kitchen facilities. The clubhouse houses the restaurant, snack bar, satellite television and books. The full-service marina attracts a lot of boaters. The resort has its own airstrip and offers charter service.

Bain Town

Cutlass Bay Club *($1590 for three nights for two, all-inclusive; 14 rooms; pb, ℜ; Port Howe, Cat Island, ☎342-3085, ⇒813-269-0556 from the US)* is The Bahamas only clothing-optional hotel, and you have to know about it because there is no sign and it is hardly in any of the tourist brochures. An old gate just under a kilometre west of Bain Town marks the entrance. Accommodations are in guest rooms and cottages that face a wide swath of green and flowers leading to the private beach. There are tennis courts, trails and a library. Snorkelling equipment is offered.

Port Howe

Greenwood Beach Resort *($99, low $85, add $40 per person for 2* *meals; 20 rooms; pb, ⊗, Port Howe, Cat Island, ☎/⇌342-3053 or 1-800-688-4752)* is owned and run by a German family. The rooms have shower stalls, king-sized beds and a bright modern decor, bordering on kitsch. There is a small pool and patio, but with eight miles of pinkish Atlantic beach at your doorstep, you can walk for miles without a soul in sight... The Atlantic breezes keep the bugs away, and coral heads just offshore make shore dives, swimming and snorkelling easy. The resort houses the Cat Island Dive Centre and offers complete scuba diving certification courses (most guests are divers), as well as bonefishing and sportfishing trips. Meals are served on the patio or inside in the informal lounge area, which looks more like a wreck-room than a dining room and puts games, television, telephone and books at your disposal. You can also rent a bicycle. Flights to New Bight and Arthur's Town are met and transfers are included; charter flights can also be organized.

Northern Cat Island

Orange Creek

Orange Creek Inn *($65-$90; 16 rooms; ≡, ⊗, pb; Orange Creek, Cat Island, ☎/⇌354-4110)* is another inexpensive option in this part of the island. It is by the creek and has a decent little swimming beach. Rooms are modern and cool. There is no restaurant, but they do run a small grocery store and laundromat.

Sea Spray Hotel *($65-$75; pb, sat tv, ℜ, ≡; 16 rooms; Orange Creek, Cat Island, ☎354-4116 or 323-5390 in Nassau, ⇌356-4161)* is tucked between the road and the surf. There is a pretty little beach nearby and each room has sliding glass doors giving onto an inviting patio overlooking the water. The decor is non-existent in both the restaurant and the rooms, but it is clean. There are plans to add a pool. MasterCard not accepted.

RESTAURANTS

New Bight and Southern Cat Island

New Bight

The **Blue Bird Club** *($-$$; on the beach side of the road)* is said to be the place to go for island "sip-sip" or gossip. Besides catching up on the latest, you can shoot some pool and savour some authentic Bahamian cooking and snacks, the fried chicken is especially good.

The **Sailing Club** *($-$$)* is most popular during the annual Cat Island Regatta, of course. Technically it serves food all day long from 8am to 10pm, reservations are required for supper, however. Saturday nights are big here with dancing into the wee hours.

The **Bridge Inn** *($$; ☎342-3013)* serves breakfast (bacon and eggs or fish stew and johnnycake), lunch (burgers, fries, pizza, fried chicken and such) and dinner where things get more creative with grouper, conch, lobster, peas 'n' rice all accompanied with fresh garden vegetables. Deserts also feature freshly picked fruits. There is a barbecue on Friday nights. The adjoining bar is a popular spot in town (see 267).

Fernandez Bay Village *($30 includes meal, dessert and coffee, cocktails begin at 7pm; ☎342-3043)* is proud to host both guests and non-guests for dinner. The bay is a popular mooring for boaters, who often row in to shore for the fine food. Tables are set up on a torch-lit, beach-side terrace, and before dinner you can fix yourself an island cocktail at the honour bar and exchange beach stories and watch the sun set with the staff and other guests. The buffet is laid and features the house's very own conch chowder, the best I tasted. The main course changes every night but is always good and there are usually two or three choices. Reservations are required, especially if you are not already staying here. Breakfast and lunch are also served daily *($)*.

Port Howe

Both lunch and supper can be had at the **Greenwood Inn** *($-$$$; reservations required for supper, ☎342-3053)*, even if you aren't a guest. Supper is the best time to come, because the sand is pinkest at dusk. The catch of the day is prepared either *à la* Bahamian or *à la* continental and served in the dining room or outside on the oceanfront terrace.

McQueen's

Hawk's Nest Club *($$-$$$; reservations required for supper, ☎357-7257)* also serves dinner to non-guests. Located as it is on the southernmost tip of the island, it is a long haul just for dinner but the restaurant and bar are decent options if you are looking for a change. Bahamian and American dishes make up the evening buffet, which is taken indoors in the air-conditioned dining room. The chef will prepare your catch if you like.

Northern Cat Island

Knowles

Ruth at **Bachelor's Rest** *($)* stores her conch in the sea in front of the restaurant, virtually guaranteeing that she serves the best and freshest conch (cracked, chowder and fritters) on the island.

Dumfries

Dumfries is known for its music and its stories and has two memorable establishments. The **Gossip Bar and Restaurant** *($-$$)* has live music on occasion, native snacks and lots of stories. The **Turning Point Club**, *($-$$)* serves a good mutton souse and also has rake 'n' scrape bands on special occasions.

Arthur's Town

The **Cookie House Restaurant** *($-$$; north of Symonette Sq., ☎354-2027)* run by Pat Rolle, serves quick meals and native dishes like sandwiches, grouper and cracked conch. They also sell freshly made rolls and sweets.

Alternately, you can tuck into Bahamian food at the **Hard Rock Cafe** *($)* (no, this is not part of the mega-chain but rather a little place built on hard rock) or burgers and fries at **Gina's Diner** *($)*, which is near the square, in town.

ENTERTAINMENT

The Cat Island Regatta is the main event on the island. Held on the August 1st Emancipation Day weekend, it is a giant homecoming for Cat Islanders from throughout The Bahamas. The island's workboats race, there are parties, fashion shows, dominoes tournaments, children's activities and musical entertainment. For information contact Wilberforce Seymour at ☎327-7029.

New Bight and Southern Cat Island

New Bight

Saturday dances at **The Bridge Inn** are an institution in New Bight.

The **Sailing Club** has a DJ on Saturday nights. On Cat Island Regatta weekend, there is nowhere else to be.

The **First and Last Chance Bar** doubles as a straw market and dominoes bar. You can quench your thirst on cold beer and smooth rhum.

Northern Cat Island

Smith Bay

In a pink building facing Smith Bay is **Hazel's Seaside Bar**, the closest thing to a sports bar on Cat Island. No giant screens here though - dominoes is the sport of choice. The kerosene freezer keeps the beers nice and cold.

Arthur's Town

Lover's Boulevard Satellite Lounge has pool tables, satellite television (!) and becomes the local discotheque on weekends.

SHOPPING

New Bight and Southern Cat Island

New Bight

Miss Iva Thompson sells her straw creations in the small blue shop next to the First & Last Chance Bar & Straw Works, she is usually at work on them in the afternoon.

On weekdays, Louise Saunders can be found at Fernandez Bay Village, stitching names into hats and bags and braiding and beading hair.

The **New Bight Food Market** is open Monday to Saturday from 8am to 6pm. Nearby, **McKinney's Bakery** has heavenly fresh bread every day.

Fernandez Bay Village's **general store** is open upon request, just go to the front desk.

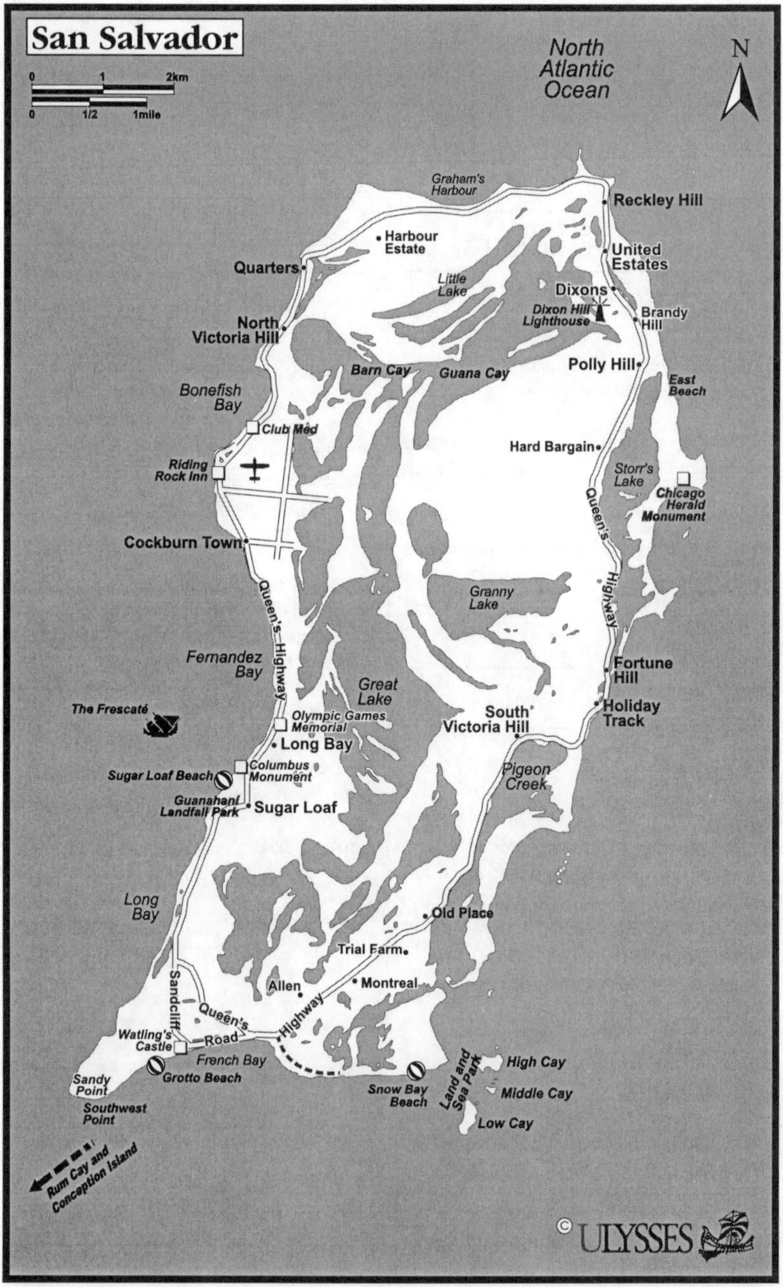
San Salvador
0
1
2km
0
1/2
1mile
North Atlantic Ocean
N
Graham's Harbour
Reckley Hill
Harbour Estate
United Estates
Quarters
Little Lake
Dixons
Dixon Hill Lighthouse
Brandy Hill
North Victoria Hill
Polly Hill
Barn Cay
Guana Cay
East Beach
Bonefish Bay
Club Med
Hard Bargain
Riding Rock Inn
Storr's Lake
Chicago Herald Monument
Queen's Highway
Cockburn Town
Granny Lake
Queen's Highway
Fernandez Bay
Fortune Hill
Great Lake
Holiday Track
The Frescaté
Olympic Games Memorial
South Victoria Hill
Long Bay
Columbus Monument
Pigeon Creek
Sugar Loaf Beach
Guanahani Landfall Park
Sugar Loaf
Long Bay
Old Place
Trial Farm
Sandcliff
Allen
Montreal
Queen's Road
Highway
Watling's Castle
French Bay
Land and Sea Park
High Cay
Sandy Point
Grotto Beach
Snow Bay Beach
Middle Cay
Southwest Point
Low Cay
Rum Cay and Conception Island
© ULYSSES

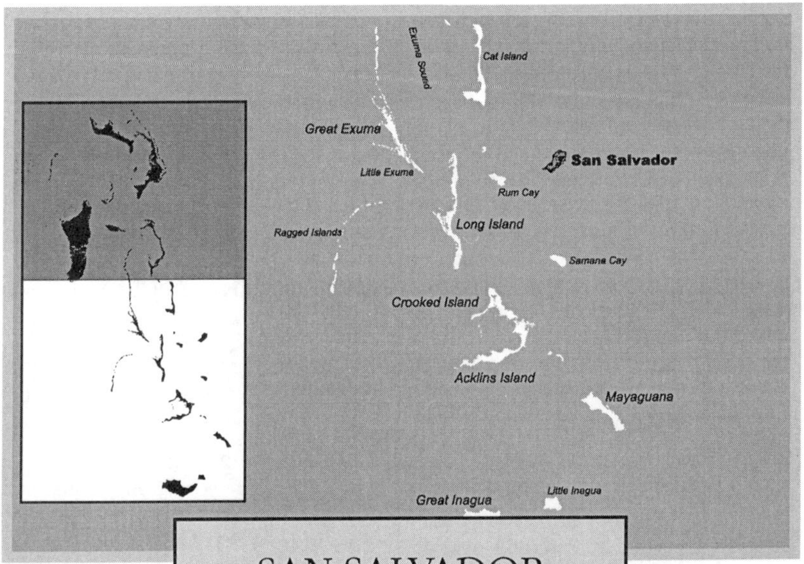

SAN SALVADOR

Riddled with lakes and trimmed with fine white sand and steep cliffs, tiny San Salvador ★★ has some of the best scuba diving in The Bahamas plus a storied past that contends this island was called Guanahaní by the Lucayans, christened San Salvador, or "holy saviour," by Christopher Columbus and dubbed Watling's Island by an eponymous religious pirate. Today, it is back to San Salvador, but the island's claim to this name may be in doubt. Was Columbus' first landfall in the New World here or wasn't it? Count the monuments on San Salvador or ask a local and there is no doubt it was, but check the facts put down in the controversial *National Geographic* magazine article (see p 270) and it would seem otherwise.

San Sal, as the island is known, is 160 square kilometres in area, most of which is water. It is actually the most water-logged island in the chain after Andros; the largest of the 28 lakes is 19-kilometre-long Great Lake. Many people still use the lakes to get between the island's two major settlements, Cockburn Town and United Estates. The rest of the island is scraggy low-lying vegetation.

A Short History

Columbus' visit may be disputed, but the holocaust that followed throughout The Bahamas is not. With the extermination of the Lucayans, the island remained deserted until the 1680s when a band of pious pirates lead by George Watling took over the island. From then on the island was known as Watling's Island. The Loyalists and cotton plantations came and went in the 18th and 19th centuries as they did throughout The Bahamas, leaving behind a population of ex-slaves and their descendants to eke out a meagre existence.

In 1791, Bishop La Casas' version of Columbus' journal was found (the original journal had been lost on its way to Queen Isabela) and the debate over the first landfall was revived. Until that time, Cat Island had held the title, but eventually scholars came to believe that Watling's Island was the rightful bearer. Reverend Chrysostrom Schreiner came to The Bahamas in 1891 to start a Catholic mission and to study the journal further. His steadfast belief in Watling's as the first landfall was central to the movement lobbying the Legislature to restore the name of San Salvador to the island – something it did in 1926. Attention focused on the island and Canadian milionaire Sir Harry Oakes built a hotel here in the 1930s, which was eventually turned over to the British Royal Navy. The United States set up a guided missile base and built an airstrip in 1951.

More recently, in 1983, pieces of Spanish pottery, beads, buckles and metal spikes of European origin, plus Arawak pottery and beads were found here and are thought to date between 1490 and 1560. All of this evidence was put into question, except in the eyes of San Salvadorans, in 1986 when the *National Geographic* magazine published an extensively researched article by its senior associate editor, Joseph Judge, which claimed to have solved the "grandest of all geographic mysteries." None of the previous calculations had taken into account leeway and current. With these two variables factored in, a new translation of the journal and a voyage across the Atlantic, the article put Columbus's first landfall some 100 kilometres to the southeast at Samana Cay. A few years later in 1989, however, another trip across the Atlantic, this time by English yachtsman Robin Knox-Johnson, using 15th-century navigational instruments landed on San Salvador... the mystery and controversy rage on.

Tourists were first drawn to the island in the 1970s by the spectacular wreck and wall diving opportunities. The industry took off in 1992 with the opening of Club Med's Columbus Isle, where divers and amateur historians alike enjoy some of the most luxurious accommodations in The Bahamas.

FINDING YOUR WAY AROUND

By Plane

Bahamasair *(☎327-5505 in Nassau)* has two flights per week from Miami and Nassau. Riding Rock offers weekly charters from Fort Lauderdale, Florida. Club Med also arranges its own charters. The airport is located north of Cockburn Town, right between the two hotels.

By Boat

By Mailboat: Departures are from Potter's Cay (under the Paradise Island Bridge) in Nassau and fares are one-way. The *Lady Francis* departs Tuesdays at 6pm for Cockburn Town, United Estates and Port Nelson (Rum Cay). Trip length varies. Fare: $40.

The **Riding Rock Inn** *(☎331-2631)* has a full-service marina, reservations are recommended.

By Car

The Queen's Highway follows the perimeter of the island and can be driven in about 45 minutes. Cars can be rented from the Riding Rock inn and from the airport for $85 a day. Scooters are also available for $60 from the airport.

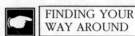

By Taxi

Both Club Med and the Riding Rock Inn offer their guests complementary airport pick-up. Taxis also meet flights, it costs about $5 to get to Cockburn Town.

By Bicycle

The island is small and flat enough to be toured by bicycle in four to five hours. Bicycles can be rented from Riding Rock for $10 for a full day and $6.50 for a half day.

PRACTICAL INFORMATION

Tourist Information and Tours: There is no tourist office here, however, Clifford Fernander, a.k.a Snake Eyes because of his domino skills, offers thorough tours of the island in his comfortable minibus. Club Med also organizes its own tours. The Riding Rock Inn organizes trips to the Exumas with snorkelling and diving.

Police: Cockburn Town, ☎331-2010.

Clinic: Government clinic with nurse in Cockburn Town, open Mon to Fri 9am to 1pm, ☎331-2105.

EXPLORING

Cockburn Town

Cockburn Town is the main settlement on the west coast. Both of the island's main resorts and the airport are located just north of the town. The town itself is nothing more than a handful of narrow streets and small houses. It is named for Governor Frances Cockburn who visited the island in the 1840s. Most of the residents gather round a big almond tree, which they call "Lazy Tree", in the centre of town.

The **San Salvador Museum** ★★ *(free admission; Mon to Fri 8am to 1pm; if doors are locked go to BaTelCo office next door)* is located in the green-shuttered, dark-salmon-pink building that once housed the prison. After ten years, islanders realized they didn't need a jail and this small museum was opened. It holds Arawak and European archaeological relics found on San Salvador that date from the time of Columbus' discovery of the New World. The interesting ceramic mural on the exterior depicting this legend was a gift from Spain in 1992. Five similar murals were erected in Spain with a sign indicating that the sixth is in San Salvador.

Cockburn Town's **Holy Saviour Roman Catholic Church** was dedicated in 1992 to commemorate the first Catholic mass held in the New World 500 years earlier. It was a gift from the Knights of Columbus of North America.

Guanahaní Landfall Park ★

Guanahaní Landfall Park lies about 4.5 kilometres south of Cockburn Town facing Long Bay and beautiful Sugar Loaf Beach. There are four monuments here, each commemorating, in one way or another, Columbus' historic visit.

The **Olympic Games Memorial** commemorates the 1968 Olympic Games in Mexico City. Runners carried the Olympic torch around the island on their way from Greece to Mexico. The metal bowl of the monument brought the flame from Greece and is lit every year on Discovery Day. Another marker was placed offshore where supposedly

Columbus dropped achor on October 12, 1492.

Right beside is the **Columbus Monument**, an oft-photographed simple cement cross erected on Christmas Day, 1956. It is supposed to mark the exact spot where Columbus came ashore. It was established by Ruth Durlacher Wolper Malvin, a Columbus scholar and widow of a Hollywood producer. She still runs the New World Museum in North Victoria Hill (see p 274).

A plaque and metal sculpture were erected in 1992 to commemorate the 500th anniversary of the voyage. The final monument was built in 1991 when a replica of the *Santa María* sailed from Barcelona to Kobe Japan, a similar monument, called the Tappan Monument, was erected 40 years earlier about 2 kilometres north of the park.

Guanahaní Landfall Park to United Estates

The southern half of the island is a succession of ruins and deserted or nearly deserted settlements. The first of these is Sugar Loaf, where sugar loaf pineapples were once grown. Its stunning beach is its biggest claim to fame these days. Continuing south along the shore the Queen's Highway cuts east, while small Sandcliff Road continues to Sandy Point and past Grotto Beach. The ruins of **Watling's Castle ★★** stand atop a hill here. This is not the former hideout of the pious pirate who named the island after himself, but rather the Loyalist-era plantation of Cade Matthews. You'll have a good view of the sea and southern shore from amidst the dense bush and the crumbling main house and slave quarters.

Before turning north, you'll pass the abandoned Belmont Church and a turn-off towards aptly named Snow Bay Beach and **High Cay Land and Sea Park** which protects High Cay, Porus Cay and Low Cay. The latter is populated by giant iguanas and the former by ospreys and boobies.

Backtrack to the Queen's Highway and continue north past **Old Place**, a virtually abandoned settlement, with just one family at last check. The old fieldstone walls were hand-built by slaves to divide Loyalist-era plantations which were plentiful across the southern half of the island. The most famous of these is **Farquarson's Plantation ★**. Charles Farquarson arrived here in the 1820s. The ruins of the main house, kitchen and what is though to have been a punishment cell can be seen. Only one family remains in **South Victoria Hill** and three in **Fortune Hill**. Lucayan artifacts were discovered along the shore between the two settlements.

Before reaching United Estates, you can venture along East Beach to the **Chicago Herald Monument**, a stone marker topped by a marble globe on a peninsula called Crab Cay. It was installed in 1892 at what, at the time, was thought to be the actual landfall site. This is virtually impossible considering the dangerous reefs offshore.

United Estates

United Estates is the second-largest settlement on the island, with not much to recommend it save the **Dixon Hill Lighthouse ★★★** *(every day 9am to noon and 2pm to 5pm, knock on the door of the adjacent cottage)*. The Dixons, who owned the United Estates plantation, are buried beside the 67-foot lighthouse. A winding set of eighty steps leads up to the top, 163 feet above sea level where you can get an

Rum Cay and Conception Island

Lying about 40 kilometres southwest of San Salvador, these two pristine and isolated isles can be visited from San Salvador (your hotel's staff can recommend a guide). If San Salvador was Columbus' first landfall, then Rum or Conception was his second and was named Santa Maria de la Concepcíon. Only Rum Cay has any inhabitants to claim the name, one that was all but defeated by *National Geographic* magazine in 1986.

Rum Cay gets its name from the rum-laden ships that were wrecked on the coral reefs that entirely surround it. After the coming and going of the Loyalists, salt was the raison d'etre of its inhabitants, who supplied the fishing fleets of Nova Scotia until hurricanes ruined the salt ponds in the early 1900s, causing most people to abandon the island. Spectacular diving and pristine beaches lead to the opening of the Rum Cay Club in 1983. But it closed in 1990 and at press time was still for sale.

The nesting grounds of seabirds and endangered green turtles are protected by the Bahamas National Trust on Conception Island Land & Sea Park, which occupies the whole island.

up-close look at the original workings of the light and step out onto the breezy balcony for a true bird's-eye view of the island. The huge Fresnel lens magnifies the light to 400,000 candle-power so that it is visible for more than 30 kilometres. A curtain, which is removed at sunset, stops the sun from hitting the lens, being magnified and igniting the grass. The mechanism that turns the light must be wound every 90 minutes throughout the night. The Bahamas Lighthouse Preservation Society is trying to save the lighthouse from automation.

Inland, you may spot the failed **Brice Memorial Flamingo Park**. An attempt was made to reintroduce flamingoes to the island, but three died shortly after arriving, so they were sent back to Inagua.

The North Shore

In the 1950s, the Americans set up a missile tracking station along this coast. Some of the station's buildings were later used as a Teachers' Training College by the Bahamian Government and are now occupied by the **Bahamian Field Station** where Bahamian and international students study archaeology and marine biology. If you want more than a cursory look around the place, it is best to plan ahead. Field courses are offered by New York State College and Oklahoma State University. For information on the station, write to it care of Twin Air, 110 Lee Wagener Blvd., Suite 113, Fort Lauderdale FL 33315. The non-profit organization Earthwatch *(680 Mount Auburn St., Watertown MA 02272, ☎1-800-776-0188, ⇛617-926-8532)* needs volunteer divers for its reef-conservation work based at the station.

Continuing west, the road follows the curve of **Graham's Harbour**. Columbus' San Salvador supposedly had a magnificent harbour that was big enough to hold as many ships as in all of Christendom, and Chrysostrom Schreiner was convinced that Graham's Harbour was that harbour. Schreiner is buried on a point overlooking the bay at the spt where he believed the navigator first stepped ashore.

The small settlement of **North Victoria Hill** on the northwest coast is home to the **New World Museum ★★** *($1; call ahead to have the curator open up the museum ☎331-2126)*, which is part of an estate called Polaris-by-the-Sea and owned by Ruth Durlacher Wolper Malvin. The museum houses Lucayan artefacts unearthed north of the town, namely pottery and rock carvings.

BEACHES

With names like Sugar Loaf and Snow Bay to describe the white sand of San Salvador need we say more? We don't but we will... Starting at Club Med is the white-sand beach of **Bonefish Bay ★★**. Lined with creepers and sparse bush, the beach is not just for Club Med guests. Anyone can get to it from just south of North Victoria Hill. **Sugar Loaf Beach ★★★** faces Fernandez Bay and Long Bay. Guanahani Landfall Park faces this long unending stretch with its clear, shallow and calm waters. Sandy Point, the southwestern tip of the island, is trimmed with more fine white sand. **Grotto Beach ★★** is backed by rolling hills and a few vacation homes. Rounding the southeastern corner of the island is deserted **Snow Bay ★★★** with its breathtaking spectacular snowy sand and superb calm waters. The Chicago Herald Monument is a good excuse to explore **East Beach ★**, an eight-kilometre-long pink-sand swath down the east coast. Offshore reefs make for good swimming here.

OUTDOOR ACTIVITIES

Scuba Diving and Snorkelling

The main activities on San Salvador are scuba diving and snorkelling. Thirty- to 60-foot visibility is the norm here, as are steep drop-offs and busy shallow reefs. The south and western sides of the island are known for their impressive walls starting at 12 metres. Spectacular creatures like hammerhead sharks, moray eels and manta rays are among the possible underwater encounters. One of the highlights of San Salvador is wreck diving. The *Frescaté*, a 261-foot freighter sunk in 1902, lies in just 20 feet of water.

Guanahani Divers *(☎331-2631 or 1-800-272-1492)* is the dive shop at Riding Rock Inn Resort & Marina and the most organized outfit on the island. They offer three dives daily, underwater, still and video camera rental, an underwater photography course plus same-day photo developing. All snorkelling and diving gear can be rented by the day or the week. One dive is $40, three dives or a full day of diving is $80. An introductory resort course is $105. Snorkelling trips are available for $20. Jean-Michel Cousteau's Out Island Snorkeling Adventures are also offered. Other options include six-day dive packages and certification courses.

The diving facilities at **Club Med Columbus Isle** *(☎331-2000)* are the most extensive in that chain. They have a daily snorkelling and diving trip for $95. Certification courses are also available.

Iguana

Fishing

San Salvador recently made a name for itself with three world-record wahoo catches. **Riding Rock Inn** *(☎331-2631)* rents sportfishing boats with a guide for $500 to $600 for a full day $300 to $400 for a half day. Club Med offers guests a daily half-day sport-fishing trip for $95.

Pigeon Creek on the southeastern coast of the island is a choice spot for bonefishing. Both the above hotels can organize trips.

Wildlife Observation

One clue that this island may well be the one the Lucayans called Guanahaní is that the name means "infested with iguanas," something the island still is to a certain extent. These endangered creatures are easy to spot around Club Med and there are hundreds of them on Low Cay in High Cay Land & Sea Park.

There are also plenty of winged species to observe here. Ospreys are ubiquitous, boobies and other seabirds nest on the north shore islets, herons and egrets wade about the shallow lakes of the interior and magnificent frigate birds can be seen scooping up flying fish at sea.

The best way to see this varied wildlife is by boat with a local guide. Hotel staff occasionally organize trips or can recommend someone.

Horseback Riding

Near Sugar Loaf, the **New Columbus Isles Riding Stables** *(☎357-9527)* offer lessons and trail rides throughout the day. An hour-and-a-half ride is $40 and a two-and-a-half-hour ride is $55.

ACCOMMODATIONS

Cockburn Town

Riding Rock Inn Resort & Marina *($95 to $120; 42 rooms; pb, ≡, ≈, ℝ, ℜ, sat tv; Cockburn Town, ☎331-2631, 1-800-272-1492 or 954-359-8353, ⇌331-2020 or 954-359-8254)*. Though the rooms were recently renovated with cool tile floors, comfortable beds, quiet air conditioners, pretty bathrooms and sofas in some, and though some of these are literally steps from the sea and face awesome sunsets, the hotel is right by the road and the poolside area lacks the atmospheric palm trees and tropical flowers of some places. But this is primarily a diver's resort, so these details don't bother guests who would rather take advantage of the excellent dive shop and its three daily scuba dives than lounge by the pool. There are also tennis courts, a full-service marina, a decent restaurant and rental cars and bicycles. The inn offers interesting all-inclusive packages for divers and non-divers.

Club Med Columbus Isle *($135 to $270 all-incl.; 286 rooms, ≡, ⊗, ≈, sat tv, ℝ, ℜ, ⊙; San Salvador, ☎331-2000 or 1-800-655-0025, ⇌331-2458)* is easily one of the Club's most refined villages. The lavish decor of the public areas is a well-achieved and exotic take on the popular sun, stars and moon look with beautiful antiques from 35 different countries, including Turkey, Brazil, Nepal and Indonesia. The collection of colourful prefab 2-story buildings is connected by wooden walkways with pretty white railings. Rooms are of average size with large closets, safes, custom-made dark-wood furnishings, vibrantly coloured bedspreads and private balconies. The large free-form pool is stunning. A network of paths leads past the giant iguanas to the fine-sand beach. The Club has three restaurants (one is non-smoking) (see p 276). A whole slew of activities is offered including waterskiing, sailing and scuba diving with the Club's own dive shop. There are no children's activities and only those over 12 years of age are permitted.

RESTAURANTS

Cockburn Town

For some real Bahamian cooking in true Bahamian surroundings there are two worthwhile options in Cockburn Town. The **Three Ships Restaurant** *($; closed Sun; ☎331-2787)* serves breakfast, lunch and dinner, with reservations required for the latter. **Charlie's Sunset Lounge** *($)* is a smaller, more rough and tumble place.

The restaurant at the **Riding Rock Inn** *(☎331-2631)* serves three meals daily at set times: breakfast *($)* 7:30am to 9:30am, lunch *($$)* 12:30pm to 2:30pm and dinner *($$$)* 6:30pm. Return guests to this hotel rave about the kitchen, which turns out simple, good and hearty American and Bahamian comfort food. That said, there is nothing fancy or really that exceptional about the food. Lunchtime features tasty macaroni and cheese, conch chowder and fresh-baked bread. There is a choice of two meals at dinner, with fresh seafood and meat somewhere in there.

For a truly enjoyable dining experience, pay a little extra to eat at **Club Med Columbus Isle** *(☎331-2000)* where

Ulysses' Favourites

Accommodations

Best Escapist Resort:

Club Med Columbus Isle (see p 276).

Best Resort for Divers:

Riding Rock Inn Resort & Marina (see p 276).

Restaurants

Best True-true Bahamian Cooking:

The Three Ships Restaurant (see p 276).

Finest Dining:

Club Med Columbus Isle (see p 276).

non-guests can dine with reservations. For one price *($40)* you can partake of the delicious buffet of either French, Italian or grilled fare, depending which restaurant you choose, enjoy the entertainment and exquisite decor and then dance the night away at their nightclub. Unlike some Club Meds, dinner does not have to be a get-to-know-ya kind of experience.

ENTERTAINMENT

Cockburn Town

The Riding Rock Inn's **Driftwood Lounge** is a casual and friendly place to end the day. Pieces of driftwood and sea glass provide the decor, complemented by a terrific ocean view.

Slide shows on San Salvador, both above and below the sea, are presented at the Riding Rock on Wednesday, Friday and Saturday evenings at 8pm. There is no admission fee.

The **Harlem Square Liquor Store** *(☎331-2777)* in Cockburn Town does double duty as San Salvador's hippest nightclub. This is a nightclub like no other, however. One where dominoes draw as many patrons as the live music and dancing and the Friday shin dig known locally as "The Rip."

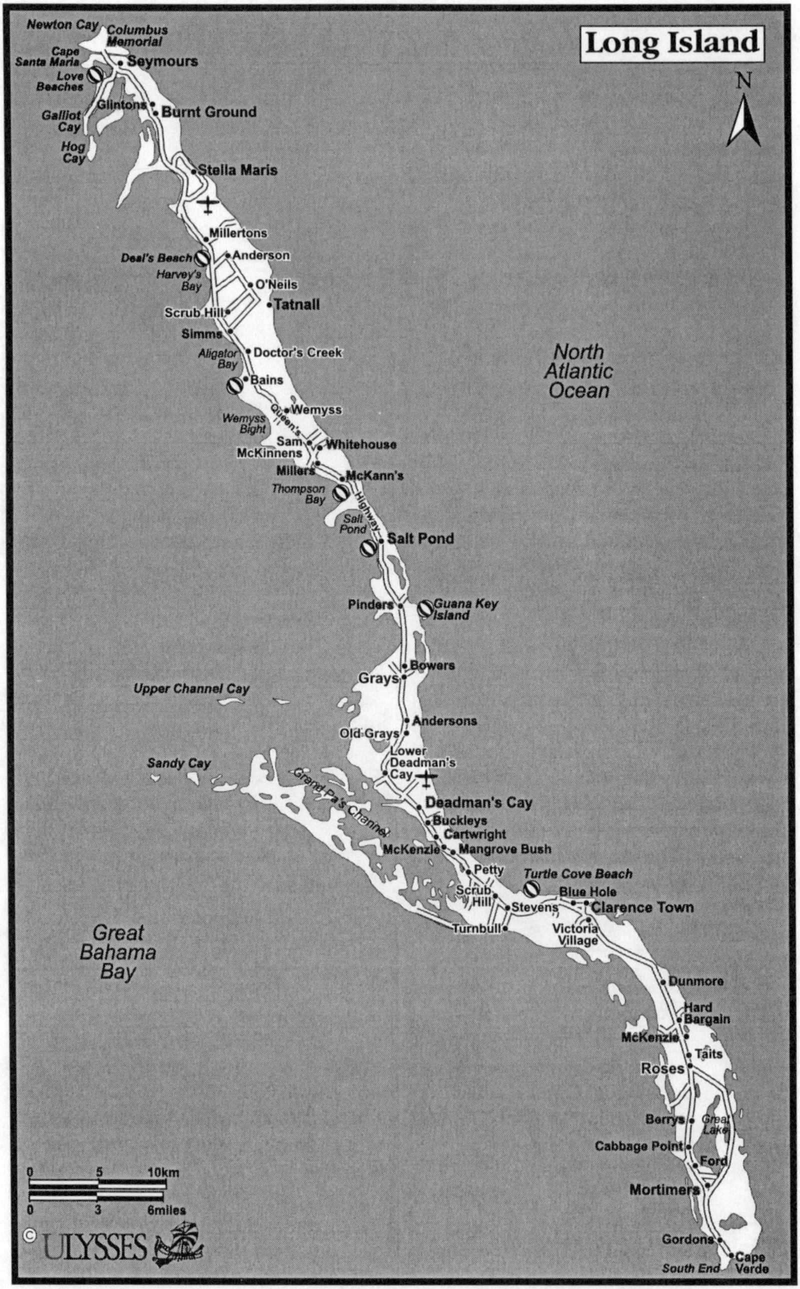
Long Island
N
Newton Cay
Columbus Memorial
Cape Santa Maria
Seymours
Love Beaches
Glintons
Burnt Ground
Galliot Cay
Hog Cay
Stella Maris
Millertons
Deal's Beach
Anderson
Harvey's Bay
O'Neils
Tatnall
Scrub Hill
Simms
Aligator Bay
Doctor's Creek
Bains
Wemyss
Queen's
Wemyss Bight
Sam McKinnens
Whitehouse
Millers
McKann's
Thompson Bay
Highway
Salt Pond
Salt Pond
North Atlantic Ocean
Pinders
Guana Key Island
Bowers
Grays
Upper Channel Cay
Andersons
Old Grays
Lower Deadman's Cay
Sandy Cay
Grand Pa's Channel
Deadman's Cay
Buckleys
Cartwright
McKenzie
Mangrove Bush
Petty
Turtle Cove Beach
Scrub Hill
Blue Hole
Stevens
Clarence Town
Turnbull
Victoria Village
Great Bahama Bay
Dunmore
Hard Bargain
McKenzie
Taits
Roses
Berrys
Great Lake
Cabbage Point
Ford
Mortimers
Gordons
Cape Verde
South End
0 5 10km
0 3 6miles
© ULYSSES

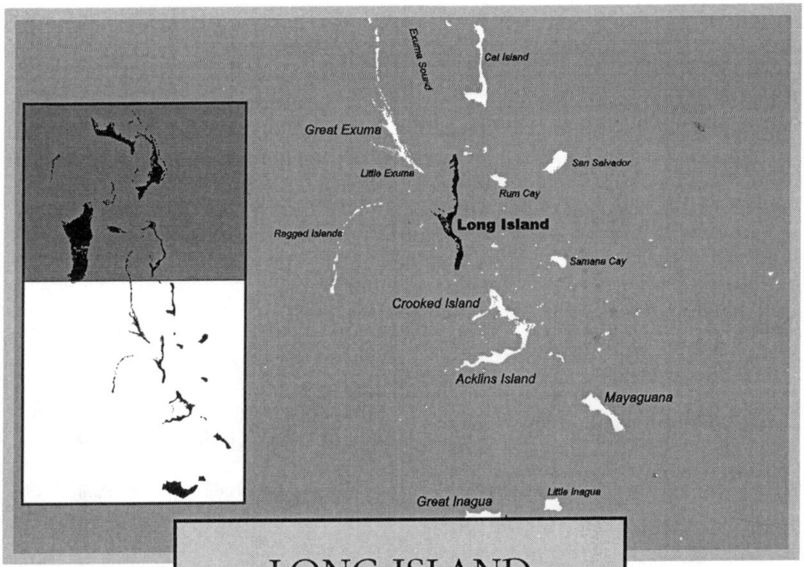

LONG ISLAND

No matter which first-landfall theory you believe, Long Island ★★ was Columbus' third stop in the New World. He described it as the "world's most beautiful island" and he may just have been right. To the north and along the windward coast, waves crash against dramatic cliffs, unlike anywhere else in the chain. Elsewhere, shallow golden and white beaches go on endlessly. Up and down the length of the island, you can explore plantation ruins, Lucayan caves, and perhaps the Out Islands' loveliest collection of churches, some the work of Father Jerome, the Hermit of Cat Island (see p 256).

A Short History

The Lucayans called this island Yuma. Long Island's caves have yielded some of the strongest evidence of Lucayan society. *Duhos*, the ceremonial stools used by native chiefs, and zemis, religious figurines, suggest a hierarchical and religious culture. Columbus seems to have been oblivious to this, reporting that the Lucayans he met had "no sect whatever."

The next people to visit Long Island were Bermudian salt gatherers who sold the salt to vessels from as far away as New York. In the early 1700s, the island probably also sheltered some Nassauvians fleeing pirates. In the late 1700s, Loyalists began pouring in. They brought their slaves and set them to work on cotton plantations and sheep and goat farms. The plantations failed and the plantation owners left the island to the slaves and their descendants. Sheep and goat rearing continued and the handmade stone enclosure walls still stand in some places. Most people continue to live off of farming and stock raising. Long Island has a large white population. This minority includes descendants of the Loyalists and "brights", those of mixed ancestry.

FINDING YOUR WAY AROUND

By Plane

There are two airports on Long Island. The Stella Maris airport in the north is the only official port of entry. It serves the Stella Maris and Cape Santa Maria resorts. **Bahamasair** *(☎327-5505 in Nassau, 338-2015 in Burnt Ground)* has four flights a week from Nassau and two from Miami. Charter flights are available from **Stella Maris Charter Service** *(☎338-2050/1)* or from **Long Island Wings** *(☎338-2006 or 357-1021)*. The other airport is at Deadman's Cay, Bahamasair touches down here after its stop at Stella Maris.

By Boat

The Stella Maris Marina is the only fully-equipped marina on the island. It is also the official port of entry.

By Mailboat: All departures are from Potter's Cay (under the Paradise Island Bridge) in Nassau and all fares are one way. The *Abilin* departs Tuesdays at noon for Clarence Town. Travel time: 17 hours. Fare: $45. The *Sherrese M* departs Tuesdays at 1pm for Seymours, Salt Pond and Deadman's Cay. Travel time: 17 hours. Fare: $45.

By Taxi

Taxis meet flights at the Stella Maris airport. The fare to the Stella Maris Resort is $3 one-way. The return trip to Cape Santa Maria Beach Resort is $25 for two people.

By Car and Scooter

One long road called the Queen's Highway runs the length of the island, with east-west roads running to both coasts at various points. The Stella Maris Resort rents cars for $65 per day plus mileage (25¢ per mile), it comes to about $100 to tour the whole island. You can make your own arrangements and save mileage through Joe Williams *(☎338-5002, Glintons)*. You can also rent a car through the Thompson Bay Inn for between $65 and $75 per day.

Scooters are available from Stella Maris Resort for $30 for a half-day and $45 for a full day.

There are gas stations in Burnt Ground, Salt Pond and Lower Deadman's Cay.

PRACTICAL INFORMATION

Burnt Ground

Post Office: near Pratt's Restaurant, ☎338-2010.

Stella Maris

Bank: Bank of Nova Scotia, open Tue and Thu 9am to 2pm, in Stella Maris General and Food Store.

Police: ☎338-8555 or 337-0999.

Simms

The government building in Simms has a **post office, police station** and **medical clinic**.

Lower Deadman's Cay

Bank: Royal Bank of Canada, open Mon to Thu 9am to 1pm, fri 9am to 5pm, ☎337-1044.

Deadman's Cay

Bank: Scotiabank, open Mon to Fri 9am to 1pm, Fri 9am to 5pm.

Clarence Town

The government building contains a **post office, medical clinic** and **BaTelCo** office *(☎337-3030)*.

★ EXPLORING

Northern Long Island

The northern settlements are easily accessible from Stella Maris Resort and Cape Santa Maria Resort. **Burnt Ground**, so named because the ground was once burnt in an effort to enrich it, **Glintons** and **Seymours**, with a good view, have a few shops and eateries, but nothing of much interest. Beyond Seymours, the winding road leads to a footbridge over a tidal creek, which leads to Newton Cay and a trail to the picturesque northern tip. Make sure you bring your camera. After about a kilometre and half over a rocky and steepish trail, you will reach the **Columbus Memorial** ★★ *(both resorts can arrange transportation to the monument)* "to the peaceful aboriginal people of Long Island and to the arrival of Christopher Columbus". The sea opens up beyond dramatic cliffs (which can be unstable so keep clear). The much calmer bay has a sandy beach.

The splendid white-sand off **Cape Santa Maria** ★★★ has good snorkelling. The Stella Maris Resort has a few beach cabanas at its southern end and offers free transportation each morning to its guests.

The Stella Maris Resort occupies what was once **Adderley's Plantation**. A sign points the way along a path to the ruins of three roofless buildings which are in the northeastern part of the resort.

South of Stella Maris is the settlement of **Millertons**, with a pretty church and a good straw market (see p 288). And just beyond that is Deal's Beach, to which the Stella Maris Resort also has daily shuttles.

Simms ★ has a few photo opportunities of its own. The diminutive pink **"Her Majesty's Prison"** ★★ and **post office** are typically Out Island, and not far are two lovely churches. **St. Peter's Anglican Church** fills with music on Sundays and the **Methodist Church** across the road is a small wooden church with a bell tower that was built around 1900.

The road continues south past pretty **Alligator Bay** ★ with a shallow beach and then to the tiny hamlet of Baines. **Wemyss** is home to **St. Andrew's Anglican Church** through a twee arched side entrance. Built in 1885, it is reminiscent of the Gothic churches of England. It has a pretty rose window.

As you head south, keep an eye peeled for the sign to the KB Resort in **McKann's** shortly before reaching **Thompson Bay**, which isn't much to rave about as far accommodations go, but enjoys one of the best locations on the island. The breezy **shore** ★★ is lined with dunes, palm trees and low scrub and ponds with lots of birdlife.

Just before reaching **Salt Pond**, yet another picture-perfect scene unfolds before you with **St. Joseph's Anglican Church** in the foreground. The Long Island Regatta sails out of Salt Pond each year, bringing with it the requisite revelry, rum and rake 'n' scrape bands. The mail boat puts in at the harbour, where a fishing and lobstering fleet is based. A road running east near the general store leads to a sublime beach and calm bay that is good for swimming and collecting shells. Salt Pond also has fascinating **caves** ★ to explore. About one-half kilometre north of general store, a short trail leads through the bush towards the western shore. Once at the shore, walk south (left) for about 10 metres and then head back into the bush to the cave entrance. You will need a flashlight.

Guana Key ★★★ is accessible from the settlement of Pinders south of Salt Pond. A rough track leads to the eastern shore where you'll find a shallow bay and beach protected by Guana Key Island, which is a short swim away. The island has semi-tame, curly-tailed iguanas that may eat right out of your hand. There is good snorkelling between the island and the beach, and if the weather is calm, the wreck of a freighter can be explored off the other side of the island.

Continuing south to **Grays** are the ruins of **Gray's Plantation** ★. The road is not easy to find so ask around for directions. Three houses and two chimneys can be picked out from the encroaching vegetation.

Southern Long Island

The southern part of Long Island is generally wealthier and whiter. The settlements are orderly places where streets are named and signposted and gardens and homes are well tended. Deadman's Cay is the largest settlement on the island with banks, shops, restaurants and an airport.

The huge medieval-looking **St. Athanatius Anglican Church** ★★ in Lower Deadman's Cay was built in 1929. Its buttressed walls and large wide nave accommodate a very large congregation. **Holy Cross Church** to the south in Deadman's Cay is another pretty house of worship.

South of Deadman's Cay, keep an eye open for **Cartwright's Cave** ★★. The Lucayan cave is now on private property and interesting tours are given by Leonard Cartwright *($5; ☎337-0235)*. There aren't any artefacts to see, just a lot of bats, though the tour is fun.

Petty's is the future home of the **Long Island Historic Museum** which was scheduled to open in 1998. Relics from the island's long history were to make up the bulk of the collection. Don't miss the turn-off for the **Wild Tamarind Pottery & Gallery** ★★★ (see p 288).

Immediately to the south in the settlement of **Petty's** a road runs east of the Hillside Tavern to a superb beach called **Turtle Cove** ★, where a joint Canadian and Bahamian residential project is planned with a golf course, hotel, pool and marina *(for information ☎337-1094 or 519-583-2494, ⇌583-3622)*. Walk south along the beach and you'll come to an awesome natural attraction, the world's deepest **blue hole** ★★★ which is also the world's 8th largest underwater cavern. These should only be explored with a guide and by experienced cave divers.

Another cave not far away in **Hamilton** is more accessible. **Hamilton's Cave** ★★ is 500 metres long and has all the things one hopes for in a cave: stalactites, stalagmites, water and bats.

Leonard Cartwright *(☎337-0235)* also offers tours of the cave. The settlement's **Our Lady of Mount Carmel Church ★**, built in 1938, features a lovely Spanish mission style, with a clean white curved exterior and thick heavy buttresses.

Clarence Town ★★ is the picturesque hub of southern Long Island. As you approach it, you'll spot the double spires of its two Father-Jerome-signed churches complementing each other beautifully from their hilltop locations. **St. Paul's Anglican Church ★★**, with its heavy stone arches and red trim, was rebuilt by hermitic architect Father Jerome (see p 256) after the 1908 hurricane. The gleaming white plaster exterior and bright blue trim of **St. Peter & Paul's Catholic Church ★★★** conjure up images of the Greek Isles. The church was designed by Father Jerome in 1946 after he had converted to Catholicism, and its towering aspect make it appear much larger than it is. If you can squeeze up the stairs of the tower, you'll have an expansive view over Clarence Town and the harbour.

Dunmore is the next settlement. A dirt track runs to **Dunmore's Plantation**, which was held by Lord Dunmore, who also lent his name to Dunmore Town, Harbour Island, where he had a vacation house. The track leads to a series of old gate posts and then to the house with its two large chimneys. Beyond Dunmore, the road passes a series of abandoned and smelly salinas. The Diamond Crystal Salt Company operated here until the 1970s. A few small-scale shrimp farms are still in operation, though. The Queen's Highway continues through the colourfully named **Hard Bargain** and then to the quaint hilltop settlement of **Roses ★** where stone enclosure walls still stand. The west-coast beach at **Cabbage Point** is good for shelling. Finally, a path leads from the southernmost settlement of **Gordons** to **Cape Verde ★**, the southern tip of the island.

BEACHES

Long Island's beaches run from powdery white, to shell-strewn gold to rocky pink. Starting in the north, the obvious favourite is **Cape Santa Maria ★★★**, which is of the powdery white variety. The water is shallow with a clean, white, sandy bottom. There are a few spots of coral for snorkelling. The Stella Maris Resort has a shuttle.

The beaches near the rooms of the Stella Maris Resort are a combination of limestone and sand. About 400 metres south of the last rooms are the four **Love Beaches ★★★**, which are best in calm weather. The first is a protected natural rock pool. The others are lovely deserted beaches between rocky bluffs and palm groves. Bring some good shoes. **Deal's Beach ★★** took a beating in Hurricane Lilly but is still worth lounging on, it is a calm spot that is good for kids. Stella Maris has a shuttle there too.

Alligator Bay ★ is another calm stretch with safe swimming for children. The beach at **McKann's ★★** facing the Kings Bay Resort is quite the opposite with beautiful waves and windswept dunes, great for scenery, less so for swimming. **Salt Pond**, though it is also on the windward side, is protected and safe for swimming. The best beach experience in the area, however, is at **Guana Key ★★** where you can swim, snorkel and explore Guana Key Island.

The last spectacular stretch of white sand worth the trip is at **Turtle Cove ★★★**, south of Petty's. The natural cove has an outlying reef that makes for calm and safe swimming and snorkelling. Be sure to walk the beach and check out the blue hole.

OUTDOOR ACTIVITIES

Fishing

Sport fishing is becoming more and more popular on Long Island thanks to a little-known ocean current, the North Equatorial Current, which carries huge schools marlin, wahoo, tuna and dorado past the Island. The offshore reefs, for their part, are teeming with snapper and grouper.

Stella Maris Resort *(☎338-2051)* offers bonefishing with a guide for $140 for a half day and $160 for a full day. Deep-sea fishing trips cost $475 per day.

Cape Santa Maria Resort *(☎338-5273)* specializes in fishing. A deep-sea fishing trip costs $600 for a full day. A day of bonefishing is $200.

There are a few local guides, including a man named Dockie *(☎338-2018)* in Burnt Ground.

Scuba Diving and Snorkelling

The island's only dive operation is at the **Stella Maris Resort** *(☎338-2051)*. A full day of diving, with two or three dives, is $75. An introductory resort course is $85. They also offer certification courses, night dives and the very popular **Shark Reef**, which is a must-see. The lowering of the dive boat's anchor attracts the reef sharks who by now know that that sound means food. Once the divers are in place, the bait bucket is emptied and the frenzy commences, lasting just a few seconds. If you aren't up to the in-your-face action, you can watch it all from the glass-bottomed dive boat. Other diving excursions include longer trips to the reefs and walls of Conception Island, Rum Cay, San Salvador and the Exumas, plus dives to the world's deepest blue hole, and a handful of wrecks. The resort offers a twice-weekly, day-long snorkelling trip for free, additional trips are $30.

Cape Santa Maria provides snorkelling equipment free of charge to its guests. Any scuba diving must be arranged through the Stella Maris Resort.

ACCOMMODATIONS

Northern Long Island

Cape Santa Maria

The friendly, Canadian-owned **Cape Santa Maria Beach Resort** *($245, low $195, AP $65; 12 rooms, pb, ⊗, ≡, ℜ; PO Box LI30117, Stella Maris, Long Island, ☎338-5273, 1-800-663-7090 or 250-598-1361, ⇒338-6013)* is the newest and most elegant place to stay on Long Island. The 20 rooms are set in 10 white beachfront cottages connected by a boardwalk. Inside are marble floors, attractive wicker furniture and spacious modern bathrooms, and each room has its own large screened-in porch (a necessary luxury on the more buggy lee side of the island). Steps from each room is the superb, secluded white-sand beach of Cape Santa Maria, the focus of the hotel, which is also big on sport fishing. The restaurant is recommended. Guests have the use of a catamaran, windsurfs, snorkelling gear and bicycles. Jean-Michel Cousteau's Out Island Snorkeling Adventures are offered here.

Ulysses' Favourites

Accommodations

Most Luxurious Accommodations:

Cape Santa Maria Beach Resort (see p 284).

Best Resort for Families:

Stella Maris Resort Club (see p 285).

Warmest Welcome:

Lochabar Beach Lodge (see p 286).

Restaurants

Best True-true Bahamian Cooking:

Barbie's (see p 286) and Harbour Restaurant Bar & Satellite (see p 287).

Finest Dining:

Stella Maris Resort Club (see p 287) and Cape Santa Maria Beach Resort (see p 286).

Funkiest Ambiance:

Thompson Bay Inn (see p 287).

Stella Maris

The **Stella Maris Resort Club** *($135, low $120, MAP $42; 60 rooms, pb, ≈, ≡, ℜ, ℝ, K, ⊗; PO Box LI30105, Stella Maris, Long Island, ☎338-2051 or 336-2106, 1-800-426-0466, ⇄338-2052)* is more like a small village than a resort when you consider the huge variety of accommodations available and the layout of the place. The resort is German-owned and attracts a number of German tourists. Set on an old plantation, the property overlooks the Atlantic shore. There are standard hotel rooms and studios or equipped cottages, bungalows and villas (some with private pools) for those who prefer the self-catering option. Prices for these range from $140 for a one-bedroom cottage for two people to $495 for a four-bedroom bungalow with a pool for six people; there are also weekly rates. The decor is a bit dated throughout but very comfortable with cool tile floors and large bathrooms and closets. The rooms have two double beds and a poolside patio. The bungalows and villas have complete kitchens, yards, driveways and lots of privacy. Some are across the road from the water, while others are just steps from it. None of the rooms are far from the three large pools. There are tennis courts, transportation to the island's best beaches, sailboats and bicycles to borrow, a very good restaurant and a whole slew of activities to choose from, including cave parties, rum punch parties, fishing excursions and snorkelling and diving trips with the resort's dive shop. The all-inclusive dive packages are a good deal.

McKann's

Kings Bay Resort *($60; 10 rooms, pb, ⊗; PO Box SM30147, McKann's, Long Island, ☎338-8945 or 338-8945, ℻338-8012)*. A winding bumpy road leads across to a superb location and an unfortunately not so superb resort. Few people venture out here and the small rooms are in need of a spit and polish, but there is no better escape than to stroll the windswept east-coast beach.

Thompson Bay

Thompson Bay Inn *($60, $65 with ≡; 9 rooms, sb, ℜ; PO Box LI30133, Thompson Bay, Long Island, ☎358-0052)* is a combination by-the-road hotel, restaurant, bar, pool hall and dance hall and isn't the place to go if you are looking for a relaxing week at the beach. Despite the very modest accommodations, a bare room with a bed and night table, the inn has a following that appreciates its unpretentious and "rollicking" atmosphere.

Southern Long Island

Clarence Town

The **Lochabar Beach Lodge** *($85; 2 rooms, pb, ⊗, K; PO Box LI30330, Clarence Town, Long Island, ☎/℻337-0331)* is further proof that Long Island has some of friendliest people in The Bahamas. This place is everything you expect in a guesthouse and more. Your hosts, the Meehans, live in the cosy beach house that also contains two hand-decorated guest rooms. French doors lead out to a deck with sea breezes and a gorgeous view of secluded Lochabar Bay, which is actually a huge blue hole. Two more cottages are planned. Bonefishing and snorkelling can be arranged.

RESTAURANTS

Northern Long Island

Cape Santa Maria

Cape Santa Maria *($$$; ☎338-5273)* serves three meals a day and non-guests are welcome, though reservations are required one day in advance for evening meals. Meals are served in the clubhouse, which, like the rooms, is only steps from the perfect white-sand beach. The menu lists Bahamian and American dishes, with some tasty seafood creations. The friendly staff and guests contribute to a lovely evening here.

Glintons

Barbie's *($-$$; at the north end of town, ☎358-5009)* was once just a simple ice cream bar, but now serves some of the freshest conch and seafood in the north. It is run by the bartender from Stella Maris and, if you call ahead, he'll prepare something special for you.

Burnt Ground

Two spots in Burnt Ground don't put on any airs for the tourists; its just real Bahamian cooking and real Bahamians: **Sabrina's Bar and Grill** *($)* serves chicken, cole slaw, peas 'n' rice and conch in all its forms, while **Pratt's Restaurant** *($; ☎338-7022)* is known for its seafood.

Stella Maris

Stella Maris Resort *($$-$$$$; ☎338-2051)* serves three delicious meals a day. For breakfast, there are sinful German apple pancakes or a buffet with fresh fruit and muffins; lunch is simple sandwiches, conch salad and the like and for dinner, the choice might be a New York sirloin, grouper with Chablis sauce or lamb with mint. The salad has perfectly crispy fresh croutons. Top it all off with the superb Long Island iced coffee sundae. There is live music for ambiance.

Potcakes Bar *($$; near the Stella Maris marina, ☎338-2016)* has a fun bar that is the scene of some of the resort's special events. This is also a fairly decent restaurant with a good selection of the typical American and Bahamian specialties.

Simms

Mario's and the **Blue Chip Bar** in picturesque Simms offer the typical Bahamian atmosphere you might be craving with native meals and drinks.

Thompson Bay

The **Thompson Bay Inn** *($-$$; ☎338-0052)* serves three meals a day, with hearty and greasy breakfasts, grouper sandwiches, pizza by the slice, pork chops, ribs and a few pasta dishes. The food is fairly standard, but things generally heat up as the evening progresses, so a good time is virtually guaranteed.

Southern Long Island

Deadman's Cay

The **Snack Corner** *($)* near the two banks at the southern end of town sells good sandwiches, salads and sweets. More complete meals can be had at the **Dew Drop** *($; ☎337-0044)*.

Clarence Town

Overlooking the pretty harbour and not-so-pretty mailboat dock, the **Harbour Restaurant Bar & Satellite Lounge** *($$)* is a large, clean, family-style restaurant. The menu is fairly extensive but pretty predictable.

The **Oriental Bakery & Restaurant** *($)* only serves Oriental food on Wednesdays! The rest of the week they have fresh-baked bread and rolls, pizzas, sweets and savoury stuffed patties.

ENTERTAINMENT

If you can, try to visit Long Island during mid-May for the annual **Long Island Regatta**. The locally-made sloops all sail out of Salt Pond, the centre of the festivities, though the whole island hops during the four-day event. For information call ☎393-3949 or 338-0333.

Stella Maris

Stella Maris Resort has a comfortable bar that attracts guests and locals alike. The resort also organizes three fun shindigs each week: the Rum Punch Cocktail Party on Wednesdays before dinner with free punch and conch fritters, a Saturday night dance, and finally the funky Cave Party on Monday nights. Drinks and meals are served in a nearby cave complete with campfire and torches, a live rake 'n' scrape band and dancing as the night wears on. The resort also plans parties at the nearby **Potcakes Bar**.

Burnt Ground

Sabrina's Bar and Grill is a lively local hangout about halfway between Stella Maris and Cape Santa Maria.

Deadman's Cay

Two local hangouts are worth checking out near Deadman's Cay. There is the waterfront **Kooter's Bar** which is actually in the hamlet of Mangrove Bush, south of town, and the **Hillside Tavern** a bit further south in the hamlet of Petty's. This last spot is one of *the* places to be during the Long Island Regatta.

SHOPPING

Stella Maris

The **Stella Maris General and Food Store** is a short bike ride from the resort. They sell foodstuffs and snacks. There is a liquor store next door.

Millertons

The **Knowles Straw Works** is a large operation with a great selection of bags, hats, baskets and handicrafts all made right on site.

Simms

Ivy Simms Super Straw Works is another good locale for handmade gifts and souvernirs.

Petty's

Wild Tamarind Pottery and Gallery *(follow the sign south of town)* is something to see even if you aren't buying. This is the studio of Dennis Darvile, an Englishman who once headed up the art department at the College of The Bahamas. He creates and sells useful things like mugs, plates, vases and such, as well as fanciful little ceramics representing elements of Bahamian folklore, like cottages, chickcharnies, duhos and Junkanoo revellers. You will only find this stuff here.

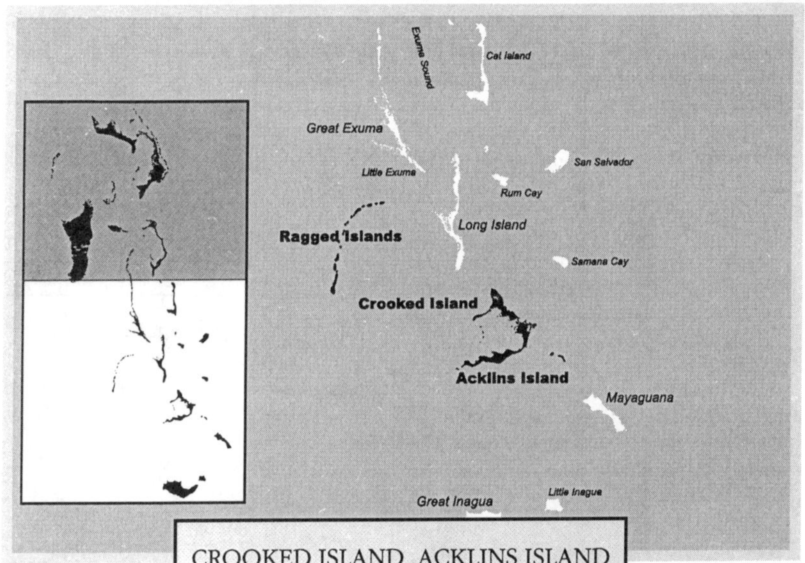

CROOKED ISLAND, ACKLINS ISLAND AND THE RAGGED ISLAND RANGE

Crooked and Acklins Islands, along with smaller Long Cay, surround a shallow bay known as the Bight of Acklins to the east of the Crooked Island Passage. The Ragged Island Range arcs across the sea on the western side of the Crooked Island Passage at the southwestern edge of The Bahamas. It starts in the north with the Jumento Cays and ends with Ragged Island, the largest of the chain, and then Little Ragged Island. The shallow turquoise waters and the sweep of islands have been compared to a South Pacific atoll, and if sunsets were marketable, this would be the centre of Bahamian tourism.

A Short History

The most recent theory of Columbus' voyage to the New World puts his first landfall at Samana Cay, his second at Crooked Island and his third at Long Cay or Fortune Island. Crooked Island is therefore Columbus' Santa María de la Concepcíon, and Long Cay, which the Lucayans called Saomete, was christened Isabela. As if to confuse matters, Long Cay is also known as Fortune Island, the origins of which are unclear. It was either wreckers and pirates who made their fortune thanks to the heavy marine traffic through the Crooked Island Passage and the many treacherous reefs of the environs, or poor Bahamians in the early 1900s who came here in search of work aboard foreign steamships en route to Mexico and Central America. Columbus also later called the islands the "Fragrant Isles", perhaps for the aromatic bark of the cascarilla tree that he smelled. The bark is used to flavour Campari and many islanders still make their living stripping and selling it.

The islands were first settled by Loyalists who set up more than 40 plantations, worked by over 1000 slaves.

These had all failed by 1803 and those who stayed probably did so because they couldn't afford to leave. They eventually turned to the salt pans of Fortune Island and to sponging to survive.

The first general post office in The Bahamas was on Crooked Island. The monthly packet stopped here on its run between Jamaica and England, a small schooner would complete the run from Crooked to Nassau.

Ragged Island is the only inhabited island in the eponymous range. Salt pans attracted the first settlers who saw prosperous times in the 1860s. Salt has always been the lifeblood of this island that receives few tourists.

FINDING YOUR WAY AROUND

By Plane

Bahamasair *(☎327-5505 in Nassau)* flies twice a week to the Colonel Hill Airfield on Crooked Island and continues on to Spring Hill Airfield on Acklins.

By Boat

By Mailboat: Departures are from Potter's Cay (under the Paradise Island Bridge) in Nassau and fares are one way. The *Lady Mathilda* goes to Landrail Point on Crooked Island and Spring Point on Acklins Island. Schedules and departures vary. Fare: $70. The *Ettiene & Cephas* departs Tuesdays at 2pm for Ragged Island. Travel time: 21 hours. Fare: $30.

There is a ferry between Cove Point, Crooked Island and Lovely Bay, near Chesters, Acklins Island. The fare is $4 one way. There is also a small passenger ferry twice a week between Church Grove Landing, Crooked Island and Albert Town, Long Cay.

PRACTICAL INFORMATION

Crooked Island

Police: Colonel Hill, ☎344-2197.

Clinic: There is a government clinic at Landrail Point.

BaTelCo: Church Grove, Crooked Island, ☎344-2590.

Post Office: In the administration building in Colonel Hill beside the police station.

Acklins Island

Clinic: There are two government clinics on Acklins, at Spring Point and Chesters Bay.

EXPLORING

Crooked Island

Crooked Island has two main settlements: the capital, **Colonel Hill**, along the northern shore with a few pretty churches in an around town, and **Landrail Point**, at the northwestern point of the island. In terms of sightseeing, the latter has much more to offer. In town the action centres around the twice-weekly arrival of the mailboat in the harbour. Heading north up the shore from the harbour, the road passes between the ocean and what is called the **Brine Pool**. In the middle of this salty lagoon are the ruins of a salt farm

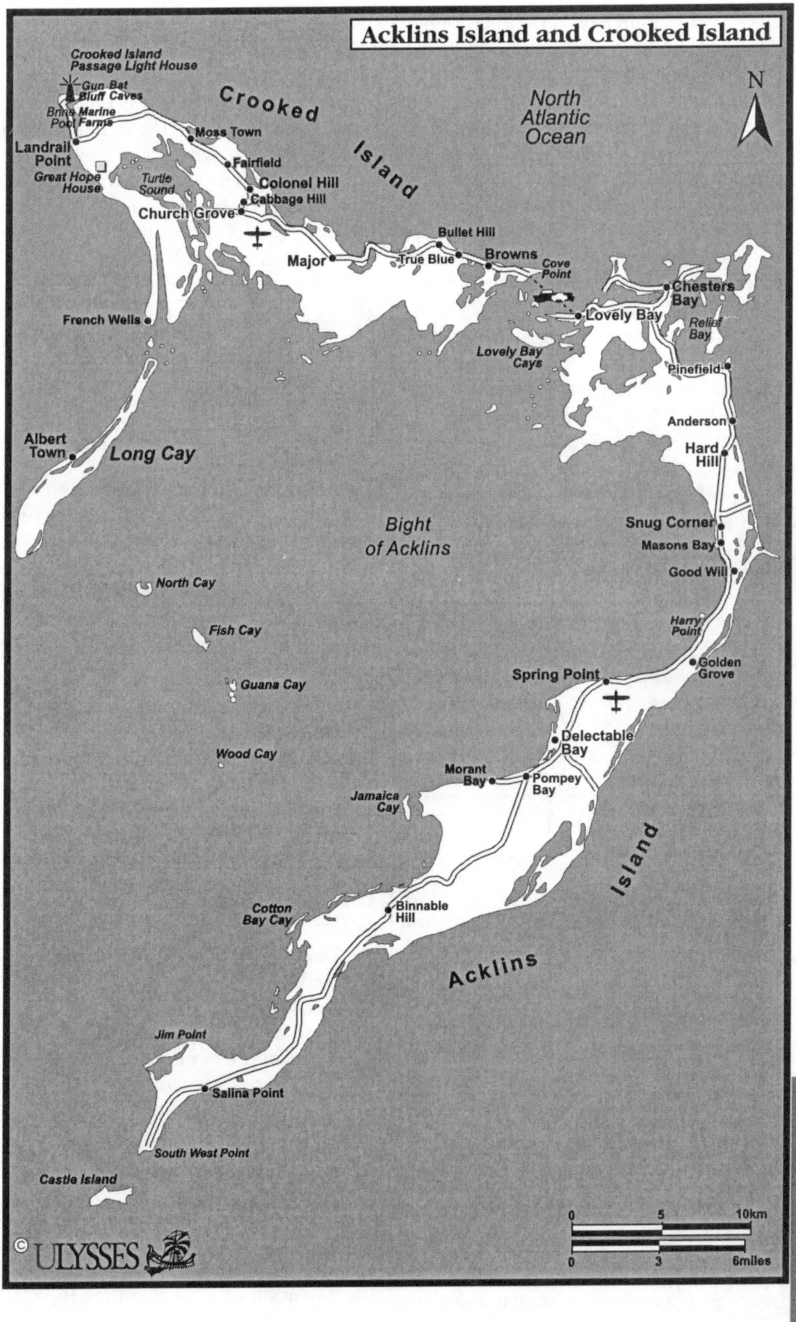
Acklins Island and Crooked Island
Crooked Island Passage Light House
Gun Bat Bluff Caves
Brine Marine Pool Farms
Crooked
Island
North Atlantic Ocean
N
Moss Town
Landrail Point
Fairfield
Great Hope House
Turtle Sound
Colonel Hill
Cabbage Hill
Church Grove
Bullet Hill
Major
True Blue
Browns
Cove Point
Chesters Bay
Lovely Bay
Relief Bay
French Wells
Lovely Bay Cays
Pinefield
Anderson
Albert Town
Long Cay
Hard Hill
Bight of Acklins
Snug Corner
Masons Bay
Good Will
North Cay
Fish Cay
Harry Point
Golden Grove
Spring Point
Guana Cay
Delectable Bay
Wood Cay
Morant Bay
Pompey Bay
Jamaica Cay
Island
Cotton Bay Cay
Binnable Hill
Acklins
Jim Point
Salina Point
South West Point
Castle Island
0 5 10km
0 3 6miles
© ULYSSES

called the **Marine Farms Fortress** which once served as a fort and supposedly saw action during the War of 1812. Continuing north, as you round the point, you can see Crooked Island Passage Light on a sandy cay offshore. Built in 1876, its historic workings have unfortunately been replaced and it is but a shadow of its former self, at least a battery-operated mechanism still marks the busy Crooked Island Passage. Back in Landrail Point, walk the dirt track across the island to **Gun Bluff ★**. Here, near the ruins of an English fort is the first Out-Island home of Evans Cottman, an American teacher who provided medical care throughout the Out Islands in the 1940s, 1950s and 1960s, amusing adventures recounted in his book *Out Island Doctor*. He later settled in the Abacos. The views from atop the bluff are great. Gordon's Bluff to the east marks the entrance to the **Bat Caves**. An easy 15 minutes should suffice to explore these caves, inhabited by crabs, bats and lots of mosquitoes. About one kilometre south of Landrail Point are the ruins of the plantation-era **Great Hope House**.

Acklins Island

The main settlement here is called **Spring Point**. At press time, electricity still had not come to Acklins. There are generators, however. Archaeological evidence suggests that the largest Lucayan settlement in The Bahamas may have been on Acklins Island. A partially excavated site lies about two kilometres south of Spring Point.

Ragged Island

Most visitors to Ragged Island arrive on their own by boat. The lack of tourist facilities precludes any tourist industry. The only settlement, Duncan Town, is a sleepy, partially boarded-up outpost with an airstrip (only used by private planes) and a dock. If you have the means to get here you'll enjoy what some claim are the most memorable sunsets in The Bahamas. Besides the brilliant yellows, pinks, oranges and purples, these sundowns sport a magnificent "green flash" just as the sun hits the horizon.

OUTDOOR ACTIVITIES

Fishing

The shallow Bight of Acklins contains renowned bonefishing flats. **Scavella Bonefish Lodge** *(☎344-2598)* rents boats. The self-proclaimed best guide on Crooked is **Robbie Gibson** *(☎344-2676 or 344-2590)* who charges $300 for a half-day and $500 for a full day.

ACCOMMODATIONS

Crooked Island

Crooked Island Beach Inn *($60; 6 rooms, ⊗, pb; Cabbage Hill, ☎344-2321)* is north of the airstrip and near a beach, but not one you'll likely be frolicking on. The rooms are almost bare and are suitable for budget travellers who don't expect or need much, mind you the price might not be to their liking. The inn is run by Revered Ezekiel Thompson and his daughter Merlene, who may also be able to rent you a car or a boat for the day.

Scavella Bonefish Lodge *($75; 3 rooms, ⊗, sb; Landrail Point, ☎344-2598)* does have boats for bonefishing the Bight of

Ulysses' Favourites

Accommodations

Best All-Inclusive Resort:

Pittsdown Point Landings (see p 293).

Restaurants

Best True-true Bahamian Cooking:

Ms. Gibson's Lunch Room (see p 293).

Finest Dining:

Pittsdown Point Landings (see p 293).

Acklins. The three rooms (one sleeps six) are very modest, there is also a shared kitchen.

Pittstown Point Landings *($95 MAP; 12 rooms, pb, ⊗, ℜ; Landrail Point, ☎/⇌344-2507, 1-800-752-2322 or 704-878-8724, ⇌704-881-0771, 238A Statesville Airport Rd., Statesville, NC 28677)*, on an isolated, sandy peninsula at the northwestern point of Crooked Island, is an escapist's dream. The rooms are in 4 bungalows, each has a screened-in porch facing the beach and palm trees. The decor is basically all white, with a tropical feel. Most guests arrive in their plane or boat, some just stopping in for a bite at the restaurant (see below).

RESTAURANTS

Crooked Island

Ms. Gibson's Lunch Room *($$, Landrail Point, ☎344-2676)* is one of the few places in The Bahamas that doesn't serve conch. They do serve the other traditional favourites like grouper, lobster, johnny cake and peas 'n' rice. Call ahead for reservations.

Pittsdown Point Landings *($$-$$$; Landrail Point, ☎344-2507)* occupies the stone-sided building that once served as barracks for British West Indies soldiers stationed at the nearby 18th-century fort, and then as Crooked Island's first post office. The breezy dining room has a maritime decor. The menu features Bahamian and American fare. Reservations are required if you are not staying here.

Acklins Island

Airport Inn and Restaurant *($; Spring Point)* is one of the only options so far on Acklins. They food is Bahamian and reasonably priced.

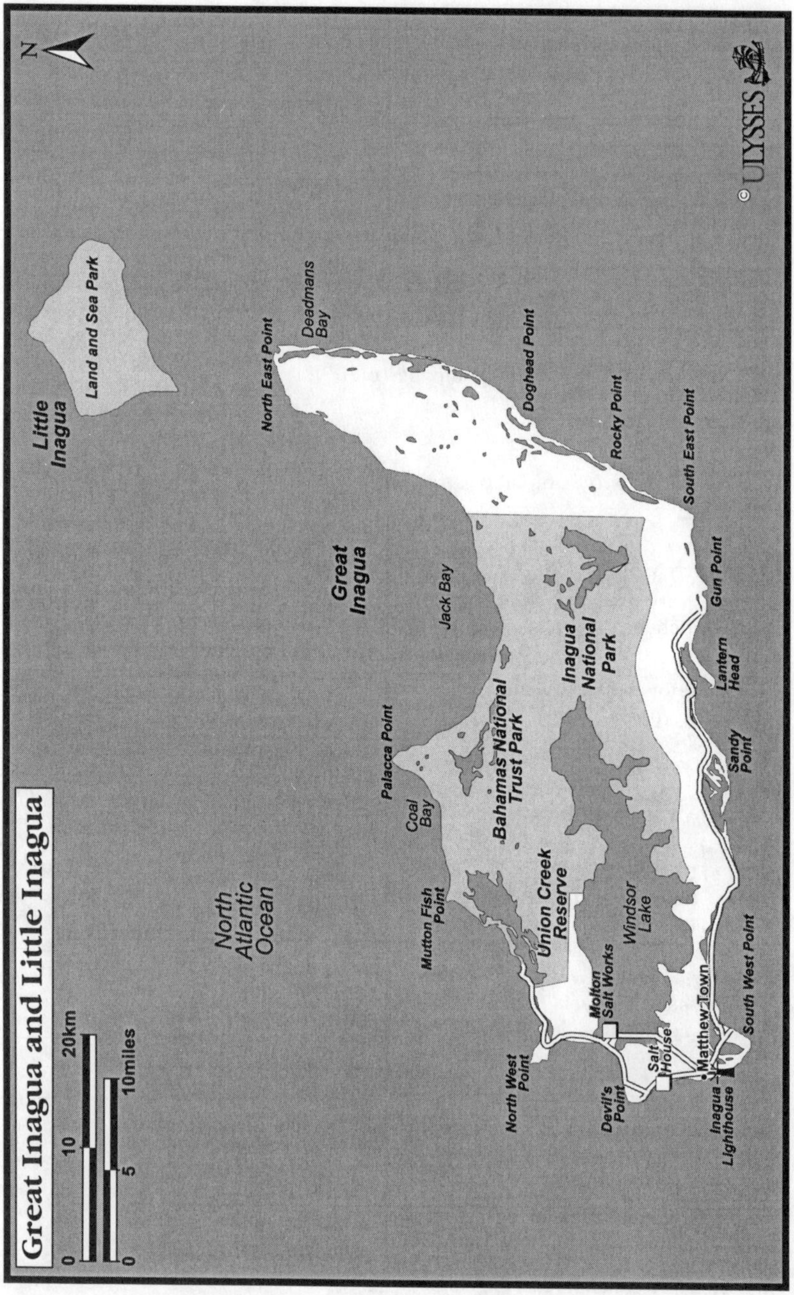
Great Inagua and Little Inagua
0
10
20km
0
5
10miles
N
Little Inagua
Land and Sea Park
North Atlantic Ocean
Great Inagua
North East Point
Deadmans Bay
Doghead Point
Rocky Point
South East Point
Gun Point
Lantern Head
Sandy Point
South West Point
Jack Bay
Palacca Point
Coal Bay
Mutton Fish Point
North West Point
Devil's Point
Inagua Lighthouse
Matthew Town
Salt House
Molton Salt Works
Windsor Lake
Union Creek Reserve
Bahamas National Trust Park
Inagua National Park
© ULYSSES

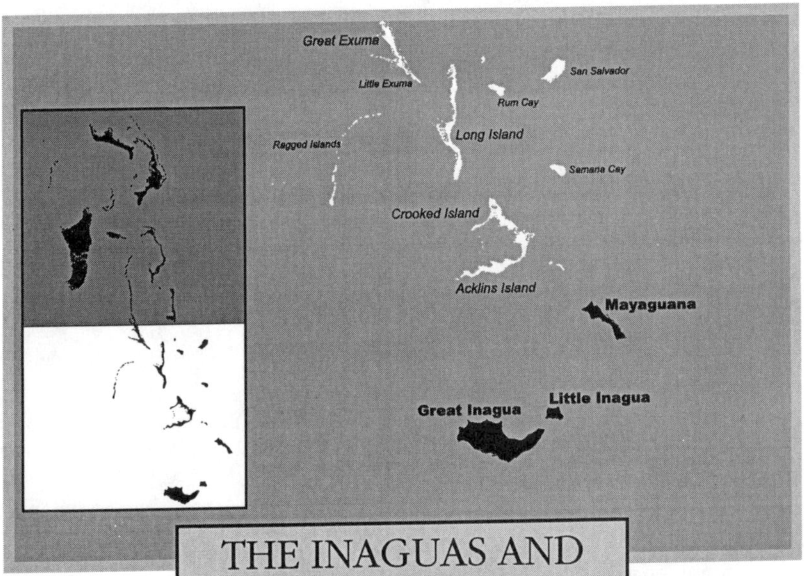

THE INAGUAS AND MAYAGUANA

These islands truly are the last outposts of The Bahamas; the Inaguas are the southernmost islands in the chain and Mayaguana, the easternmost. Few tourists ever venture this far, there are hardly any tourist facilities to welcome them. True Out Island living, huge mounds of salt and the sight of the largest West Indian flamingo colony taking flight in a flapping flurry of pink do attract a few adventurous types, however. The wildlife-viewing opportunities here are unique in the world.

Flat Great Inagua is the third largest Bahamian island. It lies 80 kilometres north of Cuba and more than 500 kilometres south of Nassau. The Bahamas National Trust protects about half of it and all of tiny neighbouring Little Inagua, which is devoid of human habitation, but has plenty of West Indian tree ducks and wild goats and donkeys. Mayaguana, about 100 kilometres north of Great Inagua, hardly ever sees any tourists. Hotel developers have considered it, but so far the only major development has been in the form of a now-defunct US missile-tracking station. The island boasts very warm year-round temperatures and pristine, untouched beaches. An eco-park is planned.

A Short History

The Lucayans called Great Inagua "Babeque". Years before settling there, though, the English called it "Heneagua", a corruption of Spanish *lleno* (full) and *agua* (water) for most of the island is covered with briny lakes. In the mid-1700s, the French took a strategic interest in the island and put up signs claiming it for the King of France. In 1802, Henri Christophe a revolutionary from Haiti, is said to have built a castle and buried a treasure here when France tried to retake Haiti. The

Salt and the Turks and Caicos

From its start, salt was vital to Bermuda's economy, and the Turks Islands were the centre of salt production. The problem was that both Bermuda and the Lords Proprietors claimed the islands. Tensions rose and the British Government finally decided in favour of the Proprietors in 1803, including the Turks in their Bahamian claim. The Turks islanders, who were Bermudians, would have nothing to do with Nassau, which imposed heavy taxes on their salt production. In 1848, the British Government changed its mind and The Bahamas lost the Turks and neighbouring Caicos Islands, along with 96% of the Bahamian salt revenue.

supposed ruins of the castle are still visible at Northeast Point; the treasure, however, has never been found.

Around this time, families were attracted to the island's salt ponds, and in 1848 there was a population of 172 working the salt ponds at Matthew Town, named for Governor George B. Matthew. Before refrigeration, salt was essential to preserve meat and fish. The loss of the Turks and Caicos Islands was a major blow to the Bahamian economy and the Heneagua Salt Pond Company was formed in 1849 to compensate. Pans were created, windmill-driven pumps were installed, iron rails over which mule-drawn trucks rolled ran from the salinas to the sea and The Salt House was built.

Prices soared during the American Civil War, and Inagua became the "El Dorado" of The Bahamas, with a million and a half bushels prouced per year. Soon the Americans got into the game and started producing their own salt. They imposed protective heavy tariffs, and it was no longer profitable to export to the US. The salt industry failed. Development projects in Mexico and Central America like the Panama Canal and the Mexican Railways, picked up the slack by creating a demand for stevedores and contract workers. Inagua's small population was not enough to supply the demand and soon people were coming here from all over The Bahamas. Matthew Town became a booming port with fine houses, churches and broad streets. The ships stopped coming with the outbreak of the First World War and stayed away until the 1930s. In 1935, the Erickson brothers from New England arrived to revive the saltworks. Not only did they revive it, they completely mechanized it and once again it flourished, overcoming competition and tariffs. In 1954 the Morton Salt Company bought, gained control of and expanded the salt works. Morton still runs the show on Great Inagua, employing just about everyone on the island.

In 1963, the Bahamas National Trust created Inagua National Park to protect the last breeding colony of West Indian flamingoes, The Bahamas' national bird, which once inhabited all of The Bahamas, but is now virtually extinct save within park. Preservation efforts have been enormously successful, and the birds have even started repopulating neighbouring islands.

Great Inagua's history contains a few juicy morsels. Shortly after the arrival of the Ericksons, two Inaguan brothers, unhappy that the economic fate of their island was controlled by two Americans, took to the streets with shotguns, killing one man, burning down several buildings and destroying the

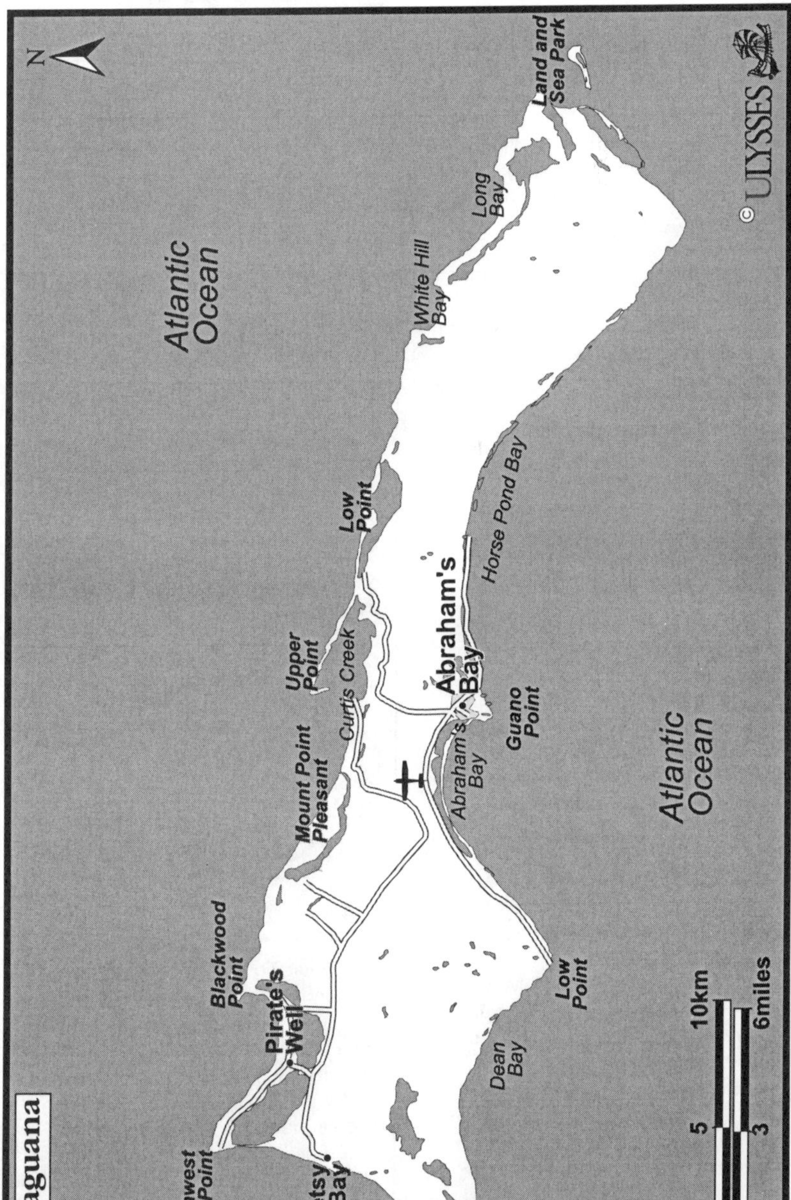
Mayaguana
N
Atlantic Ocean
Atlantic Ocean
Northwest Point
Betsy Bay
Pirate's Well
Blackwood Point
Mount Point Pleasant
Upper Point
Curtis Creek
Low Point
White Hill Bay
Long Bay
Land and Sea Park
Abraham's Bay
Abraham's Bay
Guano Point
Horse Pond Bay
Low Point
Dean Bay
Devil's Point
0 5 10km
0 3 6miles
© ULYSSES

wireless station. They fled to Haiti, but were shipped back and eventually tried and hung in Nassau. More recently, drug runners were attracted by the island's isolated southern location. In the 1980s, islanders who were profiting from the drug trade actually burned down the police station and took a policeman hostage.

Mayaguana is one of the few Bahamian islands to retain its Lucayan name. It is thickly wooded and well suited to agriculture. It remained unsettled until 1812, when Turks Islanders began drifting in and settling here. It is virtually untouched by tourism save the odd time-worn backpacker.

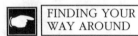

FINDING YOUR WAY AROUND

By Plane

Bahamasair *(☎327-5505 in Nassau)* has flights two to three times a week to Great Inagua and Mayaguana.

By Boat

By Mailboat: All departures are from Potter's Cay (under the Paradise Island Bridge) in Nassau and all fares are one-way. The *Abilin* departs Tuesdays at noon for Matthew Town, Great Inagua. Fare $45. Trip length: 17 hours. The *Lady Mathilda* departs for Abraham Bay, Mayaguana. Fare $70. Schedule and trip length vary.

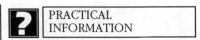

PRACTICAL INFORMATION

Great Inagua

Matthew Town

Tourist Information: There is no tourist office, however, Great Inagua Tours *(☎339-1862)* offers tours of the island that include the Morton Salt Works, but not Inagua National Park.

Bank: Bank of The Bahamas, Gregory St., open Mon, Tue, Thu and Fri 9:30am to 2pm, ☎339-1264.

Police: Gregory St., ☎339-1263.

BaTelCo: north of the police station, open Mon to Fri 9am to 5:30pm, ☎339-1000

Clinic: Government Clinic with doctor and nurse, Victoria St., ☎339-1249.

EXPLORING

Great Inagua ★★

Matthew Town

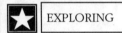

Matthew Town, Great Inagua's only settlement, is a surprisingly shiny company town. In the early 1800s a few families arrived to work the salt ponds, an activity that took off in earnest in 1849 with the creation of the Heneagua Salt Pond Company. Prosperous times followed and the town flourished. A handful of churches and administrative buildings were built. Among them, impressive **St. Phillips's Anglican Church ★** was built in 1852 of local stone with a plaster coat and a wood-shingle roof. There is a lovely font of carved stone and marble inside.

The only other sight in town, the historic **Inagua Lighthouse** ★★ *(☎339-1370)* is actually about a kilometre and a half to the south. Built in 1876, it is one of only three lighthouses in The Bahamas with a rotating mechanism that must be wound like a clock every 90 minutes. The keeper lives in one of the buildings at the base. A narrow winding staircase leads up to the top where you can see the huge lens that focuses and magnifies the kerosene-powered light. You'll also get a winning view of the whole island and, if it's clear, the coast of Cuba to the south. You'll also notice the channel cut in the shore and pump that carry water to the salt works. Hold on to your hat as it can be very windy and make sure someone points out the bathtub bolted to the top of the lighthouse that collects rainwater. Donations are appreciated to help the cause of getting the lighthouse declared a historic landmark before it is automated.

About six and a half kilometres north of town are the **Morton Salt Works** ★★ *(formal tours are not offered, but visitors are welcome and impromptu tours are often given, you can either call ahead to the company at ☎339-1847, or contact Larry Ingraham of Great Inagua Tours at ☎339-1862)*. Before you reach the present salt works, however, you will pass the original Salt House, built in the 1850s on the shore in Matthew Town. This is probably the largest historic industrial building in The Bahamas. Its walls are heavily buttressed, and the arched entrances are made from bricks salvaged from the submerged ruins of Port Royal, Jamaica, an old pirate haunt that was destroyed by an earthquake in 1692. The present Morton salt works span just under 14,000 hectares of salt pans, reservoirs, mounds of salt and storage and loading facilities. The salt-making process takes seven months, during which seawater is pumped into lagoons. The growth of algae darkens the water but also speeds up evaporation and provides a food source for brine shrimp which filter and clean the water. During the final evaporation, achieved by moving the water through channels, the sodium chloride precipitates out and the leftover water is pumped off. The 15-centimetre layer of salt crystals left behind is harvested, washed and sorted into huge mounds. These white hills will either make you want to go skiing or make you very thirsty!

Inagua National Park ★★★ *(contact the warden to arrange a visit, ☎339-1616, ⇌339-1850; you can also volunteer for the annual bird count each spring)* is one of two national parks on Great Inagua. Occupying 745 square kilometres, it covers about half of the island. The park was formally created in 1963 after more than 10 years of preservation work by Robert Porter Allen, research director of the National Audubon Society. At the time, the roseate or West Indian flamingo was in danger of extinction because of habitat destruction and overhunting, and Inagua contained was the last breeding colony. Now more than 50,000 of the birds thrive in the billowy conditions of Inagua. What little vegetation there is barely survives the barren and inhospitable terrain. The shallow salt ponds and Lake Windsor are teeming with brine shrimp and larval brine flies, tasty morsels for flamingoes and other waders, including pink egrets, cormorants, roseate spoonbills and Louisiana herons. The flamingoes are in residence from November to May when they head to Cuba, early morning and late evening are the best times to spot the birds, which can be seen prancing about near the salt works, but

Turtle

they tend to congregate in much larger numbers toward the centre of the park. They feed by turning their heads upside down and skimming the water, which is filtered through their sieve-like beaks.

Union Creek Reserve is the other national park on Great Inagua. It is located west of the northwestern park boundary of Inagua National Park. This is the only unthreatened feeding ground in this part of the world. Feeding and nesting turtles are studied at the **Archie Carr Research Centre**. Anyone interested in helping out is encouraged to volunteer *(Caribbean Conservation Corporation, PO Box 2866, Gainesville FL, 32602, ☎1-800-678-7853)*.

Mayaguana

For now, Mayaguana is the domain of hardy Out Islanders and their occasional visitors, usually intrepid backpackers. The scene is set to change, however. Electricity and telephone service are on their way to **Abraham Bay**, the main settlement, as is a new eco-park. The Mayaguana Eco-Park will occupy the eastern edge of the island and offer hiking, kayaking and canoeing, plus birdwatching and snorkelling.

OUTDOOR ACTIVITIES

Birdwatching

Besides the 50,000-odd flamingoes in Inagua National Park, there are Bahamian pintails, the Bahamian pintail

Ulysses' Favourites

Accommodations

Best Value For Your Money:

Walkine's Guest House (see p 301).

Best Flamingo Experience:

Camp Arthur Vernay (see p 301).

Restaurants

Best True-true Bahamian Cooking:

Main House (see p 302).

hummingbird, the endangered Bahama parrot, brown pelicans and burrowing owls.

ACCOMMODATIONS

Great Inagua

Matthew Town

Main House *($45-$60; 4 rooms, pb, sb, ≡, ⊛, ℜ; Matthew Town, ☎339-1267, ⇌339-1265)* is a large, casual and very modest guesthouse in the centre of town. Not all rooms have air-conditioning. The place is owned by the Morton Salt Company.

Walkine's Guest House *($65, no credit cards; 5 rooms, pb, sb, tv, ≡; Matthew Town, ☎339-1612)* is the best option in Matthew Town. It is clean, friendly, comfortable and across the street from the beach. The decor is modern but sparse and each room has a television.

If you are hoping for bit of beach action along with birdwatching, then opt for the **Crystal Beach View Hotel** *($70; 14 rooms, ℜ, pb, ≡; Matthew Town, ☎339-1550, ⇌339-1660)*, the only true beachside hotel on the island. The rooms are non-descript but acceptable nonetheless.

Inagua National Park

Camp Arthur Vernay *($25 per person; sb; contact park warden ☎339-1616, ⇌339-1850)* is located right in the park on Long Cay on Lake Windsor. There are dormitory accommodations for nine people. The camp is supervised by the park warden who sometimes spends the night and looks after guests. If this is the case, tips are appreciated. There is an outdoor kitchen, but you will have to bring all your own food.

Mayaguana

Mayaguana Inn Guest House *($45; 5 rooms, pb, ⊛; Abraham's Bay, ☎339-3065 or 339-3203 via operator)* has simple and decent motel-style rooms and a small dining room.

RESTAURANTS

Great Inagua

Matthew Town

Main House *($-$$; ☎339-1267)* serves Bahamian fare all day long, mostly fried but including a popular chicken souse for breakfast.

Topp's Restaurant *($-$$; ☎339-1465 or 339-1293)* also serves a good souse – this one made with pig's feet! Grouper, conch and other fresh catches top the menu.

INDEX

INDEX

INDEX

INDEX

INDEX

INDEX

Travel Notes

■ ULYSSES TRAVEL GUIDES

- ☐ Affordable B&Bs in Québec . . . . . $12.95 CAN $9.95 US
- ☐ Atlantic Canada $24.95 CAN $17.95 US
- ☐ Beaches of Maine $12.95 CAN $9.95 US
- ☐ Bahamas . . . . . $24.95 CAN $17.95 US
- ☐ Calgary . . . . . . $17.95 CAN $12.95 US
- ☐ Canada . . . . . . $29.95 CAN $21.95 US
- ☐ Chicago . . . . . . $19.95 CAN $14.95 US
- ☐ Chile . . . . $27.95 CAN $17.95 US
- ☐ Costa Rica . . . . $27.95 CAN $19.95 US
- ☐ Cuba . . . . $24.95 CAN $17.95 US
- ☐ Dominican Republic . . . . . . $24.95 CAN $17.95 US
- ☐ Ecuador Galapagos Islands . . . . $24.95 CAN $17.95 US
- ☐ El Salvador . . . . $22.95 CAN $14.95 US
- ☐ Guadeloupe . . . $24.95 CAN $17.95 US
- ☐ Guatemala . . . . $24.95 CAN $17.95 US
- ☐ Honduras . . . . . $24.95 CAN $17.95 US
- ☐ Jamaica . . . . . . $24.95 CAN $17.95 US
- ☐ Lisbon . . . . $18.95 CAN $13.95 US
- ☐ Louisiana . . . . . $29.95 CAN $21.95 US
- ☐ Martinique . . . . $24.95 CAN $17.95 US
- ☐ Montréal . . . . . $19.95 CAN $14.95 US
- ☐ New Orleans . . $17.95 CAN $12.95 US
- ☐ New York City . $19.95 CAN $14.95 US
- ☐ Nicaragua . . . . $24.95 CAN $16.95 US
- ☐ Ontario . . . . . . $24.95 CAN $14.95US
- ☐ Ottawa . . . . . . $17.95 CAN $12.95 US
- ☐ Panamá . . . . . . $24.95 CAN $16.95 US
- ☐ Portugal . . . . . . $24.95 CAN $16.95 US
- ☐ Provence - Côte d'Azur . . . . $29.95 CAN $21.95US
- ☐ Québec . . . . . . $29.95 CAN $21.95 US
- ☐ Québec and Ontario with Via . . . . $9.95 CAN $7.95 US
- ☐ Toronto . . . . . . $18.95 CAN $13.95 US
- ☐ Vancouver . . . . $17.95 CAN $12.95 US
- ☐ Washington D.C. $18.95 CAN $13.95 US
- ☐ Western Canada $29.95 CAN $21.95 US

■ ULYSSES DUE SOUTH

- ☐ Acapulco . . . . . $14.95 CAN $9.95 US
- ☐ Belize . . . . $16.95 CAN $12.95 US
- ☐ Cartagena (Colombia) . . . . $12.95 CAN $9.95 US
- ☐ Cancun Cozumel $17.95 CAN $12.95 US
- ☐ Puerto Vallarta . $14.95 CAN $9.95 US
- ☐ St. Martin and St. Barts . . . . . $16.95 CAN $12.95 US

■ ULYSSES GREEN ESCAPES

☐ Cycling in France $22.95 CAN
$16.95 US

☐ Hiking in the Northeastern United States . . $19.95 CAN
$13.95 US

☐ Hiking in Québec $19.95 CAN
$13.95 US

■ ULYSSES TRAVEL JOURNAL

☐ Ulysses Travel Journal (Blue, Red, Green, Yellow, Sextant) . $9.95 CAN
$7.95 US

QUANTITY	TITLES	PRICE	TOTAL

NAME:____________________

ADDRESS:____________________

____

Payment: ☐ Money Order ☐ Visa ☐ Card

Signature:____________________

Sub-total	
Postage & Handling	$8.00*
Sub-total	
G.S.T.in Canada 7%	
TOTAL	

ULYSSES TRAVEL PUBLICATIONS
4176 St-Denis, Montréal, QC, H2W 2M5
(514) 843-9447 fax (514) 843-9448
www.ulysses.ca
*$15 for overseas orders

U.S. ORDERS: **GLOBE PEQUOT PRESS**
P.O. Box 833, 6 Business Park Road,
Old Saybrook, CT 06475-0833
1-800-243-0495 fax 1-800-820-2329
www.globe-pequot.com